Frommer's®

Vienna & the Danube Valley

6th Edition

by Darwin Porter & Danforth Prince

Here's what the critics say about Frommer's:

"Amazingly easy to use. Very portable, very complete."
—*Booklist*

"Detailed, accurate, and easy-to-read information for all price ranges."
—*Glamour Magazine*

"Hotel information is close to encyclopedic."
—*Des Moines Sunday Register*

"Frommer's Guides have a way of giving you a real feel for a place."
—*Knight Ridder Newspapers*

Wiley Publishing, Inc.

About the Authors

A team of veteran travel writers, **Darwin Porter** and **Danforth Prince** have produced numerous titles for Frommer's, including best-selling guides to Italy, France, the Caribbean, England, and Germany. Porter, a former bureau chief of *The Miami Herald,* is also a Hollywood biographer, providing inside looks at the private lives of such stars as Humphrey Bogart, Katherine Hepburn, and aviator Howard Hughes. His latest bio is *Brando Unzipped.* Formerly of the Paris bureau of *The New York Times,* Prince is also president of Blood Moon Productions and other media-related firms.

Published by:

Wiley Publishing, Inc.

111 River St.
Hoboken, NJ 07030-5774

ISBN: 978-0-470-10051-6
Editor: Anuja Madar
Production Editor: M. Faunette Johnston
Cartographer: Liz Puhl
Photo Editor: Richard Fox
Anniversary Logo Design: Richard Pacifico
Production by Wiley Indianapolis Composition Services

Front cover photo: Johann Strauss Statue
Back cover photo: Vienna, Opera Ball, couples in formal attire waltzing

For information on our other products and services or to obtain technical support, please contact our Customer Care Department within the U.S. at 800/762-2974, outside the U.S. at 317/572-3993 or fax 317/572-4002.

Wiley also publishes its books in a variety of electronic formats. Some content that appears in print may not be available in electronic formats.

Manufactured in the United States of America

5 4 3 2 1

Contents

List of Maps   vi

What's New in Vienna   1

1 The Best of Vienna   4

1 Best of Vienna 4   **3** Best Dining Bets 8
2 Best Hotel Bets 7

2 Planning Your Trip to Vienna & the Danube Valley   11

1 Visitor Information 11   **5** Travel Insurance 18
2 Entry Requirements & Customs 11   **6** Health & Safety 20
 Pre-Departure Checklist 12   **7** Specialized Travel Resources 21
3 Money 13   **8** Planning Your Trip Online 24
 Emergency Cash—   **9** The 21st-Century Traveler 25
 The Fastest Way 13   Frommers.com: The Complete
 Foreign Currencies vs.   Travel Resource 25
 the U.S. Dollar 14   **10** Getting There 27
 What Things Cost in Vienna 15   **11** Packages for the Independent
4 When to Go 16   Traveler 32
 Vienna Calendar of Events 17   **12** Recommended Books 33

3 Getting to Know Vienna   34

1 Orientation .34   Transportation for Less 42
 The Neighborhoods in Brief 39   Fast Facts: Vienna 44
2 Getting Around 40

4 Where to Stay   49

1 Innere Stadt (Inner City) 50   **6** Neubau (7th District) 74
2 Leopoldstadt (2nd District) 67   **7** Josefstadt (8th District) 76
3 Landstrasse (3rd District) 70   **8** Alsergrund (9th District) 77
4 Wieden & Margareten   **9** Westbahnhof (15th District) 79
 (4th & 5th Districts) 71   **10** Near Schönbrunn 79
 Family-Friendly Hotels 72   **11** Airport Hotels 80
5 Mariahilf (6th District) 72

5 Where to Dine 81

1 Restaurants by Cuisine 81
2 Innere Stadt (Inner City) 86
   Coffeehouses & Cafes 98
3 Leopoldstadt (2nd District) 100
4 Landstrasse (3rd District) 101
   Family-Friendly Dining 101
5 Wieden & Margareten
   (4th & 5th Districts) 102
6 Mariahilf (6th District) 103

7 Neubau (7th District) 104
   Picnics & Street Food 106
8 Josefstadt (8th District) 106
9 Alsergrund (9th District) 107
10 Westbahnhof (15th District) 108
11 Near Schönbrunn 108
12 In the Outer Districts 109
13 On the Outskirts 109

6 Exploring Vienna 110

1 The Hofburg Palace Complex 110
   The Singing Ambassadors 112
   Sissi—Eternal Beauty 114
2 The MuseumsQuartier Complex . . .116
3 Other Top Attractions 117
4 Churches .125
5 Museums & Galleries 129
   In Memory of Vienna's
   Jewish Ghetto 130

6 Parks & Gardens 132
   Tales of the Vienna Woods 133
7 Especially for Kids 134
8 Musical Landmarks 135
9 Organized Tours 137
10 Sports & Active Pursuits 137
   Cruising the Danube 138

7 Vienna Walking Tours 141

Walking Tour 1: Imperial Vienna 141
Walking Tour 2: South
of the Ring .146

Walking Tour 3: Vienna's
Back Streets 153

8 Shopping 159

1 The Shopping Scene 159
2 Shopping A to Z 162

Open-Air Markets 166

9 Vienna After Dark 168

1 The Performing Arts 168
   The Toughest Ticket in Town 170
2 The Club & Music Scene 171
3 The Bar Scene 174

4 The Heurigen 177
5 More Entertainment 179
6 Only in Vienna 179

10 Side Trips from Vienna 181

1 The Wienerwald (Vienna Woods) ...182
 Twilight of the Habsburgs........188
2 The Spa Town of Baden
 bei Wien 189
3 Wiener Neustadt 192

4 The Danube Valley 194
5 Eisenstadt: Haydn's Home 202
6 Lake Neusiedl 204
 The Capricious Lake 205
7 Forchtenstein 210

Appendix A: Vienna in Depth 212

1 Vienna Today 212
2 History 101 212
 Dateline 213
3 Exploring Vienna's Architecture 220

4 Art through the Ages 223
5 Musical Vienna 225
6 A Taste of Vienna 227

Appendix B: Useful Terms & Phrases 230

1 Glossary 230

2 Menu Terms 231

General Index 234

General Index 234
Accommodations Index 242

Restaurant Index 243

List of Maps

Vienna at a Glance   36

Vienna Public Transport   41

Where to Stay in Vienna's
  Inner City   52

Where to Stay in Vienna   68

Where to Dine in Vienna   84

The Hofburg   111

Vienna Attractions   118

Schönbrunn Park & Palace   123

Walking Tour 1: Imperial Vienna   143

Walking Tour 2: South
  of the Ring   147

Walking Tour 3: Vienna's
  Back Streets   155

Vienna Shopping   160

Lower Austria, Burgenland &
  the Danube Valley   183

An Invitation to the Reader

In researching this book, we discovered many wonderful places—hotels, restaurants, shops, and more. We're sure you'll find others. Please tell us about them, so we can share the information with your fellow travelers in upcoming editions. If you were disappointed with a recommendation, we'd love to know that, too. Please write to:

Frommer's Vienna & the Danube Valley, 6th Edition
Wiley Publishing, Inc. • 111 River St. • Hoboken, NJ 07030-5774

An Additional Note

Please be advised that travel information is subject to change at any time—and this is especially true of prices. We therefore suggest that you write or call ahead for confirmation when making your travel plans. The authors, editors, and publisher cannot be held responsible for the experiences of readers while traveling. Your safety is important to us, however, so we encourage you to stay alert and be aware of your surroundings. Keep a close eye on cameras, purses, and wallets, all favorite targets of thieves and pickpockets.

Other Great Guides for Your Trip:

Frommer's Austria
Frommer's Europe
Frommer's Europe from $70 a Day

Frommer's Star Ratings, Icons & Abbreviations

Every hotel, restaurant, and attraction listing in this guide has been ranked for quality, value, service, amenities, and special features using a **star-rating system**. In country, state, and regional guides, we also rate towns and regions to help you narrow down your choices and budget your time accordingly. Hotels and restaurants are rated on a scale of zero (recommended) to three stars (exceptional). Attractions, shopping, nightlife, towns, and regions are rated according to the following scale: zero stars (recommended), one star (highly recommended), two stars (very highly recommended), and three stars (must-see).

In addition to the star-rating system, we also use **seven feature icons** that point you to the great deals, in-the-know advice, and unique experiences that separate travelers from tourists. Throughout the book, look for:

Finds	Special finds—those places only insiders know about
Fun Fact	Fun facts—details that make travelers more informed and their trips more fun
Kids	Best bets for kids and advice for the whole family
Moments	Special moments—those experiences that memories are made of
Overrated	Places or experiences not worth your time or money
Tips	Insider tips—great ways to save time and money
Value	Great values—where to get the best deals

The following **abbreviations** are used for credit cards:

AE	American Express	DISC	Discover	V	Visa
DC	Diners Club	MC	MasterCard		

Frommers.com

Now that you have this guidebook to help you plan a great trip, visit our website at **www.frommers.com** for additional travel information on more than 3,500 destinations. We update features regularly to give you instant access to the most current trip-planning information available. At Frommers.com, you'll find scoops on the best airfares, lodging rates, and car rental bargains. You can even book your travel online through our reliable travel booking partners. Other popular features include:

- Online updates of our most popular guidebooks
- Vacation sweepstakes and contest giveaways
- Newsletters highlighting the hottest travel trends
- Online travel message boards with featured travel discussions

What's New in Vienna

In the vanguard of world tourism, Vienna is forever changing, yet its imperial monuments and regal grandeur seem locked in place. At the continental crossroads between East and West, it's a volatile cityscape. Here are some of the latest developments.

ACCOMMODATIONS In hotels, one of the most sought-after new addresses is **Do & Co.**, Stephansplatz 12 (℗ **01/24188**), in the Haas Haus in the exact center of Vienna at the Dom. In one of the most avant-garde buildings in Vienna, entrepreneurs took over the upper floors and transformed them into accommodations that offer style, drama, and views.

Far more to our liking is the opening of the luxurious **Palais Coburg Hotel Residenz,** Coburgbastei 4 (℗ **01/518-180**), which was once the private palace of the Coburg dynasty. Restored in 2006, it was vandalized when the Russian army stayed here as an occupying force after World War II. Those red soldiers wouldn't recognize the "decadent capitalism" of the place today. It's a pocket of posh quite unlike any other in Vienna.

Once the headquarters of an Austrian bank, **Radisson/SAS Style Hotel,** Herrengasse 12 (℗ **01/22780-0**), has switched to hotel elegance, retaining much of the architectural style of yesterday while incorporating modern touches, such as a chic wine bar and minimalist yet comfortable bedrooms decorated in warm earth tones. As befits the old bank, the health club is found behind massive security doors.

In the new MuseumsQuartier, the best boutique hotel to open is **Das Tyrol,** Mariahilferstrasse 15 (℗ **01/587-54-15**). Originally built 175 years ago as a convent, it has been beautifully restored by its owner, a female member of Parliament. It's contemporary in style with a modern art collection to adorn its walls.

The parade of design-conscious hotel openings continues with **Parliament Levante,** Auerspergstrasse (℗ **01/535-4515**). You'd never know that this elegant bastion of comfort used to be a sanatorium and later a student dormitory. Today it's a sophisticated hotel of comfort and stylish elegance.

Among restaurants, **Do & Co.,** Stephansplatz 12 (℗ **01/24188**), not only is the most talked about new hotel in Vienna but also a deluxe restaurant. Some of the finest international dishes are served here at the controversial avant-garde building, Haas Haus. In addition to the fine food, the restaurant's Onyx bar is currently the chic place to meet for a drink.

The trendiest and most sought after dining table in Vienna at the moment is **Fabios,** Tuchlauben 6 (℗ **01/532-2222**), serving sublime Mediterranean and international cuisine. The city's glitterati compete for a table to sample the viands of the young, imaginative chef, Fabio Giacobello. We found the menu items, adjusted to what's available on any given day, to be about the freshest served in the city.

Creating a buzz is **Julius Meinl,** Graben 19 (© **01/532-3334**), near the Dom. Its upscale continental cuisine is showcased in a restaurant that also includes a wine shop, deli, and cellar-level wine bar. The cooking is bold and meticulously crafted.

Museum dining is often self-service, but not at **Österreicher in MAK Gasthof & Bar,** in the Museum der Angewanten Kunst, Stubenring 5 (© **01/714-0121**). It's not just museum-goers who stop by to sample Chef Helmut Österreicher's take on contemporary Viennese cuisine; foodies skip the exhibits and go straight for the restaurant. "I can cook classic as well as modern," Österreicher told us—and he wasn't lying. The garden terrace is also a lure in summer.

ATTRACTIONS Even the most optimistic predictions failed to estimate just how successful the opening of the **MuseumsQuartier Complex,** Museumsplatz, was. In 2006, thousands of cultural buffs flocked to Vienna just to see this post-millennium cultural city. The massive complex is one of the largest cultural complexes in the world, and has signaled a Renaissance in Vienna's museums. The treasure trove includes the **Leopold Museum** (© **01/525-700**), with its extensive collection of Austrian art, highlighted by the paintings of Egon Schiele (1890–1918); the **MUMOK (Museum of Modern Art Ludwig Foundation,** © **01/525-00**), containing one of the most outstanding collections of contemporary art in Europe; and the **Kunsthalle Wien** (© **01/521-89-33**), which combines classic modern art with the more "razor's edge" in avant-garde works.

AFTER DARK Numerous clubs are opening around the city, providing a diversity of after-dark diversions. **Passage,** Burgring 1 (© **01/961-8800**), is the dance club of the moment, found in an underground pedestrian subway station beneath the boulevards. Some of the hottest dancers in Vienna show up here to pulsate to the electronic music. **La Divina,** Hanuschgasse 3 (© **01/513-43-19**), adjacent to the Albertina, is the cocktail bar of choice for music lovers. With a link to the Vienna State Opera, it attracts the Maria Callas of tomorrow . . . and, yes, of yesterday too. Only the most talented are invited to play at its grand piano.

Sky Bar, Kärntnerstrasse 19 (© **01/513-1712**), is reached by taking an elevator to the top floor of the Steffl building. The chic and music-loving head here for the scene and the nostalgia—Mozart died in a house long ago demolished on this site.

Hip and trendy, **Mocca Club,** Linke Wienzeile 4 (© **01/587-0087**), was created from the "ruins" of a failed Starbucks. It's become a great cafe and a place to hang out, where you can enjoy 52 kinds of coffee and some 200 different cocktails.

BURGENLAND The Viennese have moved into the modern world with a vengeance, but many magazines in 2006 went searching for more nostalgic roots and discovered old-fashioned places on the doorstep of Vienna.

Following that trend, we came up with our own discoveries. In Eisenstadt, the capital of Burgenland, **Gasthof Öhr,** Ruster Strasse 51 (© **02682/62460**), opened in the dark days of World War II, facing the Communist menace of Hungary across the nearby border. It's been renewed and is now better than ever, turning out those beloved dishes of Emperor Franz Josef—*tafelspitz* (boiled beef) and Wiener schnitzel, along with freshwater fish from the lake, such as zander. You can also lodge here in well-furnished double rooms, which were modernized but still have their old-fashioned charm.

In the small lakeside resort village of Rust, the origins of **Mooslechner's Burgerhaus,** Hauptstrasse 1 (© 02685/ 6416), actually go back to the 1530s. It's been given a new lease on life by modernizing its kitchens and facilities, enough so that it can now service as many as 80 diners on a summer night. However, the old-fashioned charm has been left intact, and the preparations of zander, goose, and game dishes are just as grandmother made them.

1

The Best of Vienna

Vienna is a city of music, cafes, waltzes, parks, pastries, and wine, a true cosmopolitan center, where different tribes and nationalities have, for centuries, fused their cultural identities to produce the intriguing and, often cynical, Viennese.

From the time the Romans selected a Celtic settlement on the Danube River as one of their most important central European forts, "Vindobona," the city we now know as Vienna, has played a vital role in European history. Austria grew around the city and developed into a mighty empire. The capital became a showplace during the tumultuous reign of the Habsburg dynasty, whose court was a dazzling spectacle.

The face of the city has changed time and again because of war, siege, victory, defeat, the death of an empire and the birth of a republic, foreign occupation, and the passage of time. Fortunately, the Viennese character—a strict devotion to the good life—has remained solid.

Music, art, literature, theater, architecture, education, food, and drink are all part of Vienna's allure, all of which we bring you in the pages that follow.

1 Best of Vienna

- **Listening to Mozart:** It is said that at any time of the day or night in Vienna, someone somewhere is playing the music of Wolfgang Amadeus Mozart. You might hear it at an opera house, a church, a festival, an open-air concert, or, more romantically, performed by a Hungarian orchestra in a Belle Epoque cafe. Regardless, "the sound of music" drifting through Vienna is likely to be the creation of this prodigious genius. See section 1, "The Performing Arts," in chapter 9.
- **Cruising the Danube (Donau):** Johann Strauss used a bit of poetic license when he called the Donau "The Blue Danube"—it's actually a muddy green. Cruising the river is nevertheless a highlight of any Viennese vacation. The legendary **DDSG,** or Blue Danube Shipping Co.

(☎ **01/588800;** www.ddsg-blue-danube.at), offers 1-day trips with cruises priced for every budget. While on board, you'll pass some of the most famous sights in eastern Austria, including towns like Krems and Melk. See p. 197 and 200.
- **Watching the Lipizzaner Stallions:** Nothing evokes the heyday of imperial Vienna more than the **Spanish Riding School** (☎ **01/533-9032;** www.srs.at). Here, the sleek white stallions and their expert riders demonstrate the classic art of dressage in choreographed leaps and bounds. The stallions, a crossbreed of Spanish thoroughbreds and Karst horses, are the finest equestrian performers on earth. Riders wear black bicorn hats with doeskin breeches and brass buttons. The public is admitted to

watch; make reservations 6 to 8 weeks in advance. See p. 115.

- **Heurigen Hopping in the Vienna Woods:** *Heurigen* are rustic wine taverns that celebrate the arrival of each year's new wine *(heurig)* by placing a pine branch over the door. The Viennese rush to the taverns to drink the new local wines and feast on country buffets. Some *heurigen* have garden tables with panoramic views of the Danube Valley; others provide shaded, centuries-old courtyards where revelers enjoy live folk music. Try the red wines from Vöslau, the sylvaner of Grinzing, or the Riesling of Nussberg. See section 4, "The *Heurigen,*" in chapter 9.

- **Feasting on *Tafelspitz,* "The Emperor's Dish":** No Austrian dish is more typical than the fabled *tafelspitz* favored by Emperor Franz Joseph. Boiled beef sounds dull, but *tafelspitz* is far from bland. A tender delicacy, the "table end" cut absorbs a variety of flavors, including juniper berries, celery root, and onions. Apple-and-horseradish sauce further enlivens the dish, which is usually served with fried grated potatoes. For Vienna's best *tafelspitz,* try the **Sacher Hotel Restaurant,** in the Hotel Sacher Wien (© **01/514560**). See p. 87.

- **Revisiting the Habsburgs:** One of the great dynastic ruling families of Europe, the Habsburgs ruled the Austro-Hungarian Empire from their imperial court in Vienna. You can still witness their grandeur as you stroll through the Inner City. The Hofburg, the family's winter palace, is a living architectural textbook, dating from 1279. Also be sure to visit Schönbrunn, the sprawling summer palace, which lies on the outskirts of the city and boasts magnificent gardens. See chapter 6.

- **Biking Along the Danube:** A riverside bike trail between Vienna and Naarn links interesting villages, including Melk and Dürnstein. As you pedal along, you'll pass castles of yesteryear, medieval towns, and latticed vineyards. Route maps are available at the Vienna Tourist Office, and you can rent bikes at the ferry or train stations. See p. 43 and 137.

- **Attending an Auction at Dorotheum:** Vienna is a treasure trove of art and antiques, and as many estates break up, much of it goes on sale. The main venue for art and antiques is the state-owned auction house **Dorotheum,** Dorotheergasse 17 (© **01/5156-0200**). Founded in 1707, it remains one of the great European depositories of objets d'art. Items here are likely to be expensive; if you're looking for something more affordable, try the summer Saturday and Sunday outdoor art and antiques market along the Danube Canal (between Schwedenbrücke and Salztorbrücke). See p. 162.

- **Savoring the Legendary Sachertorte: Café Demel** (© **01/535-1717**), the most famous cafe in Vienna, has a long-standing feud with the **Sacher Hotel Restaurant,** in the Hotel Sacher Wien (© **01/514560**), over who has the right to sell the legendary and original Sachertorte, a rich chocolate cake with a layer of apricot jam. In 1965, a court ruled in favor of Hotel Sacher, but Demel still claims that the chef who invented the torte brought "the original recipe" with him when he left the Sacher to work for Demel. See p. 82 and 87.

- **Unwinding in a Viennese Coffeehouse:** The coffeehouse still flourishes here in its most perfect form.

Did You Know?

The Viennese have always been hospitable to foreigners, except during a time in the late 18th century when the emperor felt that tourists might spread pernicious ideas. Non-Austrians were limited to a 1-week stay in the capital.

You can spend hours reading newspapers (supplied free), writing memoirs, or planning the rest of your stay in Vienna. And, of course, there's the coffee, prepared 20 to 30 different ways, from *weissen ohne* (with milk) to *mocca gespritzt* (black with a shot of rum or brandy). A glass of ice-cold water always accompanies a cup of coffee in Vienna, as well as the world's most delectable pastry or slice of cake. See "Coffeehouses & Cafes," in chapter 5.

- **Strolling the Kärntnerstrasse:** Lying at the heart of Viennese life is the bustling, pedestrian-only Kärntnerstrasse. From morning to night, shoppers parade along the merchandise-laden boulevard; street performers, including musicians and magicians, are always out to amuse. For a break, retreat to one of the cafe terraces for some of the best people-watching in Vienna. See "Walking Tour 1: Imperial Vienna," in chapter 7.

- **Playing at the Prater:** Ever since Emperor Joseph II opened the Prater to the public in the 18th century, the Viennese have flocked to the park for summer fun. The Prater has abundant tree-lined paths on which to jog or stroll (the Viennese, in general, are much fonder of strolling). The amusement park boasts a looming Ferris wheel that was immortalized in the Orson Welles film *The Third Man.* Open-air cafes line the park, which also provides an array of sports facilities, including tennis courts and a golf course. See p. 133.

- **Enjoying a Night at the Opera:** Nothing is more Viennese than dressing up and heading to the Staatsoper, one of the world's greatest opera houses, where ascending the grand marble staircase is almost as exhilarating as the show. Built in the 1860s, the Staatsoper suffered severe damage during World War II. It reopened in 1955 with a production of Beethoven's *Fidelio,* marking Austria's independence from occupation. Both Richard Strauss and Gustav Mahler directed here, and the world's most renowned opera stars continue to perform, accompanied, of course, by the Vienna Philharmonic Orchestra. See p. 169.

- **Hearing the Vienna Boys' Choir:** In this city steeped in musical traditions and institutions, one group has distinguished itself among all others: the Vienna Boys' Choir, or *Wiener Sängerknaben.* Created by that great patron of the arts, Maximilian I, in 1498, the choir still performs Masses by Mozart and Haydn at the Hofburgkapelle on Sundays and holidays from September through June. See p. 112.

- **Discovering the Majesty of St. Stephan's Cathedral:** Crowned by a 137m (450-ft.) steeple, Dompfarre St. Stephan, Vienna's cathedral, is one of Europe's great Gothic structures. Albert Stifter, the acclaimed Austrian writer, wrote that its "sheer beauty lifts the spirit." The cathedral's vast tiled roof is exactly twice the height of its walls. Intricate altarpieces, stone canopies, and masterful Gothic sculptures are just some of the treasures that lie within. Climb the spiral steps to the South Tower for a panoramic view of the city. See p. 117.

2 Best Hotel Bets

For the details on these and other hotels, see chapter 4.

- **Best Historic Hotel:** Built in 1869, the **Hotel Imperial** (© **800/325-3589** in the U.S., or 01/501100; www.luxurycollection.com/imperial) is the "official guesthouse of Austria." It has presided over much of the city's history, from the heyday of the Austro-Hungarian Empire to defeat in two world wars. All the famous and infamous of the world have checked in. Wagner, for example, worked on key sections of both *Tannhäuser* and *Lohengrin* here in 1875, and some of the great cultural icons of the 20th century—from Margot Fonteyn to Herbert von Karajan—have been guests. See p. 54.
- **Best Trendy Hotel:** Created by the famous English architect Sir Terence Conran, **Hotel Das Triest** (© **01/58918;** www.dastriest.at) attracts the artistic elite to its stylish precincts near St. Stephan's. Originally a stable, it's come a long way, baby, and now is elegant, luxurious, and stylish. Rooms are decorated with a distinctive flair. See p. 59.
- **Best for Business Travelers:** With state-of-the-art business equipment and an incredibly helpful staff, the **Hotel Bristol** (© **888/625-5144** in the U.S., or 01/515160; www.westin.com/bristol) is the choice of international business travelers. Some suites are large enough for business meetings, and room service will quickly deliver hors d'oeuvres and champagne (for a price, of course) when you close the deal. Many guests like to treat their clients to dinner at the Bristol's elegant restaurant, Korso bei der Oper. See p. 51.
- **Best for a Romantic Getaway:** The outrageously ostentatious private home of the Coburg dynasty has been turned into **Palais Coburg Hotel Residenz** (© **01/518-180;** www.palais-coburg.com). Some of the suites here evoke the heyday of the Rothschilds and are as posh as anything in Vienna. You are guaranteed absolute privacy if you desire that. See p. 57.
- **Best for Families:** Only a 4-minute walk from St. Stephan's Cathedral, **Hotel Kärntnerhof** (© **01/5121923;** www.karntnerhof.com) is a small, kid-friendly hotel in the center of Vienna. It offers a superb location, attentive staff, and good prices. Rooms are spacious enough to accommodate families and come equipped with modern amenities. See p. 64.
- **Best Moderately Priced Hotel:** In the heart of Old Vienna, less than a block from the cathedral, **Hotel Royal** (© **01/515680;** www.kremslehnerhotels.at) was completely rebuilt in 1982. In this price bracket, not many hotels can compete with the Royal in terms of class. In the lobby, you'll find the piano Wagner used when he was composing *Die Meistersinger Von Nürnberg*. See p. 63.
- **Best Budget Hotel:** Near the Opera in the heart of Vienna, **Hotel-Pension Suzanne** (© **01/5132507;** www.pension-suzanne.at) offers a warm, inviting interior and affordable bedrooms furnished in a

comfortable, traditional style. The Strafinger family welcomes you to their attractive, cozy accommodations, some equipped with kitchenettes. See p. 65.

- **Best Pension (B&B):** Near the busy Mariahilferstrasse, **Pension Altstadt Vienna** (© 01/5226666; www.altstadt.at) has an elegant atmosphere exemplified by its colorful, velvet-laden Red Salon lounge. The rooms don't disappoint either: Each is the work of an individual designer and has high ceilings, antiques, and parquet floors. This is hardly a lowly pension, but a fair-priced and prestigious address with its own special charms. See p. 75.
- **Best Service:** The **Hotel de France** (© 01/31368; www.hoteldefrance. at), near the Votivkirche, is hardly the best hotel in Vienna, but the attentive and highly professional staff makes a stay here particularly delightful. Room service is efficient, messages are delivered promptly, and the housekeepers turn down your bed at night. See p. 54.
- **Best Location:** Although it's no Bristol or Imperial, the **Hotel Ambassador** (© 01/961610; www. ambassador.at) is definitely where you want to be. The hotel lies between the State Opera and St. Stephan's, with the Kärntnerstrasse on the other side. The Ambassador has enjoyed its position here since 1866, and has played host to both

Mark Twain and Theodore Roosevelt. See p. 51.

- **Best Health Club:** The **Hilton Vienna** (© 800/445-8667 in the U.S., or 01/717000; www.hilton. com) sponsors the Pytron Health Club (under different management) on its premises. This is, by far, the most professional health club in town, with state-of-the-art equipment and facilities for both men and women. See p. 67.
- **Best Hotel Pool:** Of the three hotels in town that have pools, the biggest and best is in the Euro Freizeit und Fitness spa in the windowless cellar of the **Vienna Marriott** (© 888/236-2427 in the U.S., or 01/515180; www.marriott.com). It's about 11×7.2m (36×24 ft.) and ringed with potted plants and tables. The spa has a pair of saunas, an exercise room, and massage facilities. Marriott guests enter free; nonguests pay 14€ ($17) to use the pool and fitness center, 19€ ($23) for the pool, fitness center, and sauna. It's open daily from 7am to 10pm. See p. 58.
- **Best Views:** Overlooking the Danube Canal, the 18-story **Hilton Vienna** (see "Best Health Club," above) offers panoramic views from its top floors. Plush accommodations and elegant public rooms also lure guests. The cityscape views are quite dramatic at both dawn and sunset. See p. 67.

3 Best Dining Bets

For details on these and other restaurants, see chapter 5.

- **Best Spot for a Romantic Dinner:** The **Sacher Hotel Restaurant,** in the Hotel Sacher Wien (© 01/514560), is a showcase for imperial Vienna. Franz Joseph's favorite dish was

tafelspitz, a delectable boiled beef dinner that's still served here, along with various Viennese and international dishes. And, the fabled Sachertorte was invented here. See p. 87.

- **Best Spot for a Business Lunch:** Most afternoons you'll find the movers and shakers of Vienna at

Korso bei der Oper, in the Hotel Bristol (© **01/51516546**). The refined menu features Viennese and international cuisine, and guests can conduct business with the assurance of good food and impeccable, unobtrusive service. See p. 86.

- **Best Spot for a Celebration:** When you want to take your significant other or a group of friends to a special place, **Altwienerhof** (© **01/ 8926000**), serving Austrian and French cuisine, is a discriminating choice. A private home in the 1870s, it's now one of the city's premier restaurants. Of course, if it's a real celebration, you'll order champagne, but if not, you can choose something from its wine cellar, one of Vienna's largest. See p. 108.

- **Best Cafe Dining:** Installed in the old glassed-in palm garden of Kaiser Franz Josef's palace, **Palmenhaus** (© **01/5331033**) has been restored to its original splendor. The hottest cafe restaurant in Vienna, it features well-honed Austrian cuisine. See p. 96.

- **Best Decor:** At **Steirereck** (© **01/ 7133168**), which means "corner of Styria," the decor is pristine and pure, with original beams and archways transplanted from an old Styrian castle. Murals also add to the elegant ambience, but the food is what brings most guests here. See p. 101.

- **Best Wine List:** There are far more elegant restaurants in Vienna and far better places serving haute cuisine, but the wine list at **Weibels Wirtshaus** (© **01/5123986**) is definitely for the connoisseur. Discerning Austrians flock here for the simple but tasty food and a wine list that includes some 250 varieties. All the vintages are Austrian. See p. 89.

- **Most Stylish Restaurant:** Bankers, diplomats, and Helmut Lang–clad hipsters agree on only one thing:

Mörwald im Ambassador (© **01/ 961610**) is the most fashionable joint in town. Noted for its first-rate Viennese cuisine, it virtually celebrates food itself. All the specialties are perfectly prepared and imaginative. Look your best if you show up at this stylish enclave of fine dining. See p. 87.

- **Best for Kids: Gulaschmuseum** (© **01/5121017**) will make a goulash lover out of the most stubborn of kids. Inspired by Hungary, the kitchen prepares some 15 varieties of this world-famous dish. See p. 95.

- **Best Viennese Cuisine:** There is no more traditional place to dine in all of Vienna than the **Wiener Rathauskeller** (© **01/405-1210**), a cellar-level restaurant in Vienna's Town Hall. Partake in authentic cuisine in atmospheric rooms, and dine in a style similar to that which Mozart enjoyed. Live musicians entertain as you sample your Wiener schnitzel. See p. 89.

- **Best Italian Cuisine:** Homemade pastas in savory sauces are the draw at **Firenze Enoteca,** in the Hotel Royal (© **01/5134374**), near St. Stephan's Cathedral, in the heart of Vienna. Most of the food is Tuscany-inspired, with some salutes to other regions of Italy. See p. 90.

- **Best Hungarian Cuisine:** If you can't visit neighboring Budapest, you can get a taste of Hungarian fare at **Kardos** (© **01/5126949**). Try all the Gypsy *schmaltz* favorites, including Lake Balaton–style fish soup. See p. 95.

- **Best Seafood:** The freshest seafood in Vienna—flown in from the North Sea or the Bosphorus—is available in the center of town at the **Kervansaray und Hummer Bar** (© **01/5128843**). Here, you'll find

Vienna's finest lobster catch. See p. 86.

- **Best Brew Restaurant:** How Viennese to take your affordable food (large portions) and your suds at the same complex: **Siebenstern-Bräu** (© 01/5232580). Big and bustling, it serves old-fashioned Viennese cuisine such as potato soup and *apfelstrudel*. Of course, lots of sauerkraut and potatoes accompany most dishes, and the most popular platter is an overflowing plate of Wiener schnitzel. See p. 105.

- **Best Desserts:** Sweet tooths flock to the legendary **Café Demel** (© 01/5351717), which took the Hotel Sacher to court over the recipe for the original Sachertorte. Demel also boasts Vienna's finest array of pastries and delectable desserts like *gugelhupfs* (cream-filled horns). See p. 98.

- **Best Afternoon Tea:** Situated across from the Hofburg, the grand **Café Central** (© 01/5333764) is an ideal location for a spot of tea. The decor evokes the rich trappings of late imperial Vienna. You'll find a wide selection of tea (and coffee), as well as a rich variety of pastries and desserts. See p. 98.

- **Best Brunch:** In a style that would have impressed Maria Theresa herself, **Café Imperial,** in the Hotel Imperial (© 01/50110389), prepares an outstanding breakfast buffet on Sundays beginning at 7am. See p. 99.

- **Best Music Feast:** To a true Viennese, a meal is not a meal without music. At **Wiener Rathauskeller,** in City Hall (© 01/405-1210), you'll enjoy all the schnitzel and sauerkraut you can eat while listening to musicians ramble through the world of operetta, waltz, and *schrammel*. See p. 99.

- **Best Picnic Fare:** Head for the **Naschmarkt,** the open-air food market that's a 5-minute stroll from the Karlsplatz. Here you can gather all the ingredients for a spectacular picnic and then enjoy it at the Stadtpark, the Volksgarten, or even in the Vienna Woods. See p. 103.

2

Planning Your Trip to Vienna & the Danube Valley

So, you've decided to visit Vienna. Now you need to figure out how much it will cost, how to get there, and when to go. This chapter will answer these questions, plus give you useful tips on planning your trip and getting the most from your stay.

1 Visitor Information

TOURIST OFFICES

Before you go, we recommend you contact the **Austrian National Tourist Office,** P.O. Box 1142, New York, NY 10108-1142 (© **212/944-6880;** www.austria-tourism.com).

In Canada, you'll find offices at 2 Bloor St. E., Suite 3330, Toronto, ON M4W 1A8 (© **416/967-3381**). In London, contact the Austrian National Tourist Office at 14 Cork St., W1X 1PF (© **0845/101-1818**).

As you travel throughout Vienna and Austria, you'll see signs with a fat "i"

symbol. Most often that stands for "information," and you'll be directed to a local tourist office. Chances are the office staff can help you obtain maps of the area and even assist in finding a hotel, should you arrive without a reservation.

WEBSITES

The sites for the **Austrian National Tourist Office** (www.austria-tourism.com), **Vienna Tourist Board** (www.info.wien.at), and **Mozart Concerts** (www.mozart.co.at) are good places to being your Web search.

2 Entry Requirements & Customs

ENTRY REQUIREMENTS

Citizens of the United States, Canada, the United Kingdom, Australia, Ireland, and New Zealand need only a valid passport to enter Austria. No visa is required.

CUSTOMS

Visitors who live outside Austria in general are not liable for duty on personal articles brought into the country temporarily for their own use, depending on the purpose and circumstances of each trip. Customs officials have great leeway. Travelers 17 years of age and older may carry up to 200 cigarettes, 50 cigars, or

250 grams of tobacco; 1 liter of distilled liquor; and 2 liters of wine or 3 liters of beer duty-free. Gifts not exceeding a value of 175€ ($228) are also exempt from duty.

U.S. CITIZENS Returning U.S. citizens who have been away for 48 hours or more are allowed to bring back, once every 30 days, $800 worth of merchandise duty-free. You'll pay a flat rate of 10% duty on the next $1,000 worth of purchases. Be sure to have your receipts handy. On gifts, the duty-free limit is $200. For more specific guidance, write

Pre-Departure Checklist

- Did you remember your passport? Citizens of E.U. countries can cross into Vienna or Austria for as long as they wish. Citizens of other countries must have a valid passport.
- If you purchased traveler's checks, have you recorded the check numbers and stored the documentation separately from the checks?
- Did you pack your camera and an extra set of camera batteries, and purchase enough film?
- Do you have a safe, accessible place to store money?
- Did you bring your ID cards that could entitle you to discounts, such as AAA and AARP cards and student IDs?
- Did you bring emergency drug prescriptions and extra glasses or contact lenses?
- Do you have your credit card personal identification numbers (PINs)?
- If you have an e-ticket, do you have documentation?
- Did you leave a copy of your itinerary with someone at home?
- Did you check to see if the **U.S. State Department** (http://travel.state. gov/travel_warnings.html) has issued any travel advisories regarding your destination?
- Do you have the address and phone number of your country's embassy with you?

to the **Customs & Border Protection (CBP),** 1300 Pennsylvania Ave. NW, Washington, DC 20229 (© **877/287-8667;** www.cbp.gov), and request the free pamphlet "Know Before You Go." You can also download the pamphlet from the Internet at **www.cbp.gov.**

BRITISH CITIZENS   United Kingdom citizens can buy wine, spirits, or cigarettes in an ordinary shop in Austria and bring home almost as much as they like. But if you buy goods in a duty-free shop, the old rules still apply—the allowance is 200 cigarettes and 2 liters of table wine, plus 1 liter of spirits or 2 liters of fortified wine. If you're returning home from a non–European Union country, the same allowances apply, and you must declare any goods in excess of these allowances. British Customs tends to be strict and complicated. For details, get in touch with **H.M. Customs and Excise,**

National Advice Service, Dorset House, Stamford Street, London SE1 9PY (© **0845/010-9000;** www.hmce.gov.uk).

CANADIAN CITIZENS   For a clear summary of Canadian rules, write for the booklet "I Declare," issued by **Canada Border Services Agency,** 1730 St. Laurent Blvd., Ottawa K1G 4KE (© **800/461-9999** in Canada, or 204/983-3500; www.cbsa-asfc.gc.ca). Canada allows its citizens a C$750 exemption, and you're allowed to bring back, duty-free, 200 cigarettes, 200 grams of tobacco, 1.5 liters of liquor, and 50 cigars. In addition, you may mail gifts to Canada from abroad at the rate of C$60 a day, provided they are unsolicited and aren't alcohol or tobacco (write on the package: "Unsolicited gift, under $60 value"). Before departure from Canada, declare all valuables on the Y-38 Form, including serial numbers of, for example, expensive foreign cameras that you already own. *Note:* The C$750 exemption can be used only once a year and only after an absence of 7 days.

AUSTRALIAN CITIZENS The duty-free allowance in Australia is A$900 or, for those under age 18, A$450. Personal property mailed back from Austria should be marked "Australian goods returned" to avoid duties. Upon returning to Australia, citizens can bring in 250 cigarettes or 250 grams of loose tobacco, and 2.25 liters of alcohol. If you're returning with valuable goods you already own, such as foreign-made cameras, you should file Form B263. A brochure, available from Australian consulates or Customs offices, is "Know Before You Go." For more information, contact **Australian Customs Services,** GPO Box 8, Sydney NSW 2001 (© **1300/363-263** in Australia; www.customs.gov.au).

NEW ZEALAND CITIZENS The duty-free allowance for New Zealand is NZ$700. Citizens over 17 years of age can bring in 200 cigarettes, 50 cigars, or 250 grams of tobacco (or a mixture of all three if their combined weight doesn't exceed 250 grams), plus 4.5 liters of wine and beer or 1.125 liters of liquor. New Zealand currency does not carry import or export restrictions. Fill out a certificate of export, listing the valuables you are taking out of the country; that way, you can bring them back without paying duty. Most questions are answered in a free pamphlet available at New Zealand consulates and Customs offices, "New Zealand Customs Guide for Travellers, Notice no. 4." For more information, contact **New Zealand Customs Services,** 17-21 Whitmore St., Box 2218, Wellington (© **0800/428-786;** www.customs. govt.nz).

3 Money

Foreign money and euros can be brought in and out of Vienna without any restrictions.

CURRENCY

The **euro,** the single European currency, is the official currency of Austria and 12 other participating countries. The symbol of the euro is a stylized E: €. Exchange rates of participating countries are locked into a common currency fluctuating against the U.S. dollar. For more details on the euro, check out **www.europa. eu.int**.

The relative value of the euro fluctuates against the U.S. dollar, the pound sterling, and most of the world's other

---

Tips   **Emergency Cash—The Fastest Way**

If you need emergency cash over the weekend when banks and American Express offices are closed, you can have money wired to you through **Western Union** (© **800/325-6000;** www.westernunion.com). You usually must present valid ID to pick up the cash at the Western Union office. However, in most countries, you can pick up a money transfer even if you don't have valid identification, as long as you can answer a test question provided by the sender. Be sure to let the sender know in advance that you don't have ID. If you need to use a test question instead of ID, the sender must take cash to his or her local Western Union office rather than transferring money over the phone or online.

Foreign Currencies vs. the U.S. Dollar

Conversion ratios between the U.S. dollar and other currencies fluctuate, and their differences could affect the relative cost of your holiday. The figures reflected in the currency chart below were valid at the time of this writing, but they might not be valid by the time of your departure. This chart would be useful for conversions of small amounts of money, but if you're planning on any major transactions, check for more updated rates prior to making any serious commitments.

The US Dollar and the Euro   US$1 was worth approximately .76€ at the time of this writing. Inversely stated, that means that 1€ was worth approximately US$1.30.

The British pound, the Euro, and the U.S. Dollar   At press time, £1 = approximately 1.52€, or US$1.90.

The Canadian dollar, the Euro, and the U.S. dollar   At press time, C$1 = approximately .68€, or ¢88.

Euro€	US$	U.K. £	Canadian $	Euro	US$	U.K. £	CD$
1	1.30	0.65	1.47	75	97.50	48.75	110.25
2	2.60	1.30	2.94	100	130.00	65.00	147.00
3	3.90	1.95	4.41	125	162.50	81.25	183.75
4	5.20	2.60	5.88	150	195.00	97.50	220.50
5	6.50	3.25	7.35	175	227.50	113.75	257.25
6	7.80	3.90	8.82	200	260.00	130.00	294.00
7	9.10	4.55	10.29	225	292.50	146.25	330.75
8	10.40	5.20	11.76	250	325.00	162.50	367.50
9	11.70	5.85	13.23	275	357.50	178.75	404.25
10	13.00	6.50	14.70	300	390.00	195.00	441.00
15	19.50	9.75	22.05	350	455.00	227.50	514.50
20	26.00	13.00	29.40	400	520.00	260.00	588.00
25	32.50	16.25	36.75	500	650.00	325.00	735.00
50	65.00	32.50	73.50	1000	1300.00	650.00	1470.00

currencies, and its value might not be the same by the time you travel to Vienna. We advise a last-minute check before your trip.

Exchange rates are more favorable at the point of arrival than at the departure point. Nevertheless, it's often helpful to exchange at least some money before going abroad (standing in line at the exchange bureau in the Vienna airport isn't fun after a long overseas flight). Check with any of your local American Express or Thomas Cook offices or major banks. Or, order in advance from **American Express** (© **800/221-7282,** cardholders only; www.americanexpress.com) or **Thomas Cook** (© **800/223-7373;** www.thomascook.com).

It's best to exchange currency or traveler's checks at a bank, not at a currency service, hotel, or shop. Currency and traveler's checks (for which you'll receive a better rate than cash) can be changed at all principal airports and at some travel

What Things Cost in Vienna	Euro€	US$
Bus from the airport to the city center	6.00	7.20
U-Bahn (subway) from St. Stephan's to Schönbrunn Palace	1.50	1.80
Double room at Hotel Astoria (expensive)	210.00	252.00
Double room at the Am Parkring (moderate)	165.00	198.00
Double room at the Pension Nossek (inexpensive)	110.00	132.00
Lunch for one, without wine, at Drei Husaren (expensive)	33.00	39.60
Lunch for one, without wine, at Griechenbeisl (moderate)	20.00	24.00
Dinner for one, without wine, at Plachutta (expensive)	38.00	45.60
Dinner for one, without wine, at Firenze Enoteca (moderate)	28.00	33.60
Dinner for one, without wine, at Zwölf-Apostelkeller (inexpensive)	16.00	19.20
Glass of wine	2.50–3.00	3.00–3.60
Half-liter of beer in a *beisl*	3.25	3.90
Coca-Cola in cafe	3.00	3.60
Cup of coffee *(ein kleine Braun)*	3.00	3.60
Roll of color film, 36 exp.	8.50	10.20
Movie ticket	10.00	13.00
Admission to Schönbrunn Palace	11.50	13.80

agencies, such as American Express and Thomas Cook.

If you need to prepay a deposit on hotel reservations by check, it's cheaper and easier to pay with a check drawn on an Austrian bank. You can arrange this through a large commercial bank or **Ruesch International,** 700 11th St. NW, Washington, DC 20001 (© **800/424-2923** or 202/408-1200; www.ruesch.com), which performs many conversion-related tasks, usually for only $15 per transaction.

ATMs

ATMs are prevalent in all Austrian cities and even smaller towns. ATMs are linked to a national network that most likely includes your bank at home. Both the **Cirrus** (© **800/424-7787;** www.mastercard.com) and the **PLUS** (© **800/843-7587;** www.visa.com) networks have automated ATM locators listing the banks in Austria that'll accept your card. Or, just search out any machine with your network's symbol emblazoned on it.

Important note: Make sure that the PINs on your bankcards and credit cards will work in Austria. You'll need a **four-digit code,** so if you have a six-digit code, you'll have to go into your bank and get a new PIN for your trip. If you're unsure about this, contact Cirrus or PLUS (above). Be sure to check the daily withdrawal limit at the same time.

TRAVELER'S CHECKS

You can buy traveler's checks at most banks. They are offered in denominations of $20, $50, $100, $500, and sometimes $1,000. Generally, you'll pay a service charge ranging from 1% to 4%.

The most popular traveler's checks are offered by **American Express** (© 800/221-7282 for cardholders—this number accepts collect calls, offers service in several foreign languages, and exempts Amex gold and platinum cardholders from the 1% fee); **Visa** (© 800/732-1322)—AAA members can obtain Visa checks for a $9.95 fee (for checks up to $1,500) at most AAA offices or by calling © 866/339-3378; and **MasterCard** (© 800/223-9920).

American Express, Thomas Cook, Visa, and **MasterCard** offer **foreign currency traveler's checks,** which are useful if you're traveling to one country, or to the Euro zone; they're accepted at locations where dollar checks may not be.

If you carry traveler's checks, keep a record of their serial numbers separate from your checks in the event that they are stolen or lost. You'll get a refund faster if you know the numbers.

CREDIT CARDS

Credit cards are invaluable when traveling—they're a safe way to carry money and a convenient record of all your expenses. You can also withdraw cash advances from your cards at any bank (although this should be reserved for dire emergencies only, because you'll start paying hefty interest the moment you receive the cash).

Note, however, that many banks, including Chase and Citibank, charge a 2% to 3% service fee for transactions in a foreign currency.

4 When to Go

Vienna experiences its high season from April through October, with July and August being the most crowded times. Bookings around Christmas are also heavy because many Austrians visit the capital city during this festive time. Always arrive with reservations during these peak seasons. During the off-seasons, hotel rooms are plentiful and less expensive, and there's less demand for tables in the top restaurants.

CLIMATE

Vienna has a moderate subalpine climate; the January average is 32°F (0°C), and in July it's 66°F (19°C). A New Yorker who lived in Vienna for 8 years told us that the four seasons were "about the same" as in New York. Summers in Vienna, which generally last from Easter until mid-October, are not usually as humid as those in New York City, but they can be uncomfortably sticky. The ideal times for visiting Vienna are spring and fall, when mild weather prevails, but the winter air is usually crisp and clear, with plenty of sunshine.

HOLIDAYS

Bank holidays in Vienna are as follows: New Year's Day (Jan 1); Epiphany (Jan 6); Easter Monday (Apr 9 in 2007, March 24 in 2008, Apr 12 in 2009); Labor Day (May 1); Ascension Day (May 17 in 2007, May 1 in 2008, May 21 in 2009); Whitmonday (May 28 in 2007, May 26 in 2008, May 25 in 2009); Corpus Christi Day (June 7 in 2007, May 22 in 2008, June 11 in 2009); Assumption of Mary (Aug 15); Nationalfeiertag (Oct 26); All Saints Day (Nov 1); Immaculate Conception (Dec 8); Christmas (Dec 25 and 26); and St. Stephen's Day (Dec 26).

Average Daytime Temperature & Monthly Rainfall in Vienna

	Jan	Feb	Mar	Apr	May	June	July	Aug	Sept	Oct	Nov	Dec
Temp. (°F)	30	32	38	50	58	64	68	70	60	50	41	33
Temp. (°C)	−1	0	3	10	14	18	20	21	16	10	5	1
Rainfall (in.)	1.2	1.9	3.9	1.3	2.9	1.9	.8	1.8	2.8	2.8	2.5	1.6

VIENNA CALENDAR OF EVENTS

January

New Year's Eve/New Year's Day. The famed concert of the Vienna Philharmonic Orchestra launches Vienna's biggest night. The New Year also marks the beginning of **Fasching**, the famous Vienna Carnival season, which lasts through Shrove Tuesday (Mardi Gras). For tickets and information, contact the Wiener Philharmoniker, Bösendorferstrasse 12, A-1010 Vienna (✆ 01/505-6525; www.wienerphilharmoniker.at). The **Imperial Ball** in the Hofburg follows the concert. For information and tickets, contact the Hofburg Kongressz Ent Rum, Hofburg, Heldenplatz, A-1014 Vienna (✆ 01/587-3666; www.hofburg.com). December 31/January 1.

Eistraum (Dream on Ice). During the coldest months of the Austrian winter, the monumental plaza between the Town Hall and the Burgtheater is flooded and frozen. Lights, loudspeakers, and a stage are hauled in, and the entire civic core is transformed into a gigantic ice-skating rink. Sedate waltz tunes accompany the skaters during the day, and DJs spin rock, funk, and reggae after the sun goes down. Around the rink, dozens of kiosks sell everything from hot chocolate and snacks to wine and beer. For information, call ✆ 01/319-8200; www.wienereistraum.com. Last week of January to mid-March.

February

Opera Ball. Vienna's high society gathers at the Staatsoper for the grandest ball of the Carnival season. The evening opens with a performance by the Opera House Ballet. You don't need an invitation, but you do need to buy a ticket, which, as you might guess, isn't cheap. For information, call the Opera House (✆ 01/514-44-2315; www.staatsoper.at). On the last Thursday of the Fasching.

Vienna Spring Festival. The festival has a different central theme every year, but you can always count on music by the world's greatest composers, including Mozart and Brahms, at the Konzerthaus. The booking address is Karlsplatz 6, Lothringerstrasse 20, A-1030 Vienna (✆ 01/242-002; www.konzerthaus.at). Mid-March through the first week of May.

May

International Music Festival. This traditional highlight of Vienna's concert calendar features top-class international orchestras, distinguished conductors, and classical greats. You can hear Beethoven's *Eroica* in its purest form, Mozart's *Jupiter Symphony,* and perhaps Bruckner's *Romantic.* The list of conductors and orchestras reads like a "who's who" of the international world of music. The venue and the booking address is Wiener Musikverein, Bösendorferstrasse 12, A-1010 Vienna (✆ 01/505-8190; www.musikverein-wien.at). Early May through late June.

Vienna Festival. An exciting array of operas, operettas, musicals, theater, and dances, this festival presents new productions of classics alongside avant-garde premieres, all staged by international leading directors. Celebrated productions from renowned European theaters offer guest performances. Expect such productions as Mozart's *Così Fan Tutte,* Monteverdi's *Orfeo,* and Offenbach's *La Vie Parisienne.* For bookings, contact Wiener Festwochen, Lehárgasse 11, A-1060 Vienna (*©* 01/ 589-2222; www.festwochen.at). Second week of May until mid-June.

June

Vienna Jazz Festival. This is one of the world's top jazz events, based at the Vienna State Opera. The program features more than 50 international and local stars. For information and bookings, contact the Verein Jazz Fest Wien, Lammgasse 12 (*©* 01/712-4224; www. viennajazz.org). Late June to early July.

July–August

Music Film Festival. Opera, operetta, and masterly concert performances captured on celluloid play free under a starry sky in front of the neo-Gothic City Hall on the Ringstrasse. Programs focus on works by Franz Schubert, Johannes Brahms, or other composers. You might view Rudolf Nureyev in *Swan Lake* or see Leonard Bernstein wielding the baton for Brahms. For more information, contact Ideenagentur Austria, Opernring 1R, A-1010 Vienna (*©* 01/4000-8100; www. wien-event.at). Early July and early September.

October

Wien Modern. Celebrating its 20th year in 2007, the Wien Modern was founded by Claudio Abbado and is devoted to the performance of contemporary music. You might catch works from Iceland, Romania, or Portugal, in addition to Austria. Performances are at Verein Wien Modern, Lothringerstrasse 20; the booking address is Wiener Konzerthaus, Lothringerstrasse 20 (*©* 01/242-002; www. konzerthaus.at). Late October through late November.

December

Christkindlmärkt. Between late November and New Year's, look for pockets of folk charm (and, in some cases, kitsch) associated with the Christmas holidays. Small outdoor booths known as *Christkindlmarkts*— usually adorned with evergreen boughs, red ribbons, and, in some cases, religious symbols—sprout up in clusters around the city. They sell old-fashioned toys, *tannenbaum* (tree) decorations, and gift items. Food vendors offer sausages, cookies and pastries, roasted chestnuts, and *kartoffel* (charcoal-roasted potato slices). The greatest concentration of open-air markets is in front of the Rathaus, in the Spittelberg Quarter (7th District), at Freyung, the historic square in the northwest corner of the Inner City.

5 Travel Insurance

Check your existing insurance policies and credit card coverage before you buy travel insurance. You may already be covered for lost luggage, canceled tickets, or medical expenses. The cost of travel insurance varies widely, depending on the cost and length of your trip, your age and health, and the type of trip you're taking, but expect to pay between 5% and 8% of the vacation itself. You can get estimates from various providers through **InsureMy Trip.com.** Enter your trip cost and dates, your age, and other information, for prices from more than a dozen companies.

TRIP-CANCELLATION INSURANCE Trip-cancellation insurance helps you get your money back if you have to back out

Travel in the Age of Bankruptcy

Airlines go bankrupt, so protect yourself by **buying your tickets with a credit card.** The Fair Credit Billing Act guarantees that you can get your money back from the credit card company if a travel supplier goes under (and if you request the refund within 60 days of the bankruptcy). **Travel insurance** can also help, but make sure it covers against "carrier default" for your specific travel provider. And be aware that if a U.S. airline goes bust mid-trip, a 2001 federal law requires other carriers to take you to your destination (albeit on a space-available basis) for a fee of no more than $25, provided you rebook within 60 days of the cancellation.

of a trip, if you have to go home early, or if your travel supplier goes bankrupt. Allowed reasons for cancellation can include sickness, natural disasters, and the State Department declaring your destination unsafe for travel. For information, contact one of the following recommended insurers: **Access America** (© 866/807-3982; www.accessamerica. com, **Travel Guard International** (© 800/826-4919; www.travelguard. com), **Travel Insured International** (© 800/243-3174; www.travelinsured. com), and **Travelex Insurance Services** (© 888/457-4602; www.travelex-insurance.com).

MEDICAL INSURANCE For travel overseas, most health plans (including Medicare and Medicaid) do not provide coverage, and the ones that do often require you to pay for services upfront and reimburse you only after you return home. Even if your plan does cover overseas treatment, most out-of-country hospitals make you pay your bills upfront, and send you a refund only after you've returned home and filed the necessary paperwork with your insurance company. You may want to buy travel medical insurance, particularly if you're traveling to a remote or high-risk area where emergency evacuation is a possible scenario. If you require additional medical insurance,

try **MEDEX Assistance** (© 410/453-6300; www.medexassist.com) or **Travel Assistance International** (© 800/821-2828; www.travelassistance.com; for general information on services, call the company's **Worldwide Assistance Services, Inc.,** at © 800/777-8710, or visit www.worldwideassistance.com).

LOST-LUGGAGE INSURANCE On international flights (including U.S. portions of international trips), baggage coverage is limited to approximately $9.10 per pound, up to approximately $635 per checked bag. If you plan to check items more valuable than the standard liability, see if your valuables are covered by your homeowner's policy, get baggage insurance as part of your comprehensive travel-insurance package. Don't buy insurance at the airport, as it's usually overpriced. Take any valuables or irreplaceable items with you in your carry-on, as many valuables (including books, money, and electronics) aren't covered by airline policies.

If your luggage is lost, immediately file a lost-luggage claim at the airport, detailing the luggage contents. For most airlines, you must report delayed, damaged, or lost baggage within 4 hours of arrival. The airlines are required to deliver luggage, once found, directly to your house or destination free.

6 Health & Safety

STAYING HEALTHY

You'll encounter few health problems while traveling in Austria. The tap water is generally safe to drink, the milk is pasteurized, and health services are good.

There's no need to get any shots before visiting Austria, but you might pack some antidiarrheal medications. It's not that the food or water in Austria is unhealthy; it's different and might at first cause digestive problems for those unfamiliar with it.

It's easy to get over-the-counter medicine. Fortunately, generic equivalents of common prescription drugs are available at most destinations in which you'll be traveling. It's also easy to find English-speaking doctors and to get prescriptions filled at all cities, towns, and resorts. You might experience some inconvenience, of course, if you travel in the remote hinterlands.

Before you go, contact the **International Association for Medical Assistance to Travelers** (IAMAT; © 716/754-4883, or 416/652-0137 in Canada; www.iamat.org) for tips on travel and health concerns in the countries you're visiting, and lists of local, English-speaking doctors. The United States **Centers for Disease Control and Prevention** (© 800/311-3435; www.cdc.gov) provides up-to-date information on health hazards by region or country.

WHAT TO DO IF YOU GET SICK AWAY FROM HOME

Nearly all doctors in Vienna speak English. If you get sick, consider asking your hotel concierge to recommend a local doctor—even his or her own. You can also try the emergency room at a local hospital. Many hospitals also have walk-in clinics for emergency cases that are not life-threatening; you may not get immediate attention, but you won't pay the high price of an emergency room visit.

We list hospitals and emergency numbers for Vienna under "Fast Facts" in chapter 3.

If you worry about getting sick away from home, consider purchasing **medical travel insurance** and carry your ID card in your purse or wallet. In most cases, your existing health plan will provide the coverage you need. See the section on insurance, above, for more information.

If you suffer from a chronic illness, consult your doctor before you depart. For conditions such as epilepsy, diabetes, or heart problems, wear a **Medic Alert Identification Tag** (© 888/633-4298; www.medicalert.org), which will immediately alert doctors to your condition and give them access to your records through Medic Alert's 24-hour hot line.

Pack **prescription medications** in your carry-on luggage and carry prescription medications in their original containers with pharmacy labels—otherwise they won't make it through airport security. Also, bring along copies of your prescriptions in case you lose your pills or run out. Don't forget an extra pair of contact lenses or prescription glasses. Carry the generic name of prescription medicines, in case a local pharmacist is unfamiliar with the brand name.

Contact the **International Association for Medical Assistance to Travelers** (IAMAT; © 716/754-4883 or 416/652-0137; www.iamat.org) for tips on travel and health concerns in the countries you're visiting and lists of local, English-speaking doctors. The U.S. **Centers for Disease Control and Prevention** (© 800/311-3435; www.cdc.gov) provides up-to-date information on necessary vaccines and health hazards by region or country. In Canada, contact **Health Canada** (© 613/957-2991; www.hc-sc.gc.ca). The website **www.tripprep.com**, sponsored by a consortium of travel medicine practitioners, may also offer helpful

Healthy Travels to You

The following government websites offer up-to-date health-related travel advice.
- Australia: www.dfat.gov/au/travel/
- Canada: www.hc-sc.gc.ca/index_e.html
- U.K.: www.dh.gov/uk/PolicyAndGuidance/HealthAdviceForTravellers/fs/en
- U.S.: www.cdc.gov/travel/

advice on traveling abroad. You can find listings of reliable clinics overseas at the **International Society of Travel Medicine** (www.istm.org). Any foreign consulate can provide a list of area doctors who speak English.

STAYING SAFE

Never leave valuables in a car, and never travel with your car unlocked. A U.S. State Department travel advisory warns that every car (whether parked, stopped at a traffic light, or even moving) can be a potential target for armed robbery. In these uncertain times, it is always prudent to check the U.S. State Department's travel advisories at **http://travel.state.gov**.

Austria has a low crime rate, and violent crime is rare. However, travelers can become targets of pickpockets and purse snatchers who operate where tourists tend to gather. Some of the most frequently reported spots include Vienna's two largest train stations, the plaza around St. Stephan's Cathedral, and the nearby pedestrian shopping areas (in Vienna's 1st District).

7 Specialized Travel Resources

TRAVELERS WITH DISABILITIES

Laws in Austria compel rail stations, airports, hotels, and most restaurants to follow strict regulations about **wheelchair accessibility** for restrooms, ticket counters, and the like. Museums and other attractions conform to the regulations, which mimic many of those in effect in the United States. Call ahead to check on accessibility in hotels, restaurants, and sights you want to visit.

Many travel agencies offer customized tours and itineraries for travelers with disabilities. **Flying Wheels Travel** (© 507/451-5005; www.flyingwheelstravel.com) offers escorted tours and cruises that emphasize sports and private tours in minivans with lifts. **Access-Able Travel Source** (© 303/232-2979; www.access-able.com) offers extensive access information and advice for traveling around the world with disabilities. **Accessible**

Journeys (© 800/846-4537 or 610/521-0339; www.disabilitytravel.com) caters specifically to slow walkers and wheelchair travelers and their families and friends.

Organizations that offer assistance to travelers with disabilities include **Moss-Rehab** (www.mossresourcenet.org), which provides a library of accessible-travel resources online; the **SATH (Society for Accessible Travel and Hospitality;** © 212/447-7284; www.sath.org; annual membership fees: $45 adults, $30 seniors and students), which offers a wealth of travel resources; and the **American Foundation for the Blind (AFB;** © 800/232-5463; www.afb.org), a referral resource for the blind or visually impaired that includes information on traveling with Seeing Eye dogs.

For more information specifically targeted to travelers with disabilities, the community website **iCan** (www.ican online.net/channels/travel/index.cfm) has destination guides and several regular columns on accessible travel. Also check out the quarterly magazine **Emerging Horizons** (www.emerginghorizons.com); and *Open World Magazine,* published by SATH (above; subscription: $13 per year, $21 outside the U.S.).

FOR BRITISH TRAVELERS

The **Royal Association for Disability and Rehabilitation (RADAR)**, Unit 12, City Forum, 250 City Rd., London EC1V 8AF (© **020/7250-3222;** www. radar.org.uk), publishes three holiday "fact packs" for £2 ($3.60) each or £5 ($9) for all three. The first provides general information, including tips for planning and booking a holiday, obtaining insurance, and handling finances; the second outlines transportation available when going abroad and equipment for rent; and the third deals with specialized accommodations. Another good resource is **Holiday Care Service,** Seventh Floor, Sunley House, 4 Bedford Park, Croydon, Surrey CR0 2AP (© **0845/124-9971;** www.holidaycare.org.uk), a national charity advising on accessible accommodations for the elderly and persons with disabilities.

GAY & LESBIAN TRAVELERS

Unlike Germany, Austria still has a prevailing antihomosexual attitude, in spite of the large number of gay people who live there. There is still much discrimination; gay liberation has a long way to go. Vienna, however, has a large gay community with many bars and restaurants. For information about gay-related activities in Vienna, go to **Rainbow Online** (www. gay.or.at).

In Austria, the minimum age for consensual homosexual activity is 18.

The **International Gay and Lesbian Travel Association (IGLTA;** © **800/ 448-8550** or 954/776-2626; www.iglta.

org) is the trade association for the gay and lesbian travel industry, and offers a directory of gay- and lesbian-friendly travel businesses; go to its website and click "Members."

Many agencies offer tours and travel itineraries specifically for gay and lesbian travelers. **Above and Beyond Tours** (© **800/397-2681;** www.abovebeyond tours.com) is the exclusive gay and lesbian tour operator for United Airlines. **Now, Voyager** (© **800/255-6951;** www. nowvoyager.com) is a well-known San Francisco–based gay travel service. **Olivia Cruises & Resorts** (© **800/631-6277;** www.olivia.com) charters entire resorts and ships for exclusive lesbian vacations and offers smaller group experiences for both gay and lesbian travelers. **Gay.com Travel** (© **800/929-2268** or 415/644-8044; www.gay.com/travel or www.out andabout.com), is an excellent online successor to the popular *Out & About* print magazine. It provides regularly updated information about gay-owned, gay-oriented, and gay-friendly lodging, dining, sightseeing, nightlife, and shopping establishments in every important destination worldwide. It also offers trip-planning information for gay and lesbian travelers for more than 50 destinations, along various themes, ranging from Sex & Travel to Vacations for Couples.

The following travel guides are available at many bookstores, or you can order them from any online bookseller: *Frommer's Gay & Lesbian Europe* (www.frommers.com), an excellent travel resource to the top European cities and resorts; *Spartacus International Gay Guide* (Bruno Gmünder Verlag; www.spartacusworld.com/gayguide) and *Odysseus: The International Gay Travel Planner* (Odysseus Enterprises Ltd.), both good, annual, English-language guidebooks focused on gay men; and the *Damron* guides (www.damron. com), with separate, annual books for gay men and lesbians.

SENIOR TRAVEL

Many Austrian hotels offer discounts for seniors. Mention the fact that you're a senior citizen when you make your travel reservations.

Members of **AARP** (formerly known as the American Association of Retired Persons), 601 E St. NW, Washington, DC 20049 (© **888/687-2277;** www. aarp.org), get discounts on hotels, airfares, and car rentals. AARP offers members a wide range of benefits, including *AARP: The Magazine* and a monthly newsletter. Anyone over 50 can join.

Many reliable agencies and organizations target the 50-plus market. **Elderhostel** (© **877/426-8056;** www.elder hostel.org) arranges study programs for those aged 55 and over (and a spouse or companion of any age) in the U.S. and in more than 80 countries around the world, including Austria. Most courses last 2 to 4 weeks abroad, and many include airfare, accommodations in university dormitories or modest inns, meals, and tuition. **ElderTreks** (© **800/741-7956;** www.eldertreks.com) offers small-group tours to off-the-beaten-path or adventure-travel locations, restricted to travelers 50 and older. **INTRAV** (© **800/456-8100;** www.intrav.com) is a high-end tour operator that caters to the mature, discerning traveler (not specifically seniors), with trips around the world that include guided safaris, polar expeditions, private-jet adventures, and small-boat cruises down jungle rivers.

Recommended publications offering travel resources and discounts for seniors include: the quarterly magazine *Travel 50 & Beyond* (www.travel50andbeyond. com); *Travel Unlimited: Uncommon Adventures for the Mature Traveler* (Avalon); *101 Tips for Mature Travelers,* available from Grand Circle Travel (© **800/221-2610** or 617/350-7500; www.gct.com); *The 50+ Traveler's Guidebook* (St. Martin's Press); and *Unbelievably Good Deals and Great Adventures That You Absolutely Can't Get Unless You're Over 50* (McGraw-Hill), by Joann Rattner Heilman.

FAMILY TRAVEL

If you have enough trouble getting your kids out of the house in the morning, dragging them thousands of miles away may seem like an insurmountable challenge. But family travel can be immensely rewarding, and Vienna is a great place to take your kids. The pleasures available for children (which most adults enjoy just as much) range from watching the magnificent Lipizzaner stallions at the Spanish Riding School to exploring the city's many castles and dungeons.

Another outstanding attraction is the Prater amusement park, with its giant Ferris wheel, roller coasters, merry-go-rounds, arcades, and tiny railroad. Even if your kids aren't very interested in touring palaces, take them to Schönbrunn, where the zoo and coach collection will tantalize. In summer, beaches along the Alte Donau (an arm of the Danube) are suitable for swimming. And don't forget the lure of the *Konditorei,* little shops that sell scrumptious Viennese cakes and pastries.

Babysitting services are available through most hotel desks or by applying at the tourist information office in the town where you're staying. Many hotels have children's game rooms and playgrounds.

Throughout this guide, look for the "Kids" icon, which highlights child-friendly destinations.

Familyhostel (© **800/733-9753;** www.learn.unh.edu/familyhostel) takes the whole family, including kids ages 8 to 15, on moderately priced learning vacations. Lectures, field trips, and sightseeing are guided by a team of academics.

Recommended family travel Internet sites include **Family Travel Forum** (www. familytravelforum.com), a comprehensive site that offers customized trip planning; **Family Travel Network** (www.

Traveling with Minors

It's always wise to have plenty of documentation when traveling children. For changing details on entry requirements for children traveling abroad, keep up-to-date at the U.S. State Department website: http://travel.state.gov/family. To prevent international child abduction, E.U. governments have initiated procedures at entry and exit points. These often include requiring documentary evidence of relationship and permission for the child's travel from the parent or legal guardian not present. Having such documentation on hand, even if not required, facilitates entries and exits. All children must have their own passport. To obtain a passport, the child **must** be present—that is, in person—at the center issuing the passport. Both parents must be present as well. If not, then a notarized statement from the parents is required. Any questions parents or guardians might have can be answered by calling the **National Passport Information Center** at ℰ **877/487-2778** Monday to Friday 8am to 8pm Eastern Standard Time.

familytravelnetwork.com), an award-winning site that offers travel features, deals, and tips; **Traveling Internationally with Your Kids** (www.travelwithyourkids. com), a comprehensive site offering sound advice for long-distance and international travel with children; and **Family Travel Files** (www.thefamilytravelfiles. com), which offers an online magazine and a directory of off-the-beaten-path tours and tour operators for families.

STUDENT TRAVEL

If you're planning to travel outside the U.S., you'd be wise to arm yourself with an **International Student Identity Card (ISIC),** which offers substantial savings on rail passes, plane tickets, and entrance fees. It also provides you with basic health and life insurance and a 24-hour help line. The card is available for $22 from **STA Travel** (ℰ **800/781-4040** in North America; www.sta.com; www.statravel. co.uk in the U.K.), the biggest student travel agency in the world. If you're no longer a student but are still under 26, you can get an **International Youth Travel Card (IYTC)** for the same price from the same people, which entitles you to some discounts (but not on museum admissions). **Travel CUTS** (ℰ **800/667-2887** or 888/359-2887; www.travelcuts. com) offers similar services for both Canadians and U.S. residents. Irish students may prefer to turn to **USIT** (ℰ **01/ 602-1904;** www.usitnow.ie), an Ireland-based specialist in student, youth, and independent travel.

8 Planning Your Trip Online

SURFING FOR AIRFARES

The most popular online travel agencies are **Travelocity** (www.travelocity.com or www.travelocity.co.uk); **Expedia** (www. expedia.com, www.expedia.co.uk, or www.expedia.ca); and **Orbitz** (www. orbitz.com).

In addition, most airlines now offer online-only fares that even their phone agents know nothing about. For the websites of airlines that fly to and from your destination, go to "Getting There," p. 27.

Other helpful websites for booking airline tickets online include:

- www.biddingfortravel.com
- www.cheapflights.com
- www.hotwire.com

- www.kayak.com
- www.lastminutetravel.com
- www.opodo.co.uk
- www.priceline.com
- www.sidestep.com
- www.site59.com
- www.smartertravel.com

For more info about airfares and savvy air-travel tips and advice, pick up a copy of *Frommer's Fly Safe, Fly Smart* (Wiley Publishing, Inc.).

SURFING FOR HOTELS

In addition to **Travelocity, Expedia, Orbitz, Priceline,** and **Hotwire** (see above), the following websites will help you with booking hotel rooms online:

- www.hotels.com
- www.quickbook.com
- www.travelaxe.net
- www.travelweb.com
- www.tripadvisor.com

It's a good idea to **get a confirmation number** and **make a printout** of any online booking transaction.

SURFING FOR RENTAL CARS

For booking rental cars online, the best deals are usually found at rental car company websites, although all the major online travel agencies also offer rental car reservations services. Priceline and Hotwire work well for rental cars, too; the only "mystery" is which major rental company you get, and for most travelers the difference between Hertz, Avis, and Budget is negligible.

TRAVEL BLOGS AND TRAVELOGUES

To read a few blogs about Austria, try

- www.travelblog.com
- www.travelblog.org
- www.worldhum.com
- www.writtenroad.com

9 The 21st-Century Traveler

INTERNET ACCESS AWAY FROM HOME

Travelers have any number of ways to check their e-mail and access the Internet on the road. Of course, using your own laptop—or even a PDA (personal digital assistant) or electronic organizer with a modem—gives you the most flexibility.

Frommers.com: The Complete Travel Resource

For an excellent travel-planning resource, we highly recommend **Frommers. com** (www.frommers.com), voted Best Travel Site by *PC Magazine*. We're a little biased, of course, but we guarantee that you'll find the travel tips, reviews, monthly vacation giveaways, bookstore, and online-booking capabilities to be thoroughly indispensable. Special features include our popular **Destinations** section, where you can access expert travel tips, hotel and dining recommendations, and advice on the sights to see in more than 3,500 destinations around the globe; the **Frommers.com Newsletter,** with the latest deals, travel trends, and money-saving secrets; and our **Travel Talk** area featuring **Message Boards,** where Frommer's readers post queries and share advice, and where our authors sometimes show up to answer questions. Once you finish your research, the **Book a Trip** area can lead you to Frommer's preferred online partners' websites, where you can book your vacation at affordable prices.

But if you don't have a computer, you can still access your e-mail and even your office computer from cybercafes.

WITHOUT YOUR OWN COMPUTER

It's hard nowadays to find a city that *doesn't* have a few cybercafes. Although there's no definitive directory for cyber-cafes—these are independent businesses, after all—two places to start looking are at **www.cybercaptive.com** and **www. cybercafe.com**. See "Fast Facts" in chapter 3 for information on Internet access in Vienna.

Aside from formal cybercafes, most **youth hostels** nowadays have at least one computer you can get to the Internet on. And most **public libraries** across the world offer Internet access free or for a small charge. Avoid **hotel business centers,** unless you're willing to pay exorbitant rates.

Most major airports now have **Internet kiosks** scattered throughout their gates, but we find them high-priced and clunky. These kiosks, which you'll also see in shopping malls, hotel lobbies, and tourist information offices around the world, give you basic Web access for a per-minute fee that's usually higher than cybercafe prices.

WITH YOUR OWN COMPUTER

More and more hotels, cafes, and retailers are signing on as Wi-Fi (wireless fidelity) "hotspots." Mac owners have their own networking technology: Apple AirPort. **Boingo** (www.boingo.com) and **Way-port** (www.wayport.com) have set up networks in airports and high-class hotel lobbies. iPass providers (see below) also give you access to a few hundred wireless hotel lobby setups. To locate other hotspots that provide **free wireless networks** in cities around the world, go to **www.personaltelco.net/index.cgi/ WirelessCommunities**.

For dial-up access, most business-class hotels throughout the world offer dataports for laptop modems, and a few thousand hotels in the U.S. and Europe now offer free high-speed Internet access. In addition, major Internet Service Providers (ISPs) have **local access numbers** around the world, allowing you to go online by placing a local call. The **iPass** network also has dial-up numbers around the world. You'll have to sign up with an iPass provider, who will then tell you how to set up your computer for your destination(s). For a list of iPass providers, go to www.ipass.com and click on "Individuals Buy Now." One solid provider is **i2roam** (www.i1roam.com; ℰ **866/811-6209** or 920/235-0475).

Wherever you go, bring a **connection kit** of the right power and phone adapters, a spare phone cord, and a spare Ethernet network cable—or find out whether your hotel supplies them to guests.

USING A CELLPHONE OUTSIDE THE U.S.

The three letters that define much of the world's **wireless capabilities** are GSM (Global System for Mobiles), a big, seamless network that makes for easy cross-border cellphone use throughout Europe and dozens of other countries worldwide. In the U.S., T-Mobile, AT&T Wireless, and Cingular use this quasi-universal system; in Canada, Microcell and some Rogers customers are GSM, and all Europeans and most Australians use GSM.

If your cellphone is on a GSM system, and you have a world-capable multiband phone such as many (but not all) Sony Ericsson, Motorola, or Samsung models, you can make and receive calls across civilized areas on much of the globe. Just call your wireless operator and ask for "international roaming" to be activated on your account. Unfortunately, per-minute charges can be high—usually $1 to $1.50 in western Europe.

While you can rent a phone from any number of overseas sites, including kiosks at airports and at car-rental agencies, we suggest renting the phone before you leave home. North Americans can rent one before leaving home from **InTouch USA** (ℂ **800/872-7626;** www.intouch-global.com) or **RoadPost** (ℂ **888/290-1606** or 905/272-5665; www.roadpost.com). InTouch will also, for free, advise you on whether your existing phone will work overseas; simply call ℂ **703/222-7161** between 9am and 4pm EST, or go to **http:intouchglobal.com/travel.htm**.

10 Getting There

BY PLANE

As a gateway between western and eastern Europe, Vienna has seen an increase in air traffic. Although a number of well-respected European airlines serve Vienna, most flights from America require a transfer in another European city, such as London or Frankfurt.

THE MAJOR AIRLINES FROM THE UNITED STATES

You can fly directly to Vienna on **Austrian Airlines** (ℂ **800/843-0002** in the U.S., 888/817-444 in Canada; www.austrian air.com), the national carrier of Austria. There's nonstop service from New York (approximately 9 hr.), Washington, and Toronto.

British Airways (ℂ **800/AIRWAYS** in the U.S. and Canada; www.british airways.com) provides excellent service to Vienna. Passengers fly first to London—usually nonstop—from 23 gateways in the United States, 5 in Canada, 2 in Brazil, or from Bermuda, Mexico City, or Buenos Aires. From London, British Airways has two to five daily nonstop flights to Vienna from either Gatwick or Heathrow airport.

Flights on **Lufthansa** (ℂ **800/645-3880** in the U.S. and Canada; www.lufthansa-usa.com), the German national carrier, depart from North America frequently for Frankfurt and Düsseldorf, with connections to Vienna.

Tips Getting Through the Airport

- Arrive at the airport 1 hour before a domestic flight and 2 hours before an international flight; if you show up late, tell an airline employee, and he or she will probably whisk you to the front of the line.
- Beat the ticket-counter lines by using airport electronic kiosks or even online check-in from your home computers, from where you can print out boarding passes in advance. Curbside check-in is also a good way to avoid lines.
- Bring a current, government-issued photo ID such as a driver's license or passport. Children under 18 do not need government-issued photo IDs for flights within the U.S., but they do for international flights to most countries.
- Speed up security by removing your jacket and shoes before you're screened. In addition, remove metal objects such as big belt buckles. If you've got metallic body parts, a note from your doctor can prevent a long chat with the security screeners.
- Use a TSA-approved lock for your checked luggage. Look for Travel Sentry certified locks at luggage or travel shops and Brookstone stores (or online at www.brookstone.com).

Tips **New Security Measures**

Because of increased security measures, the Transportation Security Administration has made changes to the prohibited items list. All liquids and gels—including shampoo, toothpaste, perfume, hair gel, suntan lotion and all other items with similar consistency—**are limited** within your carry-on baggage and the security checkpoint. Check the **Transportation Security Administration** site, www.tsa.gov, for the latest information.

American Airlines (✆ 800/433-7300 in the U.S. and Canada; www.aa.com) funnels Vienna-bound passengers through Zurich or London.

FROM CANADA You can usually connect from your hometown to **British Airways** (✆ 800/AIRWAYS in Canada; www.britishairways.com) gateways in Toronto, Montréal, and Vancouver. Nonstop flights from both Toronto's Pearson Airport and Montréal's Mirabelle Airport depart every day for London; flights from Vancouver depart for London three times a week. In London, you can stay for a few days (arranging discounted hotel accommodations through the British Airways tour desk) or head directly to Vienna on any of the two to five daily nonstop flights from either Heathrow or Gatwick.

FROM LONDON There are frequent flights to Vienna, the majority of which depart from London's Heathrow Airport. Flight time is 2 hours and 20 minutes. **Austrian Airlines** (✆ 0870/124-2625 from the U.K.; www.austrianair.com) has four daily nonstop flights into Vienna from Heathrow.

British Airways (✆ 0870/850-9850 in London; www.britishairways.com) offers three daily nonstops from Heathrow and two from Gatwick, with easy connections through London from virtually every other part of Britain.

GETTING INTO TOWN FROM THE AIRPORT

When you come out of Customs, signs for taxis and buses are straight ahead. A one-way **taxi** ride from the airport into the Inner City costs about 35€ ($46), or more if traffic is bad. Therefore, it's better to take the bus.

Regular **bus** service connects the airport and the **City Air Terminal,** which is adjacent to the Vienna Hilton and directly across from the **Wien Mitte/Landstrasse** rail station, where you can easily connect with subway and tramlines. Buses run every 20 minutes from 5:30am to 11:30pm, every hour from midnight until 5am. The trip takes about 25 minutes and costs 9€ ($12) per person. Tickets are sold on the bus and must be purchased with Austrian money. There's also bus service between the airport and two railroad stations, the **Westbahnhof** and the **Südbahnhof,** every 30 to 60 minutes. The fare is 6€ ($7.80).

There's also local **train** service, **Schnellbahn,** between the airport and the **Wien Nord** and **Wien Mitte** rail stations. Trains run hourly between 5am and 11:40pm and leave from the basement of the airport. Trip time is 40 to 45 minutes, and the fare is 3€ ($3.60).

FLYING FOR LESS: TIPS FOR GETTING THE BEST AIRFARE

Passengers sharing the same airplane cabin rarely pay the same fare. Travelers who need to purchase tickets at the last minute, change their itinerary at a moment's notice, or fly one-way often get stuck paying the premium rate. Here are some ways to keep your airfare costs down.

- Passengers who can book their ticket **long in advance,** who can **stay over Saturday night,** or who **fly midweek** or **at less-trafficked hours** may pay a fraction of the full fare. If your schedule is flexible, say so, and ask if you can secure a cheaper fare by changing your flight plans.
- You can also save on airfares by keeping an eye out in local newspapers for **promotional specials** or **fare wars,** when airlines lower prices on their most popular routes. You rarely see fare wars offered for peak travel times, but if you can travel in the off-months, you may snag a bargain.
- Search **the Internet** for cheap fares (see "Planning Your Trip Online," above).
- **Consolidators,** also known as bucket shops, are great sources for international tickets, although they usually can't beat the Internet on fares within North America. Start by looking in Sunday newspaper travel sections; U.S. travelers should focus on the *New York Times, Los Angeles Times,* and *Miami Herald.* For less-developed destinations, small travel agents who cater to immigrant communities in large cities often have the best deals. *Beware:* Bucket shop tickets are usually nonrefundable or rigged with stiff cancellation penalties, often as high as 50% to 75% of the ticket price, and some put you on charter airlines, which may leave at inconvenient times and experience delays.
- Several reliable consolidators are worldwide and available online. **STA Travel** (✆ 800/781-4040) has been the world's lead consolidator for students since purchasing Council Travel, but their fares are competitive for travelers of all ages. **ELTExpress (Flights.com;** ✆ 800/TRAV-800; www.eltexpress.com) has excellent fares worldwide, particularly to Europe. They also have "local" websites in 12 countries. **FlyCheap** (✆ 800/FLY-CHEAP; www.1800fly cheap.com), is owned by package-holiday megalith MyTravel and has especially good fares to sunny destinations. **Air Tickets Direct** (✆ 800/778-3447; www.airticketsdirect.com) is based in Montréal and leverages the currently weak Canadian dollar for low fares.
- Join **frequent-flier clubs.** Accrue enough miles, and you'll be rewarded with free flights and elite status. It's free, and you'll get the best choice of seats, faster response to phone inquiries, and prompter service if your luggage is stolen, your flight is canceled or delayed, or you want to change your seat. You don't need to fly to build frequent-flier miles—**frequent-flier credit cards** can provide thousands of miles for doing your everyday shopping.

BY TRAIN

If you plan to travel a lot on the European or British railroads on your way to or from Vienna, you'd do well to secure the latest copy of the *Thomas Cook European Timetable of Railroads.* It's available exclusively online at **www.thomascooktime tables.com.**

Vienna has rail links to all the major cities of Europe. From Paris, a daily train leaves the Gare de l'Est at 7:49am, arriving in Vienna at 9:18pm. From Munich, a train leaves daily at 9:24am, arriving in Vienna at 2:18pm, and at 11:19pm, arriving in Vienna at 6:47am. From Zurich, a 9:33pm train arrives in Vienna at 6:45am.

Rail travel in Austria is superb, with fast, clean trains taking you just about anywhere in the country and through some incredibly scenic regions.

Train passengers using the **Chunnel** under the English Channel can go from

---

Tips Don't Stow It—Ship It

If ease of travel is your main concern and money is no object, you can ship your luggage with one of the growing number of luggage-service companies that pick up, track, and deliver your luggage (often through couriers such as Federal Express) with minimum hassle for you. Traveling luggage-free may be ultra-convenient, but it's not cheap: One-way overnight shipping can cost from $100 to $200, depending on what you're sending. Still, for some people, especially the elderly or the infirm, it's a sensible solution to lugging heavy baggage. Specialists in door-to-door luggage delivery are **Virtual Bellhop** (© 877/BELLHOP; www.virtualbellhop.com), **SkyCap International** (© 877/775-9227; www.skycap international.com), **Luggage Express** (© 866/SHIP-BAGS; www.usxpluggage express.com), and **Sports Express** (© 800/357-4174; www.sportsexpress.com).

London to Paris in just 3 hours and then on to Vienna (see above). Le Shuttle covers the 31-mile journey in just 35 minutes. The train also accommodates passenger cars, charter buses, taxis, and motorcycles through a tunnel from Folkestone, England, to Calais, France. Service is year-round, 24 hours a day.

RAIL PASSES FOR NORTH AMERICAN TRAVELERS

EURAILPASS If you plan to travel extensively in Europe, the **Eurailpass** might be a good bet. It's valid for first-class rail travel in 18 European countries. With one ticket, you travel whenever and wherever you please; more than 100,000 rail miles are at your disposal. The pass is sold only in North America. A Eurailpass good for 15 days costs $605, a pass for 21 days is $785, a 1-month pass costs $975, a 2-month pass is $1,378, and a 3-month pass goes for $1,703. Children under 4 travel free if they don't occupy a seat; all children under 12 who take up a seat are charged half-price. If you're under 26, you can buy a **Eurail Youthpass,** which entitles you to unlimited second-class travel for 15 days ($394), 21 days ($510), 1 month ($634), 2 months ($1,018), or 3 months ($1,160). In particular, travelers considering buying a 15-day or 1-month pass should estimate how much rail travel they'll do in that amount of time. In order to reap the most cost benefit from the pass, you'd have to spend a great deal of time on the train. Eurailpass holders are entitled to substantial discounts on certain buses and ferries as well. Travel agents in all towns and railway agents in such major cities as New York, Montréal, and Los Angeles sell all of these tickets. For information on Eurailpasses and other European train data, contact **RailEurope** (© 800/438-7245; www. raileurope.com).

Eurail Saverpass offers 15% discounts to groups of three or more people traveling together between April and September, or two people traveling together between October and March. The price of a Saverpass, valid all over Europe for first class only, is $513 for 15 days, $668 for 21 days, $828 for 1 month, $1,173 for 2 months, and $1,450 for 3 months. The **Saver Flexipass** offers even more freedom; it's similar to the Eurail Saverpass, except that you are not confined to consecutive-day travel. For travel on any 10 days within 2 months, the fare is $608; any 15 days over 2 months, the fare is $800.

Eurail Flexipass allows even greater flexibility. It's valid in first class and offers the same privileges as the Eurailpass. However, it provides a number of individual travel days over a much longer period of consecutive days. Using this pass makes it possible to stay longer in one city and not lose a single day of travel. There are two Flexipasses: 10 days of travel within 2 months for $715, and 15 days of travel within 2 months for $940.

With many of the same restrictions as the Eurail Flexipass, the **Eurail Youth Flexipass** is sold only to travelers under age 25. It allows 10 days of travel within 2 months for $465 and 15 days of travel within 2 months for $611.

RAIL PASSES FOR BRITISH TRAVELERS

If you plan to do a lot of exploring, you might prefer one of the three rail passes designed for unlimited train travel within a designated region during a predetermined number of days. These passes are sold in Britain and several other European countries.

An **InterRail Pass** (www.interrail. com) is available to passengers of any nationality, with some restrictions—they must be able to prove residency in a European or North African country (Morocco, Algeria, and Tunisia) for at least 6 months before buying the pass. The pass allows unlimited travel through Europe, except Albania and the republics of the former Soviet Union. Prices are complicated and vary depending on the countries you want to include. For pricing purposes, Europe is divided into eight zones; the cost depends on the number of zones you include. For ages 25 and under, the most expensive option of £277 ($499) allows 1 month of unlimited travel in eight zones and is known to the staff as a "global." The least expensive option £140 ($252) allows 16 days of travel within only one zone.

Passengers aged 25 and older can buy an **InterRail 26-Plus Pass,** which, unfortunately, is severely limited geographically. Many countries—including France, Belgium, Switzerland, Spain, Portugal, and Italy—do not honor this pass. It is, however, accepted for travel throughout Austria, Denmark, Finland, Norway, and Sweden. Second-class travel with the pass costs £206 ($371) for 16 days or £393 ($707) for 1 month. Passengers must meet the same residency requirements that apply to the InterRail Pass (described above).

For information on buying individual rail tickets or any of the just-mentioned passes, contact **National Rail Inquiries, Victoria Station, London (© 08705/ 848-848).** Tickets and passes are also available at any of the larger railway stations as well as selected travel agencies throughout Britain and the rest of Europe.

BY CAR

If you're already on the Continent, you might want to drive to Vienna. That is especially true if you're in a neighboring country, such as Italy or Germany; however, arrangements should be made in advance with your car-rental company.

Inaugurated in 1994, the Chunnel running under the English Channel cuts driving time between England and France to 35 minutes. Passengers drive their cars aboard the train, *Le Shuttle,* at Folkestone in England, and vehicles are transported to Calais, France.

Vienna can be reached from all directions on major highways called *autobahnen* or by secondary highways. The main artery from the west is Autobahn A-1, coming in from Munich (466km/ 291 miles), Salzburg (334km/207 miles), and Linz (186km/115 miles). Autobahn A-2 runs from the south from Graz and Klagenfurt (both in Austria). Autobahn

A-4 comes in from the east, connecting with route E-58, which runs to Bratislava and Prague. Autobahn A-22 takes traffic from the northwest, and Route E-10 brings you to the cities and towns of southeastern Austria and Hungary.

Unless otherwise marked, the speed limit on *autobahnen* is 130kmph (81 mph); however, when estimating driving times, figure on 80 to 100kmph (50–62 mph) because of traffic, weather, and road conditions.

As you drive into Vienna, you can get maps, information, and hotel bookings at **Information-Zimmernachweis** at the end of the A-1 (Westautobahn) at Wientalstrasse/Auhof (© **01/211140**).

BY BUS

Because of the excellence of rail service funneling from all parts of the Continent into Vienna, bus transit is limited and not especially popular. **Eurolines,** part of National Express Coach Lines (© **0870/ 580-8080;** www.nationalexpress.com), operates two express buses per week between London's Victoria Coach Station and Vienna. The trip takes about 29 hours and makes 45-minute rest stops en route about every 4 hours. Buses depart from London at 8:15am every Friday and Sunday, traverse the Channel between Dover and Calais, and are equipped with reclining seats, toilets, and reading lights. The one-way fare is £47 ($85); a round-trip ticket costs £92 ($166). You won't need to declare your intended date of return until you actually use your ticket (although advance reservations are advisable), and the return half of your ticket will be valid for 6 months. The return to London departs from Vienna every Sunday and Friday at 7:45pm, arriving at Victoria Coach Station about 29 hours later.

BY BOAT

To arrive in Vienna with flair befitting the city's historical opulence, take advantage of the many cruise lines that navigate the Danube. One of the most accessible carriers is **DDSG Blue Danube Shipping Company,** Donaureisen, Fredrick Strasse 7, Vienna (© **01/58880;** fax 01/ 5888-0440; www.ddsg-blue-danube.at), which offers mostly 1-day trips to Vienna from as far away as Passau, Germany. It also serves Vienna from Bratislava, Budapest, and beyond, depending on the season and itinerary. Extended trips can be arranged, and cruises are priced to meet every budget. See "Cruising the Danube" in chapter 6.

11 Packages for the Independent Traveler

A sampling of some well-recommended tour operators follows, but you should always consult a good travel agent for the latest offerings.

British Airways Holidays (© **800/ AIRWAYS;** www.britishairways.com) offers a far-flung and reliable touring experience. Trips usually combine Vienna and other Austrian attractions with major sights in Germany and Switzerland. BA can arrange a stopover in London en route for an additional fee and allow extra time in Vienna before or after the beginning of any tour for no additional charge.

Other attractive options are North America's tour-industry giants. They include **Delta Vacations** (© **800/221- 6666;** www.deltavacations.com), **American Express Travel** (© **800/297-2977;** www.americanexpress.com), and an unusual, upscale (and very expensive) tour operator, **Abercrombie and Kent** (© **800/554-7016;** www.abercrombie kent.com), long known for its carriage-trade rail excursions through eastern Europe and the Swiss and Austrian Alps.

12 Recommended Books

BIOGRAPHY

Gay, Peter. *Freud: A Life for Our Times.* Norton, 1988. Gay's biography is a good introduction to the life of one of the seminal figures of the 20th century. Freud was a Viennese until he fled from the Nazis in 1938, settling with his sofa in London.

Geiringer, Karl and Irene. *Haydn: A Creative Life in Music.* University of California, 1963. This is the best biography of composer Joseph Haydn, friend of Mozart, teacher of Beethoven, and court composer of the Esterházys.

Gutman, Robert W. *Mozart: A Cultural Biography.* Harvest, 2000. Music historian Gutman places Mozart squarely in the cultural world of 18th-century Europe.

FICTION

Brandstetter, Alois. *The Abbey.* Ariadne, 1998. The search for a missing ancient chalice results in an insightful (and often humorous) assessment of post-World War II Austria.

Greene, Graham. *The Third Man.* Viking Penguin, 1949. Greene based this novel about intrigue in postwar Vienna on his screenplay for director Carol Reed's famous 1949 film starring Orson Welles and Joseph Cotten.

Hill, Carol de Chellis. *Henry James' Midnight Song.* Norton, 1993. Psychoanalysis meets feminism in this murder mystery set in Vienna around 1900 and involving such historical figures as Sigmund Freud, Carl Jung, Edith Wharton, and Henry James.

HISTORY

Brook-Shepherd, Gordon. *The Austrians: A Thousand-Year Odyssey.* Carroll & Graf, 1997. The author looks at Austria's history to explain the people and their nation, how they got there, and where they're going.

Morton, Frederic. *A Nervous Splendor: Vienna 1888–1889.* Viking Penguin, 1980. Morton uses the mysterious deaths of Archduke Rudolf and Baroness Marie Vetsera at Mayerling as a point of departure to capture Imperial Vienna at its glorious height.

Schorske, Carl E. *Fin-de-Siècle Vienna: Politics and Culture.* Vintage, 1981. This landmark book takes you into the political and social world of Vienna at the end of the 19th and beginning of the 20th centuries.

Wheatcroft, Andrew. *The Habsburgs: Embodying Empire.* Viking Penguin, 1996. Here is the full sweep of the Habsburg dynasty, from the Middle Ages to the end of World War I, focusing on such remarkable personalities as Rudolph I, Charles V, Maria Theresa, and Franz Joseph I.

3

Getting to Know Vienna

This chapter will help you get your bearings in Vienna by introducing you to Vienna's neighborhoods, explaining the layout of the city, and telling you how to get around. There's also a convenient list of "Fast Facts," covering everything from embassies to electrical outlets.

1 Orientation

ARRIVING

BY PLANE **Vienna International Airport (VIE;** ℂ **01/70070;** www.vienna airport.com) is about 19km (12 miles) southeast of the city center. Austrian Airlines and United Airlines offer nonstop service from New York (JFK), Chicago, and Washington, D.C.; Austrian Airlines and British Airways fly nonstop from London (Heathrow). Other transatlantic airlines connect to Vienna via major European hubs.

The official **Vienna Tourist Information Office** in the arrival hall of the airport is open daily 7am to 10pm.

There's regular bus service between the airport and the **City Air Terminal,** adjacent to the Vienna Hilton and directly across from the **Wien Mitte/Landstrasse** rail station, where you can easily connect with subway and tramlines. Buses run every 20 minutes from 6:30am to 11:30pm, and hourly from midnight to 5am. The trip takes about 25 minutes and costs 6€ ($7.80) per person. *Note:* Tickets are sold on the bus and must be purchased with euros. There's also bus service between the airport and two railroad stations, the Westbahnhof and the Südbahnhof, leaving every 30 minutes to an hour. Fares are also 6€ ($7.80).

There's also local train service, Schnellbahn (S-Bahn), between the airport and the Wien Nord and Wien Mitte rail stations. Trains run hourly from 5am to 11:40pm and leave from the basement of the airport. Trip time is 40 to 45 minutes, and the fare is 3€ ($3.90).

BY TRAIN Vienna has four principal rail stations with frequent connections to all Austrian cities and towns and to all major European centers, from Munich to Milan. Train information for all stations is available at ℂ **05/1717.**

Westbahnhof, on Europaplatz, is for trains arriving from western Austria, France, Germany, Switzerland, and some eastern European countries. It has frequent links to all major Austrian cities, such as Salzburg, a 3-hour ride from Vienna. The Westbahnhof connects with local trains, the U3 and U6 underground lines, and several tram and bus routes.

Südbahnhof, on Südtirolerplatz, handles train arrivals from southern and eastern Austria, Italy, Hungary, Slovenia, and Croatia. It's linked with local rail service and tram and bus routes.

Both of these stations house useful travel agencies (**Österreichisches Verkehrs-büro**) that provide tourist information and help with hotel reservations. In the West-bahnhof it's in the upper hall; at the Südbahnhof, in the lower hall.

Other stations in Vienna include **Franz-Josef Bahnhof**, on Franz-Josef-Platz, used mainly by local trains and for connections to Prague and Berlin. You can take the D tramline to the city's Ringstrasse from here. **Wien Mitte**, Landstrasser Hauptstrasse 1, is also a terminus of local trains, plus a depot for trains to the airport and the Czech Republic.

BY BUS   The **City Bus Terminal** is at the Wien Mitte rail station, Landstrasser Hauptstrasse 1. This is the arrival depot for Post and Bundesbuses from points all over the country, as well as the arrival point for private buses from various European cities. The terminal has lockers, currency-exchange kiosks, and a ticket counter open daily from 6:15am to 6pm. For bus information, call © **01/71101** daily from 6:15am to 6pm.

VISITOR INFORMATION

Once you've arrived safely in Vienna, head for either of two information points that make it their business to have up-to-the-minute data about what to see and do in Vienna. The more centrally located of the two is the **Wien Tourist-Information** office at Albertinaplatz (© **01/211-140;** tram: 1 or 2). Located directly behind the Vienna State Opera, on the corner of Philharmonikerstrasse, in the heart of the Innere Stadt (Inner City), it's open daily from 9am to 7pm. The staff will make free hotel reservations for anyone in need of lodgings. Larger and more administrative, but also willing to handle questions from the public, is the headquarters of the **Vienna Tourist Board,** at Obere Augartenstrasse (© **01/24-555;** tram: 31), open Monday to Friday 8am to 4pm. Both branches stock free copies of a tourist magazine, *Wien Monats-programm,* which lists what's going on in Vienna's concert halls, theaters, and opera houses. Also worthwhile here is *Vienna A to Z,* a general, pocket-size guide with descriptions and locations for a slew of attractions. This booklet is also free, but don't rely on its cluttered map.

For information on Vienna and Austria, including day trips from the city, visit the **Austrian National Tourist Office** (© **01/588660**) at Margaretenstrasse 1, A-1040. Lower Austria (Niederösterreich), the region surrounding the city, contains dozens of attractions worth a visit (see chapter 6). For a rundown on the Wachau (Danube Valley) and the Weinerwald (Vienna Woods), you might want to contact **Nieder-österreich Information,** Fischhof 3/3 (© **01/53-610-62-00**).

CITY LAYOUT

From its origins as a Roman village on the Danubian plain, Vienna has evolved into one of the largest metropolises of central Europe, with a surface area covering 414 sq. km (161 sq. miles). That area has been divided into 23 districts *(bezirke),* which are rather cumbersomely identified with a Roman numeral. Each district carries its own character or reputation; for example, the 9th District is known as Vienna's academic quarter, whereas the 10th, 11th, and 12th districts are home to blue-collar workers and are the most densely populated.

The 1st District, known as the **Innere Stadt (Inner City),** is where most foreign visitors first flock. This compact area is the most historic and boasts the city's astounding array of monuments, churches, palaces, and museums, in addition to the finest

Vienna at a Glance

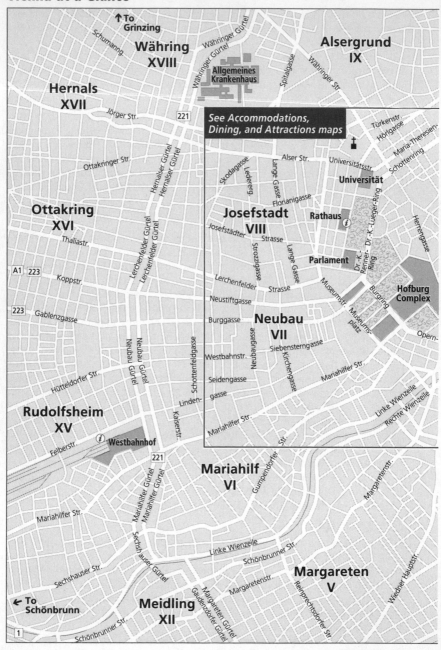

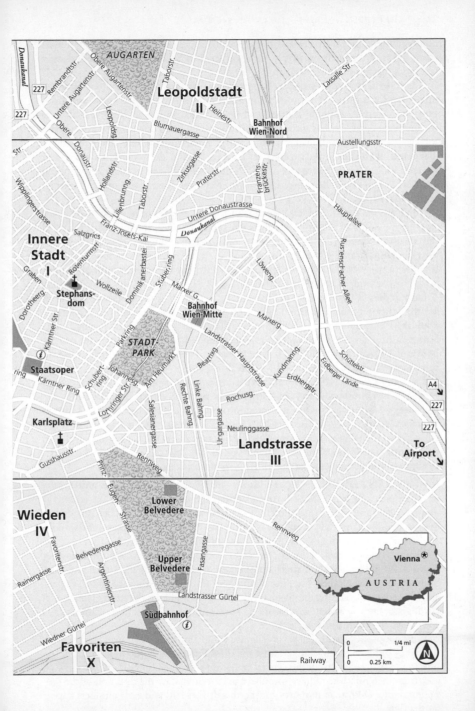

hotels and restaurants. Its size and shape roughly correspond to the original borders (then walls) of the medieval city; however, other than **St. Stephan's Cathedral,** very few buildings from that era remain.

The Inner City is surrounded by **Ringstrasse,** a circular boulevard about 4km (2½ miles) long. Constructed between 1859 and 1888, it's one of the most ambitious examples of urban planning and restoration in central European history. Built over the foundations of Vienna's medieval fortifications, the Ring opened new urban vistas for the dozens of monumental 19th-century buildings that line its edges today. The name of this boulevard changes as it moves around the Inner City, which can get confusing. Names that correspond with the boulevard end in *ring:* Schottenring, Dr.-Karl-Lueger-Ring, Burgring, Opernring, Kärntner Ring, Stubenring, Parkring, and Schubertring.

Ironically, the river for which Vienna is so famous, the **Danube,** doesn't really pass through the center of the city at all. Between 1868 and 1877, the river was channeled into its present muddy banks east of town and was replaced with a small-scale substitute, the **Donaukanal (Danube Canal),** which was dug for shipping food and other supplies to the Viennese. The canal is set against Ringstrasse's eastern edge and is traversed by five bridges in the 1st District alone.

Surrounding Ringstrasse and the Inner City, in a more or less clockwise direction, are the inner suburban districts (2–9), which contain many hotels and restaurants popular for their proximity to the city center. The villas and palaces of Vienna's 18th-century aristocrats can be found here, as well as modern apartment complexes and the homes of 19th-century middle-class entrepreneurs. These districts are profiled later in this chapter under "The Neighborhoods in Brief."

The outer districts (10–23) form another concentric ring of suburbs, comprising a variety of neighborhoods from industrial parks to rural villages. **Schönbrunn,** the Habsburg's vast summer palace, is located in these outlying areas in the 13th District, **Hietzing.** Also noteworthy is the 19th District, **Döbling,** with its famous *heurigen* villages, like Grinzing and Sievering (see "The *Heurigen,*" p. 177), and the 22nd District, **Donau-stadt,** home to the verdant Donau Park and the adjoining UNO-City, an impressive modern complex of United Nations agencies.

FINDING AN ADDRESS   Street addresses are followed by a four-digit postal code, or sometimes a Roman numeral, that identifies the district in which the address is located. Often the code is preceded by the letter A. The district number is coded in the two middle digits, so if an address is in the 1st District (01), the postal code would read A-1010; in the 7th District, A-1070; and in the 13th District, A-1130.

A rule of thumb used by hotel concierges and taxi drivers involves the following broad-based guidelines: Odd street numbers are on one side of the street, and even numbers are on the other. The lowest numbers are usually closest to the city's geographic and spiritual center, St. Stephansplatz, and get higher as the street extends outward. Naturally, this system won't work on streets running parallel to the cathedral, so you'll have to simply test your luck.

What about the broad expanses of Vienna's Ring? Traffic always moves clockwise on the Ring, and any backtracking against the direction of the traffic must be done via side streets that radiate from the general traffic flow. Numeration on the Ring always goes from high numbers to lower numbers, as determined by the direction of the prevailing traffic: Odd street numbers appear on a driver's left, and even numbers appear on the right.

STREET MAPS   You'll need a very good and detailed map to explore Vienna, as it has some 2,400km (1,488 miles) of streets (many of them narrow). Since so many places, including restaurants and hotels, lie in these alleyways, routine overview maps that are given away at hotels or the tourist office won't do. You'll need the best city map in Vienna, which is published by **Falk** and sold at all major newsstands, at bookstores, and in many upscale hotels.

THE NEIGHBORHOODS IN BRIEF

Visitors spend most of their time in the city center, and many of Vienna's hotels and restaurants are conveniently located in or just outside the 1st District. In this section, we profile the Inner City, or Innere Stadt, and the districts that immediately surround it.

Innere Stadt (1st District)   As we mentioned earlier, this compact area, bounded on all sides by the legendary Ring, is at the center of Viennese life. The Inner City has dozens of streets devoted exclusively to pedestrian traffic, including **Kärntnerstrasse,** which bypasses the Vienna State Opera House, and the nearby **Graben,** which backs up to Stephansplatz, home to the famous cathedral. Competing with both the cathedral and the Opera House as the district's most famous building is the **Hofburg,** the Habsburg palace that's now a showcase of tourist attractions, including the National Library, the Spanish Riding School, and six museums. Other significant landmarks include the Rathaus (City Hall), Parlament (Parliament), the Universität (University of Vienna), the Naturhistorisches (Natural History), and the Kunsthistorisches (Art History) museums, and Stadtpark.

Leopoldstadt (2nd District)   Once inhabited by Balkan traders, this area doesn't physically border the Ringstrasse, but lies on the eastern side of the Danube Canal, just a short subway ride (U1) from the Inner City. Here you'll find the massive **Prater** park, which boasts an amusement park, miles of tree-lined walking paths, and numerous sports facilities, including a large stadium. Vienna's renowned trade-fair exhibition site is also in this district, which has seen a spree of development along the canal in recent years.

Landstrasse (3rd District)   The bucolic **Stadtpark** spreads into this district, where you'll see more of Vienna's imperial charm. Streets are dotted with churches, monuments, and palaces, such as the grand **Schwarzenberg Palace** and the looming **Konzerthaus** (concert house). However, the top attraction remains Prince Eugene Savoy's **Belvedere Palace,** an exquisite example of baroque architecture. Several embassies are in a small section of Landstrasse that's known as Vienna's diplomatic quarter. The **Wien Mitte rail station** and the **City Air Terminal** are also here.

Wieden (4th District)   This small neighborhood extends south from Opernring and Kärntnering, and it's just as fashionable as the 1st District. Most activity centers on **Karlsplatz,** a historic square with its domed namesake, Karlskirche. Also nearby are Vienna's **Technical University** and the **Historical Museum of the City of Vienna.** Kärnerstrasse, the main boulevard of the city center, turns into **Wiedner-Hauptstrasse** as it enters this district, and the **Südbahnhof,** one of the two main train stations, lies at its southern tip.

Margareten (5th District)   Southwest of the 4th District, Wieden, this area does not border the Ring and thus

Impressions

The streets of Vienna are surfaced with culture as the streets of other cities with asphalt.

—Karl Kraus (1874–1936)

lies a bit farther from the Inner City. You'll start to see more residential neighborhoods, representing the continual growth of Vienna's middle class. The historic homes of composers Franz Schubert and Christoph Gluck still stand here among modern apartment complexes and industrial centers.

Mariahilf (6th District) One of Vienna's busiest shopping streets, **Mariahilferstrasse,** runs through this bustling neighborhood. The sprawling, lively **Naschmarkt** (produce market), selling fresh fruits, vegetables, breads, cheeses, and more, is ideal for people-watching. On Saturdays, the adjacent **Flohmarkt** (flea market) adds to the lively but sometimes seedy atmosphere as vendors sell antiques and junk. The surrounding streets are packed with *beisls* (small eateries), theaters, cafes, and pubs. Farther from the city center, you'll find that the landscape becomes more residential.

Neubau (7th District) Bordering the expansive Museum Quarter of the Inner City, this is an ideal place to stay, as it's easily accessible by public transportation. The picturesque and once neglected **Spittelberg quarter** lies atop a hill just beyond Vienna's most famous museums. The vibrant cultural community is popular with both young and old visitors. The old Spittelberg houses have been renovated into

boutiques, restaurants, theaters, and art galleries—a perfect backdrop for an afternoon stroll.

Josefstadt (8th District) The smallest of Vienna's 23 districts is named after Habsburg Emperor Joseph II and was once home to Vienna's civil servants. Like Neubau, this quiet, friendly neighborhood sits behind the City Hall and the adjacent grand museums of the Ringstrasse. Here you'll find secluded parks, charming cafes, and elaborate monuments and churches. Vienna's oldest and most intimate theater, **Josefstadt Theater,** has stood here since 1788. Josefstadt's shops and restaurants have a varied clientele, from City Hall lawmakers to university students.

Alsergrund (9th District) This area is often referred to as the Academic Quarter, not just because of nearby University of Vienna, but also because of its many hospitals and clinics. This is Freud territory, and you can visit his home, now the **Freud Museum,** on Berggasse. Here you'll also stumble upon the **Liechtenstein Palace,** one of Vienna's biggest and brightest, which today houses the federal **Museum of Modern Art.** At the northern end of Alsergrund is the **Franz-Josef Bahnhof,** an excellent depot for excursions to Lower Austria.

2 Getting Around

BY PUBLIC TRANSPORTATION

Whether you want to visit the Inner City's historic buildings or the outlying Vienna Woods, Vienna Transport (Wiener Verkehrsbetriebe) can take you there. This vast transit network—U-Bahn (subway), streetcar, or bus—is safe, clean, and easy to use.

Vienna Public Transport

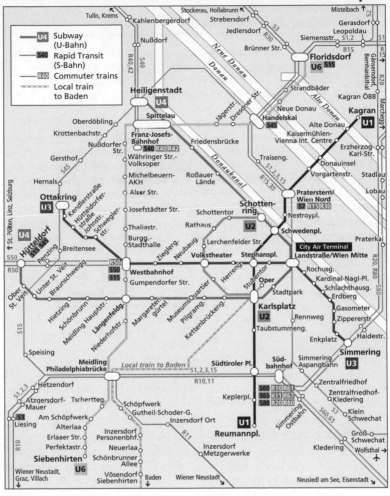

If you plan on taking full advantage of it, pay the 1€ ($1.30) for a map that outlines the U-Bahn, buses, streetcars, and local trains (Schnellbahn, or S-Bahn). It's sold at the **Vienna Public Transport Information Center (Informationdienst der Wiener Verkehrsbetriebe),** which has five locations: Opernpassage (an underground passageway adjacent to the Wiener Staatsoper), Karlsplatz, Stephansplatz (near Vienna's cathedral), Westbahnhof, and Praterstern. These offices are open Monday to Friday 6:30am to 6:30pm. For information about any of these outlets, call ✆ **01/790-9100.**

Vienna maintains a uniform fare that applies to all forms of public transport. A ticket for the bus, subway, or tram costs 1.50€ ($1.95) if you buy it in advance at a *tabac-trafiks* (a store or kiosk selling tobacco products and newspapers) or 2€ ($2.60) if you buy it onboard. Smart Viennese buy their tickets in advance, usually in blocks of at least five at a time, from any of the city's thousands of *tabac-trafiks* or at

Tips Transportation for Less

The **Vienna Card** is the best ticket to use when traveling by public transportation within the city limits. It's extremely flexible and functional for tourists because it allows unlimited travel, plus various discounts at city museums, restaurants, and shops. You can purchase a Vienna Card for 17€ ($20) at tourist information offices, public transport centers, and some hotels, or order one over the phone with a credit card (© **01/7984400148**).

You can also buy tickets that will save you money if you plan to ride a lot on the city's transport system. A ticket valid for unlimited rides during any 24-hour period costs 5€ ($6); an equivalent ticket valid for any 72-hour period goes for 12€ ($14). There's also a green ticket, priced at 24€ ($29), that contains eight individual partitions. Each of these, when stamped, is good for 1 day of unlimited travel. An individual can opt to reserve all eight of the partitions for his or her own use, thereby gaining 8 days of cost-effective travel on the city's transport system. Or the partitions can be subdivided among a group of several riders, allowing—for example—two persons 4 days each of unlimited rides.

These tickets are also available at *tabac-trafiks,* vending machines in underground stations, the airport's arrival hall (next to baggage claim), the *Reichsbrücke* (DDSG landing pier), and the *Österreichisches Verkehrsbüro* (travel agencies) of the two main train stations.

any of the public transport centers noted above. No matter what vehicle you decide to ride within Vienna, remember that once a ticket has been stamped (validated) by either a machine or a railway attendant, it's valid for one trip in one direction, anywhere in the city, including transfers.

BY U-BAHN (SUBWAY)

The U-Bahn is a fast way to get across town or reach the suburbs. It consists of five lines labeled **U1, U2, U3, U4,** and **U6** (there is no U5). Karlsplatz, in the heart of the Inner City, is the most important underground station for visitors: The U4, U2, and U1 converge there. The U2 traces part of the Ring, the U4 goes to Schönbrunn, and the U1 stops in Stephansplatz. The U3 also stops in Stephansplatz and connects with the Westbahnhof. The underground runs daily from 6am to midnight.

BY TRAM (STREETCAR)

Riding the red-and-white trams *(strassenbahn)* is not only a practical way to get around but also a great way to see the city. Tram stops are well marked. Each line bears a number or letter. Lines 1 and 2 will bring you to all the major sights on the Ringstrasse. Line D skirts the outer Ring and goes to the Südbahnhof, and line 18 goes between the Westbahnhof and the Südbahnhof. Trams run daily from 6am to midnight.

BY BUS

Buses traverse Vienna in all directions, operating daily, including at night (but with more limited service then). Night buses leave every 10 to 30 minutes from Schwedenplatz, fanning out across the city. It's usually not necessary to change lines more than once. Normal tickets are valid aboard these late night buses (no extra charge). On buses you can buy tickets from the driver.

BY TAXI

Taxis are easy to find within the city center, but be warned that fares can quickly add up. Taxi stands are marked by signs, or you can call ℭ **01/31300**, 60160, 81400, or 40100. The basic fare is 2.50€ ($3.25), plus 1.20€ ($1.55) per kilometer. There are extra charges of 1€ ($1.30) for luggage in the trunk. For night rides after 11pm, and for trips on Sunday and holidays, there is a surcharge of 1€ ($1.30). There is an additional charge of 2€ ($2.60) if ordered by phone. The fare for trips outside the Vienna area (for instance, to the airport) should be agreed upon with the driver in advance, and a 10% tip is the norm.

BY HORSE-DRAWN CARRIAGE

A horse-drawn carriage (called a *fiaker* in German) has been used as a form of transportation in the Inner City for some 3 centuries. You can clip-clop along in one for about 20 minutes at a cost of about 40€ ($52). Prices and the length of the ride must be negotiated in advance. In the 1st District, you'll find a *fiaker* for hire at the following sites: on the north side of St. Stephan's, on Heldenplatz near the Hofburg, and in front of the Albertina on Augustinerstrasse. There's also a 40-minute tour, which costs 65€ ($85).

BY BICYCLE

Vienna has more than 250km (155 miles) of marked bicycle paths within the city limits. In the summer, many Viennese leave their cars in the garage and ride bikes. You can take bicycles on specially marked U-Bahn cars for free, but only Monday through Friday from 9am to 3pm and 6:30pm to midnight, during which time you'll pay half the full-ticket price to transport a bike. On weekends in July and August, bicycles are carried free from 9am to midnight.

Rental stores abound at the Prater (see chapter 6) and along the banks of the Danube Canal, which is the favorite bike route for most Viennese. One of the best of the many sites specializing in bike rentals is **Pedal Power,** Ausstellungsstrasse 3 (ℭ **01/729-7234**), which is open March through October from 8am to 7pm. The Vienna Tourist Board can also supply a list of rental shops and more information about bike paths. Bike rentals begin at about 27€ ($35) per day.

BY CAR

See "By Car," in chapter 2, for general tips on renting a car in Austria. Use a car only for excursions outside Vienna's city limits; don't try to drive around the city. Parking is a problem; the city is a maze of congested one-way streets; and the public transportation is too good to endure the hassle of driving.

If you do venture out by car, information on road conditions is available in English 7 days a week from 6am to 8pm from the **Österreichischer Automobil-, Motorrad-und Touringclub (ÖAMTC),** Schubertring 1-3, A-1010 Vienna (ℭ **01/711-990**). This auto club also maintains a 24-hour emergency road service number (ℭ **120** or 0810/120-120).

CAR RENTALS   It's best to reserve rental cars in advance (see chapter 2), but you can rent a car once you're in Vienna. You'll need a passport and a driver's license that's at least 1 year old. Avoid renting a car at the airport, where there's an extra 6% tax, in addition to the 21% value-added tax on all rentals.

Major car-rental companies include **Avis,** Opernring 3-5 (© **01/587-62-41**); **Budget Rent-a-Car,** Hilton Air Terminal (© **01/714-6565**); and **Hertz,** Kärntner Ring 17 (© **01/512-8677**).

PARKING   Curbside parking in Vienna's 1st District, site of most of the city's major monuments, is extremely limited—almost to the point of being nonexistent. Coin-operated parking meters as they exist within North America are not common. When curbside parking is available at all, it's within one of the city's "blue zones" and is usually restricted to 90 minutes or less from 8am to 6pm. If you find an available spot within a blue zone, you'll need to display a *kurzpark scheine* (short-term parking voucher) on the dashboard of your car. Valid for time blocks of only 30, 60, or 90 minutes, they're sold at branch offices of Vienna Public Transport Information Center (see above) and, more conveniently, within tobacco/news shops. You'll have to write in the date and the time of your arrival before displaying the voucher on the right side of your car's dashboard. Be warned that towing of illegally parked cars is not an uncommon sight here. Frankly, it's much easier to simply pay the price that's charged by any of the city's dozens of underground parking garages and avoid the stress of looking for one of the virtually impossible-to-find curbside parking spots.

Parking garages are scattered throughout the city, and most of them charge between 3.50€ ($4.55) and 6€ ($7.80) per hour. Every hotel in Vienna is acutely aware of the location of the nearest parking garage—if you're confused, ask. Some convenient 24-hour garages within the 1st District include **Parkgarage Am Hof** (© **01/533-5571**); **Parkgarage Freyung,** Freyung (© **01/535-0450**); and **Tiefgarage Kärntnerstrasse,** Mahlerstrasse 8 (© **01/512-5206**).

DRIVING & TRAFFIC REGULATIONS   In general, Austria's traffic regulations do not differ much from those of other countries where you *drive on the right.* In Vienna, the speed limit is 50kmph (31 mph). Out of town, in areas like the Wienerwald, the limit is 130kmph (81 mph) on motorways and 100kmph (62 mph) on all other roads. Honking car horns is forbidden everywhere in the city.

FAST FACTS: Vienna

American Express   The office at Kärntnerstrasse 21-23 (© **01/515670**), near Stock-im-Eisenplatz, is open Monday to Friday 9am to 5pm and Saturday 9am to noon.

Babysitters   Most hotels will provide you with names of babysitters if they do not provide their own service. Sitters charge roughly 8€ to 12€ ($10–$16) per hour, and you'll need to provide transportation home, via a cab, if they sit beyond 11pm.

Business Hours   Most shops are open Monday through Friday from 9am to 6pm and Saturday from 9am to noon, 12:30pm, or 1pm, depending on the store. On the first Saturday of every month, shops customarily remain open until 4:30 or 5pm. The tradition is called *langer Samstag.*

Car Rentals   See "Getting Around," above.

Climate   See "When to Go," in chapter 2.

Crime   See "Safety," below.

Currency Exchange See "Money," in chapter 2.

Dentists For dental problems, call © **01/512-2078.**

Doctors A list of physicians can be found in the telephone directory under "Arzte." If you have a medical emergency at night, call © **141** daily from 7pm to 7am.

Driving Rules See "Getting Around," above.

Drug Laws Penalties are severe, and an infraction could lead to imprisonment or deportation. Selling drugs to minors is dealt with particularly harshly.

Drugstores Drugstores (chemist's shops) are open Monday to Friday from 8am to noon and 2 to 6pm, and Saturday from 8am to noon. At night and on Sunday, you'll find the names of the nearest open shops on a sign outside every drugstore.

Electricity Vienna operates on 220 volts AC, with the European 50-cycle circuit. That means that U.S.-made appliances will need a transformer (sometimes called a converter). Many Viennese hotels stock adapter plugs but not power transformers. Electric clocks, CD players, and tape recorders, however, will not work well, even with transformers.

Embassies & Consulates The main building of the **Embassy of the United States** is at Boltzmanngasse 16, A-1090 Vienna (© **01/313390**). However, the consular section is at Parkring 12, A-1010 Vienna (© **01/5125835**). Lost passports, tourist emergencies, and other matters are handled by the consular section. Both the embassy and the consulate are open Monday through Friday from 8:30am to noon and 1 to 2pm.

   Canada's Embassy, Laurenzerberg 2 (© **01/531-38-3321**), is open Monday to Friday 8:30am to 12:30pm and 1:30 to 3:30pm; the **United Kingdom's,** Jauresgasse 12 (© **01/716135151**), is open Monday to Friday 9am to 1pm and 2 to 5pm; **Australia's,** Mattiellistrasse 2-4 (© **01/50674**), is open Monday to Friday 8:30am to 1pm and 2 to 4pm; and **New Zealand's,** Salesianergasse 15/3 (© **01/318-8505**), is open Monday to Friday 8:30am to 5pm, but it's best to call to see if it's actually open. **Ireland's Embassy,** Rotenturmstrasse 16-18 (© **01/715-4246**), is open Monday to Friday 9 to 11:30am and 1:30 to 4pm.

Emergencies Call © **122** to report a fire, © **133** for the police, or © **144** for an ambulance.

Holidays See "When to Go," in chapter 2.

Hospitals The major hospital is **Allgemeines Krankenhaus,** Währinger Gürtel 18-20 (© **01/40400**).

Hot Lines The rape crisis hot line is Frauen Notruf (© **01/523-2222**), in service on Monday from 10am to 6pm, Tuesday from 2 to 6pm, Wednesday from 10am to 2pm, and Thursday from 5 to 9pm. Threatened or battered women can call a 24-hour emergency hot line, © **01/71719.**

Internet Access **Café Stein,** Währingerstrasse 6-8 (© **01/319-72-41**), offers Internet access at the rate of 4€ ($5.20) every half-hour, and is open Monday to Saturday 7am to 1pm, Sunday 9am to 1pm.

Language German is the official language of Austria, but because the high schools teach English, it's commonly spoken throughout the country, especially in tourist regions. Certain Austrian minorities speak Slavic languages, and Hungarian is common in Burgenland.

Legal Aid The consulate of your country is the place to turn, although consulate officers cannot interfere in the Viennese legal process. They can, however, inform you of your rights and provide a list of attorneys.

Liquor Laws Wine with meals is a normal part of family life in Vienna. Children are exposed to wine at an early age, and alcohol consumption is nothing out of the ordinary. Eighteen is the legal age for buying and ordering alcohol.

Luggage Storage & Lockers All four main train stations in Vienna have lockers available on a 24-hour basis, costing 3€ ($3.90) for 24 hours. It's also possible to store luggage at these terminals daily from 4am to midnight (1:15am at the Westbahnhof) at a cost of 2.50€ ($3.25).

Mail Post offices in Vienna can be found in the heart of every district. Addresses for these can be found in the telephone directory under "Post." Post offices are generally open for mail services Monday to Friday 8am to noon and 2 to 6pm. The central post office (Hauptpostamt), Fleischmarkt 19 (℃ **01/5138350**), and most general post offices are open 24 hours a day, 7 days a week. Postage stamps are available at all post offices and at tobacco shops, and there are stamp-vending machines outside most post offices.

Maps See "Getting Around," earlier in this chapter.

Newspapers & Magazines Most newsstands at major hotels and news kiosks along the streets sell the *International Herald Tribune* and *USA Today*, and carry the European editions of *Time* and *Newsweek*.

Police The emergency number is ℃ **133**.

Radio & TV The Austrian Radio Network (ÖRF) has English-language news broadcasts at 8:05am daily. The Voice of America broadcasts news, music, and feature programs at 1197 AM (called "middle wave" here) at least three times a day. Every Sunday at noon, the TV network FSI broadcasts the English-language "Hello, Austria," covering sightseeing suggestions and giving tips about the country. Many first-class and deluxe hotels subscribe to CNN and certain British channels. Films and programs from the United States and England are often shown in their original language with German subtitles.

Restrooms Vienna has a number of public toilets, labeled WC, at convenient locations throughout the city. Don't hesitate to use them, as they are clean, safe, and well maintained. All major sightseeing attractions also have public facilities.

Safety In recent years, purse snatchers have plagued Vienna. In the area around St. Stephan's Cathedral, signs (in German only) warn about pickpockets and purse snatchers. Small foreign children often approach sympathetic adults and ask for money. As the adult goes for his wallet or her purse, full-grown thieves rush in and grab the money, fleeing with it. Unaccompanied women are the most common victims. If you're carrying a purse, do not open it in public.

Taxes In 1993, all countries belonging to the European Union became a single market by enforcing the Single European Act and merging into a common customs and Value Added Tax (VAT) zone. VAT is a special tax applied to both goods and services. The rates vary from country to country. In Austria the rate is 20%. You can arrange for a refund of VAT if you can prove that the goods on which you paid tax were carried out of Austria. To get the refund, you must fill out Form U-34, which is available at most stores (a sign will read TAX-FREE SHOP-PING). Get one for the ÖAMTC quick refund if you plan to get your money at the border. Check whether the store gives refunds itself or uses a service. Sales personnel will help you fill out the form and will affix the store identification stamp. You will show the VAT *(MWSt)* as a separate item or will say that the tax is part of the total price. Keep your U-34 forms handy when you leave the country, and have them validated by the Viennese Customs officer at your point of departure.

Know in advance that you'll have to show the articles for which you're claiming a VAT refund. Because of this, it's wise to keep your purchases in a suitcase or carry-on bag that's separate from the rest of your luggage, with all the original tags, tickets, and receipts nearby. Don't check the item with your luggage before you process the paperwork with the Customs agent. In some instances, if your paperwork is in order, you'll receive a tax refund on the spot. If your point of departure is not equipped to issue cash on the spot, you'll have to mail the validated U-34 form or forms back to the store where you bought the merchandise after you return home. It's wise to keep a copy of each form. Within a few weeks, the store will send you a check, bank draft, or international money order covering the amount of your VAT refund. Information and help are available at the ÖAMTC (Schubertring 1-3, A-1010 Vienna; ✆ **01/711-990)**, which has instituted methods of speeding up the refund process. Before you go, call the Austrian National Tourist Office for the ÖAMTC brochure "Tax-Free Shopping in Austria."

Taxis See "Getting Around," earlier in this chapter.

Telegrams, Telex & Fax The central telegraph office is at Börseplatz 1. As for faxes and telex, virtually every hotel in Austria will have one or both of these, and will usually send a message for a nominal charge, often less than that for a long-distance phone call.

Telephone The **country code** for Austria is **43**. The **city code** for Vienna is **1**; use this code when you're calling from outside Austria. If you're within Austria but not in Vienna, use **01**. If you're calling within Vienna, simply leave off the code and dial only the regular phone number. Remember that if you dial an overseas number from your hotel room, the add-on charges imposed by the hotel might be higher (and in some cases, much higher) than you imagined, in some cases between 40% and 200% of the actual cost of the call. Therefore, do what we try to do: Either bill your call to a credit card, or briefly call your U.S.- or Canada-based friend, and ask him or her to call you back at "residential calling plan" rates that are much lower than those which will be imposed by your hotel.

Know in advance that within many Austrian hotels, either "0" or "9" is used to get an outside line. The access code for foreign (in other words, non-Austrian) countries is "00," followed by a specific country code. The international access code for both the United States and Canada is 1, followed by the area code and the seven-digit local number. Within Vienna and the rest of Austria, "08" is usually the code for direct access to an international long-distance operator. Depending on the point from which you place the call, both 1611 and 118875 are among the local numbers that will access directory assistance. If in doubt, a quick call to the hotel operator from your room will clarify any of these technical issues.

Since the changeover of Austria's monetary system from the schilling to the euro, the huge majority of Vienna's antiquated coin-operated pay phones have been replaced with machines that accept Austrian phone cards and/or international credit cards instead of coins. Phone cards are available at news kiosks and tobacco stores throughout the city, in 5-, 10-, 15-, 20-, 25-, 30-, and 35-euro denominations, with the most commonly available being the 5-, 10-, and 20-euro versions. Using one of them involves picking up the receiver, inserting your card, and dialing the correct access codes and phone numbers. (A call that's placed from a public phone will probably cost less than an equivalent call, either foreign or domestic, that's placed from your hotel room.)

A 2-minute local phone call placed in Vienna to a destination within Vienna will consume about .10€ (15¢) worth of the value of your phone card.

Time Vienna operates on Central European Time, which is 6 hours later than U.S. Eastern Standard Time. It advances its clocks 1 hour in summer.

Tipping Hotel and restaurant bills include a service charge of 10% to 15%, but it's a good policy to leave something extra for waiters and 2€ ($2.60) per day for your hotel maid.

Railroad station, airport, and hotel porters get 1.50€ ($1.80) per piece of luggage, plus a .75€ ($1) tip. Your hairdresser should be tipped 10% of the bill, and the shampoo person will be thankful for a 1.50€ ($1.95) gratuity. Toilet attendants usually receive .50€ (65¢) and coat-check attendants expect .50€ to 1.50€ (65¢–$1.95), depending on the place.

Tourist Offices See "Visitor Information," in chapter 2.

Transit Information Information, all types of tickets, and maps of the transportation system are available at Vienna Transport's main offices on Karlsplatz or at the Stephansplatz underground station Monday to Friday 8am to 6pm and Saturday, Sunday, and holidays from 8:30am to 4pm. Alternatively, you can call ℂ 01/7909100 24 hours a day for information in German and English about public transport anywhere within greater Vienna.

4

Where to Stay

Vienna has some of the greatest hotels in Europe, but finding a room can be a problem if you arrive without a reservation, especially in August and September. During these peak visiting months, you might have to stay on the outskirts, in the Grinzing or the Schönbrunn district, for example, and commute to the Inner City by streetcar, bus, or U-Bahn. If you're looking to cut costs, staying outside the Inner City is not a bad option, as you can pay a fifth to a quarter less for a hotel in the areas outside the Ringstrasse.

High season in Vienna encompasses most of the year: from May to October or early November, and during some weeks in midwinter, when the city hosts major trade fairs, conventions, and other cultural events. If you're planning a trip around Christmas and New Year's Day, room reservations should be made *at least* 1 month in advance. Some rate reductions (usually 15%–20%) are available during slower midwinter weeks—it always pays to ask.

ACCOMMODATIONS AGENCIES

Any branch of the **Austrian National Tourist Office** (© 01/588660), including the Vienna Tourist Board, will help you book a room if you arrive without a reservation. The Vienna Tourist Board has branch offices in the airport, train stations, and near major highways that access Vienna (see chapter 3, "Getting to Know Vienna").

If you prefer to deal with an Austrian travel agency, three of the city's largest are **Austropa,** Friedrichsgasse 7, A-1010 (© **01/588-00510**); **Austrobus,** Dr.-Karl-Lueger-Ring 8, A-1010 (© **01/534-110**); and **Blaguss Reisen,** Wiedner Hauptstrasse 15 A-1040 (© **01/50180**). All can reserve hotel space in Austria or anywhere else, sell airline tickets both inside and outside of Austria, and procure hard-to-get tickets for music festivals. Many of the employees speak English fluently.

SEASONAL HOTELS

In Vienna, from July to September, a number of student dormitories are transformed into fully operational hotels. Three of the most viable and popular of these are the **Academia Hotel,** Pfeilgasse 3A; the **Avis Hotel,** Pfeilgasse 4; and the **Atlas Hotel,** at Lerchenfelderstrasse 1. All are within a block of one another, and each is a rather unimaginative-looking, angular, 1960s-style building. They're comfortable and reasonably priced alternatives, only a 20-minute walk west of St. Stephan's. The lodgings will definitely take you back to your college dorm days, though each room has a phone and a private bathroom. Many of them are booked well in advance by groups, but individual travelers are welcome if space is available. Depending on the hotel, doubles cost from 65€ to 85€ ($85–$111) a night, and triples run from 87€ to 105€ ($113–$137) each. Breakfast is included in the rates. Bookings at all three hotels are arranged through the Academia Hotel, which functions as the headquarters for the entire Academia chain. For reservations and information, call ℂ **01/401-76-55,** or fax 01/401-76-20. To get to the Academia and Avis hotels, take the U-Bahn to Thaliastrasse, and then transfer to tram no. 46 and get off at Strozzistrasse. For access to the Atlas Hotel, take the U-Bahn to Lerchenfelderstrasse. These hotels accept American Express, Diners Club, MasterCard, and Visa for payment.

PRIVATE HOMES & FURNISHED APARTMENTS

For travelers who like to have more space than an average hotel room, a limited number of private homes and furnished apartments are available. These accommodations can be money-saving options, depending on the season and the size of the place. An agency that deals with rentals of apartments, villas, and chalets in both Germany and Austria is **VacationVillas.net,** GmbH, Ludwig-Erhard-Str. 4, D-34131 Kassel, Germany (ℂ **0561/920-950-10;** fax 0561/920-950-150; www.vacationvillas.net).

1 Innere Stadt (Inner City)

VERY EXPENSIVE

Do & Co. Hotel 🐸 *Finds*   In 2006, the management of one of Vienna's most consistently high-profile restaurants commandeered four floors of the Haas Haus, originally meant to be a skyscraper shopping mall, and transformed it into a stylish hotel. The result is a quirky but relentlessly upscale and obsessively design-conscious venue that almost everyone in Vienna has an opinion about. The black hulk of a building seems to grate against St. Stephan's Cathedral, which is immediately across the square. To reach the hotel reception, you'll take an elevator from a sterile-looking ground-floor entryway up to level six, where additional dramas unfold. The registration area is awkwardly positioned within a busy area that otherwise functions as a vestibule for a stylish and glossy-looking cocktail bar (Onyx Bar).

Rooms are artfully minimalist and very comfortable, with yummy but hard-to-define colors of toffee and putty Sybaritic details including showers with visible interiors. Bedrooms have mahogany louvered doors, lots of polished travertine, dark-grained hardwoods, and floor plans that follow the curved walls and tucked-away balconies of the Haas Haus. Views from your windows encompass the endlessly roiling crowds scurrying around the all-pedestrian Graben and the Stephansplatz. Critics view the hotel, with some justification, as cultish and snobbish, with lots of gloss but no particular excess or charm.

In the Haas Haus, Stephansplatz 12, 1010 Vienna. ℂ **01/24188.** Fax 01/24188444. www.doco.com. 43 units. 310€–350€ ($403–$455) double; 740€–1,250€ ($962–$1,625) suite. AE, DC, MC, V. U-Bahn: Stephansplatz. **Amenities:** Restaurant; bar; 24-hr. room service; laundry service/dry cleaning. *In room:* A/C, TV, minibar, dataport, safe, hair dryer.

Grand Hotel Wien 🐸🐸🐸   Some of the most discerning hotel guests in Europe, often music lovers, prefer this seven-story deluxe hotel to the more traditional and famous Imperial or Bristol. Only a block from the Wiener Staatsoper, it's a honey. The luxurious service begins with a doorman ushering you past the columns at the entrance into the stunning lobby and reception area. You enter a world of beveled mirrors, crystal chandeliers, marble in various hues, and brass-adorned elevators. Off the lobby is a complex of elegant shops selling expensive perfumes and pricey clothing.

The spacious soundproof accommodations are posh, with all the modern luxuries, such as heated floors, beverage makers, and phones in marble bathrooms (which contain tub/shower combinations and even antifogging mirrors). The more expensive units have more elaborate furnishings and decoration, including delicate stuccowork. The main dining room specializes in Austrian and international dishes, and there's also a Japanese restaurant that serves the town's best sushi brunch on Sunday.

Kärntner Ring 9, A-1010 Vienna. © **01/515800.** Fax 01/5151313. www.grandhotelwien.com. 205 units. 400€–480€ ($520–$624) double; from 680€ ($884) suite. AE, DC, MC, V. Parking 26€ ($34). U-Bahn: Karlsplatz. **Amenities:** 3 restaurants; 2 bars; health club; boutiques; salon; 24-hr. room service; massage; babysitting; laundry service; dry cleaning; nonsmoking rooms; rooms for those w/limited mobility. *In room:* A/C, TV, dataport, minibar, coffeemaker, hair dryer, trouser press, safe.

Hilton International Vienna Plaza *ᘓᘓ*

Vienna's third Hilton rises imposingly for 10 stories, opening onto Ringstrasse just opposite the stock exchange. Its financial-district location draws many business clients from around the world, but it's also near many attractions, such as the Burgtheater, City Hall, and the Kunsthistorisches and Naturhistorisches museums. Designed with flair for the modern traveler, the luxury hotel offers spacious guest rooms and suites. The individually designed suites are one-of-a-kind, inspired by the styles of Frank Lloyd Wright, Mies van der Rohe, and Eliel Saarinen, among others. Room rates increase with altitude and view; two floors are smoke-free. Furnishings are traditional, and many extras—electronic locks, three phones, fluffy robes—are included. Each unit has floor-to-ceiling windows and a large marble bathroom fitted with a tub/shower combination. The hotel also offers a penthouse floor with balconies. You shouldn't have trouble finding a place to eat or drink at this hotel, as it has three restaurants, a piano bar, a cocktail lounge, and a sidewalk terrace.

Schottenring 11, A-1010 Vienna. © **800/445-8667** in the U.S., or 01/313900. Fax 01/31390-22009. www. hilton.com. 255 units. 220€–376€ ($286–$489) double; from 405€ ($527) suite. AE, DC, MC, V. Parking 27€ ($35). U-Bahn: U2 to Schottentor. Tram: 2. Bus: 40A. **Amenities:** 3 restaurants; 2 bars; fitness center; Jacuzzi; sauna; business center; massage; babysitting; laundry service; dry cleaning; nonsmoking rooms; rooms for those w/limited mobility. *In room:* A/C, TV, dataport, Wi-Fi, minibar, coffeemaker (in some), hair dryer, safe.

Hotel Ambassador *ᘓᘓ*

Until it became a hotel in 1866, the six-story Ambassador was a warehouse for wheat and flour, a far cry from its status today as one of the five most glamorous hotels in Vienna. It's no Bristol or Imperial, but it's quite posh nonetheless. The Ambassador couldn't be better located: It's between the Vienna State Opera and St. Stephan's Cathedral, on the square facing the Donner Fountain. Shop-lined Kärntnerstrasse is on the other side. Mark Twain stayed here, as have a host of diplomats and celebrities, including Theodore Roosevelt.

The sumptuous accommodations are an ideal choice for devotees of rococo *fin-de-siècle* or early-20th-century decor. Bedrooms are furnished with Biedermeier and Art Nouveau period pieces. The quieter rooms open onto Neuer Markt, although you'll miss the view of lively Kärntnerstrasse. Comfortable beds, marble bathrooms with tub/shower combinations and toiletries, and ample closet space add to the hotel's allure. The restaurant, Léhar, serves high-quality Austrian and international cuisine.

Kärntnerstrasse 22, A-1010 Vienna. © **01/961610.** Fax 01/5132999. www.ambassador.at. 86 units. 289€–524€ ($376–$681) double; 554€–628€ ($720–$816) junior suite. AE, DC, MC, V. Parking 28€ ($36). U-Bahn: Stephansplatz. **Amenities:** Restaurant; bar; room service (7am–11pm); laundry service; dry cleaning; nonsmoking rooms. *In room:* A/C, TV, minibar, hair dryer, safe.

Hotel Bristol *ᘓᘓᘓ*

From the outside, this six-story landmark, a Westin hotel, looks no different from Vienna's other grand buildings, but connoisseurs of Austrian hotels maintain that this is a superb choice. Its decor evokes the height of the Habsburg Empire—only the Hotel Imperial is grander. The hotel was constructed in 1894

Where to Stay in Vienna's Inner City

Best Western Hotel Tigra **4**

Do & Co Hotel **12**

Graben Hotel **14**

Grand Hotel Wien **27**

Hilton International
Vienna Plaza **1**

Hotel Amadeus **9**

Hotel Ambassador **19**

Hotel Am Parkring **33**

Hotel Am Schubertring **29**

Hotel Astoria **20**

Hotel Austria **35**

Hotel Bristol **26**

Hotel Capricorno **37**

Hotel de France **2**

Hotel Imperial **28**

Hotel Kaiserin Elisabeth **18**

Hotel Kärntnerhof **34**

Hotel König von Ungarn **16**

Hotel Opernring **7**

Hotel-Pension Arenberg **39**

Hotel-Pension Suzanne **25**

Hotel Post **36**

Hotel Römischer Kaiser **23**

Hotel Royal **15**

Hotel Sacher Wien **21**

Hotel Wandl **10**

K + K Palais Hotel **8**

Le Meridien Vienna **6**

Mailberger Hof **24**

Palais Coburg Hotel
Residenz **31**

Pension Dr. Geissler **38**

Pension Neuer Markt **17**

Pension Nossek **11**

Pension Pertschy **13**

Radisson/SAS Palais Hotel
Vienna **30**

Radisson/SAS Style Hotel **5**

Rathauspark Hotel **3**

Vienna Marriott **32**

Zur Wiener Staatsoper **22**

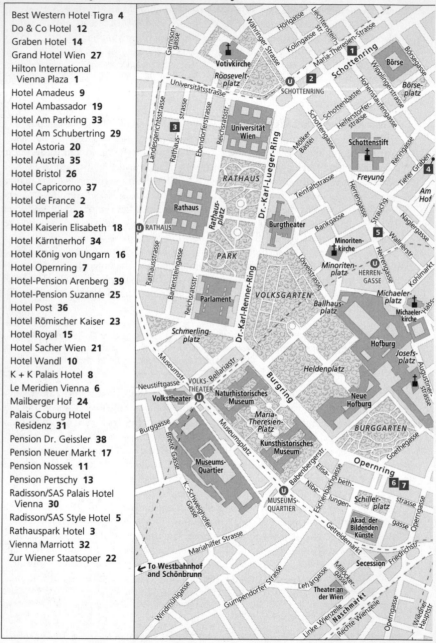

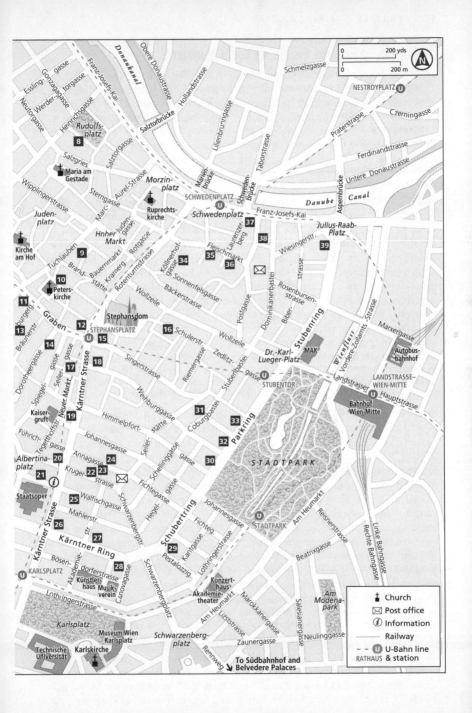

Fun Fact   What, No Palace Fit for a Queen?

The 1969 visit of England's Queen Elizabeth II to Vienna was one of the Hotel Imperial's high points. She was not initially pleased at the idea of lodging in a hotel. Wasn't there a spare palace in this former imperial city? Sure. But none of them offered the luxurious splendor of the Imperial. As it turned out, Queen Elizabeth enjoyed her stay very much. According to the hotel manager, the Queen left with warm words of gratitude and a little present for every single employee.

---

next to the Vienna State Opera, and has been updated to provide guests with black-tile bathrooms and other modern conveniences. All rooms have thermostats, bedside controls, and ample storage, plus generous marble bathrooms with scales, robes, and tub/shower combinations. Each bedroom includes a living-room area, and many have a small balcony providing a rooftop view of the Vienna State Opera and Ringstrasse.

Many of the hotel's architectural embellishments rank as objets d'art in their own right, including the black carved-marble fireplaces and the oil paintings in the salons. The Bristol Club Rooms in the tower offer comfortable chairs, an open fireplace, a self-service bar, library, stereo, deck, and sauna. Corkscrew columns of rare marble grace the Korso, Bristol's restaurant, which is one of the best in Vienna.

Kärntner Ring 1, A-1015 Vienna. © 888/625-5144 in the U.S., or 01/515160. Fax 01/51516550. www.westin.com/bristol. 146 units. 265€–345€ ($345–$449) double; from 536€ ($697) suite. Rates include breakfast. AE, DC, MC, V. Parking 28€ ($36). U-Bahn: Karlsplatz. Tram: 1 or 2. **Amenities:** 2 restaurants; bar; free access to nearby fitness center; sauna; business center; 24-hr. room service; babysitting; laundry service; dry cleaning; rooms for those w/limited mobility; nonsmoking rooms. *In room:* A/C, TV, dataport, minibar, hair dryer, safe.

Hotel de France 𝒢   Hotel de France is right on the Ring and has long been a favorite. It's neighbor to the university and the Votivkirche, which makes it a centrally located choice. Its chiseled gray facade looks basically as it did when it was first erected in 1872. After World War II, the building was transformed into a hotel. Its modern elements and unobtrusively conservative decor are the result of extensive renovation. In such a subdued and appealing ambience, you often encounter businesspeople from all over the world. They appreciate the high-ceilinged public rooms and oriental carpets, the generously padded armchairs, and the full-dress portrait of Franz Josef. The bedrooms are among the finest for their price range in Vienna. Housekeeping is of a high standard; furnishings are traditional, with firm beds and double-glazed windows that really keep noise pollution down. Roomy bathrooms have tub/shower combinations and toiletries. The best units are on the fifth floor, although windows there are too high for you to absorb the view unless you're very tall.

Schottenring 3, A-1010 Vienna. © 01/31368. Fax 01/3195969. www.hoteldefrance.at. 212 units. 290€ ($377) double; from 340€ ($442) suite. Rates include buffet breakfast. AE, DC, MC, V. Parking 18€ ($23). U-Bahn: U2 or Schottentor. Tram: 1, 2, 37, or D. Bus: 1A. **Amenities:** 2 restaurants; 3 bars; sauna; room service (7am–10pm); laundry service; dry cleaning; nonsmoking rooms. *In room:* A/C, TV, dataport, minibar, hair dryer, trouser press, safe.

Hotel Imperial 𝒢𝒢𝒢   This hotel is definitely the grandest in Vienna. Luminaries from around the world use it as their headquarters, especially music stars who prefer the location—2 blocks from the Vienna State Opera and 1 block from the Musikverein. Richard Wagner stayed here with his family for a few months in 1875 (some scholars claim that he worked out key sections of both *Tannhäuser* and *Lohengrin* during that period).

The hotel was built in 1869 as the private residence of the Duke of Württemberg. The Italian architect Zanotti designed the facade, which resembles a massive government building with a heroic frieze carved into the pediment below the roofline. It was converted into a private hotel in 1873. The Nazis commandeered it for their headquarters during World War II, and the Russians requisitioned it in 1945. Massive expenditures have returned it to its former glory, with special care paid to its fourth and fifth floors, which hold the most desirable rooms.

Accommodations vary greatly in size, as befits a hotel of this era. Those on the mezzanine and first floors are lavishly baroque; as you go higher, appointments diminish, as do bathroom sizes. Except for some top-floor rooms, bathrooms are generous in size, with heated marble floors, robes, and tub/shower combinations. Courtyard rooms are more tranquil but lack the view of the city.

On the staircase leading up from the glittering salons are archways supported by statues of gods and goddesses, along with two Winterhalter portraits of Emperor Franz Josef and his wife, Elisabeth. Everything is set against a background of polished red, yellow, and black marble; crystal chandeliers; Gobelin tapestries; and fine rugs. The salons have arched ceilings, intricately painted with garlands of fruit, ornate urns, griffins, and the smiling faces of sphinxes.

The elegant Hotel Imperial Restaurant has a turn-of-the-20th-century atmosphere, accented by antique silver, portraits of Franz Josef, and superb service.

Kärntner Ring 16, A-1015 Vienna. (C) **800/325-3589** in the U.S., or 01/501100. Fax 01/50110410. www.luxury collection.com/imperial. 138 units. 392€–669€ ($510–$870) double; from 905€ ($1,177) suite. AE, DC, MC, V. Parking 30€ ($39). U-Bahn: Karlsplatz. **Amenities:** 2 restaurants; bar; health club; sauna; salon; 24-hr. room service; massage; babysitting; laundry service; dry cleaning; nonsmoking rooms; rooms for those w/limited mobility. *In room:* A/C, TV, dataport, minibar, hair dryer, safe.

Hotel Inter-Continental Wien 🐼🐼   Opposite the Stadtpark and a few minutes from the Ringstrasse, this five-star deluxe property has forged ahead of the Marriott and the Hilton, even though it cloaks its charms in a dull "white tower." Inside, the hotel is inviting and elegant, with a tasteful lobby lit by some of the best hotel chandeliers in Vienna. Many musical stars make this their hotel of choice. Rooms are spacious and richly furnished, but are not necessarily evocative of Vienna. All the

---

Moments Dream Dates in Vienna

Imagine waking one morning to the sound of church bells from St. Stephan's Cathedral, having champagne with your sumptuous breakfast at an elegant hotel, then strolling the cobblestone streets of the city center or visiting famed museums and marveling at old masters. Not a bad way to spend a honeymoon or anniversary. Some of Vienna's most elegant hotels, such as the **Grand Hotel Wien** (p. 50) and the **Dorint Hotel Biedermeier** (p. 70), offer excellent wedding packages as well as honeymoon and anniversary arrangements. For more information on wedding and honeymoon packages, contact the Vienna Tourist Board, Obere Augartenstrasse 40, A-1025 Vienna ((C) **011-43-1-24 555;** fax 011-43-1-24-555-666; www.vienna.info).

luxuries are here: dataports with voice mail, soundproofing, comfortable beds, and robes and toiletries in bathrooms with marble sinks and tub/shower combinations.

Johannesgasse 28, A-1037 Vienna. ✆ **01/711-22-0.** Fax 01/713-44-89. www.vienna.interconti.com. 453 units. 218€–330€ ($283–$429) double; from 430€ ($559) suite. Rates include buffet breakfast. AE, DC, MC, V. Parking: 25€ ($33). U-Bahn: Johannesgasse. **Amenities:** 2 restaurants; bar; health club; sauna; 24-hr. room service; massage; babysitting; laundry service; dry cleaning; nonsmoking rooms; solarium; rooms for those w/limited mobility. *In room:* A/C, TV, dataport, coffeemaker, minibar, hair dryer, iron, safe.

Hotel Sacher Wien ✦✦✦ The Sacher was built in 1876, and despite recent improvements, partial rebuilding, and renovations which added 40 new rooms and a deluxe spa, it still has an air of Habsburg-era glory. Red velvet, crystal chandeliers, and brocaded curtains in the public rooms evoke Old Vienna. If you want truly grand, we think the Imperial and Bristol are superior, but the Sacher has its diehard admirers. Despite its popularity as a setting for spy novels, both the crowned heads of Europe and the deposed heads (especially those of eastern European countries) have safely dined and lived here.

In addition to intrigue, the Sacher has produced culinary creations that still bear its name. Franz Sacher, the celebrated chef, left the world a fabulously caloric chocolate cake called the Sacher torte.

Most rooms contain antiques or superior reproductions; those facing the Vienna State Opera have the best views. Rooms near the top are small with cramped bathrooms, but most accommodations are generous in size and often have sitting areas and midsize marble bathrooms with tub/shower combinations. Interior rooms tend to be dark, however. Thick towels are endlessly supplied by the eagle-eyed housekeeping staff. Demi-suites and chambers with drawing rooms are more expensive. The reception desk is fairly flexible about making arrangements for salons or apartments, or joining two rooms together, if possible.

Philharmonikerstrasse 4, A-1010 Vienna. ✆ **01/514560.** Fax 01/51256810. www.sacher.com. 152 units. 294€–490€ ($382–$637) double; from 650€ ($845) junior suite; from 720€ ($936) executive suite. AE, DC, MC, V. Parking 29€ ($38). U-Bahn: Karlsplatz. Tram: 1, 2, 62, 65, D, or J. Bus: 4A. **Amenities:** 2 restaurants; bar; spa; room service (7am–10pm); massage; babysitting; laundry/dry cleaning. *In room:* A/C, TV, minibar, hair dryer, safe.

Le Meridien Vienna ✦✦✦ Located directly on the famous Ringstrasse, this glamorous government-rated five-star property is only a short stroll from the Vienna State Opera and Hofburg Palace, and is the first hotel property in Austria for this popular French chain. A $120-million renovation converted an apartment block of turn-of-the-20th-century imperial Viennese architecture into this new city landmark. Luscious maple wood and satin-chrome steel and glass create an aura of understated elegance in public rooms, and special illuminations and lighting effects are used dramatically.

The midsize-to-spacious bedrooms feature designer beds, parquet floors, warm carpeting, and "sink-in" armchairs. Windows were designed to capture the most light, and decorators created drama using pinks and blues accented by earth tones. Each accommodation comes with a luxurious bathroom with tub/shower combination.

Passing through a bar with a DJ, colorful wall elements, room dividers, and special lighting effects, you arrive at the glitzy Shambala Restaurant, where award-winning Parisian chef Michel Rostang created culinary delights when he conceived the menu.

Opernring 13-A, A-1010 Vienna. ✆ **01/588900.** Fax 01/588909090. http://vienna.lemeridien.com. 294 units. 225€– 385€ ($293–$501) double; from 655€ ($852) suite. AE, DC, MC, V. U-Bahn: Karlsplatz. **Amenities:** Restaurant; 2 bars; indoor heated pool; gym; sauna; 24-hr. room service; babysitting; laundry service; dry cleaning; nonsmoking rooms; rooms for those w/limited mobility. *In room:* A/C, TV, dataport, minibar, beverage maker, hair dryer, iron/iron-ing board, safe.

Palais Coburg Hotel Residenz ✪✪✪   Originally built in 1846 as the outra-geously elegant, and even more outrageously ostentatious private home of the Coburg dynasty (who managed somehow to sire most of the monarchs of western Europe), this sprawling and staggeringly historic building—except for its exterior—was gutted and rebuilt during a six-year renovation that was completed in 2006. Prior to its pres-ent incarnation, it needed lots of time and attention. Much of its interior had been bashed and vandalized by the Russian army after their occupation of the site after World War II, and after that, it functioned as the headquarters of a dull Austrian bureaucracy associated with the State Railways. But all traces of the mundane have definitely been banished since its transformation into a multi-purpose building, only part of which is devoted to hotel accommodations.

The lavish renovation of the building's foundations, most of which date back to the Middle Ages, has created nine different meeting spaces for private dinners and con-ventions. There's both a formal restaurant (dinner only) and a somewhat less expen-sive bistro (breakfast, lunch, and dinner), which is appealingly centered within a greenhouse-inspired building on the palace's terrace, high above the street level of the nearby Marriott Hotel. The full-service spa is reserved only for residents of the hotel, and then there are those suites: The smaller and less expensive are contemporary, intensely design-conscious, and very comfortable. The more expensive evoke the hey-day of the Rothschilds and are posh, with many pale satin upholsteries and valuable antiques. Ironically, all this grandeur is the personal property of an (individual) Aus-trian investor, whose stated ambition involves the on-site compilation of the largest and most comprehensive wine collection in Europe. It's stored within the deepest of the building's medieval vaults (and they go very deep, indeed). Some, but not all, of the collection is tantalizingly visible through Plexiglas skylights set into the top of some of the cellar's vaulting.

Coburgbastei 4, 1010 Vienna. ✆ **01/518-180.** Fax 01/518-181. www.palais-coburg.com. 35 suites. 460€–1,920€ ($598–$2,496) suites. Rates include breakfast. Parking 20€ ($26). AE, DC, MC, V. **Amenities:** 2 restaurants; indoor pool; health club; spa; sauna; 24-hour room service; laundry service/dry cleaning. *In room:* A/C, TV, full kitchen w/bar, safe, personal computer.

Radisson/SAS Palais Hotel Vienna ✪   This hotel is one of Vienna's grandest ren-ovations. An unused neoclassical palace was converted into a hotel in 1985 by SAS, the Scandinavian airline; in 1994, another palace next door was added, allowing the hotel to double in size. Near Vienna's most elaborate park (the Stadtpark), the hotel boasts facades accented with cast-iron railings, reclining nymphs, and elaborate cor-nices. The interior is plushly outfitted with 19th-century architectural motifs, all impeccably restored and dramatically illuminated. The lobby contains arching palms, a soaring ceiling, and a bar with evening piano music. The result is an uncluttered, conservative, and well-maintained hotel that is managed in a breezy, highly efficient manner. Bedrooms are outfitted in either soothing pastels or, in the new wing, in summery shades of green and white. Ample closet space is an attractive feature, as are the good beds and generous-size marble bathrooms with heated floors, makeup mirrors, and tub/shower combinations. The hotel also offers several duplex suites, or *maisonettes,* conventional suites, and rooms in the Royal Club, which has upgraded luxuries and services.

Parkring 16, A-1010 Vienna. (©) **800/333-3333** in the U.S., or 01/515170. Fax 01/5122216. www.radisson.com. 247 units. 212€–276€ ($254–$331) double; from 289€ ($347) suite. AE, DC, MC, V. Parking 30€ ($36). U-Bahn: Stadtpark. Tram: 2. **Amenities:** Restaurant; 2 bars; fitness center; spa; Jacuzzi; sauna; 24-hr. room service; babysitting; laundry service; dry cleaning; nonsmoking rooms; 1 room for those w/limited mobility. *In room:* A/C, TV, dataport, minibar, hair dryer, safe, Wi-Fi.

Radisson/SAS Style Hotel ⭐   In the early 1900s, this building was the headquarters of an Austrian bank, but in 2005 it was converted into an elegant hotel. The result is a quirky and somewhat eccentric hotel with an enviable facade that's embellished with gilded, Secessionist-era bas reliefs, virtually no signage in front, and a style-conscious, avant-garde postmodern interior that challenged the creativity of a team of designers. The hotel boasts a central location deep into the heart of Imperial Vienna.

Bedrooms are comfortable, culturally neutral, and angular-minimalist, with warm earth tones that make them livable and at their best, cozy. The most appealing public area is the H-12 wine bar, a long, narrow space with hard metallic surfaces, an alabaster bar surface that's illuminated from within, and big-screen TVs showing either fashion *défilés* in Milan or the occasional soccer game. Note the massive security doors within the health club. Crafted from massive steel, and too heavy to haul away during the building's renovation, they're now ominous-looking but purely decorative reminders of the building's original function as a bank.

Herrengasse 12, 1010 Vienna. (©) **01/22780-0.** Fax 01/22780-77. www.style.vienna.radissonsas.com. 78 units. 188€–310€ ($244–$403) double; 310€–450€ ($403–$585) suite. AE, DC, MC, V. U-Bahn: Herrengasse. **Amenities:** Restaurant (Sapori); wine bar (H-12); health club w/sauna; laundry service/dry cleaning; 24-hr. room service. *In room:* A/C, TV, dataport, minibar, safe.

Vienna Marriott ⭐   The Marriott has a striking exterior and holds its own against SAS, the K + K Palais Hotel, and the Hilton, although the latter two hotels manage to evoke a more Viennese atmosphere. Opposite Stadtpark, the hotel is ideally located for visitors, as it's within walking distance of such landmarks as St. Stephan's Cathedral, the Vienna State Opera, and the Hofburg. Its Mississippi-riverboat facade displays expanses of tinted glass set in finely wrought enameled steel. About a third of the building is occupied by the American Consulate offices and a few private apartments.

The hotel's lobby culminates in a stairway whose curved sides frame a splashing waterfall that's surrounded with plants. Many of the comfortably modern bedrooms are larger than those in the city's other contemporary hotels. Spacious mirrored closets are a feature, as are great bathrooms with large sinks and tub/shower combinations. Furnishings are a bit commercial. There are four smoke-free floors and adequate soundproofing.

Parkring 12A, A-1010 Vienna. (©) **888/236-2427** in the U.S., or 01/515180. Fax 01/515186736. www.marriot.com. 313 units. 270€ ($351) double; 360€–690€ ($468–$897) suite. AE, DC, MC, V. Parking 35€ ($46). Tram: 1 or 2. **Amenities:** 3 restaurants; 3 bars; indoor heated pool; fitness center; Jacuzzi; sauna; car-rental desk; salon; 24-hr. room service; massage; babysitting; laundry service; dry cleaning; nonsmoking rooms; rooms for those w/limited mobility; solarium. *In room:* A/C, TV, dataport, minibar, hair dryer, iron/ironing board, trouser press, safe.

EXPENSIVE

Hotel Amadeus ⭐   Cozy and convenient, this boxlike hotel is only 2 minutes away from the cathedral and within walking distance of practically everything of musical or historical note in Vienna. It was built on the site of a once-legendary tavern (Zum roten Igel) that attracted the likes of Johannes Brahms, Franz Schubert, and Moritz von Schwind. Behind a dull 1960s facade, the hotel maintains its bedrooms and carpeted public rooms in reasonable shape. Bedrooms are furnished in a comfortable, modern style, and many open onto views of the cathedral. However, ceilings are uncomfortably low. Double-glazing on the windows quiets but does not obliterate street noise. Some of the carpeting and fabrics look a little worse for wear. Tiled bathrooms are midsize, but there's not enough room to lay out your toiletries. Eight rooms have showers but no tubs. Expect a somewhat dour welcome: No one on the staff will win any Mr. or Mrs. Sunshine contests.

Wildpretmarkt 5, A-1010 Vienna. ⓒ 01/5338738. Fax 01/533-87383838. www.hotel-amadeus.at. 30 units. 170€–195€ ($221–$254) double. Rates include buffet breakfast. AE, DC, MC, V. Parking 22€ ($29). U-Bahn: Stephansplatz. **Amenities:** Breakfast room; lounge; babysitting; laundry service; dry cleaning; nonsmoking rooms; rooms for those w/limited mobility. *In room:* A/C, TV, dataport, minibar, hair dryer, safe.

Hotel Astoria ⓖ   Hotel Astoria is for nostalgists who want to experience life as it was in the closing days of the Austro-Hungarian Empire. A first-class hotel, the Astoria has an eminently desirable location, lying on the shopping mall near St. Stephan's Cathedral and the Vienna State Opera. Decorated in a slightly frayed turn-of-the-20th-century style, the hotel offers well-appointed and traditionally decorated bedrooms. The interior rooms tend to be too dark, and singles are just too cramped. The place is, in fact, a bit on the melancholy side. Rooms contain built-in armoires and well-chosen linens and duvets on good beds and bathrooms that, for the most part, are spacious (although the fixtures are old) and have such extras as dual basins, heated racks, tub/shower combinations, and bidets. Of course, it has been renovated over the years, but the old style has been preserved, and management seems genuinely concerned about offering high-quality service and accommodations for what is considered a reasonable price in Vienna.

Kärntnerstrasse 32–34, A-1015 Vienna. ⓒ 01/515770. Fax 01/5157782. www.austria-trend.at. 118 units. 210€ ($273) double; 260€ ($338) suite. Rates include breakfast. AE, DC, MC, V. Parking 26€ ($34). U-Bahn: Stephansplatz. **Amenities:** Restaurant; bar; 24-hr. room service; babysitting; laundry service; dry cleaning; nonsmoking rooms. *In room:* TV, minibar, hair dryer, safe.

Hotel Das Triest ⓖⓖ *(Finds*   Sir Terence Conran, the famous English architect and designer, created the interior for this contemporary hotel in the center of Vienna, a 5-minute walk from St. Stephan's Cathedral. Conran has done for Das Triest what Philippe Starck did for New York's Paramount Hotel: created a stylish address in the heart of one of the world's most important cities. An emerging favorite with artists and musicians, this hip hotel has such grace notes as a courtyard garden. The building was originally used as a stable for horses pulling stagecoaches between Vienna and Trieste—hence its name, "City of Trieste." Its old cross-vaulted rooms, which give the structure a distinctive flair, have been transformed into lounges and suites. Bedrooms are midsize to spacious, tastefully furnished, and comfortable. The white-tiled bathrooms have heated racks, tub/shower combinations, deluxe toiletries, and vanity mirrors.

Wiedner Hauptstrasse 12, A-1040 Vienna. ⓒ 01/58918. Fax 01/5891818. www.dastriest.at. 73 units. 260€ ($338) double; from 395€ ($514) suite. Rates include buffet breakfast. AE, DC, MC, V. Parking 21€ ($27). U-Bahn: Stephansplatz. **Amenities:** Restaurant; bar; fitness center; sauna; salon; 24-hr. room service; massage; babysitting; laundry service; dry cleaning; nonsmoking rooms; solarium. *In room:* A/C, TV, dataport, minibar, hair dryer, trouser press, safe, Wi-Fi.

Hotel Kaiserin Elisabeth   This yellow-stoned hotel is conveniently located near the cathedral. The interior is decorated with oriental rugs on well-maintained marble and wood floors. The main salon has a pale-blue skylight suspended above it, with mirrors and half-columns in natural wood. The small, quiet rooms have been considerably updated since Wolfgang Mozart, Richard Wagner, Franz Liszt, and Edvard Grieg stayed here, and their musical descendants continue to patronize the place. Polished wood, clean linens, and perhaps another oriental rug grace the rooms. Bathrooms are a bit cramped, with not enough room for your toiletries, but they are tiled and equipped with tub/shower combinations, vanity mirrors, and, in some cases, bidets.

Weihburggasse 3, A-1010 Vienna. ℂ **01/515260.** Fax 01/515267. www.kaiserinelisabeth.at. 63 units. 200€ ($260) double; 220€ ($286) suite. Rates include buffet breakfast. AE, DC, MC, V. Parking 28€ ($36). U-Bahn: Stephansplatz. **Amenities:** Restaurant; bar; room service (7am–10pm); laundry service; dry cleaning. *In room:* A/C (in most units), TV, dataport, minibar, hair dryer, safe.

Hotel König Von Ungarn ⚐   On a narrow street near St. Stephan's, this hotel occupies a dormered building that dates back to the early 17th century. It's been receiving paying guests for more than 4 centuries and is Vienna's oldest continuously operated hotel—in all, an evocative, intimate, and cozy retreat. It was once a *pied-à-terre* for Hungarian noble families during their stays in the Austrian capital. In 1791, Mozart reportedly resided and wrote some of his immortal music in an apartment upstairs, where you'll find a Mozart museum.

The interior abounds with interesting architectural details, such as marble columns supporting the arched ceiling of the King of Hungary restaurant, which is one of Vienna's finest and most famous. There's also a mirrored solarium/bar area with a glass roof over the atrium, and a live tree growing out of the pavement. Tall hinged windows overlook the Old Town, and Venetian mirrors adorn some walls. Everywhere you look, you'll find low-key luxury, tradition, and modern convenience. Try for the two rooms with balconies. Guest rooms have been newly remodeled with Biedermeier accents and traditional furnishings. Some rooms—and you should try to avoid these—lack an outside window. Most bathrooms are generous in size and have dual basins, tub/shower combinations, and tiled walls. The professional staff is highly efficient, keeping the hotel spotless.

Schulerstrasse 10, A-1010 Vienna. ℂ **01/515840.** Fax 01/515848. www.kvu.at. 33 units. 203€ ($264) double; 280€–330€ ($364–$429) apt. Rates include breakfast. AE, DC, MC, V. U-Bahn: Stephansplatz. **Amenities:** Restaurant; bar; room service (7am–10pm); babysitting; laundry service; dry cleaning. *In room:* A/C, TV, dataport, minibar, hair dryer, safe.

Hotel Römischer Kaiser ⚐ 🄺ids   A Best Western affiliate, this hotel is housed in a national trust building that has seen its share of transformations. It's located in a traffic-free zone between St. Stephan's Cathedral and the Vienna State Opera, on a side street off Kärntnerstrasse. It was constructed in 1684 as the private palace of the imperial chamberlain and later housed the Imperial School of Engineering before becoming a hostelry at the turn of the 20th century. The hotel rents romantically decorated rooms (our favorite has red satin upholstery over a chaise lounge). Thick duvets and custom linens make the rooms homelike and inviting, and bathrooms are generous in size, often luxurious, with showers and half-tubs, vanity mirrors, and enough shelf space to spread out your toiletries. Double-glazed windows keep down the noise, and baroque paneling is a nice touch. Some rooms—notably nos. 12, 22, 30, and 38—can accommodate three or four beds, making this a family-friendly place. The red-carpeted sidewalk cafe has bar service and tables shaded with flowers and umbrellas. It evokes memories of Vienna in its imperial heyday.

Annagasse 16, A-1010 Vienna. ℂ **800/528-1234** in the U.S., or 01/51277510. Fax 01/512775113. www.best western.com. 23 units. 169€–229€ ($220–$298) double. Rates include buffet breakfast. AE, DC, MC, V. Parking 19€ ($25). U-Bahn: Stephansplatz. **Amenities:** Restaurant; bar; room service (7am–9pm); laundry service; dry cleaning; nonsmoking rooms. *In room:* A/C, TV/VCR, dataport, minibar, hair dryer, safe.

K + K Palais Hotel ⓖ⋆   This hotel, with its severely dignified facade, sheltered the affair of Emperor Franz Josef and his celebrated mistress, Katherina Schratt, in 1890. Occupying a desirable position near the river and a 5-minute walk from the Ring, it remained unused for 2 decades until it was renovated in 1981.

Vestiges of its imperial past remain, in spite of the contemporary but airy lobby and the lattice-covered bar. The public rooms are painted a shade of imperial Austrian yellow, and one of Ms. Schratt's antique secretaries occupies a niche near a white-sided tile stove. The bedrooms are comfortably outfitted and stylish. Rooms have a certain Far East motif, with light wood, wicker, and rattan. The tiled bathrooms are equipped with tub/shower combinations, decent shelf space, and state-of-the-art plumbing.

Rudolfsplatz 11, A-1010 Vienna. Ⓒ **800/537-8483** in the U.S., or 01/5331353. Fax 01/533135370. www. kkhotels.com. 66 units. 230€–255€ ($299–$332) double. Rates include buffet breakfast. AE, DC, MC, V. Parking 16€ ($21). U-Bahn: Schottenring. **Amenities:** Restaurant; bar; room service (6:30am–11pm); babysitting; laundry service; dry cleaning; nonsmoking rooms. *In room:* A/C, TV, dataport, minibar, hair dryer, safe.

MODERATE

Best Western Hotel Tigra ⓖ⋆ *Finds*   In the heart of Vienna, within walking distance of many historic sights, this is a comfortable, well-run hotel that's not as well known as it should be. Most rooms are midsize, furnished in a combination of modern and traditional reproductions, and have tiled bathrooms with showers. The hotel has expanded to include two historic buildings. Mozart stayed in one of these buildings in the summer of 1773, when he composed six string quartets and some marches. Fifteen one-room apartments near the main building lack air-conditioning.

Tiefer Graben 14-20, A-1010 Vienna. Ⓒ **800/528-1234** in the U.S., or 01/533-96410. Fax 01/533-9645. www.hotel-tigra.at. 79 units. 124€–195€ ($161–$254) double; 180€–210€ ($234–$273) triple. Rates include buffet breakfast. AE, DC, MC, V. U-Bahn: Herrengasse. **Amenities:** Breakfast lounge; bar; barber shop/salon; babysitting; laundry service; nonsmoking rooms. *In room:* TV, dataport, minibar, hair dryer, safe; kitchenettes in apts.

Graben Hotel   Back in the 18th century, this was called Zum Goldener Jägerhorn; over the years, it has attracted an array of bohemian writers and artists. The poet Franz Grillparzer was a regular guest, and during the dark days of World War II, it was a gathering place for such writers as Franz Kafka, Max Brod, and Peter Altenberg. There aren't too many bohemians around anymore, but what's left of them can be seen gathered at the fabled Café Hawelka across the street. The hotel stands on a narrow street off the Kärntnerstrasse, in the very center of the city. One journalist in Vienna wrote that "its staff was lent by Fawlty Towers," but we're sure he meant that lovingly, as they're helpful and bright. Guests gather around the stone fireplace in winter and look at the original postcards left by Altenberg. Rooms are high ceilinged but rather cramped, with tub/shower combinations in the bathrooms. Although there are some Art Nouveau touches, much of the furniture is a bit drab and spartan for our tastes. If there's any sunlight streaming in, it'll come from the front rooms, not the darker havens in the rear. On-site is the excellent trattoria San Stefano, serving some of the best Italian dishes in the area. The Restaurant Altenberg specializes in Austrian dishes. The chef is known for his creamy cake named in honor of Kaiser Franz Josef.

Dorotheergasse 3, A-1010 Vienna. Ⓒ **01/51215310.** Fax 01/512153120. www.kremslehnerhotels.at. 41 units. 175€–190€ ($228–$247) double. Rates include buffet breakfast. AE, DC, MC, V. Parking 22€ ($29). U-Bahn: Karlsplatz. **Amenities:** Restaurant; lounge; room service (7am–10pm); babysitting; nonsmoking rooms. *In room:* TV, dataport, minibar, hair dryer, safe.

Hotel Am Parkring   This well-maintained hotel occupies the top three floors of a 13-story office building near the edge of Vienna's Stadtpark. A semiprivate elevator services only the street-level entrance and the hotel's floors. There are sweeping views of the city from all of its bedrooms, some of which overlook nearby St. Stephan's Cathedral. Bedrooms are furnished in a conservative but comfortable style, and are favored by business travelers and tourists alike, although the atmosphere is a bit sterile if you're seeking nostalgic Vienna. Rooms here are a standard, reliable choice, but don't expect fireworks. All have well-kept bathrooms that are small but functional (some with showers instead of tubs) Eighteen units were equipped with sparkling new bathrooms in 2002. This hotel is not the kindest to the lone tourist, as single accommodations tend to be too small, and often sofa beds are used.

Parkring 12, A-1015 Vienna. ℂ **01/514800.** Fax 01/5148040. www.bestwestern.com. 64 units. 165€–233€ ($215–$303) double; 360€ ($468) suite. Rates include buffet breakfast. AE, DC, MC, V. Parking 19€ ($25). U-Bahn: Stadtpark or Stubentor. Tram: 1 or 2. **Amenities:** Restaurant; bar; room service (6:30am–10pm); babysitting; laundry service; dry cleaning; nonsmoking rooms. *In room:* A/C, TV/VCR, dataport, minibar, hair dryer.

Hotel Am Schubertring ⚛ *(Kids)*   In a historic building in the very center of town, this small hotel has a certain charm and style. On the famous Ringstrasse, next to the opera, it has Viennese flair, especially in the use of Art Nouveau and Biedermeier-style furnishings in its bedrooms. Rooms are moderate in size, comfortable, and generally quiet, and eight units are suitable for three guests or more. Bathrooms are small, with tub/shower combinations. The top-floor rooms look out over the rooftops of Vienna. At this family-friendly place, children under age 6 are housed free if sharing accommodations with a parent.

Schubertring 11, A-1010 Vienna. ℂ **01/717020.** Fax 01/7139966. www.schubertring.at. 39 units. 128€–195€ ($166–$254) double; from 142€ ($185) suite. AE, DC, MC, V. Parkring 18€ ($23). U-Bahn: Karlsplatz. **Amenities:** Restaurant; bar; room service (7am–11pm); babysitting; laundry service; dry cleaning; nonsmoking rooms. *In room:* A/C, TV, dataport, minibar, hair dryer, safe.

Hotel Capricorno   In the heart of Vienna, this government-rated four-star hotel, a short stroll from St. Stephan's and next to the Danube Canal, has more than a convenient location going for it. Outside it's a dull, cube-shape building, but inside it's rather warm and inviting, with modern Art Nouveau accents, tiles, and brass trim in the reception area. Rooms are compact—even cramped, in many cases—but are well furnished and maintained. Singles are particularly small, mainly because the beds are more spacious than most. All units have neatly kept bathrooms mostly equipped with tub/shower combinations. Some units, especially those on the lower levels, suffer from noise pollution. The hotel sends its guests to its sibling, the Hotel Stefanie, across the street, for dining in a first-class restaurant, Kronprinz Rudolph, offering both Viennese and international cuisine.

Schwedenplatz 3-4, A-1010 Vienna. ℂ **01/53331040.** Fax 01/53376714. www.schick-hotels.com. 46 units. 155€–186€ ($202–$242) double. AE, DC, MC, V. Rates include buffet breakfast. U-Bahn: Stephansplatz. **Amenities:** Breakfast room; lounge; 24-hr. room service; laundry service; dry cleaning; nonsmoking rooms. *In room:* A/C, TV, dataport, minibar, hair dryer.

Hotel Opernring *(Kids)*   Across from the Vienna State Opera, and lying along the Ring, this government-rated four-star hotel has been much improved under new owners, who have carried out a major rejuvenation of a formerly tired property. Accommodations are fairly large and tastefully furnished, with such extras as dataports, duvet-covered beds, and spacious tiled bathrooms equipped with tub/shower combinations. Double-glazed windows cut down on the noise in the front bedrooms. Some units are reserved for nonsmokers, and some of the accommodations can sleep three to four family members comfortably. Don't judge the hotel by its rather cramped

reception area or its entrance. The third-floor lounge is large and inviting; its bay window opens onto the activity of central Vienna.

Opernring 11, A-1010 Vienna. © **800/528-1234** in the U.S., or 01/5875518. Fax 01/587551829. www.opernring.at. 35 units. 150€–240€ ($195–$312) double; from 280€ ($364) suite. Rates include buffet breakfast. AE, DC, MC, V. Parking 22€ ($29). U-Bahn: Karlsplatz. **Amenities:** Breakfast room; lounge; breakfast-only room service; babysitting; laundry service; dry cleaning; nonsmoking rooms. *In room:* TV, dataport, minibar, coffeemaker, hair dryer, safe.

Hotel-Pension Arenberg ⚜ This genteel but unpretentious hotel-pension occupies the second and third floors of a six-story apartment house that was built around the turn of the 20th century. Set in a prestigious neighborhood on Ringstrasse, it offers small, soundproof bedrooms outfitted in old-world style with oriental carpets, conservative furniture, and intriguing artwork. The shower-only bathrooms are a bit cramped. Despite this, the hotel remains exceptionally appealing to those with a sense of history. One enthusiastic reader described it as a small luxury hotel where the English-speaking staff couldn't be more delightful or helpful.

Stubenring 2, A-1010 Vienna. © **800/528-1234** in the U.S., or 01/5125291. Fax 01/5139356. www.bestwestern. com. 23 units. 158€–208€ ($205–$270) double; 195€–268€ ($254–$348) triple. Rates include breakfast. AE, DC, MC, V. Parking 21€ ($27). U-Bahn: Schwedenplatz. **Amenities:** Lounge; breakfast-only room service; babysitting; laundry service; dry cleaning; nonsmoking rooms; rooms for those with limited mobility. *In room:* A/C, TV, dataport, minibar, hair dryer, safe.

Hotel Royal ⚜⚜ This dignified, nine-story hotel is on one of the more prestigious streets of the old city, less than a block from St. Stephan's Cathedral. The lobby contains the piano where Wagner composed *Die Meistersinger von Nürnberg*. Each of the good-size rooms is furnished differently, with some good reproductions of antiques and even an occasional original. Opened in 1931, the hotel was rebuilt in 1982. Try for a room with a balcony and a view of the cathedral. Corner rooms with spacious foyers are also desirable, although those facing the street tend to be noisy. The midsize bathrooms have mosaic tiles, dual basins, heated towel racks, and, in most cases, a tub bath along with a shower unit. Firenze Enoteca (p. 90), under separate management, serves savory Italian food and has the largest selection of Italian wines in Austria.

Singerstrasse 3, A-1010 Vienna. © 01/515680. Fax 01/513-9698. www.kremslehnerhotels.at. 81 units. 140€–175€ ($182–$228) double; 250€ ($325) suite. Rates include breakfast. AE, DC, MC, V. U-Bahn: Stephansplatz. **Amenities:** 2 restaurants; bar; wine bar; room service (7am–10pm); laundry service; dry cleaning; nonsmoking rooms. *In room:* TV, dataport, minibar, hair dryer.

Hotel Viennart ⚜ *Finds* More than any other hotel in Vienna, this six-story hotel, which was fully renovated, appeals to lovers of modern art. This is the most convenient place to stay for those wanting to be near the contemporary art in the newly launched MuseumsQuartier (see chapter 6). The location is at the edge of the Spittelberg, a district locals call "the Montmartre of Vienna." The decor is sock-it-to-you modern, in red, white, orange, and black. Rooms are outfitted in a functional style, with fine furnishings and tub/shower combinations in the bathrooms.

Breite Gasse 9, A-1070 Vienna. © 01/523-13-450. Fax 01/523-13-45-111. www.austrotel.at. 56 units. 190€ ($247) double; 216€ ($281) suite. Children under 12 stay free in parent's room. Rates include buffet breakfast. AE, DC, MC, V. U-Bahn: Volkstheater. **Amenities:** Breakfast room; babysitting; laundry; dry cleaning; nonsmoking rooms. *In room:* TV, dataport, hair dryer, minibar.

Mailberger Hof This old palace was built in the 14th century as a mansion for the knights of Malta and was converted into a hotel in the 1970s. Off the main drag, Kärntnerstrasse, it lies on a typical Viennese cobblestone street. The two large wooden doors at the entrance still boast a Maltese cross. The vaulted ceiling, the leather armchairs, and maybe the marbleized walls are about all that would remind the knights of their former home. Everywhere the place has been renewed, although a cobblestone court-yard, set with tables in fair weather, remains. A family-run place with a cozy atmos-phere, the hotel features moderate-size bedrooms that are often brightened with pastels, each with comfortable beds, plus tub/shower combinations in the small bath-rooms. In general, though, the public rooms are more inviting than the private ones.

Annagasse 7, A-1010 Vienna. ⓒ **01/5120641.** Fax 01/512064110. www.mailbergerhof.at. 40 units 195€–210€ ($254–$273) double; from 220€ ($286) suite. Rates include buffet breakfast. AE, DC, MC, V. Parking 22€ ($29). U-Bahn: Karlsplatz. **Amenities:** Restaurant; bar; room service (7am–10pm); babysitting; laundry service; dry cleaning; nonsmoking rooms. *In room:* A/C, TV, dataport, minibar, hair dryer, safe.

INEXPENSIVE

Drei Kronen ⓐ *Finds*   The celebrated architect Ignaz Drapala designed this splendid Art Nouveau building in a charming section of Vienna close to the famous Naschmarkt. The "three crowns" in the German name Drei Kronen refer to Austria, Hungary, and Bohemia from the old Austro-Hungarian Empire. A symbol of the crowns is displayed on top of the building. The hotel enjoys one of Vienna's best locations, close to such monuments as the Vienna State Opera and St. Stephan's Cathedral. Built in 1894, the five-story hotel was completely renovated in 1999. The midsize to spacious bedrooms are fresh and bright, with comfortable furnishings along with immaculate bathrooms with showers. Some of the rooms are large enough to contain house beds.

Schleifmuehlgasse 25, A-1040 Vienna. ⓒ **01/5873289.** Fax 01/587328911. www.hotel3kronen.at. 41 units. 90€–105€ ($117–$137) double; 106€–121€ ($138–$157) triple. AE, DC, MC, V. Parking 15€ ($20). U-Bahn: Karlsplatz. **Amenities:** Breakfast room; lounge; babysitting; nonsmoking rooms. *In room:* TV, dataport, safe (some).

Hotel Austria   The staff here always seems willing to tell you where to go in the neighborhood for a good meal or a glass of wine, and often distributes printouts explaining the medieval origins of this section of the city center. This unpretentious, family-owned hotel sits on a small, quiet street whose name will probably be unfamil-iar to many taxi drivers—a corner building on the adjoining street, Fleischmarkt 20, is the point where you'll turn onto the narrow lane. The comfortable furnishings in the lobby and in the chandeliered breakfast room are maintained in tip-top shape. Every year one of the four floors of the hotel is completely renovated with new wall-papering, furniture, and bedding. The tiled shower-only bathrooms are small but ade-quate unless you have a lot of toiletries to spread out. The decor is rather functional, and the hotel is immaculately maintained and inviting.

Wolfengasse 3A, A-1011 Vienna. ⓒ **01/51523.** Fax 01/51523506. www.hotelaustria-wien.at. 46 units, 42 w/ bathroom. 50€–90€ ($65–$117) double w/no bathroom; 109€–149€ ($142–$194) double w/bathroom; 123€–174€ ($160–$226) triple w/bathroom. Rates include buffet breakfast. AE, DC, MC, V. Parking 19€ ($25). U-Bahn: Schwedenplatz. Tram: 1 or 2. **Amenities:** Breakfast room; lounge; breakfast-only room service; massage; babysitting; laundry service; dry cleaning; nonsmoking rooms. *In room:* TV, dataport, minibar, hair dryer.

Hotel Kärntnerhof ⓐ *Kids*   Only a 4-minute walk from the cathedral, the Kärnt-nerhof has been much improved, thanks to refurbishing and renovating, and is now a more desirable address than ever. The decor of the public rooms is tastefully arranged around oriental rugs, well-upholstered chairs and couches with cabriole legs, and an occasional 19th-century portrait. The midsize to spacious units are very up to date, usually with the original parquet floors and striped or patterned wallpaper set off by curtains. Many of the guest rooms are large enough to handle an extra bed or so, mak-ing this a family favorite. The small private bathrooms glisten with tile walls and floors; about half of them contain tub/shower combinations. The owner is quite helpful, directing guests to the post office and nearby Vienna landmarks.

Grashofgasse 4, A-1011 Vienna. © **01/5121923.** Fax 01/513222833. www.karntnerhof.com. 44 units. 110€–155€ ($143–$202) double; 180€–240€ ($234–$312) suite. Rates include buffet breakfast. AE, DC, MC, V. Parking 17€ ($22). U-Bahn: Stephansplatz. **Amenities:** Breakfast room; lounge; 24-hr. room service; laundry service; dry cleaning. *In room:* TV.

Hotel-Pension Shermin
The Voshmgir family welcomes you into its small, inviting, homelike boardinghouse in the city center. Bedrooms are big and comfortable, and the hotel-pension draws many repeat guests. The location is convenient for such sights as the opera house, the Imperial Palace, and the Spanish Riding School, all a 5-minute walk away. Bathrooms are small but have good showers and well-maintained plumbing. Furnishings are modern and without much flair, but are exceedingly comfortable.

Rilkeplatz 7, A-1040 Vienna. © **01/58661830.** Fax 01/586618310. www.hotel-pension-shermin.at. 11 units. 70€–110€ ($91–$143) double. Rates include buffet breakfast. AE, DC, MC, V. Parking 16€ ($21). U-Bahn: Karlsplatz. **Amenities:** Breakfast room; lounge; breakfast-only room service. *In room:* TV, dataport, hair dryer.

Hotel-Pension Suzanne ⭐ *Kids*
Only a 45-second walk from the opera house, this is a real discovery. Once you get past its post-war facade, the interior warms considerably, brightly decorated in a comfortable, traditional style with antique beds, plush chairs, and the original molded ceilings. Now into its second generation of managers, the hotel-pension is run by the welcoming Strafinger family, who like its classic Viennese turn-of-the-20th-century styling. Rooms are midsize and exceedingly well maintained, facing either the busy street or a courtyard. Families often stay here because some of the accommodations contain three beds. Some bedrooms are like small apartments, with kitchenettes. Each unit comes with a private bathroom with a tub/shower combination.

Walfischgasse 4. © **01/5132507.** Fax 01/5132500. www.pension-suzanne.at. 26 units. 96€–108€ ($125–$140) double; 117€ ($152) double w/kitchenette; 135€–145€ ($176–$189) triple. AE, DC, MC, V. U-Bahn: Karlsplatz. **Amenities:** Breakfast room; lounge; breakfast-only room service; babysitting. *In room:* TV, hair dryer.

Hotel Post
Hotel Post lies in the medieval slaughterhouse district, today an interesting section full of hotels and restaurants. The dignified front of this hotel is constructed of gray stone, with a facade of black marble covering the street level. The manager is quick to tell you that both Mozart and Haydn frequently stayed in a former inn at this address. Those composers would probably be amused to hear recordings of their music played in the coffeehouse, Le Café, attached to the hotel. Bedrooms, most of which are midsize, are streamlined and functionally furnished, each well maintained and most with small shower-only bathrooms.

Fleischmarkt 24, A-1010 Vienna. © **01/515830.** Fax 01/51583808. www.hotel-post-wien.at. 107 units, 77 w/bathroom. 70€ ($91) double w/no bathroom; 120€ ($156) double w/bathroom; 96€ ($125) triple w/no bathroom; 145€ ($189) triple w/bathroom. Rates include buffet breakfast. AE, DC, MC, V. Parking 18€ ($23). Tram: 1 or 2. **Amenities:** Restaurant; lounge; salon; laundry service; dry cleaning; nonsmoking rooms; 1 room for those w/limited mobility. *In room:* TV, dataport, hair dryer.

Hotel Wandl
Stepping into this hotel is like stepping into a piece of a family's history—it has been under the same ownership for generations. The Wandl lies in the Inner City and offers views of the steeple of St. Stephan's Cathedral from many of its windows, which often open onto small balconies. The breakfast room is a high-ceilinged, two-toned room with hanging chandeliers and lots of ornamented plaster.

The bedrooms usually offer the kind of spacious dimensions that went out of style 60 years ago; bathrooms, most of which contain showers only, are small but adequate, tiled, and well maintained. Beds are frequently renewed—all in all, this is a comfortable choice if you're not too demanding. The hotel faces St. Peter's Church.

Petersplatz 9, A-1010 Vienna. ℂ **01/534550.** Fax 01/5345577. www.hotel-wandl.com. 138 units, 134 w/bathroom. 110€ ($143) double w/no bathroom; 150€–195€ ($195–$254) double w/bathroom. Rates include breakfast. AE, DC, MC, V. Parking 20€ ($26). U-Bahn: Stephansplatz. **Amenities:** Breakfast room, lounge, room service (7am–10pm); laundry service; dry cleaning; nonsmoking rooms. *In room:* TV, dataport, hair dryer, safe.

Pension Dr. Geissler *Value*

Unpretentious lodgings at reasonable prices are offered here, near the well-known Schwedenplatz at the edge of the Danube Canal. The bedrooms in this attractive, informal guesthouse are furnished with simple blond headboards and a few utilitarian pieces. Hallway bathrooms are generous. Most units, however, have their own private bathrooms, which are tiled and well maintained but a bit cramped. Most bathrooms have tub/shower combinations.

Postgasse 14, A-1010 Vienna. ℂ **01/5332803.** Fax 01/5332635. www.hotelpension.at. 35 units, 21 w/bathroom. 65€ ($85) double w/no bathroom; 95€ ($124) double w/bathroom. Rates include buffet breakfast. AE, DC, MC, V. U-Bahn: Schwedenplatz. **Amenities:** Breakfast room; bar; breakfast-only room service; babysitting; laundry service; dry cleaning. *In room:* TV.

Pension Neuer Markt

Near the cathedral, in the heart of Vienna, this pension is housed in a white baroque building that faces a square with an ornate fountain. The carpeted but small rooms are clean and well maintained in an updated motif of white walls and strong colors, with large windows in some. Some of the comfortable, duvet-covered beds are set into niches. Each of the units has central heating. Bathrooms with tub/shower combinations are small, seemingly added as an afterthought, but for Vienna the price is delicious. We recommend reserving 30 days in advance.

Seilergasse 9, A-1010 Vienna. ℂ **01/5122316.** Fax 01/5139105. www.hotelpension.at. 37 units. 80€–130€ ($104–$169) double. Rates include buffet breakfast. AE, DC, MC, V. Parking 10€ ($13). U-Bahn: Stephansplatz. **Amenities:** Breakfast room; bar; breakfast-only room service; babysitting; laundry service; dry cleaning; nonsmoking rooms. *In room:* TV, safe.

Pension Nossek

Mozart lived in this building in 1781 and 1782, when he wrote the *Haffner* symphony and *The Abduction from the Seraglio.* The pension lies on one of Vienna's best shopping streets, just blocks away from the major sights. In 1909, the building was converted into a guesthouse and has always been a good bet for clean, comfortable accommodations with decent (mostly comfortable) beds. Most of the bedrooms have been renovated, and all but a few singles contain small private bathrooms with tub/shower combinations.

Graben 17, A-1010 Vienna. ℂ **01/53370410.** Fax 01/5353646. www.pension-nossek.at. 26 units, 4 w/shower only, 22 w/tub. 110€ ($143) double w/tub or shower; 136€ ($177) suite w/tub or shower. Rates include breakfast. No credit cards. Free parking. U-Bahn: Stephansplatz. **Amenities:** Breakfast room; lounge; laundry service; dry cleaning. *In room:* TV, minibar, hair dryer (some).

Pension Pertschy

Well-scrubbed and reputable, this simple but historic pension was originally built in the 1700s as the Palais Carviani with a restrained baroque style. Several rooms overlook a central courtyard and are scattered among six or seven private apartments, whose residents are used to foreign visitors roaming through the building. Midsize bedrooms are high-ceilinged and outfitted in old-fashioned, almost dowdy tones of cream and pink, with good beds and rather cramped shower-only bathrooms. A free Internet terminal is found in the hall. Most appealing is its prime location in the heart of Old Vienna (between Habsburgasse and Bräunergasse, just off the Graben).

Habsburgergasse 5, A-1010 Vienna. ⓒ **01/534490.** Fax 01/5344949. 50 units, 2 w/kitchen. 102€–150€ ($133–$195) double w/no kitchen; 137€–172€ ($178–$224) suite. AE, DC, MC, V. Parking 16€ ($21). U-Bahn: Stephansplatz. **Amenities:** Breakfast room; lounge; nonsmoking rooms. *In room:* TV, dataport, minibar, hair dryer.

Zur Wiener Staatsoper 🛧 *Finds*   This simple but well-run government-rated three-star hotel has a facade that's more lavish, more ornate, and more evocative of Vienna's late 19th-century golden age than any equivalently rated hotel in town. It was built in the neo-baroque style in 1896 as a private home, and as such, contains some of the architectural charm (and many of the architectural drawbacks) of its original layout. Actually, that seems to inconvenience the kindly staff of this place more than it will you, and thanks to its reasonable prices and a location in the heart of monumental Vienna, a few steps from the all-pedestrian Kärntnerstrasse, many clients return time again.

Don't expect grandeur: Other than some elaborate replications of the gilded stucco in the original 19th-century entryway, the decor is simple but functional, all of it the hard work of its on-site owners, the Ungersböck family. You'll register within a cubbyhole-style office near the entrance, then take an elevator to any of rooms scattered over six floors. Rooms are high-ceilinged, functional, relatively comfortable, and, other than small bathrooms (with showers only), adequate for most needs. Incidentally, literary fans appreciate the fact that in earlier days, this hotel, according to the Ungersböcks, provided the inspiration to John Irving for one of the settings (an antique, run-down hotel that had evolved into a whorehouse) within his novel, *Hotel New Hampshire.*

Krugerstrasse 11, A-1010 Wien. ⓒ **01/513-12-74.** www.zurwienerstaatsoper.at. 22 units. 111€–140€ ($144–$182) double. Rates include buffet breakfast. DC, MC, V. U-Bahn: Karlsplatz. *In room:* TV, safe.

2 Leopoldstadt (2nd District)

EXPENSIVE

Hilton Vienna Danube 🛧🛧   Vienna has yet a third Hilton hotel, this one lying on the Danube River next to the exhibition ground, a 10-minute ride from the city center (free shuttle service), and near Prater park. Since it's close to many international companies, business people like this one, although it's equally suitable for vacationers as well. The hotel has the largest guest rooms of any hotel in Vienna. Each comes with a beautifully kept private bathroom with tub/shower combination. Dining is a special feature here; the Symphony Donau Restaurant serves international and Austrian cuisine with a beautiful terrace opening onto views of the river. The chef is famous for his Sunday (noon–3pm) Royal Swedish Smörgasbord, a buffet of Swedish specialties costing 30€ ($39).

Handelskai 269, A-1020 Vienna. ⓒ **800-HILTONS** or 01/727770. Fax 01/7277782200. www.vienna-danube.hilton. com. 367 units. 125€–205€ ($163–$267) double; 250€–295€ ($325–$384) suite. AE, DC, MC, V. U-Bahn: U1 to Praterstern and then tram 21 to Meiereistrasse. **Amenities:** Restaurant; bar; outdoor pool; tennis court; gym; sauna; 24-hr. room service; laundry service; dry cleaning; nonsmoking rooms; rooms for those w/limited mobility. *In room:* A/C, TV, dataport, minibar, beverage maker (some), hair dryer (some), trouser press, safe, Wi-Fi.

MODERATE

Hotel Stefanie   This updated government-rated four-star hotel is across the Danube Canal from St. Stephan's Cathedral, but it's still easily accessible to the rest of the city.

Where to Stay in Vienna

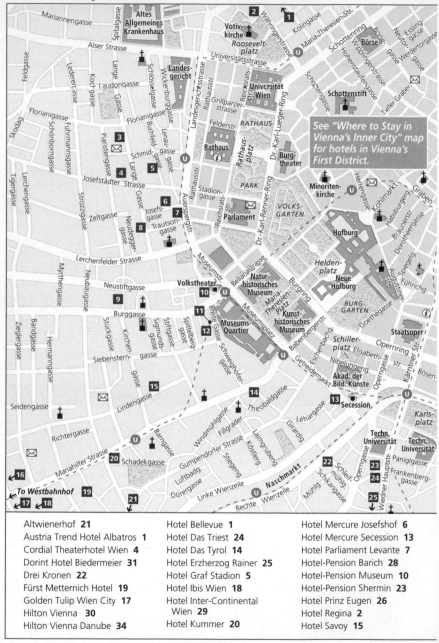

See "Where to Stay in Vienna's Inner City" map for hotels in Vienna's First District.

Altwienerhof **21**
Austria Trend Hotel Albatros **1**
Cordial Theaterhotel Wien **4**
Dorint Hotel Biedermeier **31**
Drei Kronen **22**
Fürst Metternich Hotel **19**
Golden Tulip Wien City **17**
Hilton Vienna **30**
Hilton Vienna Danube **34**

Hotel Bellevue **1**
Hotel Das Triest **24**
Hotel Das Tyrol **14**
Hotel Erzherzog Rainer **25**
Hotel Graf Stadion **5**
Hotel Ibis Wien **18**
Hotel Inter-Continental Wien **29**
Hotel Kummer **20**

Hotel Mercure Josefshof **6**
Hotel Mercure Secession **13**
Hotel Parliament Levante **7**
Hotel-Pension Barich **28**
Hotel-Pension Museum **10**
Hotel-Pension Shermin **23**
Hotel Prinz Eugen **26**
Hotel Regina **2**
Hotel Savoy **15**

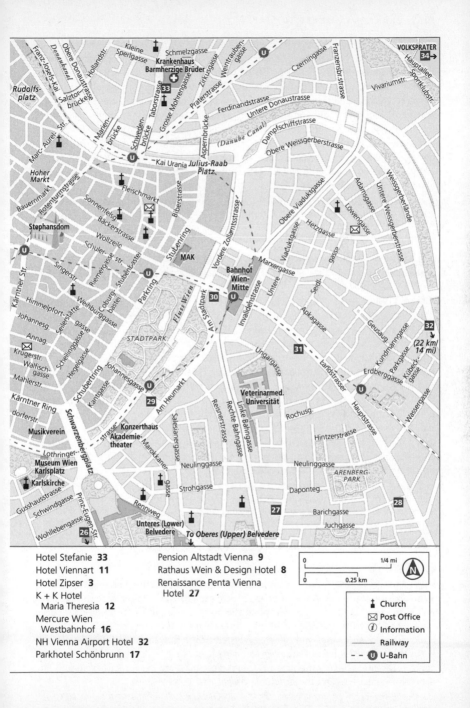

Hotel Stefanie **33**
Hotel Viennart **11**
Hotel Zipser **3**
K + K Hotel
 Maria Theresia **12**
Mercure Wien
 Westbahnhof **16**
NH Vienna Airport Hotel **32**
Parkhotel Schönbrunn **17**

Pension Altstadt Vienna **9**
Rathaus Wein & Design Hotel **8**
Renaissance Penta Vienna
 Hotel **27**

0   1/4 mi
0   0.25 km

‡ Church
✉ Post Office
ⓘ Information
.... Railway
– – Ⓤ U-Bahn

It has had a long and distinguished history, dating back to 1630. A century later, a famous inn, Weisse Rose, stood on this site. Ever since 1870, the hotel has been run by the Schick family. Over the past 20 years, all the bedrooms have had major renovations and today are well furnished in sleek Viennese styling. Some are a bit small, but they are beautifully maintained, with excellent beds and small tiled bathrooms that, for the most part, contain tub/shower combinations but not enough shelf space.

The interior is partially decorated in beautifully finished wall paneling and gilded wall sconces. Upon closer examination, much of the decor is reproductions, yet the hotel emits a hint of 19th-century rococo splendor. The bar area is filled with black leather armchairs on chrome swivel bases, and the concealed lighting throws an azure glow over the artfully displayed bottles.

Taborstrasse 12, A-1020 Vienna. © **800/528-1234** in the U.S., or 01/211500. Fax 01/21150160. www.schick-hotels.com. 131 units. 149€–211€ ($194–$274) double. Rates include buffet breakfast. AE, DC, MC, V. Parking 17€ ($22). U-Bahn: Schwedenplatz. Tram: 21. **Amenities:** Restaurant; bar; room service (7am–10pm); laundry service; dry cleaning; nonsmoking rooms. *In room:* A/C, TV, dataport, minibar, hair dryer, safe.

3 Landstrasse (3rd District)

VERY EXPENSIVE

Hilton Vienna 🕏🕏   This 18-story box overlooks the Danube Canal and offers plush accommodations and elegant public areas. The hotel reopened by the summer of 2004 after a total refurbishment, and is looking better than ever. Despite the hotel's modernity, it manages to provide plenty of Viennese flavor. Its soaring atrium and bustling nightlife make it a vibrant home for business travelers. The hotel offers well-appointed bedrooms in a range of styles, including Biedermeier, contemporary, baroque, and Art Nouveau. Regardless of the style, the hotel offers the highest level of comfort. Because the Hilton towers over the city skyline, it also affords great views from the top floors. Its suites and executive floors provide extra comfort for frequent travelers, but standard extras in all bedrooms include tub/shower combinations and a basket of toiletries in the good-size bathrooms. The adjacent Stadtpark is connected to the hotel and the City Air Terminal by a bridge, which strollers and joggers use during excursions into the landscaped and bird-filled park.

Am Stadtpark, A-1030 Vienna. © **800/445-8667** in the U.S., or 01/717000. Fax 01/7130691. www.hilton.com. 579 units. 155€–311€ ($202–$404) double; from 460€ ($598) suite. AE, DC, MC, V. Parking 24€ ($31). The Hilton is attached to the City Air Terminal, the drop-off point for buses coming in at frequent intervals from the airport. U-Bahn: Landstrasse. **Amenities:** 4 restaurants; 2 bars; indoor heated pool; fitness center; sauna; car rental desk; children's playground; business center; 24-hr. room service; babysitting; laundry service; dry cleaning; nonsmoking rooms; rooms for those w/limited mobility. *In room:* A/C, TV, dataport, minibar, hair dryer, safe, Wi-Fi.

EXPENSIVE

Dorint Hotel Biedermeier   This hotel was established in 1983 in a renovated late-19th-century apartment house. It boasts a pronounced Biedermeier style in both the public areas and the bedrooms. Although the hotel is adjacent to the Wien Mitte bus station and has roaring traffic on all sides, most bedrooms overlook a pedestrian-only walkway lined with shops and cafes. Duvets cover the firm beds, and double glazing keeps the noise level down. Bathrooms are small and tiled, with fake-marble counters and mostly tub/shower combinations. On the premises are the formal restaurant Zu den Deutschmeistern and the simpler Weissgerberstube.

Landstrasser Hauptstrasse 28, A-1030 Vienna. © **800/780-5734** in the U.S., or 01/716710. Fax 01/71671503. www.dorint.de. 203 units. 175€ ($228) double; 310€ ($403) suite. Rates include breakfast. AE, DC, MC, V. Parking

14€ ($18). U-Bahn: Rochusgasse. **Amenities:** 2 Restaurants; 2 bars; room service (7am-11pm); babysitting; laundry service; dry cleaning; nonsmoking rooms; rooms for those w/limited mobility. *In room:* A/C, TV, dataport (some), minibar, hair dryer, trouser press, safe, Wi-Fi.

Renaissance Penta Vienna Hotel ⚐   In the city's diplomatic quarter, close to the baroque Belvedere Palace, this seven-story hotel was an imperial military riding school before its conversion into a hotel in the mid-1990s. South of Stadtpark, it's an impressive mid-19th-century Tudor-style castle to which a modern glass structure has been added. The lobby sets an elegant tone, with vaulted ceilings, contemporary sculpture, and marble pillars. It holds many cozy nooks for retreating, including a library. The stylish guest rooms in the hotel's newer building hold such luxuries as oversize tubs in the tiled bathrooms.

Ungargasse 60, A-1030 Vienna. ⓒ 01/711-750. Fax 01/711-758143. www.renaissancehotels.com/viese. 342 units. 146€–227€ ($190–$295) double; 211€–257€ ($274–$334) suite. AE, DC, MC, V. Parking 18€ ($23). Tram: U3 or U4 to Landstrasse Wien Mitte. **Amenities:** Restaurant; bar; indoor pool; fitness center; sauna; 24-hr. room service; babysitting; laundry; dry cleaning; nonsmoking rooms, rooms for those w/limited mobility. *In room:* A/C, TV, dataport, minibar, hair dryer, trouser press, safe.

MODERATE

Hotel-Pension Barich   This spot might be the choice for guests who prefer serene residential surroundings. Northeast of the Südbahnhof, behind an unpretentious facade, this small hotel is quiet and well furnished. The proprietors, Ulrich and Hermine Platz, speak fluent English. Small soundproofed bedrooms have well-kept tiled bathrooms equipped with tub/shower combinations.

Barichgasse 3, A-1030 Vienna. ⓒ 01/7122275. Fax 01/712227588. www.nethotels.com/barich. 17 units. 99€–129€ ($129–$168) double. Rates include buffet breakfast. AE, DC, MC, V. Parking 17€ ($22). U-Bahn: Rochusgasse. Bus: 74A. **Amenities:** Breakfast room; lounge; laundry service; dry cleaning. *In room:* TV, minibar, hair dryer, safe.

4 Wieden & Margareten (4th & 5th Districts)

MODERATE

Hotel Erzherzog Rainer   Popular with groups and business travelers, this government-rated four-star, family-run hotel was built just before World War I and was gradually renovated room by room. It's only 5 minutes by foot to the Vienna State Opera and Kärntnerstrasse, with a U-Bahn stop just steps away. The bedrooms are well decorated and come in a variety of sizes; you'll find radios and good beds, but not soundproofing, in all. Bathrooms are tiled and small, with about half equipped with both showers and tubs. The singles are impossibly small; on certain days, air-conditioning is sorely missed. An informal brasserie serves Austrian specialties, and the cozy bar is modishly decorated with black and brass.

Wiedner Hauptstrasse 27–29, A-1040 Vienna. ⓒ 01/501110. Fax 01/50111350. www.schick-hotels.com. 84 units. 123€–191€ ($160–$248) double. Rates include breakfast. AE, MC, V. Parking 17€ ($22). U-Bahn: Taubstummengasse. **Amenities:** Restaurant; bar; room service (7am–10pm); babysitting; laundry service; dry cleaning; nonsmoking rooms; rooms for those w/limited mobility. *In room:* TV, dataport, minibar, hair dryer, safe (some).

Hotel Prinz Eugen ⚐   In a section of Vienna favored by diplomats, this hotel is immediately opposite the Belvedere Palace and the Südbahnhof rail station. Subways will carry you quickly to the center of Vienna, and there are good highway connections as well. The hotel has soundproof windows opening onto private balconies. The decor is a mixture of antiques, oriental rugs, and some glitzy touches such as glass walls with brass trim. Suites are nothing more than slightly larger double rooms with

Kids **Family-Friendly Hotels**

- **Hotel Am Schubertring** (p. 62)   Children under 6 stay free with a parent, and several rooms in this historic hotel easily accommodate three or more.
- **Hotel Graf Stadion** (p. 77)   Many of the rooms at this hotel—a longtime favorite of families on a tight budget—contain two double beds, suitable for parties of three or four.
- **Hotel Kärntnerhof** (p. 64)   A family-oriented *gutbürgerlich* hotel, this establishment lies right in the center of Vienna, and its helpful management welcomes kids.
- **Hotel Mercure Josefshof** (p. 78)   A central location and a number of rooms with kitchenettes make this a great choice for families.
- **Hotel Opernring** (p. 62)   Ample accommodations overlooking central Vienna; many rooms here sleep 3 or 4.
- **Hotel-Pension Suzanne** (p. 65)   Inexpensive and centrally located, many rooms here sleep three or more, and several feature small kitchens.
- **Hotel Römischer Kaiser** (p. 60)   The former palace of the imperial chamberlain, this Best Western affiliate offers a glimpse of imperial Vienna from around 1684. Its staff is extremely hospitable and gracious to visiting families.

an additional bathroom. Bedrooms come in a wide range of sizes, although all are comfortable and have firm, duvet-covered beds. Bathrooms, only fair in size, are well maintained, although 50 rooms have showers only (no tubs). The single accommodations, however, are decidedly small, suitable for one traveling light. All the windows are soundproof.

Wiedner Gürtel 14, A-1040 Vienna. ⓒ **01/5051741.** Fax 01/505174119. www.hotelprinzeugen.at. 110 units. 135€ ($176) double; 230€ ($299) suite. Rates include buffet breakfast. AE, DC, DISC, MC, V. Parking 17€ ($22). U-Bahn: Südtiroler Platz or Südbahnhof. **Amenities:** Restaurant; bar; room service (7am–9pm); babysitting; laundry service; dry cleaning; nonsmoking rooms. *In room:* TV, dataport, minibar, hair dryer, trouser press, safe.

5 Mariahilf (6th District)
EXPENSIVE
Hotel Das Tyrol *Kids* *Finds*   It's friendly, fairly priced, and lies within a five-minute walk of one of the densest concentrations of museums in Europe. The hotel's only drawback is that it's so good that it's often booked weeks in advance. It occupies what was originally built 175 years ago as a convent, which later functioned as a simple hotel that was the first building in its neighborhood to feature running water in each of its rooms. In 1999, it was bought by an Austrian member of Parliament, Helena von Ramsbacher, who, at the time of her election, was one of the youngest women ever to be elected to the Austrian parliament. After pouring money into the building's restoration, she justifiably defines it as a boutique-style luxury hotel. Don't expect a scaled-down version of, say, the Imperial or the Bristol. What you get are high ceilings, comfortable and contemporary furnishings, a congenial collection of contempo-

rary art, a sense of uncluttered spaciousness, and a winding central staircase that evokes the building's antique origins—all of this within a five-minute walk from the Ring.

Mariahilferstrasse 15, 1060 Vienna. 𝒞 **01/587-54-15.** Fax 01/587-54-15-49. www.das-tyrol.at. 30 units. 149€–239€ ($194–$311) double; 259€ ($337) junior suite. Extra bed 59€ ($77). Rates include breakfast. Parking 15€ ($20). U-Bahn: MuseumsQuartier, Volkstheater, or Neubaugasse. **Amenities:** Sauna; limited room service; laundry service/dry cleaning. *In room:* A/C, TV, minibar, dataport, safe.

Hotel Kummer   Established by the Kummer family in the 19th century, this hotel was built in response to the growing power of the railways as they forged new paths of commerce and tourism through central Europe. A short walk from Vienna's Westbahnhof, the hotel sits in a busy, noisy location, but looks as ornamental as any public monument constructed during those imperial days. The facade is richly embellished with Corinthian capitals on acanthus-leaf bases, urn-shape balustrades, and representations of four heroic demigods staring down from under the building's eaves. The hotel was restored and renovated in 1994 and is constantly maintained and improved.

The bedrooms have soundproof windows and often come with stone balconies. Not all rooms are alike—some feature superior appointments and deluxe furnishings. If possible, opt for a corner room—they are better lit and more spacious. Tiled bathrooms contain tubs in about half the accommodations (otherwise showers), along with vanity mirrors. Some of the singles are so small and dimly lit that they aren't recommendable.

Mariahilferstrasse 71A, A-1060 Vienna. 𝒞 **01/588950.** Fax 01/5878133. www.hotelkummer.at. 100 units. 95€–255€ ($124–$332) double. Rates include buffet breakfast. AE, DC, MC, V. Parking 18€ ($23). U-Bahn: Neubaugasse. Bus: 13A or 14A. **Amenities:** Restaurant; bar; salon; room service (7am–9pm); laundry service; dry cleaning; nonsmoking rooms. *In room:* TV, dataport, minibar, hair dryer, trouser press, safe.

MODERATE

Fürst Metternich Hotel 🖑 *Finds*   Pink-and-gray paint and ornate stone window trim identify this solidly built 19th-century hotel, formally an opulent private home. It's located between the Ring and the Westbahnhof near Mariahilferstrasse, about a 20-minute walk from the cathedral. Many of the grander architectural elements were retained, including a pair of red stone columns in the entranceway and an old-fashioned staircase guarded with griffins. The high-ceilinged bedrooms have a neutral decor, with laminated furnishings and feather pillows. The partly marbled bathrooms have modern fixtures and tubs. They aren't generally roomy, however. Windows in the front units are soundproof in theory, but not in practice. If you want a more tranquil night's sleep, opt for a room in the rear. The Barfly's Club, a popular hangout open daily, offers 120 different exotic drinks.

Esterházygasse 33, A-1060 Vienna. 𝒞 **01/58870.** Fax 01/5875268. www.austrotel.at. 55 units. 100€–150€ ($130–$195) double; 182€–210€ ($237–$273) suite. Rates include buffet breakfast. AE, DC, MC, V. Parking 14€ ($18). U-Bahn: Zieglergasse. **Amenities:** Breakfast room; bar; babysitting; laundry service; dry cleaning. *In room:* TV, minibar.

Golden Tulip Wien City   This seven-story concrete-and-glass hotel was designed in 1975 with enough angles in its facade to give each bedroom an irregular shape. Usually the units have two windows that face different skylines. Aside from the views, each of the decent-size bedrooms has comfortable furnishings and good beds. Bathrooms, though small, are well maintained, brightly lit, and equipped with tub/shower combinations. Opt for a room—really a studio with a terrace—on the seventh floor, if one is available. The hotel also has a public rooftop terrace where guests sip drinks in summer.

Wallgasse 23, A-1060 Vienna. ⓒ 800/387-8842 in the U.S., or 01/599900. Fax 01/5967646. www.goldentulipwien city.com. 77 units. 150€–230€ ($195–$299) double; from 270€ ($351) suite. Rates include buffet breakfast. AE, DC, MC, V. Parking 15€ ($20). U-Bahn: Gumpendorfer. Bus: 57A. **Amenities:** Breakfast room; bar; breakfast-only room service; babysitting; laundry service; dry cleaning; nonsmoking rooms. *In room:* A/C, TV, dataport, minibar, hair dryer, safe.

Hotel Mercure Secession 𝒢 *Kids*   Sitting at the corner of a well-known street, Lehárgasse, this hotel is in the center of Vienna between the Vienna State Opera and the famous Naschmarkt. It's a modern five-story building with panoramic windows on the ground floor and a red-tile roof. The interior is warmly decorated with some 19th-century antiques and comfortably upholstered chairs. Musicians, singers, actors, and other artists form part of a loyal clientele. This is one of Vienna's best small hotels; families are especially fond of the place as 35 of the accommodations contain kitch- enettes. All the small units have neatly kept bathrooms with tub/shower combinations.

Getreidemarkt 5, A-1060 Vienna. ⓒ 01/588380. Fax 01/58838212. www.mercure.com. 68 units. 150€–175€ ($195–$228) double. Rates include buffet breakfast. AE, DC, MC, V. Parking 18€ ($23). U-Bahn: Karlsplatz. **Ameni- ties:** Breakfast room; bar; room service (7am–10pm); babysitting; laundry; dry cleaning; nonsmoking rooms. *In room:* A/C, TV, dataport, minibar, hair dryer, safe.

INEXPENSIVE

Hotel Ibis Wien   For a reasonably priced choice near the Westbahnhof, the main rail station, this is one of your best bets. The station is about an 8-minute walk away. Although this is a chain and its units are no better than a good motel in the U.S., the rates are good for Vienna. Behind a graceless facade that looks like a small-town department store, the Ibis Wien offers modern comforts. The furnishings, though well maintained, might not always be tasteful. One guest called the upholstery "psyche- delic." The snug bedrooms are bland but inviting, with streamlined furnishings and small, neatly kept private bathrooms with shower units. The roof terrace provides a panoramic view of Vienna. Groups are booked here, and you'll meet all of them in the impersonal restaurant, where reasonably priced meals and wine are served.

Mariahilfer Gurtel 22, 1060 Vienna. ⓒ 01/59998. Fax 01/5979090. www.accorhotels.com. 341 units. 82€–102€ ($107–$133) double. Rates include buffet breakfast. AE, DC, MC, V. Parking 10€ ($13). U-Bahn: Gumpendorfer. **Amenities:** Restaurant; bar; laundry service; dry cleaning; nonsmoking rooms; rooms for those w/limited mobility. *In room:* A/C, TV, dataport, Wi-Fi.

6 Neubau (7th District)

EXPENSIVE

K + K Hotel Maria Theresia 𝒢   The hotel's initials are a reminder of the empire's dual monarchy (*Kaiserlich und Königlich*—"by appointment to the Emperor of Aus- tria and King of Hungary"). Even the surrounding neighborhood, home to some major museums that lie just outside the Ring, is reminiscent of the days of Empress Maria Theresa. The hotel is in the artists' colony of Spittelberg, within walking dis- tance of the Winter Palace gardens, the Volkstheater, and the famous shopping street Mariahilferstrasse. The hotel, built in the late 1980s, offers ample contemporary rooms. The beds (usually twins) are comfortable, and the medium-size bathrooms with tub/ shower combinations are attractively tiled.

Kirchberggasse 6–8, A-1070 Vienna. ⓒ 800/537-8483 in the U.S., or 01/52123. Fax 01/5212370. www.kkhotels. com. 123 units. 230€ ($299) double; from 280€ ($364) suite. Rates include buffet breakfast. AE, DC, MC, V. Parking 14€ ($18). U-Bahn: Volkstheater. Tram: 49. **Amenities:** Restaurant; bar; fitness center; sauna; room service

(6:30am–10pm); massage; babysitting; laundry service; dry cleaning; nonsmoking rooms. *In room:* A/C, TV, dataport, minibar, hair dryer, safe, Wi-Fi.

MODERATE

Pension Altstadt Vienna ★ *Finds*   A noted connoisseur of modern art, Otto Wiesenthal, converted a century-old private home into this charming and stylish hotel in the mid-1990s. Wiesenthal comes from a long line of artists. Grandmother Greta was an opera dancer, and works by great-great-grandfather Friedrich hang in the Vienna Historic Museum as well as the hotel. Although part of the structure remains a private home, the remainder of the building contains comfortable and cozy bedrooms. Each is outfitted with a different color scheme and contains at least one work of contemporary art, usually by an Austrian painter. Many of the good-size units are a bit quirky in decor, as exemplified by a leopard print club chair set against a sponge-painted wall. Nearly all the rooms have high ceilings, antiques, parquet floors, double-glazed windows, and good beds. Out of respect to the hotel's location within the Spittelberg, Vienna's former red light district and now a liberal and artsy residential neighborhood known for its Greenpeace affiliations, the owner has dedicated one of the best and largest bedrooms in the house to Josephina Mutzenbacher (CQ). During the final days of the Habsburgs, she was the most famous and high-profile madam in Vienna, and a hugely eccentric celebrity in her own right at the time. Naughty, a wee bit provocative, and tongue-in-cheek (*Die Liebe in Wien!/Love in Vienna!*), it is our preferred room. The white-tiled bathrooms are midsize, with a second phone and decent shelf space. About half of the accommodations contain a shower instead of a tub. The hotel added 11 new rooms stylishly designed by Matteo Thun, the famous Italian architects, and these are the best appointed and most desirable.

Kirchengasse 41, A-1070 Vienna. ⓒ **01/5226666.** Fax 01/5234901. www.altstadt.at. 47 units. 129€–169€ ($168–$220) double; 169€–299€ ($220–$389) suite. AE, DC, MC, V. Parking 18€ ($23). U-Bahn: Volkstheater. **Amenities:** Breakfast room; bar; salon; 24-hr. room service; babysitting; laundry service; dry cleaning; nonsmoking rooms. *In room:* TV, dataport, minibar, hair dryer, safe, Wi-Fi.

INEXPENSIVE

Hotel-Pension Museum *Value*   This hotel was originally built in the 17th century as the home of an aristocratic family. Its exterior was transformed around 1890 into the elegant Art Nouveau facade it has today. It's across from the Imperial Museums, and there are plenty of palaces, museums, and monuments nearby to keep you busy for days. Bedrooms come in a wide variety of sizes; some are spacious, while others are a bit cramped. Bathrooms are small but tiled, with tub/shower combinations and not much counter space. However, the rates are great for this city, and this place has its devotees for a reason.

Museumstrasse 3, A-1070 Vienna. ⓒ **01/52344260.** Fax 01/523442630. www.tiscover.com/hotel.museum. 15 units. 90€ ($117) double. Rates include breakfast. AE, DC, MC, V. Parking 12€ ($16). U-Bahn: Volkstheater. **Amenities:** Breakfast room; lounge; 24-hr. room service; nonsmoking rooms. *In room:* TV, hair dryer.

Hotel Savoy   Built in the 1960s, this well-managed hotel rises six stories above one of Vienna's busiest wholesale and retail shopping districts. Within walking distance of Ringstrasse, opposite a recently built station for the city's newest U-Bahn line (the U3), the hotel prides itself on tastefully decorated units with good beds. The small but tiled bathrooms contain only tubs. Most units offer picture-window views of the neighborhood. Although the only meal served in the hotel is breakfast, there are dozens of places to eat in the neighborhood.

Lindengasse 12, A-1070 Vienna. (© **01/5234646.** Fax 01/5234640. www.hotelsavoy.at. 43 units. 77€–115€ ($100–$150) double; 118€–145€ ($153–$189) triple. Rates include buffet breakfast. AE, DC, MC, V. Parking 15€ ($20). U-Bahn: Neubaugasse. **Amenities:** Breakfast room; babysitting; laundry service; dry cleaning; nonsmoking rooms. *In room:* TV, minibar, hair dryer, safe.

7 Josefstadt (8th District)
EXPENSIVE

Cordial Theaterhotel Wien   This hotel was created from a 19th-century core that was radically modernized in the late 1980s. Today it's a favorite of Austrian business travelers, who profit from the hotel's proximity to the city's wholesale buying outlets. Each simply furnished room contains its own small but efficient kitchenette, which allows guests to save on restaurant bills. The well-maintained bedrooms, available in a variety of sizes, have good beds and adequate tiled bathrooms with tub/shower combinations. The on-site Theater-Restaurant is especially busy before and after performances next door at Theater in der Josefstadt.

Josefstadter Strasse 22, A-1080 Vienna. (© **01/4053648.** Fax 01/4051406. www.cordial.at. 54 units. 199€–244€ ($259–$317) double; 270€–479€ ($351–$623) suite. Rates include buffet breakfast. AE, DC, MC, V. Parking 15€ ($20). U-Bahn: Rathaus. **Amenities:** Restaurant; bar; fitness center; massage; sauna; 24-hr. room service; babysitting; laundry service; dry cleaning; nonsmoking rooms. *In room:* TV, dataport, minibar, hair dryer.

Hotel Parliament Levante ♠   This is a good example of the wave of new, design-conscious hotels that opened in Vienna during 2006. It sits behind a rectilinear, five-story facade of distressed concrete which, in 1908, was chiseled into a Bauhaus-inspired design that, at least for the era, was a radical departure from the neo-Gothic facade of the Rathaus (City Hall) and the cool, elegant Greek Revival style of the Austrian Parliament, both of which lie nearby, across the boulevard. It originated as a sanatorium and later evolved into a student dormitory. After a radical reconfiguration, the hotel gives the impression that every interior angle and every interior line was meticulously plotted into a postmodern, avant-garde design that includes lots of white Turkish travertine and marble, dark-grained wood, and a (sometimes excessive) use of the photos of Austrian photographer Curt Themessl and the artfully free-form glass vases and sculptures of Romanian glass-blower Ioan Nemtoi. Most of the rooms face a quiet but dull inner courtyard, and each is comfortable, decoratively neutral, and postmodern. The on-site restaurant and wine bar is stylish and ultra-modern, with more of Nemtoi's glass sculptures and row after row of illuminated shelves holding artfully displayed bottles of wine and liquor. There's only a small plaque identifying this building as a hotel.

Auerspergstrasse 15, 1080 Vienna. (© **01/535-4515.** Fax 01/535-451515. www.thelevante.com. 70 units. 260€ ($338) double; 320€–550€ ($416–$715) suite. Extra bed 45€ ($59). Rates include breakfast. Parking 22€ ($29). AE, DC, MC, V. U-Bahn: Rathaus. **Amenities:** fitness room w/sauna; 24-hr. room service, laundry service/dry cleaning. *In room:* A/C, TV, minibar.

MODERATE

Rathauspark Hotel   A 5-minute walk from the city center, this four-star hotel stands behind an elaborate wedding cake-facade, installed in an old palace dating back to 1880. The interior doesn't quite live up to the exterior, but the hotel does tastefully combine the old with the new. Guest rooms vary in size from average to spacious, and all have been updated with contemporary furnishings. Each room has a well-kept bathroom with a tub/shower combination.

Rathausstrasse 17, A-1010 Vienna. ℂ **01/404-120.** Fax 01/404-12-761. www.austria-trend.at. 117 units. 197€–230€ ($256–$299) double; 265€–360€ ($345–$468) suite. AE, DC, MC, V. Rates include buffet breakfast. No parking. U-Bahn: Rathaus. **Amenities:** Breakfast room; bar; babysitting; laundry service/dry cleaning; nonsmoking rooms. *In room:* A/C (in some), TV, dataport (in some), minibar, hair dryer, safe.

INEXPENSIVE

Hotel Graf Stadion 🔆 *Kids*   This is one of the few genuine Biedermeier-style hotels left in Vienna. It's right behind the Rathaus, a 10-minute walk from most of the central monuments. The facade evokes the building's early-19th-century elegance, with triangular or half-rounded ornamentation above many of the windows. The bedrooms have been refurbished and are comfortably old-fashioned, and many are spacious enough to accommodate an extra bed for people traveling with small children. Bathrooms are equipped with shower units and kept sparklingly clean.

Buchfeldgasse 5, A-1080 Vienna. ℂ **01/405-5284.** Fax 01/4050111. www.graf-stadion.com. 40 units. 89€–140€ ($116–$182) double; 150€ ($195) triple. Rates include buffet breakfast. AE, DC, MC, V. Parking 15€ ($20). U-Bahn: Rathaus. **Amenities:** Breakfast room; bar; babysitting; laundry service; dry cleaning. *In room:* TV, hair dryer.

Hotel Zipser   A 5-minute walk from the Rathaus, this pension offers rooms with wall-to-wall carpeting and central heating, many overlooking a private garden. Much of the renovated interior is tastefully adorned with wood detailing. Generous-size bedrooms are furnished in a functional, modern style, with some opening onto balconies above the garden. Bathrooms with shower units are small, but housekeeping rates high marks.

Lange Gasse 49, A-1080 Vienna. ℂ **01/404540.** Fax 01/4045413. www.zipser.at. 47 units. 79€–132€ ($103–$172) double; 110€–160€ ($143–$208) suite. Rates include buffet breakfast. AE, DC, MC, V. Parking 15€ ($20). U-Bahn: Rathaus. Bus: 13A. **Amenities:** Breakfast room; bar; lounge. *In room:* TV, hair dryer, safe, Wi-Fi.

8 Alsergrund (9th District)

MODERATE

Austria Trend Hotel Albatros   A 10-minute ride from the city center, this government-rated four-star choice is dull on the outside but lively inside. Well-furnished rooms are completely renovated, medium in size, and outfitted with comfortable upholstery and small but efficient bathrooms with shower units.

Liechtensteinstrasse 89, A-1090 Vienna. ℂ **01/317-35-08.** Fax 01/317-35-08-85. www.austria-trend.at. 70 units. 120€–195€ ($156–$254) double. Rates include buffet breakfast. AE, DC, MC, V. Parking: 15€ ($20). U-Bahn: Friedensbrücke. **Amenities:** Breakfast room; bar; sauna; laundry service/dry cleaning; nonsmoking rooms. *In room:* A/C, TV, dataport (in some), minibar, hair dryer, safe.

Hotel Bellevue   This hotel was built in 1873, at about the same time as the Franz-Josefs Bahnhof, which lies a short walk away and whose passengers it was designed to house. Its wedge-shape position on the acute angle of a busy street corner is similar to that of the Flatiron Building in Manhattan.

Most of the old details have been stripped from the public rooms, leaving a clean series of lines and a handful of antiques. Some 100 guest rooms are in a wing added in 1982. All rooms are clean, functional, and well maintained, and contain comfortable low beds and utilitarian desks and chairs. Bathrooms are of medium size, and most have tub/shower combinations.

Althanstrasse 5, A-1091 Vienna. ℂ **01/313-480.** Fax 01/3134-8801. www.hotelbellevue.at. 173 units. 150€–240€ ($195–$312) double; from 250€ ($325) suite. Rates include buffet breakfast. AE, DC, MC, V. Parking 15€ ($20). U-Bahn: Friedensbrücke. Tram: 5 or D. **Amenities:** Restaurant; bar; sauna; room service (7am–10pm); babysitting; laundry service; dry cleaning; nonsmoking rooms. *In room:* TV, dataport, minibar, hair dryer, trouser press (in most), safe (in most).

Hotel Mercure Josefshof   Close to the Parliament and next to the English Theater, this Biedermeier mansion is down a narrow cobblestone street. The hotel's gilded touches include a baroque lobby with marble checkerboard floors and a lounge brimming with antiques. Standard-size rooms have double-glazed windows, and a few come with kitchenettes, which are great for families. Corner rooms are the most spacious. Bathrooms are small, and a dozen come with showers (no tubs). Several rooms are suitable for persons with disabilities. In the summer, guests can enjoy the lavish breakfast buffet in a verdant inner courtyard.

Josefsgasse 4, A-1090 Vienna. ℂ 01/404-190. Fax 01/404-191-50. www.mercure.com. 118 units. 148€–180€ ($192–$234) double; from 188€ ($244) suite. AE, DC, MC, V. U-Bahn: Rathaus. **Amenities:** Bar; fitness center; sauna; room service (7am–10pm); babysitting; laundry service; dry cleaning; nonsmoking rooms; solarium. *In room:* A/C, TV, dataport, minibar, hair dryer, Wi-Fi.

Hotel Regina   Established in 1896 near the Votive Church, this hotel was built in the recognizable (by the Viennese at least) "Ringstrasse" style. The facade is appropriately grand, reminiscent of a French Renaissance palace. The tree-lined street is usually calm, especially at night. The Regina is an old-world hotel with red salons and interminable corridors. Guest rooms are well maintained and traditionally furnished; some have half-canopied beds and elaborate furnishings. Despite variation in style and size, all have comfortable beds and small, well-maintained shower-only bathrooms.

Rooseveltplatz 15, A-1090 Vienna. ℂ 01/404-460. Fax 01/408-8392. 128 units. 145€–195€ ($189–$254) double; 185€–250€ ($241–$325) suite. Rates include buffet breakfast. AE, DC, MC, V. Parking 24€ ($31). U-Bahn: Schottenring. Tram: 1, 2, 38, 40, or 41. **Amenities:** Restaurant; cafe; bar; room service (6am–11pm); laundry service; dry cleaning; nonsmoking rooms. *In room:* TV, dataport, minibar, hair dryer, Wi-Fi.

Rathaus Wein & Design Hotel   From the outside, this government-rated, four-star hotel looks like a direct transplant from the late 18th century, thanks to a radical renovation of a once-decaying two-star hotel that had functioned here for many years. Today, the building's lavishly ornate baroque facade has meticulously applied coats of bright Schönbrunn yellow paint with white highlights. Inside, you'll find a series of photographs taken during the building's radical upgrade, a minimalist and very tasteful contemporary design, a glistening white-with-touches-of-alabaster wine bar that doubles as a breakfast room, and one of the most unusual blends of hotel and wine-industry marketing in Austria.

Bedrooms, scattered over five floors, are each dedicated to an individual Austrian wine grower and vintner, an idea that was a function of friendships that this hotel's owners (they also run a restaurant in Salzburg) developed over the years with individual wine producers. As such, each entryway has a door-size wine label identifying that room's allegiance to, say, the Triebaumer or Jamek wineries, or to any of 31 other vintners scattered across the length of Austria. Bedrooms are supremely comfortable, high-ceilinged, and surprisingly large, with a palette of neutral earth tones, high-style plumbing fixtures, and a sense of postmodern hip. In-room minibars are stocked with wine from the vineyards of whatever your room happens to have been named after, but if you absolutely insist on wines from a different vineyard, or whatever else strikes your fancy, a staff member will cheerfully oblige.

Lange Gasse 13, A-1080 Vienna. ℂ 01/400-11-22. Fax 01/400-11-22-88. www.hotel-rathaus-wien.at. 33 units. 148€–198€ ($192–$257) double. Parking 15€ ($20). AE, DC, MC, V. U-Bahn: U3 or U4 to Volkstheater. **Amenities:** Wine bar; limited room service; laundry service/dry cleaning; babysitting. *In room:* TV, minibar, safe, hair dryer, Wi-Fi.

9 Westbahnhof (15th District)

EXPENSIVE

Mercure Wien Westbahnhof Formerly the rather bleak Dorint Budget Hotel Wien, this hotel was massively improved and upgraded in the mid-1990s. Next to the Westbahnhof, it's a good middle-bracket property. While you won't get old-world Viennese charm, you'll find comfort and convenience at an affordable price. The corner building with a nine-floor turret offers completely rejuvenated rooms. Maintenance is high, and the furnishings are durable rather than stylish. The spotless bathrooms hold tub/shower combinations. Tranquillity seekers should ask for a room opening onto the patio in the rear. Deluxe units offer a little sitting area in addition to regular sleeping quarters. Two floors are for nonsmokers, and some accommodations are wheelchair accessible.

Selberstrasse 4, A-1150 Vienna. © **01/98111-0.** Fax 01/98111-930. www.mercure.com. 253 units. 129€–169€ ($168–$220) double. AE, DC, MC, V. U-Bahn: Westbahnhof. **Amenities:** Restaurant; bar; sauna; babysitting; laundry service; dry cleaning; nonsmoking rooms; rooms for those w/limited mobility. *In room:* TV, dataport (in some), minibar, hair dryer, Wi-Fi.

10 Near Schönbrunn

EXPENSIVE

Parkhotel Schönbrunn Called the "guesthouse of the Kaisers," this government-rated four-star hotel lies 2.5km (1½ miles) from the Westbahnhof and 4.8km (3 miles) from the City Air Terminal. Opposite the magical Schönbrunn Castle and its park, the hotel is only a 10-minute tram ride from the Inner City. Franz Joseph I ordered its construction in 1907. The first performances of *Loreleyklänge*, by Johann Strauss, and *Die Schönbrunner*, the famous Josef Lanner waltz, took place here. During its heyday, guests ranged from Thomas Edison to Walt Disney.

Today the hotel complex is modern and updated. The original part of the building holds public rooms, which have lost some of their past elegance. Contemporary wings and annexes include the Stöckl, Residenz, and Maximilian (which has the most boring and cramped rooms). Also in the complex is a villa formerly inhabited by Van Swieten, the personal doctor of Empress Maria Theresa. Rooms are generally spacious and well furnished, in a variety of styles ranging from classical to modern, and have small bathrooms with tub/shower combinations.

Hietzinger Hauptstrasse 10-20, A-1131 Vienna. © **01/87804.** Fax 01/8780-43220. www.austria-trend.at. 402 units. 172€–215€ ($224–$280) double; 330€ ($429) suite. Rates include breakfast. AE, DC, MC, V. Parking 19€ ($25). U-Bahn: Hietzing. Tram: 58 or 60. **Amenities:** Restaurant; cafe; 2 bars; indoor heated pool; fitness center; sauna; 24-hr. room service; babysitting; laundry service; dry cleaning; nonsmoking rooms; rooms for those w/limited mobility. *In room:* TV, dataport (in some), minibar, hair dryer.

INEXPENSIVE

Altwienerhof *Finds* This is a highly acclaimed restaurant, one of the finest and most expensive in the city, but it's also a reasonably priced hotel with traditionally furnished guest rooms. The owners, Rudolf and Ursula Kellner, and their welcoming staff enhance the hotel's old-world charm. Guest rooms are quite large, with luxurious bathrooms with separate toilets. Bathrooms are equipped with mirrors, towel warmers, double bathtubs, and showers with an aqua massage.

Herklotzgasse 6, A-1150 Vienna. © **01/892-6000.** Fax 01/892-60008. www.altwienerhof.at. 23 units. 87€–140€ ($113–$182) double; 128€–168€ ($166–$218) suite. Rates include breakfast. AE, DC, MC, V. Parking 11€ ($14).

U-Bahn: Gumpendorferstrasse. Tram: 6, 8, or 18. **Amenities:** Restaurant; lounge; room service (7am–10pm); laundry service/dry cleaning; all nonsmoking rooms. *In room:* TV.

11 Airport Hotels

MODERATE

NH Vienna Airport Hotel   Opposite the airport arrivals hall and next to Austria's World Trade Center, this is the most convenient spot to lodge if you have an early-morning flight from the Flughafen Wien. The hotel is adequate for an overnight stay, but you wouldn't want to hang out here indefinitely. The staff is clear about the category of room you're about to check into, be it standard, superior, or deluxe, each of which carries its own separate price tag. A spacious lobby of white marble with baroque appointments and furnishings anchors the airy eight-floor structure. If possible, ask for a room in the newer wing, not the older, less inviting part of the hotel. All rooms, regardless of their category, are comfortably furnished with tiled bathrooms, complete with tub and shower. To guarantee the finest accommodations, ask for one of the executive rooms, which carry a higher price tag.

Flughafen Wien, A-1300 Vienna. ℂ **01/701510.** Fax 01/70519571. www.nh-hotels.com. 498 units. 130€–187€ ($169–$243) double. AE, DC, MC, V. Parking: 16€ ($21). **Amenities:** Restaurant; bar; fitness center; sauna; 24-hr. room service; massage; laundry; dry cleaning; nonsmoking rooms; rooms for those w/limited mobility. *In room:* TV, dataport, minibar, hair dryer, Wi-Fi.

5

Where to Dine

In Vienna, dining out is a local pastime. Besides Austrian and French cuisine, you'll find restaurants serving Serbian, Slovenian, Slovakian, Hungarian, and Czech food, along with Asian, Italian, and Russian. Before dining out, refer to the section on Austrian cuisine, "A Taste of Vienna," in appendix A.

Vienna's so-called "Bermuda Triangle" is a concentration of restaurants and bars a short walk north of Stephansplatz. Schwedenplatz, Rotenturmstrasse, Hohermarkt, and Marcus Aurelius Strasse border this restaurant district.

MEALS & DINING CUSTOMS

Although Viennese meals are traditionally big and hearty, innovative chefs throughout the city now turn out lighter versions of the old classics. Even so, the Viennese love to eat, often as many as six times a day. Breakfast usually consists of bread with butter, jam, or cheese along with milk and coffee. Around 10am is *gabelfrühstück* (snack breakfast), when diners usually savor some type of meat, perhaps little finger sausages. Lunch at midday is normally a filling meal, and the afternoon *jause* consists of coffee, open-face sandwiches, and the luscious pastries that the Viennese make so well. Dinners can also be hearty, although many locals prefer a light evening meal.

Because Vienna cherishes its theaters, concert halls, and opera houses, many locals choose to dine after a performance. *Après-théâtre* is all the rage in this city, and many restaurants and cafes stay open late to cater to cultural buffs.

Unlike those in other western European capitals, many of Vienna's restaurants observe Sunday closings (marked by SONNTAG RUHETAG signs). Also beware of summer holiday closings, when chefs would rather rush to nearby lake resorts than cook for Vienna's tourist hordes. Sometimes restaurants announce vacation closings only a week or two before shutting down.

1 Restaurants by Cuisine

ASIAN
Akakiko (Innere Stadt, $, p. 92)
Hansen ✦ (Innere Stadt, $, p. 95)

AUSTRIAN
Altes Jägerhaus ✦ (Leopoldstadt, $, p. 100)
Altwienerhof ✦✦✦ (Near Schönbrunn, $$$, p. 108)
Amerlingbeisl (Neubau, $, p. 105)
Augustinerkeller (Innere Stadt, $, p. 92)
Bauer (Innere Stadt, $$$, p. 87)
Café-Restaurant Kunsthaus (Landstrasse, $, p. 101)
Die Fromme Helene ✦ (Josefstadt, $$, p. 106)
Figlmüller (Innere Stadt, $, p. 94)

Key to Abbreviations: $$$$ = Very Expensive $$$ = Expensive $$ = Moderate $ = Inexpensive

Gasthaus Ubl ✦ (Wieden &
Margareten, $, p. 103)
Gergely's (Wieden & Margareten, $,
p. 103)
Gräfin vom Naschmarkt (Mariahilf, $,
p. 103)
Griechenbeisl (Innere Stadt, $$,
p. 90)
Gulaschmuseum ✦ (Innere Stadt, $,
p. 95)
Hansen (Innere Stadt, $, p. 95)
Hietzinger Bräu (Near Schönbrunn,
$$, p. 108)
Kardos (Innere Stadt, $, p. 95)
Kern's Beisel (Innere Stadt, $, p. 96)
Leupold's Kupferdachl ✦ (Innere
Stadt, $$, p. 91)
Motto (Wieden & Margareten, $$,
p. 102)
Palmenhaus ✦ (Innere Stadt, $, p. 96)
Piaristenkeller (Josefstadt, $$, p. 107)
Plutzer Bräu ✦ (Neubau, $, p. 105)
Restaurant Salzamt ✦ (Innere Stadt,
$, p. 97)
Sacher Hotel Restaurant ✦ (Innere
Stadt, $$$$, p. 87)
Schnattl ✦ (Josefstadt, $$, p. 107)
Siebenstern-Bräu (Neubau, $$, p. 86)
Steirereck ✦✦✦ (Landstrasse, $$$$,
p. 101)
Vestibül (Innere Stadt, $$, p. 91)
Vikerl's Lokal (Westbahnhof, $$,
p. 108)
Weibels Wirtshaus ✦ (Innere Stadt,
$$$, p. 89)
Zu den 3 Hacken ✦ (Innere Stadt, $,
p. 97)
Zum Finsteren Stern (Innere Stadt,
$$, p. 91)
Zum Kuchldragoner (Innere Stadt, $,
p. 97)

BALKAN
Dubrovnik (Innere Stadt, $, p. 94)

COFFEEHOUSES, TEAROOMS & CAFES
Café Central ✦ (Innere Stadt, $,
p. 98)
Café Demel ✦✦ (Innere Stadt, $,
p. 82)
Café Diglas (Innere Stadt, $, p. 98)
Café Dommayer (Near Schönbrunn,
$, p. 98)
Café Frauenhuber (Innere Stadt, $,
p. 98)
Café Imperial ✦ (Innere Stadt, $,
p. 99)
Café Landtmann ✦ (Innere Stadt, $,
p. 99)
Café Sperl (Neubau, $, p. 99)
Café Tirolerhof (Innere Stadt, $,
p. 99)
Demmers Teehaus (Innere Stadt, $,
p. 99)

CONTINENTAL
Bauer (Innere Stadt, $$$, p. 87)
Blaustern (Outer Districts, $, p. 109)
Gasthaus Lux (Neubau, $$, p. 103)
Gräfin vom Naschmarkt (Mariahilf, $,
p. 103)
Julius Meinl (Innere Stadt, $$, p. 90)
Vincent ✦ (Leopoldstadt, $$$,
p. 100)

CROATIAN
Dubrovnik (Innere Stadt, $, p. 94)

FRENCH
Altwienerhof ✦✦✦ (Near
Schönbrunn, $$$, p. 108)

GAME
Altes Jägerhaus ✦ (Leopoldstadt, $,
p. 100)

HUNGARIAN
Alte Backstube (Josefstadt, $$, p. 106)
Gulaschmuseum ✦ (Innere Stadt, $,
p. 95)
Kardos (Innere Stadt, $, p. 95)

INTERNATIONAL

Bohème ✚ (Neubau, $$, p. 104)

Café Cuadro (Wieden & Margareten, $, p. 102)

Café Leopold ✚ (Innere Stadt, $, p. 93)

Café Restaurant Halle (Innere Stadt, $, p. 93)

Café-Restaurant Kunsthaus (Landstrasse, $, p. 101)

Do & Co. (Innere Stadt, $$$, p. 88)

Fabios (Innere Stadt, $$$, p. 88)

Gergely's (Wieden & Margareten, $, p. 103)

Hansen ✚ (Innere Stadt, $, p. 95)

König von Ungarn ✚ (Innere Stadt, $$$$, p. 86)

Korso bei der Oper ✚✚✚ (Innere Stadt, $$$$, p. 86)

Niky's Kuchlmasterei ✚ (Landstrasse, $$$, p. 101)

Restaurant Taubenkobel ✚ (On the Outskirts, $$$$, p. 109)

Sacher Hotel Restaurant ✚ (Innere Stadt, $$$$, p. 87)

Wiener Rathauskeller ✚✚ (Innere Stadt, $$$, p. 89)

Zum Schwarzen Kameel (Stiebitz) (Innere Stadt, $$, p. 92)

ITALIAN

Cantinetta Antinori ✚ (Innere Stadt, $$, p. 89)

Firenze Enoteca ✚✚ (Innere Stadt, $$, p. 90)

Motto (Wieden & Margareten, $$, p. 102)

MEDITERRANEAN

Fabios (Innere Stadt, $$$, p. 88)

Hansen ✚ (Innere Stadt, $, p. 95)

Zum Finsteren Stern (Innere Stadt, $$, p. 91)

RUSSIAN

Abend-Restaurant Feuervogel (Alsergrund, $$, p. 107)

SANDWICHES

Buffet Trzésniewski ✚ (Innere Stadt, $, p. 93)

SEAFOOD

Kervansaray und Hummer Bar ✚✚ (Innere Stadt, $$$$, p. 86)

SLOVENIAN

Kardos (Innere Stadt, $, p. 95)

THAI

Motto (Wieden & Margareten, $$, p. 102)

VIENNESE

Alfi's Goldener Spiegel (Mariahilf, $, p. 103)

Alte Backstube (Josefstadt, $$, p. 106)

Bohème ✚ (Neubau, $$, p. 104)

Dubrovnik (Innere Stadt, $, p. 94)

Gösser Bierklinik (Innere Stadt, $, p. 94)

König von Ungarn ✚ (Innere Stadt, $$$$, p. 86)

Korso bei der Oper ✚✚✚ (Innere Stadt, $$$$, p. 86)

Leupold's Kupferdachl ✚ (Innere Stadt, $$, p. 91)

Mörwald im Ambassador ✚✚✚ (Innere Stadt, $$$$, p. 87)

Niky's Kuchlmasterei ✚ (Landstrasse, $$$, p. 101)

Ofenloch (Innere Stadt, $$, p. 91)

Österreicher im MAK Gasthof & Bar ✚✚ (Innere Stadt, $, p. 96)

Plachutta ✚ (Innere Stadt, $$$, p. 89)

Sacher Hotel Restaurant ✚ (Innere Stadt, $$$$, p. 87)

Siebenstern-Bräu (Neubau, $$, p. 86)

Silberwirt (Wieden & Margareten, $$, p. 102)

Steirereck ✚✚✚ (Landstrasse, $$$$, p. 101)

Wiener Rathauskeller ✚✚ (Innere Stadt, $$$, p. 89)

Zum Weissen Rauchfangkehrer (Innere Stadt, $$, p. 92)

Zwölf-Apostelkeller (Innere Stadt, $, p. 100)

Where to Dine in Vienna

Abend-Restaurant
  Feuervogel 21
Akakiko 47
Alfi's Goldener Spiegel 20
Alte Backstube 6
Alte Jägerhaus 42
Altwienerhof 14
Amerlingbeisl 14
Augustinerkeller 11
Bauer 39
Blaustern 1
Bohème 15
Buffet Trzésniewski 32
Café Central 8
Café Cuadro 14
Café Demel 10
Café Diglas 35
Café Dommayer 16
Café Frauenhuber 51
Café Imperial 56
Café Landtmann 5
Café Leopold 13
Café Restaurant Halle 13
Café-Restaurant
  Kunsthaus 31
Café Sperl 18
Café Tirolerhof 52
Cantinetta Antinori 34
Demmers Teehaus 3
Die Fromme Helene 6
Do & Co. 33
Dubrovnik 49
Fabios 23
Figlmüller 36
Firenze Enoteca 46
Gasthaus Lux 14
Gasthaus Ubl 53
Gergely's 14
Gösser Bierklinik 26
Gräfin vom Naschmarkt 19
Griechenbeisl 38
Gulaschmuseum 44
Hansen 28
Heitzinger Braü 16
Julius Meinl 22
Kardos 40
Kern's Beisel 9
Kervansaray und
  Hummer Bar 55
König von Ungarn
  (King of Hungary) 37
Korso bei der Oper 54
Leopold & Kupferdachl 4
Mörwald im Ambassador 50
Motto 14

Votivkirche

Roosevelt-
platz

SCHOTTENRING

Hörlgasse

Schottenring

Börse

Börse-
platz

Universitätsstrasse

Universität
Wien

Dr.-Karl-Lueger-Ring

Schottenstift

Freyung

Am
Hof

RATHAUS

Rathaus

Rathaus-
platz

Burgtheater

Schottenstift

Minoriten-
kirche

PARK

Minoriten-
platz

HERREN-
GASSE

Michaeler-
platz

Michaeler-
kirche

Parlament

VOLKSGARTEN

Ballhaus-
platz

Schmerling-
platz

Dr.-Karl-Renner-Ring

Hofburg

Josefs-
platz

Heldenplatz

Burgring

VOLKS-
THEATER

Volkstheater

Naturhistorisches
Museum

Neue
Hofburg

Maria-
Theresien-
Platz

BURGGARTEN

Kunsthistorisches
Museum

Opernring

Museums-
Quartier

MUSEUMS-
QUARTIER

Schiller-
platz

Akad. der
Bildenden
Künste

Mariahilfer Strasse

To Westbahnhof
and Schönbrunn

Secession

Theater an
der Wien

Naschmarkt

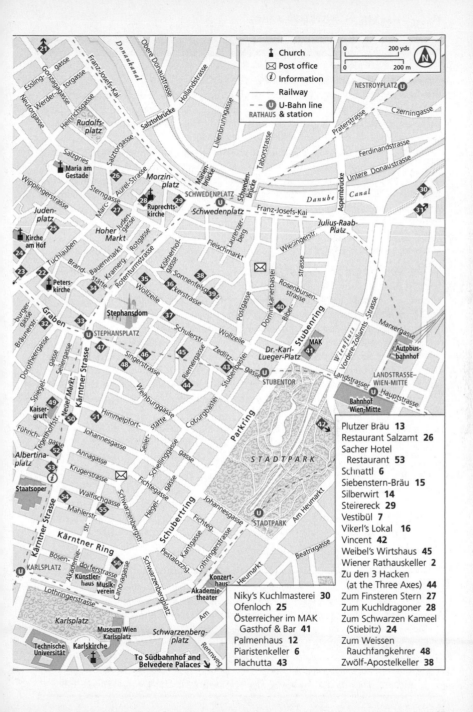

Church

Post office

Information

---------- **Railway**

– – Ⓤ **U-Bahn line**

RATHAUS **& station**

| 0 | | 200 yds |
| 0 | | 200 m |

Plutzer Bräu **13**
Restaurant Salzamt **26**
Sacher Hotel
　Restaurant **53**
Schnattl **6**
Siebenstern-Bräu **15**
Silberwirt **14**
Steirereck **29**
Vestibül **7**
Vikerl's Lokal **16**
Vincent **42**
Weibel's Wirtshaus **45**
Wiener Rathauskeller **2**
Zu den 3 Hacken
　(at the Three Axes) **44**
Zum Finsteren Stern **27**
Zum Kuchldragoner **28**
Zum Schwarzen Kameel
　(Stiebitz) **24**
Zum Weissen
　Rauchfangkehrer **48**
Zwölf-Apostelkeller **38**

Niky's Kuchlmasterei **30**
Ofenloch **25**
Österreicher im MAK
　Gasthof & Bar **41**
Palmenhaus **12**
Piaristenkeller **6**
Plachutta **43**

2 Innere Stadt (Inner City)

VERY EXPENSIVE

Kervansaray und Hummer Bar ✰✰ SEAFOOD   Here you'll sense the historic link between the Habsburgs and their 19th-century neighbor, the Ottoman Empire. On the restaurant's ground floor, polite waiters announce a changing array of daily specials and serve tempting salads from an hors d'oeuvre table. Upstairs, guests enjoy the bounties of the sea at the Lobster Bar. There's also a deli.

A meal often begins with a champagne cocktail, followed by one of many appetizers, including a lobster and salmon caviar cocktail. The menu has a short list of meat dishes such as filet mignon with Roquefort sauce, but it specializes in seafood, including grilled filet of sole with fresh asparagus, Norwegian salmon with a horseradish-and-champagne sauce, and, of course, lobster. If shellfish is your weakness, be prepared to pay for your indulgence.

Mahlerstrasse 9. ℂ 01/5128843. Reservations recommended. Main courses 22€–50€ ($29–$65). AE, DC, MC, V. Restaurant Mon–Sat noon–midnight; bar Mon–Sat 6pm–midnight. U-Bahn: Karlsplatz. Tram: 1 or 2. Bus: 3A.

König von Ungarn (King of Hungary) ✰ INTERNATIONAL/VIENNESE   Housed in the famous hotel of the same name, this restaurant evokes a rich atmosphere with crystal chandeliers, antiques, marble columns, and vaulted ceilings. If you're unsure of what to order, try the *tafelspitz*, elegantly dispensed from a cart. Other seasonal choices include a ragout of seafood with fresh mushrooms, tournedos of beef with a mustard-and-horseradish sauce, and appetizers such as scampi in caviar sauce. Chefs balance flavors, textures, and colors to create a cuisine that's long been favored by locals, who often bring out-of-town guests here. We have been dining here for years and have found the cuisine consistently good. However, in fairness and with warning, it should be noted that many of our discriminating readers have found the restaurant disappointing and the food unremarkable.

Schulerstrasse 10. ℂ 01/515840. Reservations required. Main courses 15€–19€ ($20–$25); fixed-price menu 40€–49€ ($52–$64) at lunch, 30€–40€ ($38–$51) at dinner. AE, DC, MC, V. Mon–Fri noon–2:30pm and 6–10:30pm. U-Bahn: Stephansplatz. Bus: 1A.

Korso bei der Oper ✰✰✰ INTERNATIONAL/VIENNESE   This chic and glittering choice is decorated with tasteful paneling, sparkling chandeliers, and, flanking either side of a baronial fireplace, two of the most breathtaking baroque columns in Vienna. Set in the elegant Hotel Bristol, the restaurant has its own entrance directly across from the Staatsoper, a position that has always attracted a legendary clientele of opera stars.

Impressions

The people of Vienna are completely different from western and alpine Austrians, with a different set of morals and attitudes from the rest of the country. They regard their city as incomparable—as indeed it is, after a fashion. No European capital has such a stately, imperial air . . . the double-headed eagle still broods overhead wherever you go—and no other European capital has such delightful surroundings.

—Richard Bassett, *The Austrians: Strange Tales from the Vienna Woods,* 1988

The kitchen concocts an alluring mixture of traditional and modern cuisine for discriminating palates. Your meal might feature filet of char with a sorrel sauce, saddle of veal with cèpe mushrooms and homemade noodles, or the inevitable *tafelspitz*. The rack of lamb is excellent, as are the medallions of beef with a shallot-infused butter sauce and Roquefort-flavored noodles. The wine list is extensive, and the service, as you'd expect, is impeccable.

In the Hotel Bristol, Kärtner Ring 1. 🕾 01/51516546. Reservations required. Main courses 25€–40€ ($33–$52); fixed-price menu 45€ ($59) at lunch, 76€ ($99) at dinner. AE, DC, MC, V. Mon–Fri noon–3pm and 6pm–1am. U-Bahn: Karlsplatz. Tram: 1 or 2.

Mörwald im Ambassador 😪😪😪 VIENNESE   This restaurant, in the Hotel Ambassador, is one of the best and most stylish in Vienna. Bankers, diplomats, and what one local food critic called "Helmut Lang–clad hipsters" show up here not only to see and be seen, but also to enjoy the delectable modern Viennese cuisine of Christian Domschitz. He's shown a genius for giving classic Viennese dishes a modern twist. Prepared with élan and precision, some of his best dishes include saddle of suckling pig with white cabbage dumplings, veal meat loaf with pureed spring onions, and a spicy brook char, one of the best fish offerings. You might start with the chef's velvety smooth foie gras in Kirschwasser. For dessert, we recommend the diced semolina pancakes, which sound ordinary but aren't, as they are served with a spicy apple compote and feather dumplings with a *fromage blanc* (white cheese).

In the Hotel Ambassador, Kärntnerstrasse Strasse 22. 🕾 01/961610. Reservations required. Main courses 21€–36€ ($27–$47). AE, DC, MC, V. Mon–Sat noon–3pm and 6:30–11pm. U-Bahn: Stephansplatz.

Sacher Hotel Restaurant 😪 AUSTRIAN/INTERNATIONAL/VIENNESE
Most celebrities who visit Vienna are eventually spotted in this elegant dining room, most likely enjoying the restaurant's most famous dish, *tafelspitz;* the chef at Sacher prepares the boiled beef ensemble with a savory, herb-flavored sauce that is truly fit for the emperor's table. Other delectable dishes include fish terrine and veal steak with morels. For dessert, the Sachertorte enjoys world renown. It's primarily a chocolate sponge cake that's sliced in half and filled with apricot jam. This famous pastry was supposedly created in 1832 by Franz Sacher when he served as Prince Metternich's apprentice.

Come dressed to the nines, and be sure to show up before 11pm, even though the restaurant officially closes at 1am. Despite the adherence to form and protocol here, latecomers will never go hungry, as the hotel maintains tables in the adjoining and less formal Red Bar, where the menu is available every day from noon to 11:30pm (last order). The Sacher has always been a favorite for dinner either before or after the opera.

In the Hotel Sacher Wien, Philharmonikerstrasse 4. 🕾 01/514560. Reservations required. Main courses 22€–38€ ($29–$49). AE, DC, MC, V. Daily noon–3pm and 6–11:30pm. U-Bahn: Karlsplatz.

EXPENSIVE

Bauer 😪😪 AUSTRIAN/CONTINENTAL   It's upscale, it's *gemütlich*, and it's on the short list of restaurants that concierges at some of Vienna's most upscale hotels recommend to their clients. You'll find it on a narrow street a few blocks northeast of the Cathedral, beneath 500-year-old ceiling vaults, now painted a dark shade of pink, that evoke a venue that's more folksy and rustic than this sophisticated restaurant really is. Recent clients have included Jose Carreras, race-car celeb Nicki Lauda, Keith Richards, and the President of Austria (Heinz Fischer). The fact that there are only 30 seats enhances the coziness of a venue that was established in its present format in 1989. Expect glamorous food. The finest examples include carpaccio of beef with mustard sauce; sweetbreads with vanilla sauce and braised chicory; and stuffed squid with lemon sauce and pepper-flavored cream sauce.

Sonnenfelsgasse 17. ⓒ **01/512-9871.** Reservations recommended. Main courses 26€–31€ ($34–$40); 4-course set-price menu 59€ ($77). AE, DC, MC, V. Mon 6–11pm, Tues-Fri noon–2pm and 6–11pm, Closed Sat and Sun, and one week at Easter and mid-July to mid-Aug. U-Bahn: Stephansplatz, Schwedenplatz, or Stubentor.

Do & Co. 𝔊 INTERNATIONAL   Positioned on the 7th floor of a radically angular hypermodern building that's set across from Vienna's cathedral, this restaurant is the crown jewel of an also-recommended hotel. It's difficult to overstate its fame within the complicated but steely hierarchy of fine and/or stylish Viennese dining. So great is its demand that even if there happens to be a space available during the city's key dining hours (roughly defined as between 7 and 10pm), management will simply not release that space to walk-ins who haven't pre-reserved a table, saving it instead for last-minute calls from the aides of either "celebrities of the minute" or genuinely grand Imperial dragons. At its best, it will provide a high-pressure insight into Vienna's social priorities.

Consider a pre-dinner cocktail at the stylish and sometimes overcrowded Onyx Bar on the building's 6th floor, then climb a circular staircase through cramped hallways to the 7th-floor dining room. Here, *if you've reserved,* you'll be presented with a slightly claustrophobic table and a confusingly diverse set of menu items that the menus divide into categories that include "Tastes of the World" (Tataki of Atlantic tuna); "Catch of the Day" (potpourri of scallops with beans, comfit of tomato, and *crème fraîche*); "Beef & Co." (French breast of duck with green beans and creamy kumquat polenta); "Kebab, Wok & Curries" (dishes inspired by Asia, especially Thailand); "Austrian Classics" (deep-fried monkfish with potato salad); and many different kinds of sushi.

In the Haas Haus, Stephansplatz 12. ⓒ **01/24188.** Reservations required. Main courses 16€–24€ ($21–$31). AE, DC, MC, V. Daily noon–3pm and 6–11:45pm. U-Bahn: Stephansplatz.

Fabios 𝔊𝔊 INTERNATIONAL/MEDITERRANEAN   This is the trendiest and most sought-after restaurant in Vienna, with considerable jockeying among the city's glitterati. The creation of the young and fun Fabio Giacobello, the space is bigger inside than you might think. Most of the visual distraction in this mostly black but plush and artfully lit environment comes from its fashion-conscious and usually good-looking clients, and from walls of glass that seem to bring the visual details of Vienna's historic core directly inside. Menu items change frequently, but might include warm octopus marinated with olive oil and parsley served on a bed of cold gazpacho cream sauce, crispy sesame leaves stuffed with warm goat cheese served with Treviso radicchio and honeydew melon, and roasted rack of lamb with cold marinated eggplant and tomatoes served with deep-fried polenta gnocchetti. Our favorite dessert? The panna cotta with apricot ragout and caramelized pistachios, although a selection of cheeses is equally tempting. Incidentally, don't overlook the value of this place's wine bar as a nightlife option. There's enough drama unfolding around its rectangular surface to keep a few tabloid writers busy, and someone famous within the inner workings of Vienna's media and politics always seems to be popping up for air and a drink or two.

Tuchlauben 6. ⓒ **01/532-2222.** Reservations recommended. Main courses 19€–29€ ($25–$38). AE, MC, V. Mon-Sat noon–11:30pm. U-Bahn: Stephansplatz.

Plachutta ⟨ VIENNESE   Few restaurants have built such a fetish around one dish as Plachutta has done with *tafelspitz*, offering 10 variations of the boiled beef dish, which was the favorite of Emperor Franz Josef throughout his prolonged reign. The differences between the versions are a function of the cut of beef you request. We recommend *schulterscherzel* (shoulder of beef) and *beinfleisch* (shank of beef), but if you're in doubt, the waitstaff is knowledgeable about one of the most oft-debated subjects in Viennese cuisine. Hash brown potatoes, chives, and an appealing mixture of horseradish and chopped apples accompany each order. Other Viennese staples such as goulash soup, calf's liver, and braised pork with cabbage are also available. Although we have been here on several occasions and have been welcomed graciously, some readers have complained about their reception.

Wollzeile 38. ℂ 01/5121577. Reservations recommended. Main courses 18€–25€ ($23–$33). DC, MC, V. Daily 11:30am–midnight. U-Bahn: Stubentor.

Weibels Wirtshaus ⟨ *Finds* AUSTRIAN   Don't be fooled by the unpretentious and cozy feel to this place, which at first glance might look like a simple tavern. Food is considerably better than the *wirtshaus* (tavern) appellation implies, and the clientele is a lot more upscale than the usual wurst-with-potatoes-and-beer crowd. There are only two rooms (and about 40 seats) within this wood-paneled restaurant, each on a separate floor of a building whose age is estimated to be around 400 years old. During clement weather, another 30 seats become available within a garden in back. Former clients have included the mayor of Vienna, and the wine list, with more than 250 varieties of Austrian wine, looks like a patriotic, pro-Austrian statement in its own right. Menu items change seasonally, but during our visit they included pumpkinseed soup, sliced breast of duck with lentils, well-prepared schnitzels of veal and chicken, and a superb saddle of lamb with polenta and spinach.

Kumpfgasse 2. ℂ 01/5123986. Reservations recommended. Main courses 14€–23€ ($18–$30); fixed-price menu 35€ ($46). AE, MC, V. Daily 11:30am–midnight. U-Bahn: Stephansplatz.

Wiener Rathauskeller ⟨⟨ INTERNATIONAL/VIENNESE   City halls throughout the Teutonic world have traditionally maintained restaurants in their basements, and Vienna is no exception. Although Vienna's famous Rathaus was built between 1871 and 1883, its cellar-level restaurant wasn't added until 1899. Today, in half a dozen richly atmospheric dining rooms, with high vaulted ceilings and stained-glass windows, you can enjoy good and reasonably priced food. The chef's specialty is a *rathauskellerplatte* for two, consisting of various cuts of meat, including a veal schnitzel, lamb cutlets, and pork medallions. One section of the cellar is devoted every evening to a Viennese musical soiree beginning at 8pm. Live musicians ramble through the world of operetta, waltz, and *schrammel* (traditional Viennese music) as you dine.

Rathausplatz 1. ℂ 01/405-1210. Reservations required. Main courses 11€–39€ ($14–$51); Vienna music evening with dinner (Tues–Sat 8pm) 44€ ($57). AE, DC, MC, V. Mon–Sat 11:30am–3pm and 6–11pm. U-Bahn: Rathaus.

MODERATE

Cantinetta Antinori ⟨ ITALIAN   This is one of three European restaurants run by the Antinori family, who own Tuscan vineyards and whose name is nearly synonymous with Chianti. The traditions and aesthetics of the original restaurant, in Florence, have been reproduced here to showcase Antinori wines and the culinary zest of Tuscany. Within a 140-year-old building overlooking the Stephansplatz and the cathedral, you'll find a high-ceilinged dining room, as well as a greenhouse-style "winter garden" that transports you straight to Tuscany. Start off with an order of *antipasti tipico*, a medley of marinated vegetables and seafood arranged by the staff. This might be followed with sumptuous ravioli stuffed with porcini mushrooms and summer truffles or perfectly grilled lamb steaks with sun-dried tomatoes and Mediterranean herbs. *Panna cotta*, a creamy flan, is a simple but flavorful way to finish a meal. A huge selection of wines is served by the glass.

Jasomirgottstrasse 3–5. ℂ 01/5337722. Reservations required. Main courses 14€–29€ ($18–$38). AE, DC, MC, V. Daily 11:30am–11pm. U-Bahn: Stephansplatz.

Firenze Enoteca ✿✿ ITALIAN   This is one of Vienna's premier Italian restaurants. Located near St. Stephan's next to the Royal Hotel, it's furnished in Tuscan Renaissance style, with frescoes by Benozzo Gozzoli. The kitchen specializes in homemade pasta served with zesty sauces. According to the chef, the cuisine is "80% Tuscan, 20% from the rest of Italy." Start with selections from the antipasti table, and then choose among spaghetti with "fruits of the sea"; veal cutlet with ham, cheese, and sardines; or perhaps filet mignon in a tomato-garlic sauce. Be sure to complement any meal here with a classic bottle of Chianti.

Singerstrasse 3. ℂ 01/5134374. Reservations recommended. Main courses 8€–26€ ($10–$34). AE, DC, MC, V. Daily noon–3pm and 6pm–midnight. U-Bahn: Stephansplatz.

Griechenbeisl AUSTRIAN   Astonishingly, Griechenbeisl was established in 1450 and is still one of the city's leading restaurants. There's a maze of dining areas on three different floors, all with low vaulted ceilings, smoky paneling, and wrought-iron chandeliers. Watch out for the Styrian-vested waiters who scurry around with large trays of food. As you enter, look down at the grate under your feet for an illuminated view of a pirate counting his money. Inside, check out the so-called inner sanctum, with signatures of former patrons such as Mozart, Beethoven, and Mark Twain. The Pilsen beer is well chilled, and the food is hearty and ample. Menu items include fried breaded filet of chicken with cucumber-potatoes salad; and roast filet of pikeperch with almonds. As an added treat, the restaurant features nighttime accordion and zither music.

Fleischmarkt 11. ℂ 01/5331941. Reservations required. Main courses 16€–25€ ($21–$33). AE, DC, MC, V. Daily 11am–1am (last order at 11:30pm). Tram: N, 1, 2, or 21.

Julius Meinl ✿ CONTINENTAL   This upscale and appealingly formal restaurant is the most sought-after of the three elements within the Julius Meinl trio, which includes, on the same premises, one of the most comprehensive delicatessens and wine shops in Austria, and a cellar-level wine bar. The restaurant occupies a site immediately upstairs from street level, with big-windowed views that sweep out over the all-pedestrian grandeur of the Graben. Although the restaurant looks as upscale as any other of the city's dining competitors, with dark paneling, touches of gilt, a voluptuous-looking service bar, and a sense of Habsburgundian charm, it's positioned within a few steps of the bustling and brightly illuminated premises of its associated delicatessen. Menu items change with the availability of fresh ingredients, but might include tuna with avocado cream and a carrot and ginger-flavored vinaigrette or marinated gratin of lobster with fennel. Our favorite is a platter containing two different preparations of quail accompanied with goose liver and marinated *boletus* mushrooms. Desserts? They're divine. Consider a praline mousse with raspberries and tonka-bean ice cream, or a semolina soufflé with plums and elderberries. And then, there's the cheese trolley, a movable feast and a work of art in its own right.

Graben 19. 🕿 **01/532-3334.** Reservations recommended. Main courses 25€–34€ ($33–$44). Mon-Sat 8:30am-10pm. U-Bahn: Stephansplatz.

Leupold's Kupferdachl 🏆 VIENNESE/AUSTRIAN   Run by the Leopold family since the 1950s, this choice is known for "new Austrian" cuisine, although the chef does prepare traditional dishes. Recommended menu items include beef tenderloin (Old Viennese style) with dumplings boiled in a napkin, lamb loin breaded and served with potatoes, and chicken breast Kiev. The interior is both rustic and elegant, decorated with oriental rugs and cozy banquettes with intricate straight-back chairs. The restaurant operates a beer pub, with good music and better prices. The pub is open daily from 10am to midnight.

Schottengasse 7. 🕿 **01/5339381.** Reservations recommended. Main courses 8€–18€ ($10–$23). AE, DC, MC, V. Mon–Fri 10am–3pm; Mon–Sat 6pm–midnight. U-Bahn: Schottentor. Tram: 2, 43, or 44.

Ofenloch VIENNESE   Viennese have frequented this spot since the 1600s, when it functioned as a simple tavern. The present management dates from the mid-1970s and maintains a well-deserved reputation for its nostalgic, old-fashioned eating house. Waitresses wear classic Austrian regalia and will give you a menu that looks more like a magazine, with some amusing mock-medieval illustrations inside. The hearty soup dishes are popular, as is the schnitzel. For smaller appetites, the menu offers salads and cheese platters, plus an entire page devoted to one-dish meals. For dessert, choose from old-style Viennese specialties.

Kurrentgasse 8. 🕿 **01/5338844.** Reservations required. Main courses 10€–19€ ($13–$25). AE, DC, MC, V. Tues–Sat 11am–midnight. U-Bahn: Stephansplatz. Bus: 1A.

Vestibül *Finds* AUSTRIAN   For theater buffs in particular, this is a real discovery. You can not only attend performances at the Burgtheater, but enjoy good food and drink as well. The restaurant entrance originally existed for the emperor's coach. Architect Luigi Blau took the basic structure and enlarged it, creating a setting that is both antique and modern. Before or after the theater, guests gather in the elegant bar for an aperitif, digestif, or coffee. Tapas are also served here, with tables opening onto a view of the City Hall and Ringstrasse.

Beginning on the first warm spring day and lasting until the mild afternoons of autumn, tables are also placed outside in the garden. A team of skilled chefs present classic cuisine with market-fresh ingredients. An appetizer of fresh oysters might be followed by such main dishes as traditional paprika chicken (inspired by nearby Hungary) or a traditional *beuschel* (a Viennese style hash made of heart and lung). Styrian beef is also a local favorite.

Dr.-Karl-Lueger-Ring 2. 🕿 **01/5324999.** Reservations recommended. Main courses 14€–24€ ($18–$31); fixed-price lunch 17€ ($22); fixed-price dinner 39€–45€ ($51–$59). AE, DC, MC, V. Mon–Fri 11am–midnight; Sat 6pm–midnight, July-Aug closed Sat. U-Bahn: Herrangosset.

Zum Finsteren Stern AUSTRIAN/MEDITERRANEAN   Although primarily a wine bar, this restaurant is also notable for its refined cuisine. Of an intimate, rather discreet appeal, it appears from the outside to be just a store selling wine. Inside, there are tables and chairs for dining. Vintages are from Austria, France, Italy, California, Australia, and South Africa. We are especially fond of the wide selection of Austrian schnapps. It's a perfect place for a glass of wine, a cheese plate, or some cold snacks, but if you visit for lunch or dinner, you can enjoy hot food as well. The chef seems to prefer homemade pasta dishes and fresh fish. Another specialty is chicken with apple stuffing or pasta with black mushrooms.

Sterngasse 2. ✆ 01/5358152. Reservations necessary for lunch or dinner. Main courses 15€–20€ ($20–$26); 6-course fixed-price menu 35€ $46). MC, V. Mon–Fri 3:30pm–midnight; Sat 2:30pm–midnight. U-Bahn: Schwedenplatz.

Zum Schwarzen Kameel (Stiebitz) INTERNATIONAL
This restaurant has remained in the same family since 1618. A delicatessen against one of the walls sells wine, liquor, and specialty meat items, although most of the action takes place among the chic clientele in the cafe. On Saturday mornings, the cafe is packed with locals trying to recover from a late night. Uniformed waiters will bring you a beverage here, and you can select open-face sandwiches from the trays on the black countertops.

Beyond the cafe is a perfectly preserved Art Deco dining room, where jeweled copper chandeliers hang from beaded strings. The walls are a combination of polished paneling, yellowed ceramic tiles, and a dusky plaster ceiling frieze of grape leaves. The restaurant has just 11 tables, and it's the perfect place for a nostalgic lunch in Vienna. The hearty and well-flavored cuisine features herring filet Oslo, potato soup, tournedos, Roman saltimbocca (veal with ham), and an array of daily fish specials.

Bognergasse 5. ✆ 01/5338125. Main courses 16€–25€ ($21–$33). AE, DC, MC, V. Mon–Sat 8:30am–3pm and 6–10:30pm. U-Bahn: Schottentor. Bus: 2A or 3A.

Zum Weissen Rauchfangkehrer VIENNESE
Established in the 1860s, this dinner-only place is the former guildhall for Vienna's chimney sweeps. In fact, the restaurant's name (translated as the "white chimney sweep") comes from the story of a drunken and blackened chimney sweep who fell into a kneading trough and woke up the next day covered in flour. The dining room is rustic, with deer antlers, fanciful chandeliers, and pine banquettes that vaguely resemble church pews. A piano in one of the inner rooms provides nighttime music and adds to the comfortable ambience. Big street-level windows let in lots of light. The hearty, flavorful menu offers Viennese fried chicken, both Tyrolean and Wiener schnitzel, wild game, veal goulash, bratwurst, and several kinds of strudel. You'll certainly want to finish with the house specialty, a fabulously rich chocolate cream puff.

Weihburggasse 4. ✆ 01/5123471. Reservations required. Main courses 15€–26€ ($20–$34). DC, MC, V. Tues–Sat 5pm–1am. Closed July and Aug. U-Bahn: Stephansplatz.

INEXPENSIVE

Akakiko (Value) ASIAN
It's busy and loaded with Asians living permanently or temporarily within Vienna. And as a member of a chain with eight equivalent branches throughout Vienna, it boasts a carefully rehearsed and inexpensive formula for Asian food within an otherwise very expensive neighborhood. To reach its dining room, you'll pass by an open kitchen, where everything gives the impression of wholesomeness and a recent scrubbing. Within the brightly lit modern dining room, outfitted in tones of white and bamboo green, you'll pick from menu items that include sushi, sashimi, teppanyaki, bento boxes, and wok versions of duck, chicken, beef, fish, and vegetarian dishes inspired by the cuisines of China. Staff is polite, even charming.

Singerstrasse 4. ✆ 057/333-140. Reservations not accepted. Main courses 8€–14€ ($10–$18). MC, V. Daily 10:30am–11:30pm. U-Bahn: Stephansplatz.

Augustinerkeller AUSTRIAN
Since 1857, the Augustinerkeller has served wine, beer, and food from the basement of one of the grand Hofburg palaces. It attracts a lively and diverse crowd that gets more boisterous as the *schrammel* (traditional Viennese

music) is played late into the night. The vaulted brick room, with worn pine-board floors and wooden banquettes, is an inviting place to grab a drink and a simple meal. Be aware that this long and narrow dining room is usually as packed with people as it is with character. Roaming accordion players add to the festive atmosphere. An upstairs room is quieter and less crowded. This place offers one of the best values for wine tasting in Vienna. The ground-floor lobby lists prices of vintage local wines by the glass. Tasters can sample from hundreds of bottles near the stand-up stainless-steel counter. Aside from the wine and beer, the kitchen serves simple food, including roast chicken, schnitzel, and *tafelspitz*.

Augustinerstrasse 1. ✆ 01/5331026. Main courses 8€–20€ ($10–$26). AE, DC, MC, V. Daily 10am–midnight. U-Bahn: Stephansplatz.

Buffet Trzésniewski ✿ SANDWICHES   Everyone in Vienna, from the most hurried office worker to the most elite hostess, knows about this spot. Franz Kafka lived next door and used to come here for sandwiches and beer. It's unlike any buffet you've seen, with six or seven cramped tables and a rapidly moving line of people, all jostling for space next to the glass counters. Indicate to the waitress the kind of sandwich you want (if you can't read German, just point). Most people hurriedly devour the delicious finger sandwiches, which come in 18 different combinations of cream cheese, egg, onion, salami, herring, tomatoes, lobster, and many other tasty ingredients. You can also order small glasses of fruit juice, beer, or wine with your snack. If you do order a drink, the cashier will give you a rubber token, which you'll present to the person at the far end of the counter.

Dorotheergasse 1. ✆ 01/5123291. Reservations not accepted. Sandwiches .90€ ($1.15). No credit cards. Mon–Fri 9:30am–7:30pm; Sat 9am–5pm. U-Bahn: Stephansplatz.

Café Leopold ✿ *Finds* INTERNATIONAL   Even before it was built, everyone expected that the cafe and restaurant within one of Vienna's newest museums would be trendsetting. And indeed, critics have defined the place as a postmodern version, in architectural form, of the Viennese expressionist paintings (including many by Egon Schiele) that are exhibited within the museum that contains it. Set one floor above street level in the Leopold Museum, and with a schedule that operates long after the museum is closed for the night, it's sheathed in the same pale pink sandstone as the museum's exterior, but enhanced with three tones (jet black, "Sahara cream," and russet) of marble. There are a minimalist-looking oak-trimmed bar, huge windows, vague and simplified references to 18th-century baroque architecture, and a chandelier that cynics say looks like a lost UFO suspended from the ceiling. During the day, the place functions as a conventional cafe and restaurant, serving a postmodern blend of *mitteleuropäische* (central European) and Asian food. Examples include roasted shoulder of veal with Mediterranean vegetables, Thai curries, Vietnamese spring rolls, and arugula-studded risottos. Three nights a week, however, from around 10pm till at least 2am, any hints of kitsch and coziness are banished as soon as a DJ begins cranking out dance tunes for a hard-drinking denizens-of-the-night crowd. For more on this cafe's role as a nightclub, see "Vienna After Dark," in chapter 9.

In the Leopold Museum, Museumsplatz 1. ✆ 01/5236732. Main courses 4.50€–11€ ($5.85–$14); 2-course fixed-price menu 9€ ($12). AE, DC, MC, V. Sun–Wed 10am–2am, Fri–Sat 10am–4pm. U-Bahn: Volkstheater or Babenbergstrasse/MuseumsQuartier.

Café Restaurant Halle INTERNATIONAL   Set within the Kunsthalle, this is the direct competitor of the also-recommended Café Leopold (above). Larger and with a more sophisticated menu than the Leopold, but without any of its late-night emphasis on dance music, this is a postmodern, airy, big-windowed quartet of wood-trimmed, cream-color rooms. The menu changes every 2 weeks, and service is efficient, conscientious, and in the old-world style. The first thing you'll see when you enter is a spartan-looking cafe area, with a trio of more formal dining rooms at the top of a short flight of stairs. Despite the commitment of its staff to changing the *carte* very frequently, the menu will always contain a half-dozen meal-size salads, many garnished with strips of steak, chicken, or shrimp; two daily homemade soups; and a rotating series of platters that, on the day of our last visit, included tasty braised filets of shark and roasted lamb, prepared delectably in the Greek style, with yogurt-and-herb dressing.

In the Kunsthalle Wien, Museumsplatz 1, in the MuseumsQuartier. (Ⓒ **01/5237001.** Main courses 7€–16€ ($9.10–$21). MC, V. Daily 10am–2am. U-Bahn: MuseumsQuartier.

Dubrovnik BALKAN/CROATIAN/VIENNESE Dubrovnik's allegiance is to the culinary (and cultural) traditions of Croatia. The restaurant, founded in 1965, consists of three dining rooms on either side of a central vestibule filled with busy waiters in Croat costume. The menu lists a lengthy choice of Balkan dishes, including gooseliver pâté; stuffed cabbage; and filet of veal with boiled potatoes, sour cream, and sauerkraut. Among the fish dishes, the most exotic is *Fogosch* (a whitefish) served with potatoes and garlic. For dessert, try baklava or an assortment of Bulgarian cheeses. The restaurant schedules live piano entertainment nightly from 7:30 to 11pm. The hip and internationally minded management of this place recently added an unconventional-looking cafe (the Kono-Bar) that serves drinks and many of the main courses available during the grander restaurant's daily midafternoon closing.

Am Heumarkt 5. (Ⓒ **01/713-7102.** Reservations recommended. Main courses 8€–18€ ($11–$23). AE, DC, MC, V. Daily 11am–3pm and 6pm–midnight; cafe Mon–Fri 11am–midnight. U-Bahn: Stadtpark.

Figlmüller AUSTRIAN This is the latest branch of a wine tavern whose original home, established in 1905, lies only a few blocks away. This new branch, thanks to a location on three floors of a thick-walled 200-year-old building and lots of old-world memorabilia attached to the walls, evokes Old Vienna with style and panache. Austrian Airlines referred to its black-and-white uniformed waiters as "unflappable," and we believe that its schnitzels are the kind of plate-filling, golden-brown delicacies that people always associate with schmaltzy Vienna. Menu items include goulash soup, onion-flavored roast beef, Vienna-style fried chicken, and strudels. During mushroom season (autumn and early winter), expect many variations, perhaps most deliciously served in an herbed cream sauce over noodles. This restaurant's nearby twin, at Wollzeile 5 (Ⓒ **01/5126177**), offers basically the same menu, prices, and richly nostalgic wine-tavern ambience.

Bäckerstrasse 6. (Ⓒ **01/5121760.** Reservations recommended. Main courses 10€–14€ ($13–$18). AE, DC, MC, V. Daily 11am–11:30pm. Closed Aug. U-Bahn: Stephansplatz.

Gösser Bierklinik VIENNESE Also known as the Güldene Drache (Golden Dragon), this restaurant serves the Styrian-brewed Gösser, reportedly the finest beer in the city. The rustic institution occupies a building that, according to tradition, dates from Roman times. An inn operated here in the early 16th century, when Maximilian I ruled the empire, and the decor is strictly medieval. The harried and somewhat unresponsive waitstaff are usually carrying ample mugs of Gösser beer. When you finally get their attention, order some hearty Austrian fare, such as veal chops with dumplings.

Steindlgasse 4. ℂ 01/535-6897. Reservations recommended for parties of 3 or more. Main courses 9€–16€ ($12–$21). DC, MC, V. Mon–Sat 10am–11:30pm. U-Bahn: Stephansplatz. Tram: 31 or 32.

Gulaschmuseum 🍴 (Kids) AUSTRIAN/HUNGARIAN   If you thought that goulash was available in only one form, think again. This restaurant celebrates at least 15 varieties of it, each an authentic survivor of the culinary traditions of Hungary, and each redolent with the taste of the national spice, paprika. The Viennese adopted goulash from their former vassal centuries ago, and have long since added it to their culinary repertoire. You can order versions of goulash made with roast beef, veal, pork, or even fried chicken livers. Vegetarians rejoice: Versions made with potatoes, beans, or mushrooms are also available. Boiled potatoes and rough-textured brown or black bread will usually accompany your choice. An excellent starter is the Magyar national crepe, *Hortobágy Palatschinken,* stuffed with minced beef and paprika-flavored cream sauce. If you prefer an Austrian dish, there are *tafelspitz,* Wiener schnitzel, fresh fish from Austria's lakes, and such dessert specialties as homemade *apfelstrudel* and Sachertorte.

Schulerstrasse 20. ℂ 01/5121017. Reservations recommended. Main courses 8€–14€ ($10–$18). MC, V. Mon–Fri 9am–midnight; Sat–Sun 10am–midnight. U-Bahn: Wollzeile or Stephansplatz.

Hansen 🍴 (Finds) ASIAN/AUSTRIAN/INTERNATIONAL/MEDITERRANEAN   One of the most intriguing and stylish restaurants in Vienna opened as a partnership between a time-tested culinary team and the downtown showrooms of one of Austria's most famous horticulturists and gardening stores (Lederleitner, GmbH). You'll find them cheek-by-jowl in the vaulted cellars of Vienna's stock exchange, a Beaux Arts pile designed in the 1890s by the restaurant's namesake, Theophile Hansen. Part of the charm of this place involves trekking through masses of plants and elaborate garden ornaments on your way to your dining table. Expect to be joined by the movers and shakers of corporate Vienna at lunch and at relatively early dinners, when the place is likely to be very busy. Choose from a small but savory menu that changes weekly. Examples include a spicy bean salad with strips of chicken breast served in a summer broth, risotto with cheese and sour cherries, and poached *Saibling* (something akin to trout from the coldwater streams of the Austrian Alps) with a potato and celery puree and watercress.

In the cellar of the Börsegebäude (Vienna Stock Exchange), Wipplingerstrasse 34 at the Schottenring. ℂ 01/5320542. Reservations recommended. Main courses 8€–17€ ($10–$22). AE, DC, MC, V. Mon–Fri 9am–8pm (last order); Sat 9am–3:30pm (last order). U-Bahn: Schottenring.

Kardos AUSTRIAN/HUNGARIAN/SLOVENIAN   This folkloric restaurant specializes in the strong flavors and potent traditions that developed in different parts of what used to be the Austro-Hungarian Empire. Similarly, the setting celebrates the idiosyncratic folklore of various regions of the Balkans and the Great Hungarian Plain. Newcomers are welcomed with piquant little rolls known as *grammel,* seasoned with minced pork and spices, and a choice of grilled meats. Other specialties include Hungarian *Fogosch* (a form of pikeperch) that's baked with vegetables and parsley potatoes; Hungarian goulash; and braised cabbage. The cellar atmosphere is Gypsy schmaltz— pine-wood accents and brightly colored Hungarian accessories. During the winter, you're likely to find a strolling violinist. To begin, try a glass of *Barack,* an aperitif made from fermented apricots.

Dominikaner Bastei 8. ℂ 01/5126949. Reservations recommended. Main courses 7€–20€ ($9.10–$26). AE, DC, MC, V. Mon–Sat 11:30am–2:30pm and 6–11pm. U-Bahn: Schwedenplatz.

Kern's Beisel *Value* AUSTRIAN   The term *beisl* implies an aggressively unpretentious tavern where food is plentiful and cheap, and the staff has minimal attitude. That's very much the case with this neighborhood favorite, although in this case, the "neighborhood" happens to be within a few steps of the city's tourist and cultural core, Stephansplatz. You'll dine in an old-fashioned wood-paneled dining room darkened by smoke throughout the ages. The tables in back, near the kitchen and separated from the front with a wooden partition, are a wee bit cozier than those near the front, which are more brightly lit. Here, you might discover groups of five or more wine-drinking friends, sometimes middle-aged ladies, celebrating their after-work rituals. Overall, it's fine, and charming in kind of a rough and mountain way. The dinner menu changes weekly and might feature a starter platter of mixed Austrian appetizers, including vegetable terrine, cooked ham, and strips of fried chicken; cream of garlic soup; and roulades of poached chicken with pumpkinseed sauce. There are also wurst with dumplings, beefsteaks, goulash soup, and Wiener schnitzels of both veal and pork, and, in autumn, some well-prepared game dishes.

Kleeplattgasse 4. ℭ 01/533-9188. Reservations recommended. 6.80€–13€ ($8.85–$17) at lunch, 8.50€–17€ ($11–$21) at dinner. MC, V. Mon–Fri 9am–11pm. Closed Sat-Sun. U-Bahn: Stephansplatz.

Palmenhaus ♠ AUSTRIAN   Many architectural critics consider the Jugendstil glass canopy of this greenhouse the most beautiful in Austria. Overlooking the formal terraces of the Burggarten, it was built between 1901 and 1904 by the Habsburgs' court architect Friedrich Ohmann as a graceful architectural transition between the Albertina and the National Library. Damaged during wartime bombings, it was restored in 1998. Today, its central section functions as a chic cafe and, despite the lavishly historic setting, an appealingly informal venue. No one will mind if you drop in for just a drink and one of the voluptuous pastries displayed near the entrance. But if you want a meal, there's a sophisticated menu that changes monthly and might include fresh Austrian goat cheese with stewed peppers and zucchini salad; young herring with sour cream, horseradish, and deep-fried beignets stuffed with apples and cabbage; and squash blossoms stuffed with salmon mousse.

In the Burggarten. ℭ 01/5331033. Reservations recommended for dinner. Main courses 14€–18€ ($18–$23); pastries 6.20€–7€ ($8.05–$9.10). AE, DC, MC. V. Daily 10am–2am. U-Bahn: Opera.

Österreicher im MAK Gasthof & Bar ♠♠ VIENNESE   The food and beverage facilities within many of Vienna's museums are often simple, self-service snack bars, but this one, nestled within the MAK, is a deeply respected culinary destination in its own right. It occupies a pair of rooms on the museums' street level, one of them an enormous and echoing room that's capped with one of the most elaborate coffered and frescoed ceilings in town; the other a smaller, postmodern, glass-sided room with a ceiling that rolls back during clement weather for a view of the sky. There's also a garden terrace that's not immediately visible when you first enter, so if you want to dine outside (and in summer, almost everyone does), be sure to make your wishes known. Since 2006, the culinary inspiration behind all this is Helmut Österreicher, a chef who has helped to redefine the tenets of modern Viennese cuisine—a lighter interpretation of what dining with the Habsburgs really meant. The menu is divided into two categories, one featuring "classical" and the other "modern" Viennese cuisine. Favored dishes (for example, personally recommended by Herr Österreicher) among the classical choices include *zwiebelrostbraten,* roast beef with onions and sautéed potatoes; Wiener schnitzel, and *tafelspitz*—in this case, two types of prime boiled beef with fried grated potatoes, apple horseradish, and chive sauce. Recommended from the list of modern choices include artfully presented versions of roasted chicken in a creamy paprika sauce (utterly delicious) with small creamed dumplings; salmon-trout in a muesli crust served with potato-based noodles; and pike-perch on a bed of tomato-flavored cabbage with parsley potatoes. Menu items change frequently with the inspiration of this gifted chef.

In the MAK (*Museum der Angewanten Kunst*), Stubenring 5. $\copyright$ 01/714-0121. Reservations recommended. Main courses 11€–18€ ($14–$23). AE, DC, MC, V. Daily 11:30am–11:30pm. U-Bahn: Stubentor or Schwedenplatz.

Restaurant Salzamt $\maltese$ AUSTRIAN   This is the best restaurant in a neighborhood— the "Bermuda Triangle"—that's loaded with less desirable competitors. It evokes a turn-of-the-20th-century Viennese bistro, replete with Wiener Werkstatte-inspired chairs and lighting fixtures, cream-color walls, and dark tables and banquettes where you're likely to see an arts-involved, sometimes surprisingly prominent clientele of loyal repeat diners, including Karl Lagerfeld and the Prince of Monaco. Sit within its vaulted interior or—if weather permits—move out to any of the tables on the square, overlooking Vienna's oldest church, St. Ruprecht. Well-prepared items include a terrine of broccoli and artichoke hearts, light-textured pastas, filets of pork with a Gorgonzola-enriched cream sauce, several kinds of goulash, and fresh fish. One of the most noteworthy of these is fried filets of *Saibling*, a fish native to the coldwater streams of western Austria, served with lemon or tartar sauce.

Ruprechtsplatz 1. $\copyright$ 01/5335332. Reservations recommended. Main courses 8€–19€ ($10–$25). V. Mon–Fri 11am–2am; Sat–Sun 3pm–2am. U-Bahn: Schwedenplatz.

Zu den 3 Hacken (at the Three Axes) $\maltese$ AUSTRIAN   Cozy, small-scale, and charming, this restaurant was established 350 years ago and today bears the reputation as the oldest *gasthaus* (tavern) in Vienna. In 1827, Franz Schubert had an ongoing claim to one of the establishment's tables as a site for entertaining his cronies. Today, the establishment maintains midsummer barriers of green-painted lattices and potted ivy for tables that jut onto the sidewalk. During inclement weather, head for one of three dining rooms, each paneled and each evocative of an inn high in the Austrian Alps. Expect an old-fashioned menu replete with the kind of dishes that fueled the Austro-Hungarian Empire. Examples include *tafelspitz,* beef goulash, mixed grills piled high with chops and sausages, and desserts that include Hungarian-inspired *palatschinken* (crepes) with chocolate-hazelnut sauce. The Czech and Austrian beer here seems to taste especially good when it's dispensed from a keg.

Singerstrasse 28. $\copyright$ 01/5125895. Reservations recommended. Main courses 7€–17€ ($9.10–$22). AE, DC, MC, V. Mon–Sat 11am–11pm. U-Bahn: Stephansplatz.

Zum Kuchldragoner AUSTRIAN   Some aspects of this place will remind you of an old-fashioned Austrian tavern, perhaps one that's perched high in the mountains, far from any congested city neighborhood. The feeling is enhanced by the pine trim and the battered *gemütlichkeit* of what you'll soon discover is a bustling, irreverent, and sometimes jaded approach to feeding old-fashioned, flavorful, but far-from-cutting-edge cuisine to large numbers of urban clients, usually late into the night after everyone has had more than a drink or two. You can settle for a table inside, but our preferred venue is an outdoor table, immediately adjacent to the Romanesque foundation of Vienna's oldest church, St. Ruprechts. Come here for foaming steins of beer and such Viennese staples as Wiener schnitzel, schnitzel cordon bleu, baked eggplant layered with ham and cheese, and grilled lamb cutlets.

Coffeehouses & Cafes

Café Central 🌟, Herrengasse 14 (© **01/5333764**; U-Bahn: Herrengasse), stands in the center of Vienna across from the Hofburg and the Spanish Riding School. This grand cafe offers a glimpse into 19th-century Viennese life–it was once the center of Austria's literati. Even Lenin is said to have met his colleagues here. The Central offers a variety of Viennese coffees, a vast selection of pastries and desserts, and Viennese and provincial dishes. It's a delightful spot for lunch. The cafe is open Monday through Saturday from 8am to 10pm, Sunday 10am to 6pm.

The windows of the venerated **Café Demel** 🌟🌟, Kohlmarkt 14 (© **01/5351717**; U-Bahn: Herrengasse; Bus: 1A or 2A), are filled with fanciful spun-sugar creations of characters from folk legends. Inside you'll find a splendidly baroque landmark where dozens of pastries are available daily, including the *Pralinen,* Senegal, truffle, *Sand,* and *Maximilian* tortes, as well as *Gugelhupfs* (cream-filled horns). Demel also serves a mammoth variety of tea sandwiches made with smoked salmon, egg salad, caviar, or shrimp. If you want to be traditional, ask for a Demel-Coffee, which is filtered coffee served with milk, cream, or whipped cream. It's open daily from 10am to 7pm.

Café Diglas, Wollzeile 10 (© **01/5125765**; U-Bahn: Stubentor), evokes prewar Vienna better than many of its competitors, thanks to a decor that retains some of the accessories from 1934, when it first opened. The cafe prides itself on its long association with composer Franz Léhar. It offers everything in the way of run-of-the-mill caffeine fixes, as well as more elaborate, liqueur-enriched concoctions such as a Biedermeier (with apricot schnapps and cream). If you're hungry, ask for a menu (foremost among the platters is an excellent Wiener schnitzel). The cafe is open daily from 7am to midnight.

Café Dommayer, Dommayergasse 1 (© **01/8775465**; U-Bahn: Schönbrunn), boasts a reputation for courtliness that goes back to 1787. In 1844, Johann Strauss, Jr., made his musical debut here, and beginning in 1924, the site became known as *the* place in Vienna for tea dancing. During clement weather, a garden with seats for 300 opens in back. The rest of the year, the venue is restricted to a high-ceilinged black-and-white old-world room. Every Saturday from 2 to 4pm, a pianist and violinist perform; and every third Saturday, an all-woman orchestra plays mostly Strauss. Most patrons come for coffee, tea, and pastries, but if you have a more substantial appetite, try the platters of food, including Wiener schnitzel, *Rostbraten,* and fish. It's open daily from 7am to midnight.

Even the Viennese debate the age of **Café Frauenhuber,** Himmelpfortgasse 6 (© **01/5128383**; U-Bahn: Stephansplatz). But regardless of whether 1788 or 1824 is correct, it has a justifiable claim to being the oldest continuously operating coffeehouse in the city. The old-time decor is a bit battered and more than a bit smoke-stained. Wiener schnitzel, served with potato salad and greens, is a good bet, as are any of the ice cream dishes and pastries. It's open daily from 8am to 11pm.

Housed in the deluxe Hotel Imperial, **Café Imperial** ⓕ, Kärntner Ring 16 (© **01/50110389;** U-Bahn: Karlsplatz), was a favorite of Gustav Mahler and a host of other celebrities. The "Imperial Toast" is a small meal in itself: white bread with veal, chicken, and leaf spinach topped with a gratin, baked in an oven, and served with hollandaise sauce. A daily breakfast/brunch buffet for 35€ ($46) is served Habsburg-style on Sunday from 7am to 11pm. It's said to be the only hotel buffet breakfast in Vienna that comes with champagne. The cafe is open daily from 7am to 11pm.

One of the Ring's great coffeehouses, **Café Landtmann** ⓕ, Dr.-Karl-Lueger-Ring 4 (© **01/241000;** tram: 1, 2, or D), has a history dating to the 1880s and has long drawn a mix of politicians, journalists, and actors. It was also Freud's favorite. The original chandeliers and the prewar chairs have been refurbished. We highly suggest spending an hour or so here, perusing the newspapers, sipping on coffee, or planning the day's itinerary. The cafe is open daily from 7:30am to midnight (lunch is served 11:30am to 3pm and dinner is served 5 to 11pm).

Part of the success of **Café Sperl,** Gumpendorferstrasse 11 (© **01/5864158;** U-Bahn: Karlsplatz), derives from the fact that the Gilded Age panels and accessories that were installed in 1880 are still in place. These details also contributed to Sperl's designation in 1998 as "Austria's best coffeehouse of the year." If you opt for a black coffee, you'll be in good company. Platters include salads; toast; baked noodles with ham, mushrooms, and cream sauce; omelets; steaks; and Wiener schnitzels. The staff evokes a bemused kind of courtliness, but in a concession to modern tastes, there's a billiard table and some dartboards on the premises. It's open Monday through Saturday 7am to 11pm and Sunday 11am to 8pm (closed Sunday July to August).

Café Tirolerhof, Fürichgasse 8 (© **01/5127833;** U-Bahn: Stephansplatz or Karlsplatz), which has been under the same management for decades, makes for a convenient sightseeing break, particularly from a tour of the nearby Hofburg complex. One coffee specialty is the Maria Theresia, a large cup of mocha flavored with apricot liqueur and topped with whipped cream. If coffee sounds too hot, try the tasty milkshakes. You can also order a Viennese breakfast of coffee, tea, hot chocolate, two Viennese rolls, butter, jam, and honey. It's open daily 7am to midnight.

Thirty kinds of tea are served at **Demmers Teehaus,** Mölker Bastei 5 (© **01/5335995;** U-Bahn: Schottentor), along with dozens of pastries, cakes, toasts, and English sandwiches. Demmer's is managed by the previously recommended restaurant, Buffet Trzésniewski; however, the teahouse offers you a chance to sit down, relax, and enjoy your drink or snack. It's open Monday to Friday from 10am to 6:30pm.

Impressions

What if the Turks had taken Vienna, as they nearly did, and advanced west-ward? . . . Martial spoils apart, the great contest has left little trace. It was the beginning of coffee-drinking in the West, or so the Viennese maintain. The ear-liest coffeehouses, they insist, were kept by some of the Sultan's Greek and Ser-bian subjects who had sought sanctuary in Vienna. But the rolls which the Viennese dipped in the new drink were modeled on the half-moons of the Sul-tan's flag. The shape caught on all over the world. They mark the end of the age-old struggle between the hot-cross-bun and the croissant.

—Patrick Leigh Fermor, A Time of Gifts, 1977

Seitenstettengasse 3 or Ruprechtsplatz 4–5. ℭ 015338371. Reservations recommended. Main courses 7€–13€ ($9.10–$17). MC, V. Mon–Thurs 11am–2am; Fri–Sun 11am–4am. U-Bahn: Schwedenplatz.

Zwölf-Apostelkeller VIENNESE   For those seeking a taste of old Vienna, this is the place. Sections of this wine tavern's walls predate 1561. Rows of wooden tables stand under vaulted ceilings, with lighting partially provided by streetlights set into the masonry floor. It's so deep that you feel you're entering a dungeon. Students love this place for its low prices and proximity to St. Stephan's. In addition to beer and wine, you can get hearty Austrian fare. Specialties include Hungarian goulash soup, meat dumplings, and a *schlachtplatte* (a selection of hot black pudding, liverwurst, pork, and pork sausage with a hot bacon and cabbage salad). The cooking is hardly refined, but it's very well prepared.

Sonnenfelsgasse 3. ℭ 01/5126777. Main courses 5€–10€ ($6.50–$13). AE, DC, MC, V. Daily 4:30pm–midnight. Closed July. U-Bahn: Stephansplatz. Tram: 1, 2, 21, D, or N. Bus: 1A.

3 Leopoldstadt (2nd District)

EXPENSIVE

Vincent ✿ CONTINENTAL   The decor of this restaurant is smooth and cozy, and guests can opt for a seat in three different dining rooms, any of which might remind you of a richly upholstered, carefully decorated private home that's accented with flickering candles, flowers, and crystal. The menu here changes with the season and the whim of the chef. Food here is elegant, upscale, and served in convivial surroundings. The finest examples include a well-prepared rack of lamb flavored with bacon, whitefish or pikeperch in white-wine sauce, turbot with saffron sauce, filet of butter-fish with tiger prawns served with a consommé of shrimp, and, in season, many different game dishes, including quail and venison.

Grosse-Pfarrgasse 7. ℭ 01/2141516. Reservations required. Main courses 18€–29€ ($23–$38). AE, DC, MC, V. Mon–Sat 5pm–1am. U-Bahn: Schwedenplatz.

INEXPENSIVE

Altes Jägerhaus ✿ AUSTRIAN/GAME   Little about the decor here has changed since this place opened in 1899. Located 1.5km (1 mile) from the entrance to the Prater in a verdant park, it's a welcome escape from the more crowded restaurants of the Inner City. Grab a seat in any of the four old-fashioned dining rooms, where the beverage of choice is equally divided between beer and wine. Seasonal game like pheasant and venison are the house specialty, but you'll also find an array of seafood dishes that might include freshwater and saltwater trout, zander, or salmon. The menu also features a delicious repertoire of Austrian staples such as *tafelspitz* and schnitzel.

Freudenau 255. © **01/72895770.** Reservations recommended. Main courses 7€–18€ ($9.10–$23). AE, DC, MC, V. Daily 9am–11pm. U-Bahn: Schlachthausgasse, then bus 77A.

4 Landstrasse (3rd District)

VERY EXPENSIVE

Steirereck ✶✶✶ AUSTRIAN/VIENNESE *Steirereck* means "corner of Styria," which is exactly what Heinz and Birgit Reitbauer have created in this intimate and rustic restaurant. Traditional Viennese dishes and "new Austrian" selections appear on the menu. Begin with a caviar-semolina dumpling or roasted turbot with fennel (served as an appetizer), or opt for the most elegant and expensive item of all, goose-liver Steirereck. Some enticing main courses include asparagus with pigeon, saddle of lamb for two, prime Styrian roast beef, and red-pepper risotto with rabbit. The menu is wisely limited and well prepared, changing daily depending on what's fresh at the market. The restaurant is popular with after-theater diners, and the large wine cellar holds some 35,000 bottles.

Am Heumarkt 2A. © **01/7133168.** Reservations required. Main courses 15€–25€ ($20–$33); 4-course fixed-price lunch 45€ ($59); 5-course fixed-price dinner 95€ ($124). AE, DC, MC, V. Mon–Fri noon–3pm and 7–11pm. Closed holidays. Tram: N. Bus: 4.

EXPENSIVE

Niky's Kuchlmasterei ✶ INTERNATIONAL/VIENNESE The decor features old stonework with some modern architectural innovations, and the extensive menu boasts well-prepared food. The lively crowd of loyal habitués adds to the welcoming ambience, making Niky's a good choice for an evening meal, especially in summer when you can dine on its unforgettable terrace. After a long and pleasant meal, your bill will arrive in an elaborate box suitable for jewels, along with an amusing message in German that offers a tongue-in-cheek apology for cashing your check.

Obere Weissgerberstrasse 6. © **01/7129000.** Reservations recommended. Main courses 17€–36€ ($21–$47); 3-course fixed-price lunch 30€ ($39); 7-course fixed-price dinner 51€ ($66). AE, DC, MC, V. Mon–Sat noon–midnight. U-Bahn: Schwedenplatz.

INEXPENSIVE

Café-Restaurant Kunsthaus AUSTRIAN/INTERNATIONAL Come here for the visuals and the artsy, chit-chatting crowd, which spills over into the garden summer, but don't expect anything terribly innovative in the cuisine.

This restaurant was designed by one of the most distinctive architects in Austrian history, the late Friedensreich Hundertwasser, as a whimsical, tongue-in-cheek answer

---

Kids Family-Friendly Dining

- **Gulaschmuseum (p. 95)** If your kids think ordering hamburgers in a foreign country is adventurous eating, this is a great place to introduce them to goulash—it comes in at least 15 delicious varieties. Few youngsters will turn down the homemade apfelstrudel.

to the awesomely portentous collections of the Kunsthaus, the museum that contains it. The cafe occupies the street level of the museum, in a location overlooking a lavish garden through large sliding windows that remain completely open whenever the weather is clement. Hundreds of verdant potted plants, the complete absence of any 90-degree angles, the artful mismatching of chairs, and a defiant lack of symmetry have made the place a hot conversational topic in Vienna. The food, less likely to spark conversation, is competent and well prepared, but much more traditional than the bizarre decor might imply. Standard menu items include roast beef with onions, schnitzels of veal or pork, goulash or potato soup, fried chicken, wursts, and strudels.

In the Kunsthaus, 14 Weissgerberlande. ℂ 01/7120497. Main courses 7.20€–14€ ($9.35–$18). No credit cards. Daily 10am–9pm. U-Bahn: Schwedenplatz. Tram: N to Radetskyplatz.

5 Wieden & Margareten (4th & 5th Districts)

MODERATE

Motto AUSTRIAN/ITALIAN/THAI   This is the premier gay-friendly restaurant of Austria, with a cavernous red-and-black interior, a busy bar, and a clientele that has included many of the glam figures (Thierry Mugler, John Galliano, and lots of theater people) of the international circuit. Even Helmut Lang worked here briefly as a waiter. It's set behind green doors and a sign that's so small and discreet as to be nearly invisible. In summer, it's enhanced with tables set up in a garden. No one will mind if you pop in just to chat, as it's a busy nightlife entity in its own right. But if you're hungry, cuisine is about as eclectic as it gets, ranging from sushi and Thai-inspired curries to *gutbürgerlich* (home and hearth) food like grandma used to make.

Schönbrunnerstrasse 30 (entrance on Rudigergasse). ℂ 01/5870672. Reservations recommended. Main courses 6€–21€ ($7.80–$27). MC, V. Daily 6pm–4am. U-Bahn: Pilgrimgasse.

Silberwirt VIENNESE   Despite the fact that it opened a quarter of a century ago, this restaurant oozes with Old Viennese style and resembles the traditional *beisl* (bistro) with its copious portions of conservative, time-honored Viennese food. You can dine within a pair of dining rooms or move into the beer garden. Menu items include stuffed mushrooms, *tafelspitz*, schnitzels, and filets of zander, salmon, and trout. Be aware that this establishment shares the same building and address as the restaurant Schlossgasse 21 listed above.

Schlossgasse 21. ℂ 01/5444907. Reservations recommended. Main courses 8€–22€ ($10–$29). V. Daily noon–11pm. U-Bahn: Pilgrimgasse.

INEXPENSIVE

Café Cuadro INTERNATIONAL   Trendy, countercultural, and arts-oriented, this café and bistro is little more than a long, glassed-in corridor with vaguely Bauhaus-inspired detailing. There are clusters of industrial-looking tables, but many clients opt for a seat at the long, luncheonette-style counter above a Plexiglas floor with four-sided geometric patterns illuminated from below. In keeping with the establishment's name (Cuadro), the menu features four of everything—salads (including a very good Caesar option), juicy burgers, homemade soups, steak, and—if you're an early riser—breakfasts.

Margaretenstrasse 77. ℂ 01/544-7550. Breakfast 4.50€ ($5.85); main courses 4€–10€ ($5.20–$13). V. Mon–Sat 8am–midnight; Sun 9am–11pm. U-Bahn: Pilgramgasse.

Tips **A Veggie Tale**

The president of the People for the Ethical Treatment of Animals, Ingrid E. Newkirk, informed us that she fared well in Vienna kitchens, long known as a bastion of animal fats. She reported that at the ubiquitous McDonald's, she could always order a veggie burger (a GemuseMac), and even some Gemuse Nuggets. She claimed that most restaurants will go out of their way to please if you simply say what you want. She had particular praise for **Firenze Enoteca** (p. 90), citing the superb pastas, "exquisite" white-bean soup, and a fresh asparagus starter.

Gasthaus Ubl 🛧 *Finds* AUSTRIAN   This is a closely guarded Viennese secret. It's where locals who want to enjoy some of the famous dishes enjoyed by their last great emperor, Franz Josef, go. This is an authentic guesthouse-like atmosphere with an old Viennese stove. Three sisters run it, and the whole place screams Old Vienna—nothing flashy or touristy here. Begin with one of the freshly made salads or soups, then follow with the classics—the best *tafelspitz* in the area or such old favorites as *schweinebraten* (a perfectly roasted pork). Desserts are old-fashioned and yummy. The staff is most welcoming.

Pressgasse 26. ℂ **01/5876437.** Reservations recommended. Main courses: 9€–15€ ($12–$20). AE, DC, MC, V. Daily noon-3pm and 6-10pm. U-Bahn: Karlsplatz. Bus: 59A.

Gergely's AUSTRIAN/INTERNATIONAL   This cozy restaurant is in a turn-of-the-century building, decorated with a pleasant mishmash of old and new furnishings, much like you would find in someone's home. It serves classic Austrian fare as well as some interesting, palate-pleasing Asian dishes, such as Indonesian satay and Chinese stir-fry. An enduring favorite is the tender, well-flavored steak.

Schlossgasse 21. ℂ **01/544-0767.** Reservations recommended. Main courses 8€–20€ ($10–$26). V. Mon-Sat 6pm-2am. U-Bahn: Pilgrimgasse.

6 Mariahilf (6th District)

INEXPENSIVE

Alfi's Goldener Spiegel VIENNESE   By everyone's account, this is the most prominent gay restaurant in Vienna, where a mostly gay clientele enjoys food and ambience that might remind you of a simple Viennese *beisl* in a working-class district. (Many of the young European men you'll see here come with a price tag.) If you do decide to sit down for a meal, expect large portions of traditional Viennese specialties such as Wiener schnitzel, roulade of beef, filet steaks with pepper sauce, and *tafelspitz*. Its position near Vienna's Naschmarkt, the city's biggest food market, ensures that the food served is impeccably fresh.

Linke Wienzeile 46 (entrance on Stiegengasse). ℂ **01/5866608.** Main courses 6.50€–15€ ($8.45–$20). No credit cards. Wed–Mon 7pm–2am. U-Bahn: U4 to Kettenbruckengasse.

Gräfin vom Naschmarkt AUSTRIAN/CONTINENTAL   For night owls, this restaurant is set almost immediately adjacent to Vienna's largest food and vegetable market (the Naschmarkt), behind a facade that's lit up with thousands of whimsically cheerful strands of tiny light bulbs. This all-day, all-night restaurant seems very far removed from the Habsburgundian grandeur of central Vienna, despite the fact that it has been a local institution for the past 125 years. It's famous among those who make it either their business or their hobby to stay out very late at night. An equal-opportunity feeder, it caters to more than just the entertainment industries: Early-morning truckers loading and unloading vegetables at the nearby market sometimes drop in for beer and Wiener schnitzel, sitting more or less amicably next to soggy and perspiration-drenched or beer-soaked insomniacs from the neighborhood's many straight and gay bars. It also does a roaring business from the after-theater crowd at the nearby Theater an der Wien, and by 4am the place is usually packed. Staff tends to be cheerful and philosophical about the role they play in feeding and caring for the needs of Vienna's dark side. The ambience evokes an amicably battered inn whose woodsy decor hasn't changed much since the 1960s, except for a replica of a bare-branched tree, draped with glittering lights, near the bar at the entrance. Menu items are *hausmannskost,* substantial, traditional, and comfort food. Examples include Styr-ian-style chicken salad with pine nuts, bacon-studded dumplings with green salad, pork cutlets with potato salad, and what a local paper (*Kurier*) defined as "Vienna's best *gulaschsuppe.*"

Linke Wienzeile 14. © 01/586-3389. Reservations not necessary. Main courses 6€–29€ ($7.80–$38). No credit cards. 24 hours a day, although service and menu items are reduced as the restaurant is cleaned, every morning between 2 4am. U-Bahn: Karlsplatz or Kettenbrückengasse.

7 Neubau (7th District)

MODERATE

Bohème 🦆 INTERNATIONAL/VIENNESE   This one-time bakery was originally built in 1750 in the baroque style. Today its historic street is an all-pedestrian walk-way loaded with shops. Since opening in 1989, Bohème has attracted a crowd that's knowledgeable about the nuances of wine, food, and the opera music that reverber-ates throughout the two dining rooms. Even the decor is theatrical; it looks like a cross between a severely dignified stage set and an artsy, turn-of-the-19th-century cafe. Menu items are listed as movements in an opera, with overtures (aperitifs), prologues (appe-tizers), and first and second acts (soups and main courses). As you'd guess, desserts provide the finales. Some tempting items include Andalusian gazpacho, platters of mixed fish filets with tomato risotto, *tafelspitz* with horseradish, and vegetarian dishes such as soya schnitzels in sesame sauce.

Spittelberggasse 19. © 01/5233173. Reservations recommended. Main courses 10€–22€ ($13–$29). AE, DC, MC, V. Mon–Sat 6–11:30pm. Closed Jan 7–23. U-Bahn: Volkstheater.

Gasthaus Lux CONTINENTAL   Dark, labyrinthine, and evocative of turn-of-the-20th-century Vienna, this place attracts an artsy crowd that appreciates the flavorful food and conspiratorial atmosphere. Most of the rooms here are richly outfitted with deep red walls and brown, sometimes leather, upholsteries, with dog-eared newspapers lying around. There's also a heated glassed-in area within what used to be an open-air courtyard. The clientele includes the kind of gregarious, arts-conscious souls you might have expected to meet in a German-speaking neighborhood of New York City's Greenwich Village. The menu changes at least every 2 weeks, and might include air-dried venison with cranberry sauce and mushroom dumplings; phyllo pastry stuffed with black pudding and apple chutney; a confit of pumpkins with fried goat cheese and tomato marmalade; smoked trout on a bed of shredded beet root; and medallions of venison with cranberry preserve. Vegetarians appreciate a choice of all-vegetarian risottos, gnocchis, and lasagnas. And "because everyone is interested lately in reminisces from their childhood" (according to the charming manager, Dagmar), there's even a dish that many Viennese remember from their earliest days: rice pudding with mascarpone cheese and rosemary, served with an apple-flavored cream sauce.

Schrankgasse 4 or Spittelberggasse 3. ⓒ 01/526-9491. Reservations recommended. Main courses 8.50€–17€ ($11–$22); 2-course set lunch 5.90€ ($7.65). DC, MC, V. Mon–Fri 11am–2am, Sat–Sun 10am–2am. U-Bahn: Volkstheater.

INEXPENSIVE

Amerlingbeisl AUSTRIAN   The hip clientele, occasionally blasé staff, and minimalist, somewhat industrial-looking decor give Amerlingbeisl a modern sensibility. If you get nostalgic, you can opt for a table out on the cobblestones of the early-19th-century building's glassed-in courtyard, beneath a grape arbor, where horses used to be stabled. Come to this neighborhood spot for simple but good food and a glass of beer or wine. The menu ranges from simple sandwiches and salads to more elaborate fare such as Argentinean steak with rice, turkey or pork schnitzels with potato salad, and dessert crepes stuffed with marmalade.

Stiftgasse 8. ⓒ 01/526-1660. Main courses 5.70€–8.70€ ($7.40–$11). DC, MC, V. Daily 9am–2am. U-Bahn: Volkstheater.

Plutzer Bräu ⓡ *(Finds* AUSTRIAN   This is one of the best examples in Vienna of the explosion of hip and trendy restaurants within the city's 7th district. Maintained by the Plutzer Brewery, it occupies the cavernous cellar of an imposing 19th-century building. Any antique references are quickly lost once you're inside, thanks to an industrial-looking decor with exposed heating ducts, burnished stainless steel, and accessories that might remind you of the cafeteria in a central European factory. You can stay at the long, accommodating bar and drink fresh-brewed Plutzer beer, but if you're hungry (and this very good beer will probably encourage an appetite), head for the well-scrubbed dining room, where the menu reflects Old Viennese traditions. Food is excellent and includes veal stew in beer sauce with dumplings, "brewmaster's-style" pork steak, and pasta with herbs and feta cheese. Dessert might include curd dumplings with poppy seeds and sweet bread crumbs.

Schrankgasse 2. ⓒ 01/5261215. Reservations not necessary. Main courses 7.50€–12€ ($9.75–$16); 2-course fixed-price lunch served daily 11:30am–3pm, 6€ ($7.80). MC, V. Mon–Sat 11am–11:45pm. U-Bahn: Volkstheater.

Siebenstern-Bräu *(Value* AUSTRIAN/VIENNESE   This is the greatest brewpub in town. Relatively new, it's a big, bustling dive with good food, affordable prices, and large portions. Faced with a choice of brews, and seeking guidance, you might enjoy the Prager Dunkle, a Czech-style dry dark lager that's one of Austria's more intriguing brews. For a more Viennese-style lager, order the amber-colored Märzen, the only one of its type brewed in Austria. Oh, yes, the staff serves old-fashioned food as well. You might begin with an *altwiener kartoffelsuppe* (potato soup) and go through the menu, ending with an *apfelstrudel*. Lots of sauerkraut is consumed here daily along with a classic Wiener schnitzel. For something spicier, opt for the spareribs with chile sauce. Vegetarian dishes are also available.

Siebensterngasse 19. ⓒ 01/5232580. Main courses 6€–15€ ($7.80–$20). DC, MC, V. Tues–Sat 10am–1am; Sun–Mon 10am–midnight. U-Bahn: Volkstheater.

> ## *Tips* Picnics & Street Food
>
> Picnickers will find that Vienna is among the best-stocked cities in Europe for food supplies. The best—and least expensive—place is the **Naschmarkt,** an open-air market that's only a 5-minute stroll from Karlsplatz (the nearest U-Bahn stop). Here you'll find hundreds of stalls selling fresh produce, breads, meats, cheeses, flowers, tea, and more. Fast-food counters and other stands peddle ready-made foods such as grilled chicken, Austrian and German sausages, sandwiches, and even beer. The market is open Monday to Friday from 6am to 6:30pm, Saturday from 6am to 1pm. You can also buy your picnic at one of Vienna's many delis, such as **Konditorei Oberlaa,** Neuer Markt 16 (✆ **01/513-2936**), or **Gerstner,** Kärntnerstrasse 15 (✆ **01/5124-9630**).
>
> With your picnic basket in hand, head for Stadtpark or the Volksgarten, both on the famous Ring. Even better, if the weather is right, plan an excursion into the Vienna Woods.
>
> On street corners throughout Vienna, you'll find one of the city's most popular snack spots, the **Würstelstand.** These small stands sell beer and soda, plus frankfurters, bratwurst, curry wurst, and other Austrian sausages, usually served on a roll *mit senf* (with mustard). Try the *käsekrainer,* a fat frankfurter with tasty bits of cheese. Conveniently located stands are on Seilergasse (just off Stephansplatz) and Kupferschmiedgasse (just off Kärntnerstrasse).

8 Josefstadt (8th District)

MODERATE

Alte Backstube HUNGARIAN/VIENNESE   This spot is worth visiting just to admire the baroque sculptures that crown the top of the doorway. The building was originally designed as a private home in 1697, and 4 years later it was transformed into a bakery, complete with wood-burning stoves. For more than 2½ centuries, the establishment served the baking needs of the neighborhood. In 1963, the owners added a dining room, a dainty front room for drinking beer and tea, and a collection of baking-related artifacts. Once seated, you can order such wholesome, robust specialties as braised pork with cabbage, Viennese-style goulash, and roast venison with cranberry sauce and bread dumplings. There's an English-language menu if you need it. Try the house special dessert, cream-cheese strudel with hot vanilla sauce.

Lange Gasse 34. ✆ **01/4061101.** Reservations required. Main courses 10€–18€ ($13–$23). MC, V. Tues–Thurs and Sat–Sun 11am–midnight; Fri 5pm–midnight. Closed mid-July to Aug 30. U-Bahn: Rathaus. Go east along Schmidgasse to Lange Gasse.

Die Fromme Helene ☆ AUSTRIAN   This is the kind of upscale tavern where the food is traditional and excellent, the crowd is animated and creative, and the staff is hip enough to recognize and recall the names of the many actors, writers, and politicians who come here regularly. Part of its theatrical allure derives from a location that's close to several of the city's theaters (including the English Theater), and to prove it, there are signed and framed photographs of many of the quasi-celebrity clients who have eaten and made merry here. Expect a wide range of traditional and well-prepared

Austrian dishes, including schnitzels of both veal and pork, pastas, and a chocolate pudding (whose name translates as "Moor in a Shirt") served with hot chocolate sauce and whipped cream. The establishment's enduring specialty is *Alt Wiener Backfleisch,* a long-marinated and spicy version of steak that's breaded, fried, and served with potato salad. There's a range of pasta and vegetarian dishes as well. The restaurant's name, incidentally, derives from the comic-book creation of a 19th-century illustrator, Wilhelm Busch, whose hard-drinking but well-meaning heroine, "pious Helen," captivated the imagination of the German-speaking world.

15 Josefstädter Strasse. (*C*) 01/4069144. Reservations recommended. Main courses 7€–19€ ($9.10–$25). AE, DC, MC, V. Mon–Sat 11:30am–1am. Tram: J to Theater in der Josefstadt.

Piaristenkeller AUSTRIAN   Erich Emberger has successfully renovated and reassembled this wine tavern with centuries-old vaulted ceilings in a vast cellar room. The place was founded in 1697 by Piarist monks as a tavern and wine cellar. The kitchen, which once served the cloisters, still dishes out traditional Austrian specialties based on original recipes. Zither music is played beginning at 7:30pm, and in summer the garden at the church square is open from 11am to midnight. Wine and beer are available whenever the cellar is open. Advance booking is required for a guided tour of the cloister's old wine vaults. Groups of six or more pay 12€ ($18) per person for the tour.

Piaristengasse 45. (*C*) 01/4059152. Reservations recommended. Main courses 14€–22€ ($18–$29). AE, DC, MC, V. Daily 6pm–midnight. U-Bahn: Rathaus.

Schnattl (*✿* AUSTRIAN   Even the justifiably proud owner of this place, Wilhelm (Willy) Schnattl, dismisses its decor as a mere foil for the presentation of his sublime food. Schnattl is near Town Hall, in a location that's convenient for most of the city's journalists and politicians, and features a cozy bar area and a medium-size dining room, an inviting, intimate green-painted and wood-paneled space of enormous comfort and charm. Menu items show intense attention to detail and—in some cases—a megalomaniacal fervor from a chef whom the press has called a "mad culinary genius." Roasted sweetbreads are served with a purée of green peas; marinated freshwater fish (a species known locally as *Hochen*) comes with a parfait of cucumbers. Wild duck and a purée of celery are perfectly cooked, as is a celebrated parfait of pickled tongue (a terrine of foie gras and a mousse of tongue, blended and wrapped in strips of tongue and served with a toasted corn brioche).

40 Lange Gasse. (*C*) 01/405-3400. Reservations required. Main courses 15€–22€ ($20–$29). AE, DC, MC, V. Mon–Fri 11:30am–3pm and 6–11pm. Closed for 2 weeks at Easter, 2 weeks late Aug. U-Bahn: Rathaus.

9 Alsergrund (9th District)

MODERATE

Abend-Restaurant Feuervogel RUSSIAN   Since World War I, this restaurant has been a Viennese landmark, bringing Russian cuisine to a location across from the palace of the Prince of Liechtenstein. You'll eat in romantically Slavic surroundings with Gypsy violins playing Russian and Viennese music. Specialties include chicken Kiev, beef Stroganoff, veal Dolgoruki, borscht, and many other dishes that taste as if they came right off the steppes. For an hors d'oeuvre try *sakkuska*, a variety platter that's popular in Russia. You can also order a gourmet fixed-price dinner with five courses. Be sure to sample the Russian ice cream known as *plombier*.

ɔachstrasse 21. ℂ **01/3175391.** Reservations recommended. Main courses 11€–16€ ($14–$21); 5-course f..ed-price menu 45€ ($59). AE, DC, MC, V. Mon–Sat 6pm–midnight. Closed July 20–Aug 8. U-Bahn: Friedensbrücke. Bus: 32.

10 Westbahnhof (15th District)

MODERATE

Vikerl's Lokal AUSTRIAN   This cozy tavern has been a neighborhood fixture since before World War II, when it got its name from the nickname of its since-departed founder, Victor. In 1994, its reputation took a soaring turn for the better when Bettina and Adi Bittermann took over and began serving food that was a lot more sophisticated than the simple setting. In two intricately paneled dining rooms, you'll find a menu that changes every 2 weeks. During our visit, it featured a starter of slices from a dish you might not relish as a main course, but which locals consider a delicacy: roasted veal's head. (It's a great introduction to a flavorful dish that might not appeal to many Americans in its earthier form.) Other dishes include carpaccio of venison with horseradish and lentil salad; roasted leg of lamb with fried zucchini slices and roasted potatoes; and imaginative variations of *tafelspitz*. One particularly luscious dish is a thick-sliced calf's liver, served on a bed of crisp-fried tripe prepared with ginger. Chocolate-walnut cake makes a satisfying dessert.

4 Würffelgasse. ℂ **01/894-3430.** Reservations recommended. Main courses 12€–20€ ($16–$26). MC, V. Tues–Sat 5–11pm; Sun 11:30am–4pm. U-Bahn: Westbahnhof, then tram 52 or 58 to Würffelgasse.

11 Near Schönbrunn

EXPENSIVE

Altwienerhof ✦✦✦ AUSTRIAN/FRENCH   A short walk from Schönbrunn Palace lies one of the premier dining spots in Vienna. The building is completely modernized, but it was originally designed as a private home in the 1870s. Mr. Günter brings sophistication and charm to the dining rooms, which retain many Biedermeier embellishments from the original construction. The chef prepares nouvelle cuisine using only the freshest and highest-quality ingredients. The menu changes frequently, and the maître d' is always willing to assist with recommendations. Each night the chef prepares a tasting menu, which is a sampling of the kitchen's best nightly dishes. The wine list consists of more than 700 selections, each of which is chosen by Mr. Günter himself. The cellar below houses about 18,000 bottles.

In the Altwienerhof Hotel, Herklotzgasse 6. ℂ **01/8926000.** Reservations recommended. Main courses 12€–21€ ($15–$27). AE, DC, MC, V. Mon–Sat 5–11pm. Closed first 3 weeks in Jan. U-Bahn: Gumpendorferstrasse.

MODERATE

Hietzinger Brau AUSTRIAN   Established in 1743, this is the most famous and best-recommended restaurant in the vicinity of Schönbrunn Palace. Everything about it evokes a sense of bourgeois stability—wood paneling, a staff wearing folkloric costume, and platters heaped high with *gutbürgerlich* cuisine. The menu lists more than a dozen preparations of beef, including the time-tested favorite, *tafelspitz*, as well as mixed grills, all kinds of steaks, and fish that includes lobster, salmon, crab, and zander. Homage to the cuisine of Franz Josef appears in the form of very large Wiener schnitzels, a creamy goulash, and even a very old-fashioned form of braised calf's head. Wine is available, but by far the most popular beverage here is a foaming stein of the local brew, Hietzinger.

Auhofstrasse 1. ℂ **01/87770870.** Reservations not necessary. Main courses 13€–23€ ($17–$30). DC, MC, V. Daily 11:30am–3pm and 6–11:30pm. U-Bahn: Hietzing.

12 In the Outer Districts

INEXPENSIVE

Blaustern CONTINENTAL   It's well managed, hip, and stylish, but because of its location in Vienna's outlying 19th District, Blaustern almost exclusively attracts local residents. The Sunday-morning breakfast crowd might include local celebrity and race-car champ Niki Lauda. Expect bacon and eggs, light fare such as pastas and salads, and daily specials that include braised scampi with vegetable beignets and avocado sauce. The name comes from the *blau stern* (blue star) that used to adorn sacks of coffee imported from South America by the restaurant's owners.

Döblinger Gürtel 2. ℂ **01/369-6564.** Main courses 7.50€–12€ ($9.75–$16). No credit cards. Daily 7am–1am. U-Bahn: Nussdorfer Strasse.

13 On the Outskirts

VERY EXPENSIVE

Restaurant Taubenkobel ✿ INTERNATIONAL   This increasingly well-known restaurant lies beside the main street of the hamlet of Schützen, about 25 miles southeast of Vienna. In a 200-year-old *maison bourgeoise* with a quintet of tastefully rustic dining rooms, self-taught chef and owner Wazlter Eselböck (Austrian Chef of the Year in 1995) prepares artful, idiosyncratic cuisine.

The menu items change according to the season and Eselböck's whim. Expect a meal that's more sophisticated and upscale than anything else in the region. Dishes might include a salad of marinated salmon trout and eel, Asian-style corn soup with sweetwater crab, and Austrian Angus steak served with mushrooms and butter-enriched mashed potatoes with fresh truffles.

Hauptstrasse 33, Schützen. ℂ **02684/2297.** Reservations recommended. Set menus 78€–88€ ($101–$114). AE, DC, MC, V. Wed–Fri 6–10pm, Sat–Sun noon–1pm. From Vienna, take the A-2 highway, then the A-3 highway, heading south. Exit at the signs for Schützen.

6

Exploring Vienna

"**A**sia begins at Landstrasse," Austria's renowned statesman Prince von Metternich said, suggesting the power and influence of the far-flung Austrian Empire, whose destiny the Habsburg dynasty controlled from 1273 to 1918.

Viennese prosperity under the Habsburgs reached its peak during the long reign of Maria Theresa in the late 18th century. Many of the sights described below originated under the great empress who escorted Vienna through the Age of Enlightenment. She welcomed Mozart, the child prodigy, to her court at Schönbrunn when he was just 6 years old.

With the collapse of the Napoleonic Empire, Vienna took over Paris's long-held position as "the center of Europe." At the Congress of Vienna (1814–15), the crowned heads of Europe met to restructure the continent's political boundaries. But they devoted so much time to galas that Prince de Ligne remarked, "The Congress doesn't make progress, it dances."

In this chapter we'll explore the many sights of Vienna. It's possible to spend a week here and only scratch the surface of this multifaceted city. We'll take you through the highlights, but even this venture will take more than a week of fast-paced walking.

1 The Hofburg Palace Complex ★★★

Once the winter palace of the Habsburgs, the vast and impressive **Hofburg** sits in the heart of Vienna. To reach it (you can hardly miss it), head up Kohlmarkt to Michaelerplatz 1, Burgring (© **01/587-5554** for general information), where you'll stumble across two enormous fountains embellished with statuary. You can also take the U-Bahn to Stephansplatz, Herrengasse, or Mariahilferstrasse, or Tram nos. 1, 2, D, or J to Burgring.

This complex of imperial edifices, the first of which was constructed in 1279, grew with the empire, and today the palace is virtually a city within a city. The earliest parts surround a courtyard, the **Swiss Court,** named for the Swiss mercenaries who performed guard duty here. The Hofburg's styles, which are not always harmonious, result from each emperor's opting to add to or take away some of the work done by his or her predecessors. Called simply *die Burg,* or "the Palace," by the Viennese, the Hofburg has withstood three major sieges and a great fire. Of its more than 2,600 rooms, fewer than two dozen are open to the public.

Albertina ★ This Hofburg museum, named for a son-in-law of Maria Theresa, explores the development of graphic arts since the 14th century. It houses one of the world's greatest graphics collections. Dürer's *Hare* and *Clasped Hands,* which the Albertina has owned for centuries, are two of the most frequently reproduced works in the world. Among the Albertina's 60,000 drawings and one million prints, the children's

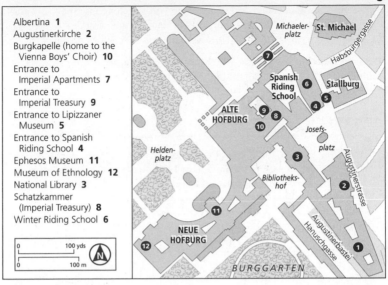

Albertina **1**
Augustinerkirche **2**
Burgkapelle (home to the
   Vienna Boys' Choir) **10**
Entrance to
   Imperial Apartments **7**
Entrance to
   Imperial Treasury **9**
Entrance to Lipizzaner
   Museum **5**
Entrance to Spanish
   Riding School **4**
Ephesos Museum **11**
Museum of Ethnology **12**
National Library **3**
Schatzkammer
   (Imperial Treasury) **8**
Winter Riding School **6**

studies of Rubens as well as the masterpieces of Schiele, Cézanne, Klimt, Kokoschka, Picasso, and Rauschenberg are among the best known. Located in the center of Vienna, the former Habsburg residence is one of the most beautiful classical palaces in the world. The Albertina's state apartments are among the most valuable examples of classical architecture. Visitors who remember the old Albertina are often surprised at the $110-million overhaul. Today there are three airy new galleries on four floors constructed into a former city wall.

Albertinaplatz. ✆ **01/534830.** www.albertina.at. Admission 10€ ($13) adults, 7.50€ ($9.75) students, free for children under 6. Thurs–Tues 10am–6pm; Wed 10am–9pm.

Augustinerkirche (Church of the Augustinians) ✿

This 14th-century church was built within the Hofburg complex to serve as the parish church for the imperial court. In the latter part of the 18th century, it was stripped of its baroque embellishments and returned to the original Gothic features. The Chapel of St. George, dating from 1337, is entered from the right aisle. The **Tomb of Maria Christina** ✿, the favorite daughter of Maria Theresa, is housed in the main nave near the rear entrance, but there's no body in it. (The princess was actually buried in the Imperial Crypt, described later in this section.) This richly ornamented empty tomb is one of Canova's masterpieces. A small room in the Loreto Chapel is filled with urns containing the hearts of the imperial Habsburg family. They can be viewed through a window in an iron door. The Chapel of St. George and the Loreto Chapel are open to the public by prearranged guided tour.

Not everything in the church belongs to the macabre. Maria Theresa married François of Lorraine here in 1736, and the Augustinerkirche was also the site of other royal weddings: Marie Antoinette to Louis XVI of France in 1770, Marie-Louise of Austria to Napoleon in 1810 (by proxy—he didn't show up), and Franz Joseph to Elisabeth of Bavaria in 1854.

The most convenient and dramatic time to visit the church is on Sunday at 11am, when a high Mass is accompanied by a choir, soloists, and an orchestra.

Augustinerstrasse 3. ℭ 01/533-70-99. Free admission. Daily 6:30am–6pm. U-Bahn: Stephansplatz.

Die Burgkapelle (Home of the Vienna Boys' Choir)   Construction of this Gothic chapel began in 1447 during the reign of Emperor Frederick III, but it was

The Singing Ambassadors

The Vienna Boys' Choir is one of the oldest boys choirs in the world, and has been a symbol of Austria for more than 5 centuries. In 1498, Emperor Maximilian I, who was a great supporter of the arts, especially music, moved his court orchestra from Innsbruck to Vienna and added a dozen choirboys to the new musical group. At first, their primary task was to participate in the Mass at the Imperial Chapel of Hofburg Palace every Sunday. Since that time, the Vienna Boys' Choir has occupied a prominent position in Austrian musical life. Its first-class training has produced many highly qualified vocalists, violinists, and pianists. A number of famous composers also have emerged from its ranks.

Joseph Haydn, a member of the Cathedral Choir of St. Stephan's, sang with the court choirboys in the chapel of the Hofburg and in the newly built palace of Schönbrunn. **Franz Schubert** wrote his first compositions as a member of the Court Choir Boys. He was always in trouble with his teachers because he was more interested in composing and making music than in getting good grades. After Schubert's voice lost its alto quality in 1812, he had to leave the choir. At his departure, he noted on a musical score, which is now in Austria's National Library: *F. Schubert, zum letzten Mal gekräht* (F. Schubert has crowed for the last time).

Great composers and teachers, such as Johann Joseph Fux, Antonio Salieri, and Joseph and Michael Haydn, greatly contributed to the musical quality of the Vienna Boys' Choir. As court organist, **Anton Bruckner** also rehearsed his own Masses with the choir. If a performance went particularly well, it was his custom to reward the boys with cake.

With the end of the monarchy in 1918, the choir changed its name and relinquished the imperial uniform (complete with swords) in favor of sailor suits. As early as 1924, the Vienna Boys' Choir, now consisting of four separate choirs, was performing in most of the world's famous concert halls. In the days of the First Republic, between 1918 and 1938, they acquired the sobriquet "Austria's singing ambassadors." Since that time, the Vienna Boys' Choir has performed with some of the world's best orchestras and nearly all the great conductors: Claudio Abbado, Leonard Bernstein, Herbert von Karajan, Carlos Kleiber, Lorin Maazel, Riccardo Muti, and Sir Georg Solti. The choir has also made numerous recordings and participated in many opera and film productions. And, continuing a tradition that dates to 1498, the Vienna Boys' Choir performs every Sunday during the solemn Mass in Vienna's Imperial Chapel.

later massively renovated. Today, the Burgkapelle hosts the **Hofmusikkapelle** ⭐⭐, an ensemble of the Vienna Boys' Choir and members of the Vienna State Opera chorus and orchestra, which performs works by classical and modern composers. Written applications for reserved seats should be sent at least 8 weeks in advance. Use a credit card; do not send cash or checks. For reservations, write to Verwaltung der Hofmusikkapelle, Hofburg, A-1010 Vienna. If you failed to reserve in advance, you might be lucky enough to secure tickets from a block sold at the Burgkapelle box office every Friday from 11am to 1pm or 3 to 5pm, plus Sunday from 8:15 to 8:45am. The line starts forming at least half an hour before that. If you're willing to settle for standing room, it's free.

Hofburg (entrance on Schweizerhof). ⓒ **01/533-9927**. Mass: Seats and concerts 5€–29€ ($6.50–$38); standing room free. Masses (performances) held only Jan–June and mid-Sept to Dec, Sun and holidays 9:15am. Concerts May–June and Sept–Oct Fri 4pm.

Kaiserappartements (Imperial Apartments) ⭐⭐   The Kaiserappartements, on the first floor, are where the emperors and their wives and children lived. To reach the apartments, enter through the rotunda of Michaelerplatz. The apartments are richly decorated with tapestries, many from Aubusson in France. Unfortunately, you can't visit the quarters once occupied by Empress Maria Theresa and now used by the president of Austria. The court tableware and silver are outrageously ornate, reflecting the pomp and splendor of a bygone era. The **Imperial Silver and Porcelain Collection,** from the Habsburg household of the 18th and 19th centuries, provides a window into court etiquette.

The Imperial Apartments seem to be most closely associated with the long reign of Franz Joseph. A famous portrait of his beautiful wife, Elisabeth of Bavaria (Sissi), hangs in the apartments. You'll see the "iron bed" of Franz Joseph, who claimed he slept like his own soldiers. (Maybe that explains why his wife spent so much time traveling.) The Sissi Museum opened in 2004 with six rooms devoted to the life and complex personality of this famous, tragic empress.

Michaeler Platz 1 (inside the Ring, about a 7-min. walk from Stephansplatz; entrance via the Kasertor in the Inneren Burghof). ⓒ **01/533-7570**. www.hofburg-wien.at. Admission 9€ ($12) adults, 7€ ($9.10) students under 25, 4.50€ ($5.85) children 6–15, free for children 5 and under. Daily 9am–5pm. U-Bahn: U1 or U3 to Stephansplatz. Tram: 1, 2, 3, or J to Burgring.

Lipizzaner Museum   The latest attraction at Hofburg Palace is this museum near the stables of the famous white stallions. This permanent exhibition begins with the historic inception of the Spanish Riding School in the 16th century and extends to the stallions' near destruction in the closing weeks of World War II. Paintings, historic engravings, drawings, photographs, uniforms, bridles, and video and film presentations bring to life the history of the Spanish Riding School, offering an insight into the breeding and training of the champion horses. Visitors to the museum are also able to see through a window into the stallions' stables while they are being fed and saddled.

Reitschulgasse 2, Stallburg. ⓒ **01/525-24583**. www.lipizzaner.at. Admission 5€ ($6.50) adults, 3.60€ ($4.70) children. Daily 9am–6pm. U-Bahn: Stephansplatz.

Neue Hofburg   The most recent addition to the Hofburg complex is the Neue Hofburg, or New Château. Construction was started in 1881 and continued through 1913. The palace was the residence of Archduke Franz Ferdinand, the nephew and heir apparent of Franz Joseph, whose assassination at Sarajevo by Serbian nationalists set off the chain of events that led to World War I.

The arms and armor collection, second only to that of the Metropolitan Museum of Art in New York, is in the **Hofjagd und Rüstkammer** ⭐⭐, on the second floor of

Sissi—Eternal Beauty

Empress Elisabeth of Austria (1837–98), affectionately known to her subjects as Sissi, is remembered as one of history's most tragic and fascinating women. An "empress against her will," she was at once a fairytale princess and a liberated woman. It's not surprising that she has frequently been compared to Britain's Princess Diana—both were elegant women, dedicated to social causes, who suffered through unhappy marriages and won a special place in the hearts of their subjects.

Elisabeth was born in Munich on Christmas Day 1837. She grew up away from the ceremony of court and developed an unconventional, freedom-loving spirit. When Emperor Franz Joseph of Austria met the 15-year-old, he fell in love at once. Franz Joseph and Elisabeth were married on April 24, 1854, in Vienna.

With her beauty and natural grace, Elisabeth soon charmed the public, but in her private life, she had serious problems. Living under a strict court regime and her domineering aunt and mother-in-law, the Grand Duchess Sophie, she felt constrained and unhappy. She saw little of her husband—"I wish he were not emperor," she once declared.

She was liberal and forward-minded, and in the nationality conflict with Hungary, she was decisively for the Hungarians. The respect and affection with which she was regarded in Hungary has lasted until the present day.

Personal blows left heavy marks on Sissi's life. The most terrible tragedy was the death of her son, Rudolf, in 1889. From that time on, she dressed only in black and stayed away from the pomp and ceremony of the Viennese court.

On September 10, 1898, as she was walking along the promenade by Lake Geneva, a 24-year-old anarchist stabbed her to death. To the assassin, Elisabeth represented the monarchic order that he despised; he was unaware that Elisabeth's contempt for the monarchy, which she considered a "ruin," matched his own.

Even a century after her death, Sissi's hold on the popular imagination remains undiminished. A TV series about her life achieved unprecedented popularity, and the musical *Elisabeth* has run for years in Vienna.

the Neue Hofburg. On display are crossbows, swords, helmets, pistols, and other armor, mostly the property of Habsburg emperors and princes. Some of the items, such as scimitars, were captured from the Turks as they fled their unsuccessful siege of Vienna. Of bizarre interest is the armor worn by the young (and small) Habsburg princes.

The **Sammlung alter Musikinstrumente** ✸ (✆ 01/52524, ext. 471), is devoted to old musical instruments, mainly from the 17th and 18th centuries, but some from the 16th century. Some of these instruments, especially among the pianos and harpsichords, were played by Brahms, Schubert, Mahler, Beethoven, and Austrian emperors who fancied themselves as having an ear for music.

In the **Ephesos-Museum (Museum of Ephesian Sculpture),** with an entrance behind the Prince Eugene monument, you'll see high-quality finds from Ephesus in Turkey and the Greek island of Samothrace. Here the prize exhibit is the Parthian monument, the most important relief frieze from Roman times ever found in Asia Minor. It was erected to celebrate Rome's victory in the Parthian wars (A.D. 161–65).

Visit the **Museum für Völkerkunde (Museum of Ethnology)** for no other reason than to see the only original Aztec feather headdress in the world. Also on display are Benin bronzes, Cook's collections of Polynesian art, and Indonesian, African, Eskimo, and pre-Columbian exhibits.

Heldenplatz. ⓒ 01/525-24-484. Admission for each museum 8€ ($10) adults, 2€ ($2.60) for children. Wed–Mon 10am–6pm.

Österreichische Nationalbibliothek (Austrian National Library)   The royal library of the Habsburgs dates from the 14th century, and the library building, developed on the premises of the court from 1723 on, is still expanding to the Neue Hofburg. The **Great Hall** ✦✦ of the present-day library was ordered by Karl VI and designed by those masters of the baroque, the von Erlachs. The complete collection of Prince Eugene of Savoy is the core of the precious holdings. With its manuscripts, rare autographs, globes, maps, and other historic memorabilia, this is among the finest libraries in the world.

Josefsplatz 1. ⓒ 01/5341-0202. www.onb.ac.at. Admission 1.45€ ($1.90) for all. July–Sept Mon–Fri 9am–4pm, Sat 9am–12:45pm; Oct–June Mon–Fri 9am–9pm, Sat 9am–12:45pm.

Schatzkammer (Imperial Treasury) ✦✦✦   Reached by a staircase from the Swiss Court, the Schatzkammer is the greatest treasury in the world. It's divided into two sections: the Imperial Profane and the Sacerdotal Treasuries. The first displays the crown jewels and an assortment of imperial riches, while the other contains ecclesiastical treasures.

The most outstanding exhibit in the Schatzkammer is the imperial crown, which dates from 962. It's so big that, though padded, it probably slipped down over the ears of many a Habsburg at his coronation. Studded with emeralds, sapphires, diamonds, and rubies, this 1,000-year-old symbol of sovereignty is a priceless treasure, a fact recognized by Adolf Hitler, who had it taken to Nürnberg in 1938 (the American army returned it to Vienna after World War II). Be sure to have a look at the coronation robes of the imperial family, some of which date from the 12th century.

You can also view the 9th-century saber of Charlemagne and the 8th-century holy lance. The latter, a sacred emblem of imperial authority, was thought in medieval times to be the weapon that pierced the side of Christ on the cross. Among the great Schatzkammer prizes is the Burgundian Treasure. Seized in the 15th century, it's rich in vestments, oil paintings, and gems. Highlighting this collection of loot are artifacts connected with the Order of the Golden Fleece, the romantic medieval order of chivalry.

Hofburg, Schweizerhof. ⓒ 01/525-240. www.khm.at. Admission 8€ ($10) adults, 2€ ($2.60) children 10–18, 6€ ($7.80) seniors and students, free for children under 6. Wed–Mon 10am–6pm.

Spanische Reitschule (Spanish Riding School) ✦   This riding school is a reminder that horses were an important part of everyday Vienna life for many centuries, particularly during the imperial heyday. The school is housed in a white, crystal-chandeliered ballroom in an 18th-century building. You'll marvel at the skill and beauty of the sleek Lipizzaner stallions as their adept trainers put them through their paces in a show that hasn't changed for 4 centuries. These are the world's most famous

classically styled equine performers. To watch the Lipizzaners prance to the music of Johann Strauss or a Chopin polonaise in their home setting is a pleasure you shouldn't miss.

Reservations for performances must be made in advance, as early as possible. Order your tickets for the Sunday and Wednesday shows by writing to Spanische Reitschule, Hofburg, A-1010 Vienna (fax 01/533-903-240), or through a travel agency in Vienna. (Tickets for Sat shows can be ordered only through a travel agency.) Tickets for training sessions with no advance reservations can be purchased at the entrance.

Michaelerplatz 1, Hofburg. ☎ 01/533-9032. www.srs.at. Regular performances 40€–160€ ($52–$208) seats, 25€ ($33) standing room. Classical art of riding with music 12€ ($16) adults, 5€ ($6.50) children 3–6 with an adult; children under age 3 not admitted. Regular shows Mar–June, Sept–Oct, and Dec, most Sun 11am and some Fri 6pm. Classical dressage with music performances Apr–June and Sept, Tues–Sat 10am–noon.

2 The MuseumsQuartier Complex ★★★

The giant modern art complex **MuseumsQuartier** (www.mqw.at; U-Bahn: Museums-Quartier) opened in 2001. Art critics proclaimed that the assemblage of art installed in former Habsburg stables tipped the city's cultural center of gravity from Habsburgian pomp into the new millennium. One of the 10 largest cultural complexes in the world, it is like combining New York's Guggenheim Museum, Museum of Modern Art, and Brooklyn Academy of Music, plus a children's museum, an architecture and design center, theaters, art galleries, video workshops, and much more. There's even an ecology center, architecture museum, and, yes, a tobacco museum.

Kunsthalle Wien ★   This is a showcase for cutting-edge contemporary and classic modern art. You'll find works by everyone from Picasso, Joán Miró, and Jackson Pollock to Paul Klee, Andy Warhol, and, surprise, Yoko Ono. From expressionism to cubism, exhibits reveal the major movements in contemporary art since the mid-20th century. Exploring the five floors takes 1 to 2 hours, depending on what interests you.

Museumsplatz 1. ☎ 01/521-89-33. Admission 11€ ($14) adults, 8.50€ ($11) seniors, students, and children 6–18. Fri–Wed 10am–7pm; Thurs 10am–10pm.

Leopold Museum ★★   This extensive collection of Austrian art includes the world's largest treasure trove of the works of Egon Schiele (1890–1918), who was once forgotten in art history but now stands alongside van Gogh and Modigliani in the ranks of great doomed artists. The Leopold's collection includes more than 2,500 Schiele drawings and watercolors and 330 oil canvases. Other Austrian modernist masterpieces include paintings by Oskar Kokoschka, the great Gustav Klimt, Anton Romaki, and Richard Gerstl. Major statements in Arts and Crafts from the late 19th

---

Impressions

The weight of the imperial past is a burden felt by millions of Viennese; how to bear it gracefully is a question that never quite seems to go away. A group of architects, curators, conservators, and cultural impresarios have attempted to find an answer in an ambitious new arts and performance complex called the MuseumsQuartier, known affectionately as the MQ. Weaving past and present together in a seamless and thought-provoking whole, it may just be the most "Viennese" edifice ever built.

—Author and historian Daniel Mendelsohn, 2001

and 20th centuries include works by Josef Hoffmann, Kolo Moser, Adolf Loos, and Franz Hagenauer.

Museumsplatz 1. © 01/525-700. Admission 9€ ($12) adults, 6€ ($7.80) students and children over 7. Daily 10am–7pm, Thurs 10am–9pm, closed Tues.

MUMOK (Museum of Modern Art Ludwig Foundation) ⚝ This gallery presents one of the most outstanding collections of contemporary art in central Europe. It exhibits mainly American pop art, mixed with concurrent Continental movements such as hyperrealism of the 1960s and 1970s. The museum features five exhibition levels (three above ground, two underground).

Museumsplatz 1. © 01/525-00. Admission 8€ ($10) adults, 6.50€ ($8.45) children. Fri–Wed 10am–6pm; Thurs 10am–9pm.

3 Other Top Attractions
THE INNER CITY

Domkirche St. Stephan (St. Stephan's Cathedral) ⚝⚝⚝ *Kids* A basilica built on the site of a Romanesque sanctuary, this cathedral was founded in the 12th century in what was, even in the Middle Ages, the town's center.

A 1258 fire that swept through Vienna virtually destroyed Stephansdom, and toward the dawn of the 14th century, a Gothic building replaced the basilica's ruins. The cathedral suffered terribly during the Turkish siege of 1683, then experienced peace until Russian bombardments in 1945. Destruction continued when the Germans fired on Vienna as they fled the city at the close of World War II. Restored and reopened in 1948, the cathedral is one of the greatest Gothic structures in Europe, rich in woodcarvings, altars, sculptures, and paintings. The 135m (450-ft.) steeple has come to symbolize the spirit of Vienna.

The 106m-long (352-ft.) cathedral is inextricably entwined with Viennese and Austrian history. Mourners attended Mozart's "pauper's funeral" here in 1791, and Napoleon posted his farewell edict on the door in 1805.

The **pulpit** of St. Stephan's is the enduring masterpiece of stonecarver Anton Pilgrim, but the chief treasure of the cathedral is the carved wooden **Wiener Neustadt altarpiece** ⚝⚝, which dates from 1447. The richly painted and gilded altar, in the left chapel of the choir, depicts the Virgin Mary between St. Catherine and St. Barbara. In the Apostles' Choir, look for the curious **tomb of Emperor Frederick III** ⚝⚝. Made of pinkish Salzburg marble in the 17th century, the carved tomb depicts hideous hobgoblins trying to wake the emperor from his eternal sleep. The entrance to the catacombs or crypt is on the north side next to the Capistran pulpit. Here you'll see the funeral urns that contain the entrails of 56 members of the Habsburg family. You can climb the 343-step South Tower of St. Stephan's for a view of the Vienna Woods. Called **Alter Steffl (Old Steve),** the tower, marked by a needlelike spire, dominates the city's skyline. It was originally built between 1350 and 1433, and reconstructed after heavy damage in World War II. The North Tower (Nordturm), reached by elevator, was never finished to match the South Tower, but was crowned in the Renaissance style in 1579. From here you get a panoramic view of the city and the Danube.

Stephansplatz 1. © 01/515-523526. Cathedral free admission; tour of catacombs 4€ ($5.20) adults, 1.50€ ($1.95) children under 15. Guided tour of cathedral 4€ ($5.20) adults, 1.50€ ($1.95) children under 15. North Tower 3.50€ ($4.55) adults, 1.50€ ($1.95) children under 15. South Tower 3.50€ ($4.55) adults, 1€ ($1.30) students and children under 15. Evening tours, including tour of the roof, 10€ ($13) adults, 3.50€ ($4.55) children under 15. Cathedral daily

Vienna Attractions

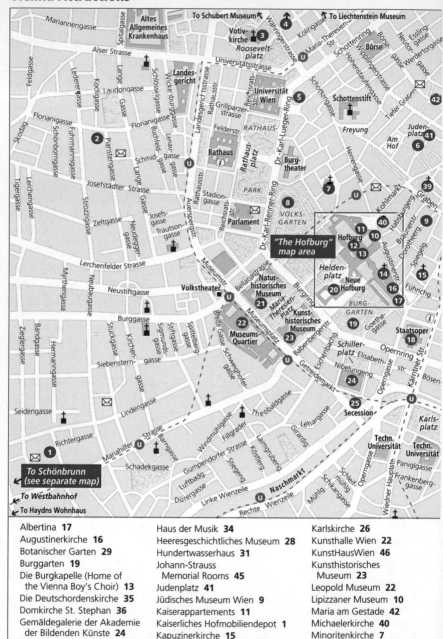

Albertina **17**
Augustinerkirche **16**
Botanischer Garten **29**
Burggarten **19**
Die Burgkapelle (Home of
  the Vienna Boy's Choir) **13**
Die Deutschordenskirche **35**
Domkirche St. Stephan **36**
Gemäldegalerie der Akademie
  der Bildenden Künste **24**

Haus der Musik **34**
Heeresgeschichtliches Museum **28**
Hundertwasserhaus **31**
Johann-Strauss
  Memorial Rooms **45**
Judenplatz **41**
Jüdisches Museum Wien **9**
Kaiserappartements **11**
Kaiserliches Hofmobiliendepot **1**
Kapuzinerkirche **15**

Karlskirche **26**
Kunsthalle Wien **22**
KunstHausWien **46**
Kunsthistorisches
  Museum **23**
Leopold Museum **22**
Lipizzaner Museum **10**
Maria am Gestade **42**
Michaelerkirche **40**
Minoritenkirche **7**

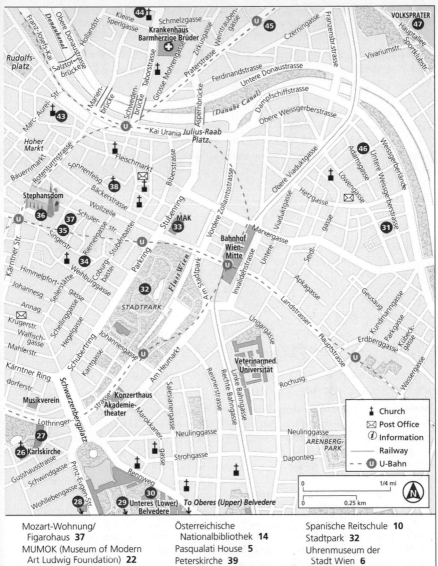

Mozart-Wohnung/
  Figarohaus **37**
MUMOK (Museum of Modern
  Art Ludwig Foundation) **22**
Naturhistorisches Museum **21**
Neue Hofburg **20**
Österreichische Galerie
  Belvedere **30**
Österreichisches Museum für
  Angewandte Kunst **33**

Österreichische
  Nationalbibliothek **14**
Pasqualati House **5**
Peterskirche **39**
Piaristenkirche **2**
Praterverband (The Prater) **47**
Ruprechtskirche **43**
Schatzkammer **12**
Secession Building **25**
Sigmund Freud Haus **4**

Spanische Reitschule **10**
Stadtpark **32**
Uhrenmuseum der
  Stadt Wien **6**
Universitätskirche **38**
Volksgarten **8**
Votivkirche **3**
Wien Museum Karlsplatz **27**
Wiener Staatsoper **18**
Zirkus und Clownmuseum **44**

6am–10pm except times of service. Tour of catacombs Mon–Sat 10am–4:30pm; Sun 2–4:30pm. Guided tour of cathedral Mon–Sat 10:30am and 3pm; Sun at 3pm. Special evening tour Sat 7pm (June–Sept). North Tower Oct–Mar daily 8:30am–5pm; Apr–Sept daily 9am–6pm. South Tower daily 9am–5:30pm. Bus: 1A, 2A, or 3A. U-Bahn: Stephansplatz.

Gemäldegalerie der Akademie der Bildenden Künste (Gallery of Painting and Fine Arts) ⟨★⟩

This gallery is home to the *Last Judgment* ⟨★★⟩ triptych by Hieronymus Bosch. In this masterpiece, the artist conjured up all the demons of hell for a terrifying view of the suffering and sins that humankind must endure. You'll also be able to view many Dutch and Flemish paintings, some from as far back as the 15th century, although the academy is noted for its 17th-century art. The gallery boasts works by Van Dyck, Rembrandt, and a host of others. There are several works by Lucas Cranach the Elder, the most outstanding being his *Lucretia* from 1532. Some say it's as enigmatic as *Mona Lisa*. Rubens is represented here by more than a dozen oil sketches. You can see Rembrandt's *Portrait of a Woman* and scrutinize Guardi's scenes from 18th-century Venice.

Schillerplatz 3. ⟨✆⟩ 01/58816. Admission 7€ ($9.10) adults, 4€ ($5.20) students and children 6–18. Tues–Sun 10am–6pm. U-Bahn: Karlsplatz.

Haus der Musik ⟨★⟩

This full-scale museum devoted to music is both hands-on and high-tech. You can take to the podium and conduct the Vienna Philharmonic. Wandering the building's halls and niches, you encounter reminders of the great composers who have lived in Vienna—not only Mozart, but also Beethoven, Schubert, Brahms, and others. In the rooms, you can listen to your favorite renditions of their works or explore memorabilia. A memorial, "Exodus," pays tribute to the Viennese musicians driven into exile or murdered by the Nazis. At the Musicantino Restaurant on the top floor, enjoy a panoramic view of the city and some good food. There's a coffeehouse on the ground floor.

Seilerstätte 30. ⟨✆⟩ 01/516-48. Admission 10€ ($13) adults, 8.50€ ($11) students and seniors, 5.50€ ($6.60) children 10–18. Open daily 10am–10pm.

Kaiserliches Hofmobiliendepot (Imperial Furniture Collection) ⟨★⟩

A collection spanning 3 centuries of royal acquisitions, this museum is a treasure house of the Habsburg attics. Exhibits range from the throne of the Emperor Francis Joseph and Prince Rudolf's cradle to a forest of coat racks and some 15,000 chairs. At the end of World War I, with the collapse of the Austro-Hungarian Empire, the new republic inherited this horde of property. Empress Maria Theresa established the collection in 1747; it now totals some 55,000 objects.

The collection includes prized examples of decorative and applied arts, and is particularly rich in Biedermeier furnishings, which characterized the era from 1815 to 1848. Particularly stunning is Maria Theresa's imposing desk of palissander (an exotic wood) marquetry with a delicate bone inlay. The modern world also intrudes, with pieces designed by such 20th-century Viennese architects such as Adolf Loos and Otto Wagner. The collection occupies a century-old warehouse complex halfway between Hofburg Palace and Schönbrunn Palace. Allow about 2½ hours to visit the three floors. Expect cheek-by-jowl bric-a-brac.

Andreasgasse 7. ⟨✆⟩ 01/524-33570. Admission 6.90€ ($8.95) adults, 4.50€ ($5.85) students, 3.60€ ($4.70) children under 18. Tues–Sun 10am–6pm. U-Bahn: Zieglergasse.

Kunsthistorisches Museum (Museum of Fine Arts) ⟨★★★⟩

Across from Hofburg Palace, this huge building houses many of the fabulous art collections gathered

THE TRAVELOCITY GUARANTEE

...THAT SAYS EVERYTHING YOU BOOK WILL BE RIGHT, OR WE'LL WORK WITH OUR TRAVEL PARTNERS TO MAKE IT RIGHT, RIGHT AWAY.

*To drive home the point,
we're going to use the word "right" in every single sentence.*

Let's get right to it. Right to the meat! Only Travelocity guarantees everything about your booking will be right, or we'll work with our travel partners to make it right, right away. Right on!

Here's a picture taken smack dab right in the middle of Antigua, where the Guarantee also covers you.

The Guarantee covers all but one of the items pictured to the right.

Now, you may be thinking, "Yeah, right, I'm so sure." That's OK; you have the right to remain skeptical. That is until we mention help is always right around the corner. Call us right off the bat, knowing our customer service reps are there for you 24/7. Righting wrongs. Left and right.

For example, what if the ocean view you booked actually looks out at a downright ugly parking lot? You'd be right to call – we're there for you. And no one in their right mind would be pleased to learn the rental car place has closed and left them stranded. Call Travelocity and we'll help get you back on the right track.

Now if you're guessing there are some things we can't control, like the weather, well you're right. But we can help you with most things – to get all the details in righting,* visit travelocity.com/guarantee.

*Sorry, spelling things right is one of the few things not covered under the Guarantee.

I'd give my right arm for a guarantee like this, although I'm glad I don't have to.

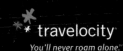

travelocity
You'll never roam alone.

©2006 Travelocity.com LP. CST# 2056372-50.

An Indestructible Legacy of the Third Reich

As you stroll about Vienna, you'll come across six anti-aircraft towers with walls up to 16 feet thick, a legacy of the Third Reich. These watchtowers, built during World War II, were designed to shoot down Allied aircraft. After the war, there was some attempt to rid the city of these horrors, but the citadels remained, their proportions as thick as the Arc de Triomphe in Paris. "We live with them," a local resident, Josef Hoffmann, told us. "We try our best to ignore them. No one wants to remember what they were. But even dynamite doesn't work against them. They truly have walls of steel."

by the Habsburgs as they added new territories to their empire. One highlight is the fine collection of ancient Egyptian and Greek art. The museum also has works by many of the great European masters, such as Velásquez and Titian.

On display here are Roger van der Weyden's *Crucifixion* triptych, a Memling altarpiece, and Jan van Eyck's portrait of Cardinal Albergati. The museum is renowned for the works of **Pieter Bruegel the Elder,** known for his sensitive yet vigorous landscapes and lively studies of peasant life. Don't leave without a glimpse of Bruegel's *Children's Games* and his *Hunters in the Snow,* one of his most celebrated works.

Don't miss the work of Van Dyck, especially his *Venus in the Forge of Vulcan,* or Peter Paul Rubens's *Self-Portrait* and *Woman with a Cape,* for which he is said to have used the face of his second wife, Helen Fourment. The Rembrandt collection includes two remarkable self-portraits as well as a moving portrait of his mother and one of his sons, Titus.

A highlight of any trip to Vienna is the museum's **Albrecht Dürer** collection. The Renaissance German painter and engraver (1471–1528) is known for his innovative art and his painstakingly detailed workmanship. *Blue Madonna* is here, as are some of his landscapes, such as *Martyrdom of 10,000 Christians.*

Maria-Theresien-Platz, Burgring 5. ⓒ 01/525-240. Admission 10€ ($13) adults, 7.50€ ($9.75) students and seniors, free for children under 6. Fri–Wed 10am–6pm; Thurs 10am–9pm. U-Bahn: Mariahilferstrasse. Tram: 1, 2, D, or J.

Liechtenstein Museum ✮✮✮ The rare collection of art treasures from the Liechtenstein's princely collections went on display in 2004 in the royal family palace in the Rossau district. For the first time visitors can see this fabled collection of Raphaels, Rubens, and Rembrandts, one of the world's greatest private art collections.

In 2003, a decision was made to open the palace and its treasures to the public. This meant restoring frescoes, relandscaping the gardens, and rejuvenating the palace. Art, such as works by Frans Hals and Van Dyck, are displayed in the neoclassical Garden Palace, which became Vienna's first museum when it opened its doors in 1807. There are some 1,700 works of art in the collection, although not all of them can be displayed at once, of course.

On your visit you're likely to see some 200 works spread over eight galleries. Works range from the 13th to the 19th centuries, such as *Venus in Front of the Mirror* (ca. 1613) by Peter Paul Rubens. Rubens, as you'll soon see, is clearly the star of the museum. Of spectacular beauty is the splendid **Hercules Hall** ✮, the largest secular baroque room in Vienna. Frescoes were painted between 1704 and 1708 by Andrea Pozzo.

The palace also has two new restaurants, including Ruben's Brasserie, serving both traditional Viennese and Liechtenstein fare (some based on princely recipes) and

Ruben's Palais, offering more haute cuisine. Both restaurants have gardens in the palace's baroque courtyard.

Liechtenstein Garden Palace, Fürstengasse 1. ℂ 01/3195767252. www.liechtensteinmuseum.at. Admission 10€ ($13) adults, 8€ ($10) seniors, 5€ ($6.50) students, 2€ ($2.60) children under 14. Family ticket 20€ ($26). Wed–Mon 10am–5pm. U-Bahn: Rossauer Lände. Tram: D to Porzellangasse.

Secession Building ✿   Come here if for no other reason than to see Gustav Klimt's *Beethoven Frieze*, a 30m-long (98-ft.) visual interpretation of Beethoven's Ninth Symphony. This building—a virtual art manifesto proclamation—stands south of the Opernring, beside the Academy of Fine Arts. The Secession building was the home of the Viennese avant-garde, which extolled the glories of Jugendstil (Art Nouveau). A young group of painters and architects launched the Secessionist movement in 1897 in rebellion against the strict, conservative ideas of the official Academy of Fine Arts. Gustav Klimt was a leader of the movement, which defied the historicism favored by the Emperor Franz Joseph. The works of Kokoschka were featured here, as was the "barbarian" Paul Gauguin.

Today works by the Secessionist artists are on display in the Belvedere Palace, and the Secession Building is used for substantial contemporary exhibits. It was constructed in 1898 and is crowned by a dome once called "outrageous in its useless luxury." The empty dome—covered in triumphal laurel leaves—echoes that of the Karlskirche on the other side of Vienna.

Friedrichstrasse 12 (on the western side of Karlsplatz). ℂ 01/587-53070. www.secession.at. Admission 6€ ($7.80) adults, 3.50€ ($4.55) children 6–18. Tues–Sun 10am–6pm; Thurs 10am–8pm. U-Bahn: Karlsplatz.

Wiener Staatsoper (Vienna State Opera) ✿   This is one of the most important opera houses in the world. When it was built in the 1860s, critics apparently upset one of the architects, Eduard van der Null, so much that he killed himself. In 1945, at the end of World War II, Vienna started restoration work on the theater (despite other pressing needs such as public housing), finishing it in time to celebrate the country's independence from occupation forces in 1955. (See also chapter 9, "Vienna After Dark.")

Opernring 2. ℂ 01/5144-42250. Tours daily year-round, 2–5 times a day, depending on demand. Tour times are posted on a board outside the entrance. Tours 4.50€ ($5.85) per person. U-Bahn: Karlsplatz.

OUTSIDE THE INNER CITY

Hundertwasserhaus   In a city filled with baroque palaces and numerous architectural adornments, this sprawling public-housing project in the rather bleak 3rd District is visited—or at least seen from the window of a tour bus—by about a million visitors annually. Completed in 1985, it was the work of self-styled "eco-architect" Friedensreich Hundertwasser. The complex, which has a facade like a gigantic black-and-white game board, is relieved with scattered splotches of red, yellow, and blue. Trees stick out at 45-degree angles from apartments among the foliage.

There are 50 apartments here, and signs warn not to go inside. However, there's a tiny gift shop (ℂ 01/715-15-53) at the entrance where you can buy Hundertwasser posters and postcards, plus a coffee shop on the first floor.

Löwengasse and Kegelgasse 3. ℂ 01/715-15-53. www.hundertwasserhaus.at. U-Bahn: Landstrasse. Tram: N.

Österreichische Galerie Belvedere ✿✿   Southeast of Karlsplatz, the Belvedere sits on a slope above Vienna. The approach to the palace is memorable—through a long garden with a huge circular pond that reflects the sky and the looming palace buildings. Designed by Johann Lukas von Hildebrandt, the last major Austrian

Schönbrunn Park & Palace

THE PARK

1. Main Gate
2. Courtyard
3. Theater
4. Mews
5. Chapel
6. Restaurant
7. Hietzing Church
8. Naiad's Fountains
9. Joseph II Monument
10. Palm House
11. Neptune's Fountain
12. Schöner Brunnen
13. Gloriette
14. Small Gloriette
15. Spring
16. Octagonal Pavilion

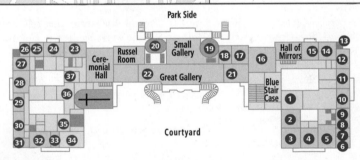

THE PALACE

1. Guard Room
2. Billiard Room
3. Walnut Room
4. Franz Joseph's Study
5. Franz Joseph's Bedroom
6. Cabinet
7. Stairs Cabinet
8. Dressing Room
9. Bedroom of Franz Joseph I & Elisabeth
10. Empress Elisabeth's Salon
11. Marie Antoinette's Room
12. Nursery
13. Breakfast Room
14. Yellow Salon
15. Balcony Room

16 17 18. Rosa Rooms

19 20. Round and Oval Chinese Cabinets

21. Lantern Room
22. Carousel Room
23. Blue Chinese Salon
24. Vieux-Laque Room
25. Napoleon Room
26. Porcelain Room
27. Millions Room
28. Gobelin Tapestry Room
29. Archduchess Sophie's Study
30. Red Drawing Room
31. East Terrace Cabinet
32. Bed-of-State Room
33. Writing Room
34. Drawing Room
35. Wild Boar Room
36. Passage Chamber
37. Bergl-Zimmer

124 CHAPTER 6 · EXPLORING VIENNA

baroque architect, the Belvedere was built as a summer home for Prince Eugene of Savoy. It consists of two palatial buildings made up of a series of interlocking cubes. Two great, flowing staircases dominate the interior. The Gold Salon in Lower Belvedere is one of the most beautiful rooms in the palace. A regal French-style garden lies between the two buildings.

Unteres Belvedere (Lower Belvedere), Rennweg 6A, was constructed from 1714 to 1716. **Oberes Belvedere (Upper Belvedere)** was started in 1721 and completed in 1723. Anton Bruckner, the composer, lived in one of the buildings until his death in 1896. The palace was the residence of Archduke Franz Ferdinand, whose assassination sparked World War I. In May 1955, the Allied powers signed the peace treaty recognizing Austria as a sovereign state in Upper Belvedere. The treaty is on display in a large salon decorated in red marble.

Lower Belvedere houses the **Barockmuseum (Museum of Baroque Art).** The original sculptures from the Neuer Markt fountain (replaced now by copies), the work of Georg Raphael Donner, who died in 1741, are displayed here. During his life, Donner dominated the development of Austrian sculpture. The fountain's four figures represent the four major tributaries of the Danube. Works by Franz Anton Maulbertsch, an 18th-century painter, are also exhibited here. Maulbertsch, strongly influenced by Tiepolo, was the greatest and most original Austrian painter of his day. He was best known for his iridescent colors and flowing brushwork.

Museum Mittelalterlicher Kunst (Museum of Medieval Art) is in the Orangery at Lower Belvedere. Here you'll see art from the Gothic period as well as a Tyrolean Romanesque crucifix that dates from the 12th century.

Upper Belvedere houses the **Galerie des 19. und 20. Jahrhunderts (Gallery of 19th- and 20th-Century Art)** ⊛. Here you also find works by the artists of the 1897 Secessionist movement. Most outstanding are those by Gustav Klimt (1862–1918), one of the movement's founders. Sharing almost equal billing with Klimt is Egon Schiele (1890–1918), whose masterpieces here include *The Wife of an Artist.*

Prinz-Eugen-Strasse 27. ℭ 01/79557. www.belvedere.at. Admission 9€ ($12) adults, free for children 11 and under. Tues–Sun 10am–6pm. Tram: D to Schloss Belvedere.

Schönbrunn Palace ⊛⊛⊛

The 1,441-room Schönbrunn Palace was designed for the Habsburgs by those masters of the baroque, the von Erlachs. It was built between 1696 and 1712 at the request of Emperor Leopold I for his son, Joseph I. Leopold envisioned a palace whose grandeur would surpass that of Versailles. However, Austria's treasury, drained by the cost of wars, would not support the ambitious undertaking, and the original plans were never carried out.

Art-School Reject

One Austrian painter whose canvases will never grace any museum wall is Adolph Hitler. Aspiring to be an artist, Hitler had his traditional paintings, including one of the Auersberg Palace, rejected by the Academy of Fine Arts in Vienna. The building was accurate, but the figures were way out of proportion. Hitler did not take this failure well, denouncing the board as a "lot of old-fashioned fossilized civil servants, bureaucrats, devoid lumps of officials. The whole academy ought to be blown up!"

When Maria Theresa became empress, she changed the original plans, and Schön-brunn looks today much as she conceived it. Done in "Maria Theresa ochre," with delicate rococo touches designed for her by Austrian Nikolaus Pacassi, the palace is in complete contrast to the grim, forbidding Hofburg. Schönbrunn was the imperial summer palace during Maria Theresa's 40-year reign, and it was the scene of great cer-emonial balls, lavish banquets, and fabulous receptions held during the Congress of Vienna. At the age of 6, Mozart performed in the Hall of Mirrors before Maria Theresa and her court. The empress held secret meetings with her chancellor, Prince Kaunitz, in the round Chinese Room.

Franz Joseph was born within the palace walls. It was the setting for the lavish court life associated with his reign, and he spent the final years of his life here. The last of the Habsburg rulers, Karl I, signed a document here on November 11, 1918, renounc-ing his participation in affairs of state—not quite an abdication, but tantamount to one. Allied bombs damaged the palace during World War II, but restoration has oblit-erated the scars.

The **Gloriette** ✮✮, a marble summerhouse topped by a stone canopy with an imperial eagle, embellishes the palace's **Imperial Gardens** ✮. The so-called Roman Ruins (a collection of marble statues and fountains) date from the late 18th century, when it was fashionable to simulate the ravaged grandeur of Rome. Adria van Steck-hoven laid out the park, which contains many fountains and heroic statues, often depicting Greek mythological characters. Visitors may enter until sunset daily.

The **State Apartments** ✮✮✮ are the most stunning display in the palace. Much of the interior ornamentation is in the rococo style, with red, white, and 23½-karat gold predominating. Of the 40 rooms that you can visit, particularly fascinating is the Room of Millions, decorated with Indian and Persian miniatures—a truly grand rococo salon. English-language guided tours of many of the palace rooms, lasting 50 minutes, start every half-hour beginning at 9:30am. You should tip the guide 1€ ($1.30).

Also on the grounds is the baroque **Schlosstheater (Palace Theater;** ✆ **01/876-4272),** which stages summer performances. The **Wagenburg (Carriage Museum)** ✮ (✆ **01/877-3244)** is also worth a visit. It contains a fine display of imperial coaches from the 17th to 20th centuries.

Called the **Schloss Schönbrunn Experience,** 60- to 90-minute children's tours are conducted. First, kids are dressed in imperial clothing, then led by English-speaking guides through rooms that offer hands-on displays.

Admission price to the palace includes a tour (the Grand Tour) of 40 state rooms with audio guide.

Schönbrunner Schlossstrasse. ✆ **01/811-132-39.** www.schoenbrunn.at. Admission 12€ ($15) adults, 6€ ($7.80) children 6–15, free for children under 6; Wagenburg 5€ ($6.50) adults, 3.50€ ($4.55) seniors and children 10 and under; Schloss Schönbrunn Experience 4.50€ ($5.85) children. Apartments Apr–Oct daily 8:30am–5pm; Nov–Mar daily 9am–4:30pm. Wagenburg Apr–Oct daily 9am–6pm; Nov–Mar Tues–Sun 10am–4pm. U-Bahn: Schönbrunn.

4 Churches

See section 1 of this chapter for information on the Burgkapelle, where the Vienna Boys' Choir performs, and the Augustinerkirche. Section 3, "Other Top Attractions," contains the description of St. Stephan's Cathedral.

THE INNER CITY

Die Deutschordenskirche (Church of the Teutonic Order)   The Order of the Teutonic Knights was a German society founded in 1190 in the Holy Land. The order came to Vienna in 1205, and the church dates from 1395. The building never fell prey to the baroque madness that swept the city after the Counter-Reformation, so you see it pretty much in its original form, a Gothic church dedicated to St. Elizabeth. The 16th-century Flemish altarpiece standing at the main altar is richly decorated with woodcarving, gilt, and painted panel inserts. Many knights of the Teutonic Order are buried here, their heraldic shields still mounted on some of the upper walls.

In the knights' treasury, on the second floor of the church, you'll see mementos such as seals and coins illustrating the history of the order, as well as a collection of arms, vases, gold, crystal, and precious stones. Also on display are the charter given to the Teutonic Order by Henry IV of England and a collection of medieval paintings. A curious exhibit is the Viper Tongue Credenza, said to have the power to detect poison in food and render it harmless.

Singerstrasse 7. ℂ 01/512-1065. Free admission to church; treasury 3.60€ ($4.70) adults, 2.20€ ($2.85) children under 11. Church daily 7am–7pm; treasury Mon and Wed 3–5pm, Thurs 10am–noon, Fri 3–5pm, Sat 10am–noon and 3–5pm. U-Bahn: Stephansplatz.

Kapuzinerkirche   The Kapuziner Church (just inside the ring behind the Opera) has housed the Imperial Crypt, the burial vault of the Habsburgs, for some 3 centuries. Capuchin friars guard the final resting place of 12 emperors, 17 empresses, and dozens of archdukes. Only their bodies are here: Their hearts are in urns in the Loreto Chapel of the Augustinerkirche in the Hofburg complex, and their entrails are similarly enshrined in a crypt below St. Stephan's Cathedral.

Most outstanding of the imperial tombs is the double sarcophagus of Maria Theresa and her consort, Francis Stephen (François, duke of Lorraine, or, in German, Franz von Lothringen, 1708–65), the parents of Marie Antoinette. The "King of Rome," the ill-fated son of Napoleon and Marie-Louise of Austria, was buried here in a bronze coffin after his death at age 21. (Hitler managed to anger both the Austrians and the French by having the remains of Napoleon's son transferred to Paris in 1940.)

Emperor Franz Joseph was interred here in 1916. He was a frail old man who outlived his time and died just before the final collapse of his empire. His wife, Empress Elisabeth, was also buried here after her assassination in Geneva in 1898, as was their son, Archduke Rudolf, who died at Mayerling (see the "Twilight of the Habsburgs" box, in chapter 10).

Neuer Markt. ℂ 01/512-6853. Admission 4€ ($5.20) adults, 3€ ($3.90) children 10–15. Daily 9:30am–4pm. U-Bahn: Stephansplatz.

Maria am Gestade (St. Mary's on the Bank)   This church, also known as the Church of Our Lady of the Riverbank, was once just that. With an arm of the Danube flowing by, it was a favorite place of worship for fishermen. The river was redirected, and now the church relies on its beauty to draw people. A Romanesque church on this site was rebuilt in the Gothic style between 1394 and 1427. The western facade is flamboyant, with a remarkable seven-sided Gothic tower surmounted by a dome that culminates in a lacelike crown.

At Passauer Platz. ℂ 01/5339-5940. Free admission. Daily 7am–7pm. U-Bahn: Stephansplatz.

Michaelerkirche (Church of St. Michael)   Over its long history this church has felt the hand of many architects and designers, resulting in a medley of styles, not all harmonious. Some of the remaining Romanesque sections date to the early 1200s. The exact date of the chancel is not known, but it's probably from the mid-14th century. The catacombs remain as they were in the Middle Ages.

Impressions

This is one of the most perplexing cities that I was ever in. It is extensive, irregular, crowded, dusty, dissipated, magnificent, and to me disagreeable. It has immense palaces, superb galleries of paintings, several theaters, public walks, and drives crowded with equipages. In short, everything bears the stamp of luxury and ostentation; for here is assembled and concentrated all the wealth, fashion, and nobility of the Austrian empire.

—Washington Irving, letter to his sister, from *Tales of a Traveller,* 1824

Most of St. Michael's as it appears today dates from 1792, when the facade was redone in neoclassical style; the spire is from the 16th century. The main altar is richly decorated in baroque style, and the altarpiece, entitled *The Collapse of the Angels* (1781), was the last major baroque work completed in Vienna.

Michaelerplatz. 🕐 01/533-8000. Free admission. Mon–Sat 6:45am–8pm; Sun 8am–6:30pm. U-Bahn: Herrengasse. Bus: 1A, 2A, or 3A.

Minoritenkirche (Church of the Minorites)   If you're tired of baroque ornamentation, visit this church of the Friar Minor Conventual, a Franciscan order also called the Minorite friars (inferior brothers). Construction began in 1250 but was not completed until the early 14th century. The Turks damaged the tower in their two sieges of Vienna, and the church later fell prey to baroque architects and designers. But in 1784, Ferdinand von Hohenberg ordered the baroque additions removed, and the simple lines of the original Gothic church returned, complete with cloisters. Inside you'll see a mosaic copy of da Vinci's *The Last Supper.* Masses are held on Sunday at 8:30 and 11am.

Minoritenplatz 2A. 🕐 01/533-4162. Free admission. Apr–Oct Mon–Sat 8am–6pm; Nov–Mar Mon–Sat 9am–5pm. U-Bahn: Herrengasse.

Peterskirche (St. Peter's Church)   This is the second-oldest church in Vienna, and the spot on which it stands could well be Vienna's oldest Christian church site. It's believed that a place of worship stood here in the second half of the 4th century. Charlemagne is credited with having founded a church on the site during the late 8th or early 9th century.

The present St. Peter's is the most lavishly decorated baroque church in Vienna. Gabriel Montani designed it in 1702. Hildebrandt, the noted architect of the Belvedere Palace, is believed to have finished the building in 1732. The fresco in the dome is a masterpiece by J. M. Rottmayr depicting the coronation of the Virgin. The church contains many frescoes and much gilded carved wood, plus altarpieces done by well-known artists of the period.

Peterplatz. 🕐 01/533-6433. Free admission. Daily 9am–6:30pm. U-Bahn: Stephansplatz.

Ruprechtskirche (St. Rupert's Church)   The oldest church in Vienna, Ruprechtskirche has stood here since 740, although much that you see now, such as the aisle, is from the 11th century. Beautiful new stained-glass windows, the work of Lydia Roppolt, were installed in 1993. It's believed that much of the masonry from a Roman shrine on this spot was used in the present church. The tower and nave are Romanesque; the rest of the church is Gothic. St. Rupert is the patron saint of the Danube's salt merchants.

Ruprechtsplatz. ℭ 01/535-6003. Free admission. Day after Easter to Oct Mon–Fri 10am–noon. Closed Nov–Easter. U-Bahn: Schwedenplatz.

Universitätskirche (Church of the Jesuits)   Built at the time of the Counter-Reformation, this church is rich in baroque embellishments. This was the university church, dedicated to the Jesuit saints Ignatius of Loyola and Franciscus Xaverius. The high-baroque decorations— galleries, columns, and the *trompe l'oeil* painting on the ceiling, which gives the illusion of a dome—were added from 1703 to 1705. The embellishments were the work of a Jesuit lay brother, Andrea Pozzo, on the orders of Emperor Leopold I. Look for Pozzo's painting of Mary behind the main altar. Choir and orchestra services (mostly classical) are celebrated on Sunday and holy days at 10am.

Dr.-Ignaz-Seipel-Platz 1. ℭ 01/512-13350. Free admission. Daily 8am–7pm. U-Bahn: Stephansplatz or Stubentor. Tram: 1 or 2. Bus: 1A.

OUTSIDE THE INNER CITY

Karlskirche (Church of St. Charles)   The Black Plague swept Vienna in 1713, and Emperor Charles VI vowed to build this church if the disease abated. Construction on Karlskirche, dedicated to St. Charles Borromeo, began in 1716. The master of the baroque, Johann Bernard Fischer von Erlach, did the original work from 1716 to 1722, and his son, Joseph Emanuel, completed it between 1723 and 1737. The lavishly decorated interior stands as a testament to the father-and-son duo. J. M. Rottmayr painted many of the frescoes inside the church from 1725 to 1730.

The green copper dome is 72m (236 ft.) high, a dramatic landmark on the Viennese skyline. Two columns, spinoffs from Trajan's Column in Rome, flank the front of the church, which opens onto Karlsplatz. There's also a sculpture by Henry Moore in a little pool.

Karlsplatz. ℭ 01/504-6187. Admission 4€ ($5.20) adults, free for children under 12. Mon–Fri 9am–12:30pm; Sat–Sun 1–6pm. U-Bahn: Karlsplatz.

Piaristenkirche (Church of the Piarist Order)   A Roman Catholic teaching congregation known as the Piarists (fathers of religious schools) launched work on the Piaristenkirche in 1716. The church, more popularly known as Piaristenplatz, was not consecrated until 1771. Some of the designs submitted during that long period are believed to have been drawn by von Hildebrandt, the noted architect who designed the Belvedere Palace, but many builders had a hand in its construction. This church is noteworthy for its fine classic facade as well as the frescoes by F. A. Maulbertsch, which adorn the inside of the circular cupolas.

Piaristengasse 54. ℭ 01/406-14530. Free admission. Mon–Fri 3–6pm; Sat 10am–noon. U-Bahn: Rathaus.

Votivkirche   After a failed assassination attempt on Emperor Franz Joseph, a collection was taken for the construction of the Votive Church, which sits across from the site of the attempt. Heinrich von Ferstel began work on the neo-Gothic church in 1856, but it was not consecrated until 1879. The magnificent facade features awesome lacy spires and intricate sculpture.

Rooseveltplatz 8. ℭ 01/406-1192. Free admission. Tues–Sun 9am–1pm and 4–6:30pm. U-Bahn: Schottenor.

5 Museums & Galleries
THE INNER CITY

Jüdisches Museum Wien   This is the main museum tracing the history of Viennese Jewry. Don't confuse it with its annex at Judenplatz (p. 130). This museum opened in 1993 in the former Eskeles Palace, once one of the most patrician of town houses in Vienna. Both temporary and permanent exhibitions are on view here. The permanent exhibitions trace the major role that Jews played in the history of Vienna until their expulsion or deaths in the Holocaust beginning in 1938. Displays note their valuable contributions in such fields as philosophy, music, medicine, and, of course, psychiatry. Sigmund Freud escaped the Holocaust by fleeing to London. Many objects were rescued from Vienna's private synagogues and prayer houses, which were concealed from the Nazis in 1938. Many other exhibits are from Vienna's old Jewish Museum, which closed that same year.

Dorotheergasse 11. (✆ 01/535-0431. Admission 5€ ($6.50) adults, 2.90€ ($3.75) students and children 10–18. Sun–Fri 10am–6pm. U-Bahn: Stephansplatz.

Naturhistorisches Museum (Natural History Museum) *Kids*   Housed in a handsome neo-Renaissance building near the Museum of Fine Arts, this is the third-largest natural history museum (after its counterparts in New York and London) in the world, and holds the oldest collections. It was established by the husband of Empress Maria Theresa (Franz Stephan von Lothringen) in 1748, who donated one of its major art objects (a personal gift to him from his wife) to the collections at the time of his death. Located in Room no. 4 of the Mineralogy Department, and known as Der Juwelen Strauss, it's a 60cm-tall (24-in.) bouquet of flowers crafted from more than 2,000 gemstones, each of which was even rarer at the time of the object's creation than they are today. The museum also holds an important collection of early Stone Age artifacts, the best-known and most evocative of which is the **Venus of Willendorf,** whose discovery in Lower Austria in 1906 attests to the area's ancient habitation.

Maria-Theresien Platz, Burgring 7. (✆ 01/521770. Admission 8€ ($10) adults, 3.50€ ($4.55) students. Thurs–Mon 9am–6:30pm; Wed 9am–9pm. U-Bahn: Volkstheater. Tram: 1, 2, D, J.

Österreichisches Museum für Angewandte Kunst (Museum of Applied Art)   Of special interest here is a rich collection of tapestries, some from the 16th century, and the most outstanding assemblage of Viennese porcelain in the world. Look for a Persian carpet depicting *The Hunt,* as well as the group of 13th-century Limoges enamels. Biedermeier furniture and other antiques, glassware, crystal, and large collections of lace and textiles are also on display. An entire hall is devoted to Art Nouveau. There are outstanding objects from the Wiener Werkstatte (Vienna Workshop), founded in 1903 by architect Josef Hoffman. In the workshop, many well-known artists and craftsmen created a variety of objects—glass, porcelain, textiles, wooden articles, and jewelry.

Stubenring 5. (✆ 01/711360. www.mak.at. Admission 7.90€ ($10) adults, 4€ ($5.20) children 6–18, free for children under 6. Wed–Sun 10am–6pm; Tues 10am–midnight. Free admission on Sat. U-Bahn: Stubentor. Tram: 1 or 2.

Uhrenmuseum der Stadt Wien (Municipal Clock Museum)   A wide-ranging group of timepieces—some ancient, some modern—is on view here. Housed in what was once the Obizzi town house, the museum dates from 1917 and attracts clock collectors from all over Europe and North America. Check out Rutschmann's 18th-century

In Memory of Vienna's Jewish Ghetto

Judenplatz (U-Bahn: Stephansplatz), off Wiplingerstrase, was the heart of the Jewish ghetto from the 13th to the 15th centuries. The opening of a Holocaust memorial on this square revived that memory.

The memorial, a new museum, and excavations have re-created a center of Jewish culture on the Judenplatz. It is a place of remembrance unique to Europe.

The architect of the Holocaust memorial, Rachel Whitehead, designed it like a stylized stack of books signifying the strive toward education. The outer sides of the reinforced concrete cube take the form of library shelves. Around the base of the monument are engraved the names of the places in which Austrian Jews were put to death during the Nazi era. Nearby is a statue of Gotthold Ephraim Lessing (1729–81), the Jewish playwright.

Museum Judenplatz, Judenplatz 8 (✆ 01/535-0431), is a new annex of Vienna's Jewish Museum. Exhibits tell of the major role Viennese Jews played in all aspects of city life, from music to medicine, until a reign of terror began in 1938. The main section of the museum holds an exhibition on medieval Jewry in Vienna. The exhibition features a multimedia presentation on the religious, cultural, and social life of the Viennese Jews in the Middle Ages until their expulsion and death in 1420 and 1421. The three exhibition rooms are in the basement of the Misrachi house. An underground passage connects them to the exhibitions of the medieval synagogue. The museum is open Sunday through Thursday from 10am to 6pm and Friday from 10am to 2pm; admission is 3€ ($3.90) for adults and 2.90€ ($3.75) for students and children under 16.

An exhibition room has been installed in the **Mittelalterliche Synagogue (Medieval Synagogue)** nearby. It is visited on the same ticket as the Jewish Museum. The late-medieval synagogue was built around the middle of the 13th century, and was one of the largest synagogues of its time. After the pogrom in 1420 to 1421, the synagogue was systematically destroyed so that only the foundations and the floor remained. These were excavated by the City of Vienna Department of Urban Archaeology from 1995 to 1998. The exhibition room shows the remnants of the central room, or "men's shul" (the room where men studied and prayed), and a smaller room annexed to it, which might have been used by women. In the middle of the central room is the foundation of the hexagonal bimah (raised podium from which the Torah was read). *Note:* Combined ticket (Jewish Museum, Museum Judenplatz, and Synagogue) 7€ ($9.10) adults, 4€ ($5.20) students and children ages 6 to 18.

astronomical clock. Also here are several interesting cuckoo clocks and a gigantic timepiece that was once mounted in the tower of St. Stephan's.

Schulhof 2. ✆ 01/533-2265. Admission 4€ ($5.20) adults, 2€ ($2.60) children 10–18. Tues–Sun 9am–4:30pm. U-Bahn: Stephansplatz.

OUTSIDE THE INNER CITY

Heeresgeschichtliches Museum (Museum of Military History)   The oldest state museum in Vienna, this building was constructed from 1850 to 1856, a precursor to the Ringstrasse style. Inside, exhibits delineate Habsburg military history—defeats as well as triumphs.

A special display case in front of the Franz-Josef Hall contains the six orders of the House of Habsburg that Franz Josef sported on all public occasions. The fascinating Sarajevo room contains mementos of the assassination of Archduke Franz Ferdinand and his wife on June 28, 1914, the event that sparked World War I. The archduke's bloodstained uniform is displayed, along with the bullet-scarred car in which the couple rode. Many exhibits focus on the Austro-Hungarian navy, and frescoes depict important battles, including those against the Turks in and around Vienna.

Arsenal 3. © 01/79561. Admission 5.10€ ($6.65) adults, 3.30€ ($4.30) children under 14. www.hgm.or.at. Sat–Thurs 9am–5pm. Closed Jan 1, Easter, May 1, Nov 1, and Dec 24–25 and 31. Tram: 18 or D.

Historisches Museum der Stadt Wien (Historical Museum of Vienna)   History buffs should seek out this fascinating but little-visited collection. Here the full panorama of Old Vienna's history unfolds, beginning with the settlement of prehistoric tribes in the Danube basin. Roman relics, artifacts from the reign of the dukes of Babenberg, and a wealth of leftovers from the Habsburg sovereignty are on display, as well as arms and armor from various eras. A scale model shows Vienna as it looked in the Habsburg heyday. You'll see pottery and ceramics dating from the Roman era, 14th-century stained-glass windows, mementos of the Turkish sieges of 1529 and 1683, and Biedermeier furniture. There's also a section on Vienna's Art Nouveau.

Karlsplatz 4. © 01/505-8747. www.museum.vienna.at. Admission 6€ ($7.80) adults, 3€ ($3.90) children 10–18. Tues–Sun 9am–6pm. U-Bahn: Karlsplatz.

KunstHausWien _Finds_   Vienna's most whimsical museum, a former Thonet chair factory, shows the imaginative, fantastical works of painter and designer Friedensreich Hundertwasser (1928–2000). Hundertwasser was one of the world's most famous architects, and this is a fitting memorial. It's filled with his paintings, drawings, and architectural projects (many of which were never built). The museum is also a venue for temporary exhibitions of international artists. Previous shows have focused on such artists as Chagall, Picasso, and Cecil Beaton.

The tiled black-and-white checkerboard exterior has been compared to a Klimt painting seen through a kaleidoscope. Inside, the architect created uneven floors, irregular corners, trees growing out of the roof and windows, and oddly shaped, different size windows. After leaving the museum, you can walk 5 minutes to the **Hundertwasserhaus** (see listing earlier in this chapter).

Untere Weissgerberstrasse 13. © 01/712-04-91. Admission 9€ ($12) adults, 7€ ($9.10) for students and children 10–18, free for children under 10. Extra charge for temporary exhibits. Daily 10am–7pm. Tram: N or O.

Sigmund Freud Haus   Walking through this museum, you can almost imagine the good doctor ushering you in and telling you to make yourself comfortable on the couch. Antiques and mementos, including his velour hat and dark walking stick with ivory handle, fill the study and waiting room he used during his residence here from 1891 to 1938.

The museum also has a bookshop with a variety of postcards of the apartment, books by Freud, posters, prints, and pens.

Berggasse 19. © 01/319-1596. Admission 8.50€ ($11) adults, 6€ ($7.80) seniors, 5€ ($6.50) students, 3€ ($3.90) children 12–18. Free for children 11 and under. Daily 9am–6pm. Tram: D to Schlickgasse.

6 Parks & Gardens

When the weather is fine, Vienna's residents shun city parks in favor of the **Wiener-wald (Vienna Woods),** a wide arc of forested countryside that surrounds northwest and southwest Vienna (for more details, see chapter 10, "Side Trips from Vienna"). If you love parks, you'll find some magnificent ones in Vienna. Within the city limits are more than 1,600 hectares (3,952 acres) of gardens and parks, and no fewer than 770 sports fields and playgrounds. You can, of course, visit the grounds of **Schönbrunn Park** and **Belvedere Park** when you tour those palaces. Below, we highlight Vienna's most popular parks.

THE INNER CITY

Burggarten   These are the former gardens of the Habsburg emperors. They were laid out soon after the Volksgarten (see below) was completed. Look for the monument to Mozart, as well as an equestrian statue of Francis Stephen, Maria Theresa's beloved husband. The only open-air statue of Franz Joseph in Vienna is also here, and there's a statue of Goethe at the park entrance.

Opernring-Burgring, next to the Hofburg. Tram: 1, 2, 52, 58, or D.

Stadtpark   This lovely park lies on the slope where the Danube used to overflow into the Inner City before the construction of the Danube Canal. Many memorial statues stand in the park; the best known depicts Johann Strauss, Jr., composer of operettas and waltzes like "The Blue Danube Waltz." Here, too, are monuments to Franz Schubert and Hans Makart, a well-known artist whose work you'll see in churches and museums throughout Vienna. Verdant squares of grass, well-manicured flower gardens, and plenty of benches surround the monuments. The park is open 24 hours daily.

Volksgarten (People's Park)   Laid out in 1820 on the site of the old city wall fortifications, this is Vienna's oldest public garden. It's dotted with monuments, including a 1907 memorial to assassinated Empress Elisabeth and the so-called Temple of Theseus, a copy of the Theseion in Athens.

Dr.-Karl-Renner-Ring, between the Hofburg and the Burgtheater. Tram: 1, 2, or D.

OUTSIDE THE INNER CITY

Botanischer Garten (Botanical Garden of the University of Vienna)   These lush gardens contain exotic and sometimes rare plants from all over the world. Located in Landstrasse (3rd District) right next to the Belvedere Park, the Botanical Garden developed on a spot where Maria Theresa once ordered medicinal herbs to be planted. Always call in advance if the weather is doubtful.

Rennweg 14. © 01/4277-54100. Free admission. Late May to late Oct daily 9am–dusk. Tram: 71 to Unteres Belvedere.

Donaupark   This 99-hectare (245-acre) park, in the 22nd District between the Danube Canal and the Alte Donau (Old Danube), was converted in 1964 from a garbage dump to a park with flowers, shrubs, and walks, as well as a bird sanctuary. You'll find a bee house, an aviary with native and exotic birds, a small-animal paddock, a horse-riding course, playgrounds, and games. An outstanding feature of the park is the **Donauturm (Danube Tower),** Donauturmstrasse 4 (© **01/2633-5720**), a 253m (830-ft.) tower with two rotating cafe-restaurants from which you have a panoramic view of Vienna. One restaurant is at the 161m (528-ft.) level; the other is at 171m (561 ft.). International specialties and Viennese cuisine are served in both. There's also a sightseeing terrace at 151m (495 ft.). Two express elevators take people up in the tower. It's open daily in summer from 10am to midnight and in winter from 10am to 10pm. The charge for the elevator is 5.30€ ($6.90) for adults and 3.90€ ($5.05) for children.

Wagramer Strasse. U-Bahn to Reichsbrücke.

Praterverband (The Prater) ⭐ *Kids*   This extensive tract of woods and meadowland in the 2nd District has been Vienna's favorite recreation area since 1766, when

---

(Fun Fact   Tales of the Vienna Woods

The Vienna Woods (*Wienerwald* in German) weren't something Johann Strauss (II) dreamed up to enliven his musical tales told in waltz time. The Wienerwald is a delightful hilly landscape of gentle paths and trees that borders Vienna on the southwest and northwest. If you stroll through this area, a weekend playground for the Viennese, you'll be following in the footsteps of Strauss and Schubert. Beethoven, when his hearing was failing, claimed that the chirping birds, the trees, and leafy vineyards of the Wienerwald made it easier for him to compose.

A round-trip through the woods takes about 3½ hours by car, a distance of some 80km (48 miles). Even if you don't have a car, the woods can be visited relatively easily. Board tram no. 1 near the Staatsoper, going to Schottentor; here, switch to tram no. 38 (the same ticket is valid) going out to **Grinzing,** home of the famous *heurigen* (wine taverns). Here you can board bus no. 38A to go through the Wienerwald to **Kahlenberg.** The whole trip takes about 1 hour each way. You might rent a bicycle nearby to explore the woods.

Kahlenberg is located on a hill that is part of the northeasternmost spur of the Alps (483m/1,584 ft.). If the weather is clear, you can see all the way to Hungary and Slovakia. At the top of the hill is the small Church of St. Joseph, where King John Sobieski of Poland stopped to pray before leading his troops to the defense of Vienna against the Turks. For one of the best views overlooking Vienna, go to the right of the Kahlenberg restaurant. From the terrace here, you'll have a panoramic sweep, including the spires of St. Stephan's. You can also go directly to Kahlenberg from the city center in about 20 minutes by U-Bahn to Heiligenstadt; then take bus no. 38A.

A favorite pastime, especially in summer, involves fleeing the congested city and taking tram no. D to either Heiligenstadt (a 30-min. ride from Stephansplatz) or Nussdorf (a 45-min. ride from Stephansplatz). At either of these points you'll see a string of *heurigen* and a series of footpaths perfect for a relaxing stroll.

For more about the Wienerwald, see chapter 10, "Side Trips from Vienna."

Emperor Joseph II opened it to the public. Before it became a public park, it had been a hunting preserve and riding ground for the aristocracy.

The Prater is an open fairground, without barricades or an entrance gate. Its attractions are independently operated and maintained by individual entrepreneurs who determine their own hours, prices, and, to a large extent, policies and priorities.

Few other spots in Vienna convey such a sense of the decadent end of the Habsburg Empire—it's turn-of-the-century nostalgia, with a touch of 1950s-era tawdriness. The Prater is the birthplace of the waltz, first introduced here in 1820 by Johann Strauss (I) and Josef Lanner. However, it was under Johann Strauss (II), "the King of the Waltz," that the musical form reached its greatest popularity.

The best-known part of the huge park is at the end nearest the entrance from the Ring. Here you'll find the **Riesenrad** (© **01/729-5430;** www.wienerriesenrad.com), the giant Ferris wheel, which was constructed in 1897 and reaches 67m (220 ft.) at its highest point. In 1997, the Ferris wheel celebrated its 100th anniversary, and it remains, after St. Stephan's Cathedral, the most famous landmark in Vienna. Erected at a time when European engineers were showing off their "high technology," the wheel was designed by Walter Basset, the British engineer, who, trying to outdo Eiffel, had constructed his tower in Paris a decade earlier. The wheel was designed for the Universal Exhibition (1896–97), marking the golden anniversary of Franz Joseph's coronation in 1848. Like the Eiffel Tower, it was supposed to be a temporary exhibition. Except for World War II damage, the Ferris wheel has been going around without interruption since 1897.

Just beside the Riesenrad is the terminus of the Lilliputian railroad, the 4km (2.5-mile) narrow-gauge line that operates in summer using vintage steam locomotives. The amusement park, right behind the Ferris wheel, has all the typical attractions—roller coasters, merry-go-rounds, tunnels of love, and game arcades. Swimming pools, riding schools, and racecourses are interspersed between woodland and meadows. International soccer matches are held in the Prater stadium.

The latest attraction includes "Volare—The Flying Coaster," which flies face down along a 435m (1,437-ft.) labyrinth of track at a height of 23m (75 ft.); and "Starflyer," a tower ride where passengers are whirled around at 70m (230 ft.) above the ground at speeds of up to 70kmph (43 mph).

The Prater is not a fenced-in park, but not all amusements are open throughout the year. The season lasts from March or April to October, but the Ferris wheel operates all year round. Some of the more than 150 booths and restaurants stay open in winter, including the pony merry-go-round and the gambling venues. If you drive here, don't forget to observe the no-entry and no-parking signs, which apply after 3pm daily. The place is usually jammed on Sunday afternoons in summer.

Admission to the park is free, but you'll pay for games and rides. The Ferris wheel costs 7.50€ ($9.75) for adults and 3€ ($3.90) for children ages 4 to 14; it's free for children 1 to 3.

Prater 9. © **01/728-0516.** Free admission; price for rides and amusements varies. May–Sept daily 10am–1am; Oct–Nov 3 daily 10am–10pm; Nov 4–Dec 1 daily 10am–8pm. Closed Dec 2–April. U-Bahn: Praterstern.

7 Especially for Kids

The greatest attraction for kids is the **Prater Amusement Park** (p. 133), but kids will also enjoy performances at the **Spanish Riding School** (p. 115); climbing the tower of **St. Stephan's Cathedral** (p. 117); and visiting the exhibition at the **Natural History Museum** (p. 129). And nothing quite tops a day like a picnic in the **Vienna Woods** (p. 133).

Other worthwhile museums for children include the **Zirkus und Clownmuseum (Circus and Clown Museum),** Karmelitergasse 9 (✆ **01/21106**), a tribute to clowns and circus performers throughout the centuries; and the **Wiener Straasenbahnmuseum (Streetcar Museum),** Ludwig-Koessler-Platz (✆ **01/7909-44900**), which commemorates the public conveyances that helped usher Vienna and the Habsburg Empire into the Industrial Age.

In addition to the below, see "Sports & Active Pursuits," at the end of this chapter.

Schönbrunner Tiergarten *Kids*   The world's oldest zoo was founded by the husband of Empress Maria Theresa. She liked to have breakfast here with her brood, favoring animal antics with her eggs. The baroque buildings in the historic park landscape make a unique setting for modern animal keeping; the tranquillity makes for a relaxing yet interesting outing.

Schönbrunn Gardens. ✆ **01/8779-2940.** Admission 12€ ($16) adults, 5€ ($6.50) students and children, free for children under 3. Mar–Sept daily 9am–6:30pm; Oct–Feb daily 9am–5pm. U-Bahn: Hietzing.

8 Musical Landmarks

If you're a fan of Mozart, Schubert, Beethoven, Strauss, or Haydn, you've landed in the right city. Not only will you be able to hear their music in the concert halls and palaces where they performed, but you can also visit the houses and apartments in which they lived and worked, as well as the cemeteries where they were buried.

Haydns Wohnhaus (Haydn's House)   This is where (Franz) Joseph Haydn (1732–1809) conceived and wrote his magnificent later oratorios *The Seasons* and *The Creation.* He lived in this house from 1797 until his death. Haydn also gave lessons to Beethoven here. There's a room in the house, which is a branch of the Historical Museum of Vienna, honoring Johannes Brahms.

Haydngasse 19. ✆ **01/596-1307.** Admission 2€ ($2.60) adults, 1€ ($1.30) students and children 10–16. Wed–Thurs 10am–1pm and 2–6pm; Fri–Sun 10am–1pm. Closed Mon and Tues. U-Bahn: Nestroyplatz.

Fun Fact **Now It Can Be Told: Porky Pig Murdered Mozart**

New theories about what caused the death of Mozart in 1791 have led to increased attendance at the **Mozart-Wohnung/Figarohaus** museum. The composer resided here from 1784 to 1787.

Dr. Jan V. Hirschmann, a distinguished physician, now believes he knows what caused Mozart's death at the age of 35. It was pork cutlets—that is, trichinosis, which wasn't identified until the 19th century. Hirschmann has discovered that Mozart wrote to his wife 44 days before his illness began, "What do I smell? Pork cutlets!" The doctor's eight-page report, based on an examination of medical literature and historical documents, appeared in 2001 in the *Archives of Internal Medicine.*

Fun Fact **Irascible Beethoven & His Beautiful Music**

Ludwig von Beethoven (1770–1827), a native of Bonn, Germany, paid his first visit to Vienna in 1787 to study under Mozart. After 2 weeks, however, his mother's deteriorating health prompted him to return to Germany. Five years later, after Mozart's death, he embarked on his second journey to Vienna to continue his studies with J. G. Albrechtsberger, Antonio Salieri, and Joseph Haydn. According to Count Waldstein, one of his later patrons, Beethoven came to Vienna to receive "Mozart's spirit from the hands of Haydn." As the protégé of Count Waldstein, he found that the doors of Viennese society were open to him. In spite of his republican leanings and at times irascible behavior, he soon became the darling of the aristocracy. His restless nature caused him to change residences 79 times during his 35 years in Vienna. In his last works—his famous *Ninth Symphony* as well as the late quartets and piano sonatas—Beethoven took the forms of music he had inherited into bold new directions.

Johann-Strauss Memorial Rooms   "The King of the Waltz," Johann Strauss, Jr. (1825–99), lived at this address for a number of years, composing "The Blue Danube Waltz" here in 1867. The house is now part of the Historical Museum of Vienna.

Praterstrasse 54. (C) 01/214-0121. Admission 2€ ($2.60) adults, 1€ ($1.30) children 10–18. Tues–Thurs 2–6pm, Fri–Sun 10am–1pm. U-Bahn: Nestroyplatz.

Mozart-Wohnung/Figarohaus (Mozart Memorial)   This 17th-century house is called the House of Figaro because Mozart (1756–91) composed his opera *The Marriage of Figaro* here. The composer resided here from 1784 to 1787, a relatively happy period in what was otherwise a rather tragic life. It was here that he often played chamber-music concerts with Haydn. Over the years he lived in a dozen houses in all, which became more squalid as he aged. He died in poverty and was given a "pauper's" blessing at St. Stephan's Cathedral and then buried in St. Marx Cemetery. The Domgasse apartment has been turned into a museum.

Domgasse 5. (C) 01/513-6294. Admission 9€ ($12) adults, 7€ ($9.10) students and children. Tues–Sun 10am–8pm. U-Bahn: Stephansplatz.

Pasqualati House   Beethoven (1770–1827) lived in this building on and off from 1804 to 1814. Beethoven is known to have composed his Fourth, Fifth, and Seventh Symphonies here, as well as *Fidelio* and other works. There isn't much to see except some family portraits and the composer's scores, but you might feel it's worth the climb to the fourth floor (there's no elevator).

Mölker Bastei 8. (C) 01/535-8905. Admission 2€ ($2.60) adults, 1€ ($1.30) children 6–18. Tues–Sun 10am–1pm and 2–6pm. U-Bahn: Schottentor.

Schubert Museum   The son of a poor schoolmaster, Franz Schubert (1797–1828) was born here in a house built earlier in that century. Many Schubert mementos are on view. You can also visit the house at Kettenbrückengasse 6, where he died at age 31.

Nussdorferstrasse 54. (C) 01/317-3601. Admission 2€ ($2.60) adults, 1€ ($1.30) students and children 10–16. Tues–Sun 10am–1pm and 2–6pm. S-Bahn: Canisiusgasse.

9 Organized Tours

Wiener Rundfahrten (Vienna Sightseeing Tours), Starhemberggasse 25 (© 01/
7124-6830; www.viennasightseeingtours.com), offers the best tours, including a 1-
day motor-coach excursion to Budapest costing 100€ ($130) per person. The histor-
ical city tour costs 34€ ($44) for adults and is free for children 12 and under. It's ideal
for visitors who are pressed for time and yet want to be shown the major (and most
frequently photographed) monuments of Vienna. Tours leave the Staatsoper daily at
9:45 and 10:30am and 2:45pm. The tour lasts 3½ hours (U-Bahn: Karlsplatz).

"Vienna Woods—Mayerling," another popular excursion, lasting about 4 hours,
leaves from the Staatsoper and takes you to the towns of Perchtoldsdorf and Modling,
and to the Abbey of Heiligenkreuz, a center of Christian culture since medieval times.
The tour also takes you for a short walk through Baden, the spa that was once a
favorite summer resort of the aristocracy. Tours cost 42€ ($55) for adults and 15€
($20) for children ages 10 to 16.

A **"Historical City Tour,"** which includes visits to Schönbrunn and Belvedere
palaces, leaves the Staatsoper daily at 9:45 and 10:30am and 2:45pm. It lasts about 3
hours and costs 35€ ($46) for adults and 15€ ($20) for children ages 10 to 18.

A variation on the city tour includes an optional visit to the Spanish Riding School.
This tour is offered Tuesday through Saturday, leaving from the Staatsoper building at
8:30am. Tickets are 59€ ($77) for adults, 30€ ($39) for children 13 and older, and
free for children 3 to 12.

Information and booking for these tours can be obtained either through Vienna
Sightseeing Tours (see above) or through its affiliate, **Elite Tours,** Operngasse 4
(© 01/5132225).

10 Sports & Active Pursuits
ACTIVE SPORTS
BIKING   Vienna maintains almost 322km (200 miles) of cycling lanes and paths,
many of which meander through some of the most elegant parks in Europe. Depending on their location, they're identified by a yellow image of a cyclist either stenciled
directly onto the pavement or crafted from rows of red bricks set amid the cobblestones or concrete of the busy boulevards of the city center. Some of the most popular bike paths run parallel to both the Danube and the Danube Canal.

You can carry your bike onto specially marked cars of the Vienna subway system,
but only during nonrush hours. Subway cars marked with a blue shield are the ones
you should use for this purpose. Bicycles are *not* permitted on the system's escalators—
take the stairs.

You can rent a bike for 3€ to 5€ ($3.90–$6.50) per hour. You'll usually be asked
to leave either your passport or a form of ID as a deposit. One rental possibility is
Pedal Power, Ausstellungsstrasse 3 (© 01/729-7234). There are rental shops at the
Prater and along the banks of the Danube Canal. You can also rent a bike at **Bicycle
Rental Hochschaubahn,** Prater 113 (© 01/729-5888).

One terrific bike itinerary, and quite popular since it has almost no interruptions,
encompasses the long, skinny island that separates the Danube from the Neue Donau
Canal. Low-lying and occasionally marshy, but with paved paths along most of its
length, it provides clear views of central Europe's industrial landscape and the endless
river traffic that flows by on either side.

Tips **Cruising the Danube**

Its waters aren't as idyllic as the Strauss waltz would lead you to believe, and its color is usually muddy brown rather than blue, but visitors to Austria still view a day cruise along the Danube as a highlight of their trip. Until the advent of railroads and highways, the Danube played a vital role in Austria's history, helping to build the complex mercantile society that eventually became the Habsburg Empire.

The most professional of the cruises are operated by the **DDSG Blue Danube Shipping Co.**, whose main offices are at Fredrickstrasse 7, A-1010 Vienna (© 01/588800; www.ddsg-blue-danube.at). The most appealing cruise focuses on the Wachau region east of Vienna, between Vienna and Dürnstein. The cruise departs April through October every Sunday at 8:30am from the company's piers at Handelskai 265, 1020 Vienna (U-Bahn: Vorgartenstrasse), arriving in Dürnstein 6 hours later. The cost is 50€ ($65) for adults; it's half-price for children 10 to 15.

April through October, DDSG operates a daily hydrofoil that departs from the Vienna piers at 9am and arrives in Budapest at 2:30pm. One-way transit is 79€ ($103) for adults; it's half-price for children 15 and under.

BOATING   Wear a straw boating hat and hum a few bars of a Strauss waltz as you paddle your way around the quiet eddies of the Alte Donau. This gently curving stream bisects residential neighborhoods to the north of the Danube and is preferable to the muddy and swift-moving currents of the river itself.

At An der Obere along the Danube, you'll find some kiosks in summer, where you can negotiate for the rental of a boat, perhaps a canoe or a kayak. There are, of course, organized tours of the Danube, but it's more fun to do it yourself.

GOLF   The two golf courses in or near Vienna are chronically overbooked, forcing even long-term members to be highly flexible about their starting times. The busier, and more challenging, of the region's two golf courses lies within a 15-minute drive north of Vienna, on the grounds of the Prater, at the 18-hole **Golfplatz Wien-Freudenau 65A** (© 01/728-9564). If there's an available tee-off time, nonmembers with a minimum handicap of 28 can play for a fee of 70€ ($91) per person. More likely to have an available tee-off time on a weekday (but rarely on a weekend), is **Golfplatz Föhrenwald** (© 02622/29171), an 18-hole course that's positioned about 48km (30 miles) south of Vienna, at Bodenstrasse 54 in the hamlet of Klein Wolkersdorf, just outside the suburb of Weiner Neustadt. If space is available, greens fees there cost 55€ ($72) for tee-offs Monday to Friday, 70€ ($91) for tee-offs on Saturday or Sunday, and require that prospective players have a handicap of at least 45.

HEALTH CLUBS   Even if you're not registered there, you may use the exercise facilities at the popular health club, **Health & Fitness (Living Well Express)**, in the Vienna Hilton, Am Stadtpark (© 01/717-00-12800). Positioned on the third floor (designed in the access elevators as level "M1") of the also-recommended hotel, it charges nonresidents of the hotel 12€ ($16) to use the fitness equipment, with a supplement of 5€ ($6.50) for access to the sauna and steam rooms. Know in advance that men and women share the same sauna and steam room facilities, either with or without the discreet covering of a towel, so if you're feeling shy or modest at the time of your visit, plan your sauna rituals accordingly. (Women who prefer to have their sauna alone are directed, by appointment only, to a private room.) Between September and May it's open daily from 11am to 10pm; between June and August it's open daily from 2 to 10pm. Hotel residents, without charge, can use the exercise facilities at this place 24 hours a day, but if they opt for the sauna and steam room, their visits will be limited to the hours noted above, and they'll be asked to pay the 5€ ($6.50) supplement.

HIKING   You're likely to expend plenty of shoe leather simply walking around Vienna, but if you yearn for a more isolated setting, the city tourist offices will provide information about its eight **Stadt-Wander-Wege.** These marked hiking paths usually originate at a stop on the city's far-flung network of trams.

You can also head east of town into the vast precincts of the **Lainzer Tiergarten,** where hiking trails meander amid forested hills, colonies of deer, and abundant bird life. To get there, first take the U-Bahn to the Kennedy Brücke/Hietzing station, which lies a few steps from the entrance to Schönbrunn Palace. Take tram no. 60, then bus no. 60B.

ICE SKATING   There's a public rink, the **Wiener Eislaufverein,** Lothringer Strasse 22 (© 01/713-6353), within a 20-minute walk southeast of the cathedral. Located just outside the famous Am Stadtpark, near the Inter-Continental Hotel, and especially crowded on weekends, the rink rents skates and is open from late October to early March daily from 8am to 8pm. Monday through Saturday, the charge is 7€ ($9.10) for adults and 5.50€ ($7.15) for children 7 to 18. On Sunday, the price goes up to 8€ ($10) for adults and 6€ ($7.80) for children. Skates rent for 6€ ($7.80). The rest of the year (Apr to Sept), the site is transformed into seven public tennis courts available to anyone who wants to play. The price for rental of a court is 8.50€ ($11) for daily sessions from 8am to noon, 11€ ($14) for sessions from noon to 5pm, and 15€ ($20) for sessions from 5 to 8pm.

SKIING   We strongly recommend that if you're an avid skier, avoid the flatlands of Vienna completely and head for mountainous regions in western and southern Austria, particularly the Tyrol, Land Salzburg, the Vorarlberg, or perhaps Styria. (For more about the ski resorts of those regions, refer to this edition's companion guide, *Frommer's Austria.*)

If you're absolutely dying to go skiing and you're not able to wander far from the relatively flat landscapes in and around Vienna, there's a limited amount of skiing within about an hour's drive of the city, on the gentle slopes of Mount Semmering (the Hirschenkogl Ski Lifts) and Mount Schneeberg (the Rax am Schneeberg Lifts; © 02664/20025 for information about either venue). Most visitors find it infinitely easier to reach these areas by car, but in a serious pinch, you can ride the U4 subway to the Hütteldorf station, then take bus no. 49B to the city's far-flung 14th district. For additional information about skiing in Austria, either near Vienna or within the more appealing zones of the country's western regions, contact the Austrian National Tourist Office, Margaretenstrasse 1, A-1040 Vienna (© 01/588660).

SWIMMING   Despite the popularity of certain beaches on islands in the Alte Donau Canal in summer, swimming in either the Danube or any of its satellite canals is not recommended because of pollution and a dangerous undertow in the main river.

To compensate, Vienna has dozens of swimming pools. Your hotel's receptionist can tell you about options in your neighborhood. One of the most modern is in the Prater. For locations of any of the city's many indoor or outdoor pools, contact the Vienna Tourist Office, Obere Augartenstrasse 40 (℃ **01/24-555**).

TENNIS   Your hotel might have a connection to a tennis court in Vienna, or might be able to steer you to a court nearby. Also see the listing for "Ice Skating," earlier in this section, for information about the courts at Wiener Eislaufverein. The **Askoe-Tennis-Centrum-Schmelz,** Auf der Schmelz 10 (℃ **01/982-1333;** take U3 to Jungstrasse), is a modern complex with about a dozen outdoor courts. Depending on the time of day, prices range from 8.80€ to 12€ ($11–$16) per hour. An indoor court costs 14€ ($18) per hour. If nothing is available, we recommend that you contact one of the city's largest tennis agencies, **Askoe Wien,** Hafenleitengasse 73, in the 11th District (℃ **01/545-3131**). It will direct you to one of several tennis courts it manages throughout the city and might charge a small referral fee.

SPECTATOR SPORTS

HORSE RACING   There are three racetracks in Vienna, but by far the oldest, most venerable, and most prestigious is the **Rennbahn Freudenau, at Trapprenbahnplatz** on the grounds of the Prater (℃ **01/728-9531**). Established in 1836, it operates from April to November, and traditionally includes both trotting and flat racing. The Vienna Derby, one of the season's highlights, takes place here in late June. A "competing" racetrack, smaller and less interesting in terms of architecture, lies on the opposite side of the Prater fairgrounds: **Rennbahn Krieau** (℃ **01/728-0046**) operates trotting races every week of the year, except for during July and August, when the venue is closed, and when race fans head to a racetrack in the outlying resort of Baden for a short, 2-month season. Newer than any of the above-mentioned racetracks, and permeated with a deliberate dose of hypermodern style that's directly influenced by Las Vegas, is the **Magna Racino** racetrack and casino complex in the Viennese suburb of A-2483 Ebreichsdorf (℃ **02254/9000;** www.magnaracino.at), 30km (19 miles) south of Vienna. Inaugurated in 2004 and funded by a Canadian billionaire of Austrian descent, it's the site of a casino, several restaurants, an ongoing series of cabaret with girls-and-glitter shows, and horse races, which run between April and early November. At press time, it was fighting for market shares in the tight-knit world of Austrian horseracing. It's the home of the **Austrian Derby,** presented in late June.

SOCCER   Football, as it's known in Europe, tends to draw a slightly less impassioned response in Austria than it does in Germany or Italy, but it still exerts a powerful appeal on sports fans throughout town. The city's two soccer teams are **Rapide-Wien,** Hannappi Stadion, Keisslergasse (℃ **01/91001;** U-Bahn: Hütteldorf), and the Austrian national team (Österreichische National Team), based at the **Horr Stadion,** Fischhofgasse (℃ **01/688-0150;** U-Bahn: Reumannplatz). Bigger than either of those stadiums, and usually used for soccer matches of above-average international interest drawing massive crowds, is the **Ernst-Happel-Stadion** (sometimes known simply as **Weiner Stadion**), Meiereistrasse 7 (℃ **01/728-0854;** U-Bahn: Praterstern, then tram no. 21 to Meiereistrasse). For tickets and information about upcoming events, call the stadiums.

7

Vienna Walking Tours

Vienna's architecture is a treasure trove that includes buildings erected during virtually every period of the city's history. Although it suffered extensive damage during World War II, Vienna retained many of its important buildings, and reconstruction has been meticulous. All this makes Vienna a natural place for rewarding walking tours.

Each of the three walking tours below is geared toward a different kind of experience. Note that many of the streets in the revered 1st District are pedestrian malls, and cars have been banished except for early morning deliveries; however, on the streets where there's still traffic, beware of cars because drivers sometimes roar through narrow streets at relatively high speeds.

WALKING TOUR 1 — IMPERIAL VIENNA

Start:	Staatsoper (State Opera House).
Finish:	Staatsoper.
Time:	3 hours.
Best Time:	During daylight hours or at dusk.
Worst Time:	Rainy days.

One of dozens of potential paths through Vienna's historic center, this meandering tour will give you at least an exterior view of the Habsburgs' urban haunts. This tour also reveals lesser-known sights best seen from the outside on foot. Later, you can pick the attractions you want to revisit. (For details on many of these sights, see chapter 6.)

Our tour begins at the southernmost loop of Ringstrasse, the beltway that encircles most of the historic core of the city, in the shadow of the very symbol of Austrian culture, the:

❶ Staatsoper (State Opera House)
Built between 1861 and 1865 in a style inspired by the French Renaissance (and faithfully reconstructed after World War II), it was so severely criticized when it was unveiled that one of its architects, Eduard van der Null, committed suicide. (See "Walking Tour 2," later in this chapter, for a more extensive discussion.)

On Opernring, walk 1 block north on Austria's most famous pedestrian street, Kärntner Strasse. We'll eventually walk past the glamorous shops and famous houses, but for the moment, turn left behind the arcaded bulk of the State Opera onto Philharmonikerstrasse. On the right side, you'll see the lushly carved caryatids and globe lights of Vienna's best-known hotel, the:

❷ Hotel Sacher
A confectionery store with a separate street entrance sells the hotel's namesake, Sachertorte, which can be shipped anywhere in the world.

A few steps later you'll find yourself amid the irregular angles of Albertinaplatz, where you'll be able to plunge into the purely Viennese experience of the *kaffeehaus*.

TAKE A BREAK
If you'd rather indulge in heartier fare than the coffeehouses offer, try the **Augustinerkeller**, Augustinerstrasse 1 ((C) **01/533-1026**), in the basement of the Hofburg palace sheltering the Albertina collection. This popular wine tavern, open daily from 11am to midnight, offers wine, beer, and Austrian food.

In the same building as your rest stop is the:

❸ Albertina

A monumental staircase in the building's side supports the equestrian statue that dominates the square. Its subject is Field Marshal Archduke Albrecht, in honor of a battle he won in 1866.

Adjacent to Albertinaplatz, at Lobkowitzplatz 2, lies one of the many baroque jewels of Vienna. Its position is confusing because of the rows of buildings partially concealing it. To get here, walk about 50 paces to the right of the Albertina. This is the:

❹ Lobkowitz Palace

This privately owned building existed in smaller form at the time of the second Turkish siege of Vienna. After the Turks were driven from the outskirts of the city, the palace was enlarged by the reigning architect of his day, Fischer von Erlach. In 1735, it passed into the hands of Prince Lobkowitz, a great patron of the arts; Beethoven's Third Symphony premiered here in 1803.

At the far end of Lobkowitzplatz, take Gluckgasse past a series of antiques shops filled with Art Deco jewelry and silverware. At the end of the block, at Tegetthoffstrasse, go left. About 50 paces later, you'll be in front of the deceptively simple facade of the:

❺ Church of the Capuchin Friars

Originally constructed in the 1620s, its facade was rebuilt in 1935 along a severely simple design following old illustrations. Despite its humble appearance, the Kapuzinerkirche contains the burial vaults of every Habsburg ruler since 1633. The heavily sculpted double casket of Maria Theresa and her husband, Francis, is flanked with weeping nymphs and skulls but capped with a triumphant cherub reuniting the couple.

The portal of this church marks the beginning of the Neuer Markt, whose perimeter is lined with rows of elegant baroque houses. The square's centerpiece is one of the most beautiful works of outdoor art in Austria, the:

❻ Donner Fountain

Holding a snake, the gracefully undraped Goddess of Providence is attended by four laughing cherubs struggling with fish. Beside the waters flowing into the basin of the fountain are four allegorical figures representing nearby tributaries of the Danube. The fountain is a copy of the original, which was moved to the Baroque Museum in the Belvedere Palace. The original was commissioned by the City Council in 1737 and executed by Georg Raphael Donner, but judged obscene and immoral when Maria Theresa viewed it for the first time. Today it's considered a masterpiece.

Take the street stretching west from the side of the fountain, Plankengasse, where a yellow baroque church fills the space at the end of the street. As you approach it, you'll pass an array of shops filled with alluring old-fashioned merchandise. Even the pharmacy at the corner of Spiegelgasse has a vaulted ceiling and rows of antique bottles. Museum-quality antique clocks fill the store at Plankengasse 6 and its next-door neighbor at the corner of Dorotheergasse.

Turn left when you reach Dorotheergasse, past the Italianate bulk of no. 17. This is one of the most historic auction houses of Europe, the:

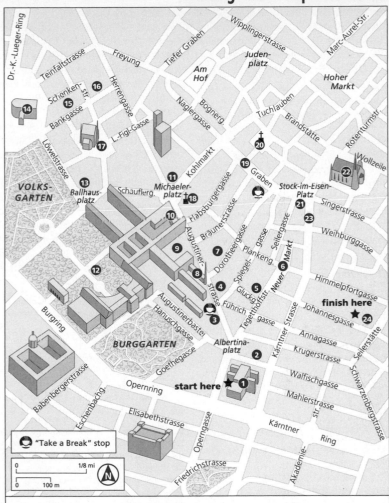

🔵 "Take a Break" stop

0	1/8 mi
0	100 m

1 Staatsoper	**9** Josefsplatz	**18** St. Michael's Church
2 Hotel Sacher	**10** Spanish Riding School	**19** Plague Column
3 Albertina Collection	**11** Loos House	**20** Peterskirche
4 Lobkowitz Palace	**12** Heldenplatz	**21** Stock-im-Eisen
5 Church of the Capuchin Friars	**13** Chancellery	**22** St. Stephan's Cathedral
6 Donner Fountain	**14** Burgtheater	**23** Kärntner Strasse
7 Dorotheum	**15** Palais Liechtenstein	**24** Savoy Foundation for Noble Ladies
8 Hofburg	**16** Hungarian Embassy	
	17 Church of the Minorites	

⓻ Dorotheum

Established in 1707, it was rebuilt in the neo-baroque style in 1901. Here, members of Austria's impoverished aristocracy could discreetly liquidate their estates.

About half a block later, turn right onto Augustinerstrasse, which borders the labyrinth of palaces, museums, and public buildings known as the:

⓼ Hofburg

Roaring traffic usually diminishes the grime-encrusted grandeur of this narrow street with darkened stone walls. Despite that modern intrusion, this group of buildings is the single most impressive symbol of the majesty and might of the Habsburgs.

In about half a block you'll arrive at:

⓽ Josefsplatz

A huge equestrian statue of Joseph II seems to be storming the gate of no. 5, the Palffy Palace, originally built around 1575 with a combination of classical and Renaissance motifs. Two pairs of relaxed caryatids guard the entrance. Next door, at no. 6, is another once-glittering private residence, the Palavicini Palace. Completed in 1784 for members of the Fries family, it was later purchased by the family whose name it bears today.

A few steps later, a pedestrian tunnel leads past the:

⓾ Spanish Riding School (Spanische Reitschule)

The district becomes increasingly filled with slightly decayed vestiges of a vanished empire whose baroque monuments sit on outmoded, too-narrow streets amid thundering traffic.

Michaelerplatz now opens to your view. At Michaelerplatz 3, opposite the six groups of combative statues, is a streamlined building with rows of unadorned windows. This is the:

⓫ Loos House

Designed in 1910, it immediately became the most violently condemned building in town. That almost certainly stemmed from

the unabashed (some would say provocative) contrast between the lavishly ornamented facade of the Michaelerplatz entrance to the Hofburg and what contemporary critics compared to "the gridwork of a sewer." Franz Joseph hated the building so much that he used the Michaelerplatz exit as infrequently as possible.

A covered tunnel that empties both pedestrians and automobiles into the square takes you beneath the Hofburg complex. Notice the passageway's elaborate ceiling: spears, capes, and shields crowning the supports of the elaborate dome. This must be one of the most heavily embellished traffic tunnels in the world. As you walk through the tunnel, a series of awesomely proportioned courtyards reveals the Imperial Age's addiction to conspicuous grandeur.

When you eventually emerge from the tunnel, you'll find yourself surrounded by the magnificent curves of:

⓬ Heldenplatz

Its carefully constructed symmetry seems to dictate that each of the stately buildings bordering it, as well as each of its equestrian statues and ornate lampposts, has a well-balanced mate.

Gardens stretch out in well-maintained splendor. Enjoy the gardens if you want, but to continue the tour, put the rhythmically spaced columns of the Hofburg's curved facade behind you, and walk cater-corner to the far end of the palace's right wing. At Ballhausplatz 2, notice the:

⓭ Chancellery

It's an elegant building, erected in 1720, yet its facade is modest in comparison with the ornamentation of its royal neighbor. Here, Count Kaunitz plotted with Maria Theresa to expand the influence of her monarchy. Prince Metternich used these rooms as his headquarters during the Congress of Vienna (1814–15). Many of the decisions made here were links in the chain of events leading to World War I. In 1934, Austrian Nazis murdered Dollfuss here. Four years later,

Hermann Goering, threatening a military attack, forced the ouster of the Austrian cabinet with telephone calls to an office in this building. Rebuilt after the bombings of World War II, this battle-scarred edifice has housed Austria's Foreign Ministry and its federal chancellor's office since 1945.

Walk along the side of the Chancellery's adjacent gardens, along Lowelstrasse. Notice the window trim of some of the buildings along the way, each of which seems to have its own ox, satyr, cherub, or Neptune carved above it. Continue until you reach the:

⑭ Burgtheater

This is the national theater of Austria. Destroyed in World War II, it reopened in 1955.

At the Burgtheater, make a sharp right turn onto Bankgasse. On your right at no. 9 is the:

⑮ Palais Liechtenstein

An ornate beauty, the building was completed in the early 18th century.

A few buildings farther on, pause at nos. 4–6, the:

⑯ Hungarian Embassy

You'll see stone garlands and catch glimpses of crystal chandeliers.

Now retrace your steps for about half a block until you reach Abraham-a-Sancta-Clara-Gasse. At its end, on Minoritenplatz, you'll see the severe Gothic facade of the:

⑰ Church of the Minorites

Its 14th-century severity contrasts sharply with the group of stone warriors struggling to support the gilt-edged portico of the baroque palace facing it.

Walk behind the blackened bulk of the church to the curve of the building's rear. At this point some maps might lead you astray. Regardless of the markings on your map, look for Leopold-Figl-Gasse and walk down it. You'll pass between two sprawling buildings, each of which belongs to one of the Austrian bureaucracies linked by a bridge. A block later, turn right onto Herrengasse. Within a few minutes, you'll be on the now-familiar Michaelerplatz. This time you'll have a better view of:

⑱ St. Michael's Church

Winged angels carved by Lorenzo Mattielli in 1792 fly above the entranceway, and a single pointed tower rises. Turn left (north) along Kohlmarkt, noticing the elegant houses along the way: No. 14 houses **Café Demel,** the most famous coffeehouse in Vienna; no. 9 and no. 11 bear plaques for Chopin and Haydn, respectively.

At the broad pedestrian walkway known as the Graben, turn right. In the center is the:

⑲ Plague Column

The baroque structure has chiseled representations of clouds piled high like whipped cream. It's dotted profusely with statues of ecstatic saints fervently thanking God for relief from an outbreak of the Black Plague that erupted in Vienna in 1679 and may have killed as many as 150,000 people. Carved between 1682 and 1693 by a team of the most famous artists of the era, this column eventually inspired the erection of many similar monuments throughout Austria.

A few feet before the Plague Column, turn left onto Jungferngasse and enter our favorite church in Vienna:

⑳ Peterskirche

Believed to be on the site of a crude wooden church built during the Christianization of Austria around A.D. 350, it was later (according to legend) rebuilt by Charlemagne. A lavish upgrade by baroque artists during the 1700s incorporated the work of the famous painter J. M. Rottmayr.

Return to the Graben, passing the Plague Column. A few steps beyond it, pass the bronze statue of a beneficent saint leading a small child. You might, after all this, enjoy a sandwich. Leave the Graben at one of the first intersections on the right, Dorotheergasse, where you'll find a fine choice.

Impressions

This is a town for walkers: nearly every street inside the inner city, within the semicircle of the linked series of avenues known collectively as the Ringstrasse, holds something of interest.

—Novelist William Murray, 1999

 TAKE A BREAK
Despite its functional simplicity, **Buffet Trzesniewski,** Dorotheergasse 1 (*(©)* 01/512-3291), has satisfied the hunger pangs of everyone who was anyone in Vienna in the last century. For more info, see chapter 5, "Where to Dine."

After your break, continue southeast down the Graben to its terminus. Here you'll find a vaguely defined section of pavement that signs identify as:

㉑ Stock-im-Eisen

Here two pedestrian thoroughfares, the Graben and Kärntner Strasse, meet at the southernmost corner of Stephansplatz. To your right, notice the sheet of curved Plexiglas bolted to the corner of an unobtrusive building at the periphery of the square. Behind it are the preserved remains of a **tree.** In it, 16th-century blacksmiths would drive a nail for luck each time they left Vienna. Today the gnarled and dusty log is covered with an almost uninterrupted casing of angular, hand-forged nails.

By now, it will be difficult to avoid a full view of Vienna's most symbolic building:

㉒ St. Stephan's Cathedral

Newcomers should circumnavigate the building's exterior to check out its 12th- and 13th-century stonework before going inside.

When you exit, turn left after passing through the main portal and head down the most famous street in Vienna's Inner City, the pedestrian-only:

㉓ Kärntnerstrasse

As you wander through the street, don't miss the mini museum of glassmaking that decorates the second floor of the world-famous glassmaker **Lobmeyr,** at no. 26.

If you still have the energy, detour off Kärntnerstrasse, turning left on Johannesgasse. You'll pass some old and very interesting facades before reaching the baroque carvings and stone lions that guard the 17th-century portals of the:

㉔ Savoy Foundation for Noble Ladies (Savoysches Damenstift)

Countless generations of well-born Austrian damsels struggled to learn "the gentle arts of womanhood" here, at no. 15. Established by the duchess of Savoy-Carignan and originally built in 1688, its facade is adorned with a lead statue by the baroque sculptor F. X. Messerschmidt.

As you retrace your steps to the shops and the pedestrian crush of Kärntner Strasse, you might hear strains of music cascading into the street from the **Vienna Conservatory of Music,** which occupies several buildings on Johannesgasse. Turn left as you re-enter Kärntner Strasse, enjoying the sights until you eventually return to your point of origin, the **State Opera House.**

WALKING TOUR 2   SOUTH OF THE RING

Start:	Staatsoper (State Opera House).
Finish:	Gumpendorferstrasse (on Sat, Flohmarkt).
Time:	3½ hours, not counting visits to museums.
Best Time:	Saturday morning, when the Flohmarkt is open.
Worst Time:	After dark or in the rain.

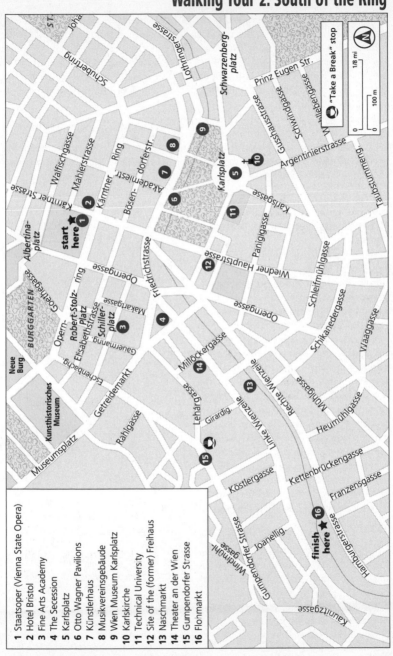

1 Staatsoper (Vienna State Opera)
2 Hotel Bristol
3 Fine Arts Academy
4 The Secession
5 Karlsplatz
6 Otto Wagner Pavilions
7 Künstlerhaus
8 Musikvereinsgebäude
9 Wien Museum Karlsplatz
10 Karlskirche
11 Technical University
12 Site of the (former) Freihaus
13 Naschmarkt
14 Theater an der Wien
15 Gumpendorfer Strasse
16 Flohmarkt

"Take a Break" stop

The temptation is strong, especially for first-time visitors to Vienna, to limit exploration to the monuments within the Ring—the city's medieval core, the 1st District.

You'll discover a different side of Vienna by following this tour, which incorporates the sometime surreal manifestations of *fin-de-siècle* Habsburg majesty a short distance south of the Ring. The tour also includes less celebrated late-19th-century buildings that don't seem as striking today as when they were designed, but which, for their era, were almost revolutionary.

Regrettably, parts of the 6th District, the area of this tour, were heavily damaged and then rebuilt after the horrors of World War II. Parts of the tour take you along busy, less-than-inspiring boulevards. Fortunately, a network of underground walkways, designed by city planners as part of Vienna's subway system, makes navigating the densest traffic a lot easier.

Begin your tour near the southern facade of:

❶ The Staatsoper (Vienna State Opera)

This French Renaissance structure was the first of the many monuments built during the massive Ringstrasse project. Franz Joseph began the development around 1850 on land reclaimed from the razing of Vienna's medieval fortifications. Controversy and cost overruns plagued the construction from the moment the foundations were laid. On the building's southern edge, the roaring traffic of the nearby Ringstrasse is several feet higher than the building's foundation, a result of bad overall planning. This error, coupled with an offhand—but widely reported—criticism of the situation by Franz Joseph, is believed to have contributed to the suicide (by hanging) of one of the building's architects, van der Null, and the death by stroke a few weeks later of its other architect, von Sicardsburg.

The roof and much of the interior were largely rebuilt after a night bombing on March 12, 1945, sent the original building up in flames. Ironically, the last performance before its near-destruction was a rousing version of Wagner's *Götterdammerung*, with its immolation scene. Since its reconstruction, the Staatsoper has nurtured such luminaries as Bruno Walter and Herbert von Karajan.

Across the avenue, on your left as you face the Ring, at the intersection of the Kärntner Ring and the Kärntner Strasse, is one of Europe's grandest hotels, the:

❷ Hotel Bristol

Ornate and socially impeccable, the Bristol reigns alongside the Sacher and the Imperial as the *grandes dames* of Viennese hotels. A deceptively unpretentious lobby might disappoint; a labyrinth of upstairs corridors conceals the most impressive reception areas. Consider returning later for a midafternoon coffee or a drink in one of the bars.

Now descend into the depths of an underground passageway that begins at the corner of the Kärntner Strasse and the Kärntner Ring, just south of the Opera House. (You'll find it's a lot easier and safer than trying to cross the roaring traffic of the Ring as an unarmed pedestrian.) You'll pass some underground boutiques before climbing out on the southern edge of the Opernring.

Walk west along the Opernring, using another of those underground tunnels to cross beneath the Operngasse, until you reach the Robert-Stolz-Platz, named after an Austrian composer who died nearby in 1975. If you glance north, across the Opernring, you'll see a faraway statue of Goethe, brooding in a bronze chair, usually garnished with a roosting pigeon. The Robert-Stolz-Platz opens southward into the Schillerplatz, where, as you'd expect, an equivalent statue features an image of Schiller. The building on Schillerplatz's southern edge (Schillerplatz 3) is the:

❸ Akademie der Bildenden Künste (Fine Arts Academy)

Erected between 1872 and 1876, it's a design by the Danish architect Theophil Hansen in a mix of Greek Revival and Italian Renaissance styles. Here the artistic dreams of 18-year-old Adolf Hitler were dashed in 1907 and 1908 when he twice failed to gain admission to what was at the time the ultimate arbiter of the nation's artistic taste and vision. A few years later, painter Egon Schiele, an artist of Hitler's age, eventually seceded from the same academy because of its academic restrictions and pomposity. For details about the exhibits in this building, refer to chapter 6.

Now walk east for a half block along the Niebelungengasse and then south along the Makartgasse, skirting the side of the Academy. Makartgasse bears the name of Hans Makart, the most admired and sought-after painter in 19th-century Vienna, and the darling of the Academy you've just visited. His soaring studio, which Franz Joseph himself subsidized, became a salon every afternoon at 4pm to receive every prominent newcomer in town. Exhibitions of his huge historical canvases attracted up to 34,000 people at a time. Young Adolf Hitler is said to have idolized Makart's grandiloquent sense of flamboyance; Klimt and Schiele of the Secessionist school at first admired him, then abandoned his presuppositions and forged a bold new path. Rumor and innuendo swirled about the identities of the models, who appeared as artfully undressed figures in the handsome and promiscuous artist's paintings. He fell from social grace after defying upper-class conventions by marrying a ballet dancer; then he contracted a case of syphilis that killed him at age 44.

At the end of Makartgasse, turn left (east) and go a half block. Then turn right onto the

Friedrichstrasse. Before the end of the block, at Friedrichstrasse 12, is the Jugendstil (Art Nouveau) facade of a building that launched one of the most admired and envied artistic statements of the early 20th century:

❹ The Secession

At the time of its construction in 1898, its design was much more controversial than it is today, and hundreds of passersby would literally gawk. Its severe cubic lines, Assyrian-looking corner towers, and gilded dome caused its detractors to refer to it as "the Gilded Cabbage" and "Mahdi's Tomb." It was immediately interpreted as an insult to bourgeois sensibilities. Despite (or perhaps because of) the controversy, 57,000 people attended the inaugural exhibition of Secessionist works. The Secession's location, within a short walk of the organization it defied (stop no. 3, the Fine Arts Academy), was an accident, prompted only by the availability of real estate. Inside, a roster of innovative display techniques—revolutionary for their time—included movable panels, unadorned walls, and natural light pouring in through skylights. The inscription above the door, *Jeder Zein sein Kunst, Jeder Kunst sein Freiheit,* translates as, "To every age its art, to every art its freedom." Damaged during World War II and looted in 1945, it lay derelict until 1973, when it was bought and later restored as a municipal treasure.

From here, retrace your steps northeasterly beside the dense traffic of the Friedrichstrasse for 2 blocks. At the corner of the Niebelungengasse and the Friedrichstrasse (which forks gently into the Operngasse nearby), you'll find the entrance to an underground tunnel, part of Vienna's subway network, that will lead you safely beneath roaring traffic for several blocks to your next point of interest.

Follow the underground signs to the subway and to the Wiedner Hauptstrasse. Turn right at the first major underground intersection, again following signs to the Wiedner Hauptstrasse. After a rather long walk, you'll ascend into

daylight near the sprawling and sunken perimeter of the:

❺ Karlsplatz

For many generations, this sunken bowl contained Vienna's fruit-and-vegetable markets. Too large to be called a square and too small to be a park, it's an awkward space that's valued today mainly as a means of showcasing the important buildings that surround it.

Climb from the Karlsplatz up a flight of stone steps to the platform that skirts the Karlsplatz's northern edge, and walk east for a minute or two. The small-scale pair of Jugendstil (Art Nouveau) pavilions you'll notice are among the most famous of their type in Vienna, the:

❻ Otto Wagner Pavilions

Originally designed by Otto Wagner as a station for his *Stadtbahn* (the subway system he laid out), they are gems of applied Secessionist theory and preserved as monuments by the city. After their construction, many of their decorative adornments were copied throughout other districts of the Austro-Hungarian Empire as part of the late-19th-century building booms. Regrettably, many were later demolished as part of the Soviet regime's control of the Iron Curtain countries during the Cold War. Art historians consider them Vienna's response to the Métro stations of Paris built around the same time.

From here, continue walking east. The first building across the avenue on your left, at Friedrichstrasse 5, is the:

❼ Künstlerhaus

Around 1900, its name was associated with conservative art and tended to enrage the iconoclastic rebels who later formed the Secessionist movement. Completed in 1868, this not particularly striking building functioned for years as the exhibition hall for students at the Fine Arts Academy. Today, it's used for temporary exhibitions and devotes some of its space to film and theater experiments.

Immediately to the right (east) of the Künstlerhaus, at Karlsplatz 13, is the Renaissance-inspired:

❽ Musikvereinsgebäude (Friends of Music Building)

Home of the Vienna Philharmonic, this is the site of concerts that often sell out years in advance through fiercely protected private subscriptions. Constructed between 1867 and 1869, and designed by the same Theophil Hansen who built the Fine Arts Academy (stop no. 3), it's another example of the way architects dabbled in the great historical styles of the past during the late-19th-century revitalization of the Ringstrasse.

At Karlsplatz 4, a short walk southeast from the Musikverein, is a monument that serves, better than any other, to bind the complicated worlds, subcultures, and historic periods that form the city of Vienna, the:

❾ Wien Museum Karlsplatz

Its holdings are so vast, it deserves a separate visit.

Continue your clockwise circumnavigation of the Karlsplatz to the majestic confines of the:

❿ Karlskirche (Church of St. Charles)

Built by Emperor Charles VI, father of Maria Theresa, who mourned the loss of Austria's vast domains in Spain, this church was conceived as a means of recapturing some of Vienna's imperial glory. It is the monument for which the baroque architect Fischer von Erlach the Elder is best remembered today, and the most impressive baroque building in Austria. Built between 1716 and 1737, nominally in thanks for Vienna's surviving another disastrous bout with the plague, it combines aspects of a votive church with images of imperial grandeur. At the time of its construction, the Ringstrasse was not yet in place, and it lay within an easy stroll of the emperor's residence in the Hofburg. Rather coyly, Charles didn't name the church after himself, but after a Milanese prelate (St. Charles Borromeo), although the confusion that ensued was almost certainly deliberate.

To construct the skeleton of the church's dome, 300 massive oak trees were felled. The twin towers in front were inspired by Trajan's Column in Rome, the Pillars of Hercules (Gibraltar) in Spain, and Mannerist renderings of what contemporary historians imagined as the long-lost Temple of Jerusalem. The reflecting fountain in front of the church, site of a parking lot in recent times, contains a statue donated by Henry Moore in 1978.

Now continue walking clockwise around the perimeter of the square to the southern edge of the Karlsplatz. A short side street running into the Karlsplatz here is the Karlsgasse. At Karlsgasse 4, you'll see a plaque announcing that in a building that once stood here, Johannes Brahms died in 1897. The next major building you'll see is the showcase of Austria's justifiably famous reputation for scientific and engineering excellence, the:

⓫ Technische Universität (Technical University)

Its Ionic portico overlooks a public park with portrait busts of the great names associated with this center of Austrian inventiveness. Josef Madersperger, original inventor of the sewing machine in 1815 (who died impoverished while others, such as the Singer family, profited from his invention), and Siegfried Marcus, inventor of a crude version of the gasoline-powered automobile in 1864, were graduates of the school. Other Austrians associated with the institution are Ernst Mach, for whom the speed at which an aircraft breaks the sound barrier is named, and Josef Weineck, whose experiments with the solidification of fats laid the groundwork for the cosmetics industry.

Continue walking west along the southern perimeter of the Karlsplatz, past the Resselpark, and across the Wiedner Hauptstrasse, a modern manifestation of an ancient road that originally linked Vienna to Venice and Trieste. Urban historians consider this neighborhood Vienna's first suburb, although wartime damage from as early as the Turkish sieges of 1683 has largely destroyed its antique character. Sprawling annexes of the Technical University and bland modern buildings now occupy the neighborhood to your left, stretching for about 4 blocks between the Wiedner Hauptstrasse and the Naschmarkt (which you'll soon visit). But historians value it as the 18th-century site of one of the largest communal housing projects in Europe, the long-gone:

⓬ Freihaus

In the 18th century, more than 1,000 people inhabited apartments here. In 1782, the Theater auf der Wieden, where Mozart's *Magic Flute* premiered, opened in a wing of the building. During the 19th century, when the Freihaus degenerated into an industrial slum and became a civic embarrassment in close proximity to the Karlskirche and the State Opera House, much of it was demolished to make room for the Operngasse. World War II bombings finished off the rest.

Continue walking along the Treitlstrasse, the westward extension of Resselpark, until you reach the Rechte Wienzeile, a broad boulevard that once flanked the quays of the Danube before the river was diverted as part of 19th-century urban renewal. In the filled-in riverbed, you'll see the congested booths and labyrinthine stalls of Vienna's largest food-and-vegetable market, the:

⓭ Naschmarkt

Wander through the produce, meat, and dairy stalls. If you want to buy, there are more appealing and more expensive shops near the Naschmarkt's eastern end. The center is devoted to housewares and less glamorous food outlets, including lots of butcher shops. After exploring the food market, walk along the market's northern fringe, the Linke Wienzeile.

At the corner of the Millöckergasse, at Linke Wienzeile 6, you'll see a historic theater that, during the decade-long renovation of the State Opera House, functioned as Vienna's primary venue for the performing arts, the:

⓮ Theater an der Wien

Despite its modern facade (the result of an unfortunate demolition and rebuilding around 1900 as well as damage during World War II), it's the oldest theater in Vienna, dating to 1801. To get an idea of its age, bypass the front entrance and walk northwest along Millöckergasse—named after an overwhelmingly popular composer of Viennese operettas, Karl Millöcker (1842–99). At no. 8 is the theater's famous *Pappagenotor,* a stage door entrance capped with an homage to Pappageno, the Panlike character in Mozart's *Magic Flute.* The likeness was deliberately modeled after Emanuel Schikaneder, the first actor to play the role, the author of most of the libretto, and the first manager, in 1801, of the theater. Attached to the wall near the *Pappagenotor* is a plaque recognizing that Beethoven lived and composed parts of his Third Symphony and the *Kreuzer* sonata inside. An early—later rewritten—version of Beethoven's *Fidelio* premiered at this theater, but after an uncharitable reception, the composer revised it into its current form.

Continue walking northwest along Millöckergasse, then turn left onto the Lehárgasse. (The massive building on the Lehárgasse's north side is yet another annex of the Technical University.) Within about 3 blocks, Lehárgasse merges into the:

⓫ Gumpendorferstrasse

Here you see the same sort of historically eclectic houses, on a smaller scale, that you'll find on the Ringstrasse. Previously the medieval village of Gumpendorf, the neighborhood was incorporated into the city of Vienna as the 6th District in 1850. Modern Viennese refer to the neighborhood as Mariahilf. At this point, it's time to:

TAKE A BREAK
Café Sperl, Gumpendorferstrasse 11 (℡ **01/586-4158**), is one of the most historic cafes in the district. From the time of its establishment in the mid-1800s until renovations in the 1960s ripped away some of its ornate interior, it functioned as a hub of social and intellectual life in this monument-rich district. The artists who initiated the Secession maintained a more or less permanent table in the cafe.

After your break, walk southwest along Gumpendorferstrasse, admiring the eclectic Ringstrasse-style houses and apartment buildings that line the sidewalks. At Köstlergasse, turn left and walk for about a block past some more ornate 19th-century architecture. At the end of Köstlergasse (at nos. 1 and 3) are apartment houses designed by Otto Wagner. Around the corner at Linke Wienzeile 40, you'll see yet another of his designs, an apartment house referred to by architecture students around the world as the **Majolikahaus.** Adjacent to the Majolikahaus, at 38 Linke Wienzeile, is the **Medallion House,** with a Secession-style floral display crafted from tiles set into its facade. It was designed by Koloman Moser, creator of the stained-glass windows in the Am Steinhof church.

Your tour is about over, unless it happens to be Saturday, between 7am and around 4pm. If it is, continue southwest along Linke Wienzeile (cross over the Kettenbrückengasse) toward the enchantingly seedy site of one of Europe's most nostalgic flea markets, the:

⓰ Flohmarkt

Don't expect glamour, or even merchants who are particularly polite. But scattered amid the racks of cheap clothing, kitchenware, and hardware, you're likely to find plenty of imperial kitsch: porcelain figures of Franz Joseph, medallions of Empress Maria Theresa, drawings of the Hofburg, soldier figurines of the Imperial Guard, paintings of St. Stephan's Cathedral, and faded portraits of the Empress Elisabeth.

WALKING TOUR 3   VIENNA'S BACK STREETS

Start:	Maria am Gestade.
Finish:	St. Stephan's Cathedral.
Time:	2½ hours (not counting visits to interiors).
Best Time:	Daylight hours, when you can visit shops and cafes.
Worst Time:	In the rain and between 4 and 6pm.

In 1192, the English king Richard I (the Lion-Hearted) was captured trespassing on Babenburg lands in the village of Erdberg—now part of Vienna's 3rd District—after his return to England from the Third Crusade. The funds the English handed over for his ransom were used for the enlargement of Vienna's fortifications, which eventually incorporated some of the neighborhoods you'll cover on this walking tour. Horrified, the pope excommunicated the Babenburg potentate who held a Christian crusader, but not before some of medieval London was mortgaged to ransom him and, eventually, pay for Vienna's city walls.

Much of this tour focuses on smaller buildings and lesser-known landmarks on distinctive streets where some of the most influential characters of Viennese history have walked. Prepare yourself for a labyrinth of medieval streets and covered passages, and insights into the age-old Viennese congestion that sociologists claim helped catalyze the artistic output of the Habsburg Empire.

Begin your promenade slightly northwest of Stephansplatz with a visit to one of the least-visited churches of central Vienna:

❶ Maria am Gestade

The edifice, at Salvatorgasse 1, is also known as "Maria-Stiegen-Kirche," or the Church of St. Mary on the Strand. Designated centuries ago as the Czech national church in Vienna, it replaced a wooden church, erected in the 800s, with the 14th-century stonework you see today. Restricted by the narrowness of the medieval streets around it, the church's unusual floor plan is only 30 feet wide, but it's capped with one of the neighborhood's most distinctive features, an elaborate pierced Gothic steeple. Since the early 19th century, when the first of at least five renovations began, art historians have considered the church one of the most distinctive but underrated buildings in town.

From here, walk south along the alleyway that flanks the church's eastern edge, turning left (east) at the Wipplingerstrasse for an eventual view of the:

❷ Altes Rathaus

The Habsburg ruler Duke Frederick the Fair confiscated the building in 1316 from the leader of an anti-Habsburg revolt and subsequently donated it to the city. It later gained a baroque facade (1700) and a courtyard fountain (1740–41) that's famous for being one of Raphael Donner's last works. The building, at Wipplingerstrasse 3, functioned as Vienna's Town Hall until 1885, when the city's municipal functions moved to grander, neo-Gothic quarters on the Ring. Today, the Altes Rathaus contains a minor museum dedicated to the Austrian resistance to the Turks.

Wipplingerstrasse runs east into the:

❸ Hoher Markt

The city's oldest marketplace, this was the location of a public gallows until the early 1700s, and of a pillory used to punish dishonest bakers until the early 1800s. Hoher Markt was originally the forum of the ancient Roman settlement of Vindobona. Some excavations of what's believed to be a Roman barracks are visible in the courtyard of the building at no. 3. It's likely, according to scholars, that Marcus Aurelius died of the plague here in A.D. 180. In the 1700s, several generations of plague columns (erected in thanksgiving for deliverance from the Turks and from the plague) replaced the instruments of torture that dominated the square. The present version was designed by Josef Emanuele von Ehrlach in 1732 and sculpted by Italian-born Antonio Corradini. An important scene from the film *The Third Man* was filmed at the base of the Hoher Markt's famous clock, the Ankeruhr, which—to everyone's amazement—escaped destruction during aerial bombardments of the square in 1945.

From here, walk a short block east along the Liechtensteingasse, then turn left and walk northeast along one of Vienna's most prominent shopping streets, the Rotenturmstrasse, for 2 blocks. Then turn right (east) onto the:

❹ Griechengasse

The construction of this narrow street in the 1100s was representative of the almost desperate need for expansion away from the city's earlier perimeter, which more or less followed the ancient configuration of the Roman settlement of Vindobona. Griechengasse's name comes from the 18th-century influx of Greek merchants, precursor of the waves of immigrants flooding into modern Vienna from eastern Europe and the Middle East today. At Griechengasse 5, notice the unpretentious exterior of the Greek Orthodox church, built in 1805 with the plain facade that was legally required of all non-Catholic churches until the 19th century. At Griechengasse 7, occupying the point where the street turns sharply at an angle, stands a 14th-century watchtower. One of the few medieval vestiges of the old city walls, it was incorporated long ago into the antique architecture that surrounds it.

The Griechengasse narrows at this point, and in some places buttresses supporting the walls of the buildings on either side span it. Griechengasse soon intersects with a thoroughfare where, during the 12th century, you'd have been affronted with the stench of rancid blood from the nearby slaughterhouses.

Turn right and head to:

❺ Fleischmarkt

Notice the heroic frieze above the facade of the antique apartment house at no. 18 ("The Tolerance House"), which depicts in symbolic form Joseph II, son of Maria Theresa, granting freedom of worship to what was at the time a mostly Greek Orthodox neighborhood. No. 9, opened in the 1400s and improved and enlarged during the next 300 years, was used as an inn (or, more likely, a flophouse) and warehouse for traders from the Balkans and the Middle East during the age of Mozart.

TAKE A BREAK
Griechenbeisl, Fleischmarkt 11 (☎ 01/533-1941), is an inn named for the many Greeks who made it their regular dining spot for hundreds of years. Established in 1450 and divided into a warren of cozy dining rooms, it's described more fully in chapter 5, "Where to Dine."

The walls of another Greek Orthodox church rise adjacent to the Griechenbeisl. It was embellished in 1858 by Theophil Hansen, the Danish-born architect of many of the grand buildings of the Ringstrasse.

At Fleischmarkt 15, notice the baroque facade of the birthplace of an obscure Biedermeier painter, Moritz von Schwind. His claim to fame is his membership in the circle of friends who attended the Schubertiades, evenings of music and philosophy organized by Franz Schubert in Vienna during the early 19th century.

Walking Tour 3: Vienna's Back Streets

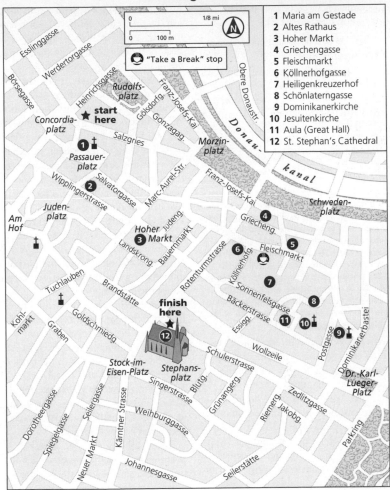

1 Maria am Gestade
2 Altes Rathaus
3 Hoher Markt
4 Griechengasse
5 Fleischmarkt
6 Köllnerhofgasse
7 Heiligenkreuzerhof
8 Schönlaterngasse
9 Dominikanerkirche
10 Jesuitenkirche
11 Aula (Great Hall)
12 St. Stephan's Cathedral

A branch of the Vienna post office lies at no. 19, on the premises of a monastery confiscated from the Dominicans by Joseph II as part of his campaign to secularize the Austrian government. The only ecclesiastical trappings left in this bureaucratic setting are the skeletons of dozens of dead brethren, buried in the building's crypt many generations ago.

The uninspired modern facade of the building at Fleischmarkt 24 was the long-ago site of a now-defunct hotel, Zur Stadt London, whose musical guests included the family of young Mozart as well as Franz Liszt, Richard Wagner (when he wasn't fleeing his creditors), and the Polish exile Chopin. The building at Fleischmarkt 14 shows a rich use of Jugendstil (Art Nouveau) detailing, and a plaque commemorating it as the birthplace of one of the directors of the Court Opera in the latter days of the Habsburg dynasty. At Fleischmarkt 1, residents will tell you about the birth here of a later director of the same opera company, after its reorganization into the State Opera.

Turn left and walk for about a half block on the:

⑥ Köllnerhofgasse

Nos. 1 through 3 functioned long ago as the headquarters of a group of merchants, based on the Rhine in Cologne, who set up a trading operation in Vienna in response to fiscal and legal perks and privileges granted to merchants during medieval times. The building you'll see today—remarkable for the number of windows in its facade—dates from 1792.

At this point, turn left into a cul-de-sac that funnels through a wide gate into a courtyard that's always open to pedestrians. The cul-de-sac is Grashofgasse, at the end of which is a wall painted with a restored fresco of the Stift Heiligenkreuz (Holy Cross Abbey), a well-known 12th-century Cistercian monastery 15 miles west of town. A covered arcade, which is usually open, pierces the wall of Grashofgasse 3 and leads into the cobbled public courtyard of the:

⑦ Heiligenkreuzerhof

This ecclesiastical complex incorporates a 17th-century cluster of monks' apartments, lodging for an abbot, and the diminutive baroque chapel of St. Bernard, which is usually closed to the public except for wedding ceremonies. The courtyard's continued existence in the heart of Vienna is unusual: Many equivalent tracts formerly owned by abbeys were converted long ago into building sites and public parks after sale or confiscation by the government.

Exit the monastery's courtyard from its opposite (southeastern) edge onto the:

⑧ Schönlaterngasse

Its name derives from the ornate wrought-iron street lamp that adorns the facade of the 16th-century building at no. 6. What hangs there now is a copy; the original is in the Historical Museum of Vienna. This well-maintained street is part of a designated historic preservation district. Renovation loans to facilitate

such preservation were issued at rock-bottom interest rates and have been referred to ever since as *kultur schillings*. The neighborhood you're in is a prime example of these loans in action.

At Schönlaterngasse 7 lies the **Basilikenhaus,** a 13th-century bakery supported by 12th-century foundations. When foul odors began emanating from the building's well, the medieval residents assumed that it was sheltering a basilisk (a mythological reptile from the Sahara Desert whose breath and gaze were fatal). The building's facade incorporates a stone replica of the beast, who was killed, according to a wall plaque, by a local baker who bravely showed the creature its own reflection in a mirror. A modern interpretation involves the possibility of methane gas or sulfurous vapors seeping out of the building's well.

Schönlaterngasse 7A was the home of Robert Schumann from 1838 to 1839, the winter he rediscovered some of the unpublished compositions of Franz Schubert. Schumann, basking in the glory of a successful musical and social career, did more than anyone else to elevate Schubert to posthumous star status. The groundwork for the renaissance of Schubert's music was laid at this spot.

The building at no. 9 (Die Alte Schmiede) on the same street has functioned as a smithy since the Middle Ages. From outside, you can glimpse a collection of antique blacksmith tools.

Continue walking east along the Schönlaterngasse, where you'll see the back of the Jesuit Church, which you'll visit in a moment. Continue walking (the street turns sharply right) until the street widens into the broad plaza of the Postgasse, where you turn right. The monument that rises in front of you, at Postgasse 4, is the:

⑨ Dominikanerkirche

This is the third of three Dominican churches on this site. The earliest, constructed around 1237, burned down. The Turks demolished the second, completed around 1300, during the siege of 1529. The building you see today was completed in 1632 and is the most important early baroque church in Vienna. The rather murky-looking frescoes in the side chapels are artistically noteworthy; some are the 1726 statement of baroque artist Françoise Roettiers. However, the church is mainly attractive as an example of baroque architecture and for the pomp of its high altar. Elevated to the rank of what the Viennese clergy calls a "minor basilica" in 1927, it's officially the "Rosary Basilica ad S. Mariam Rotundam." Don't confuse the Dominikanerkirche with the less architecturally significant Greek Orthodox Church of St. Barbara, a few steps to the north at Postgasse 10, with its simple facade and elaborate liturgical rituals. Beethoven lived for about a year in a building adjacent to St. Barbara's, Postgasse 8.

Now, walk south along the Postgasse to its dead end, and turn right into a narrow alley interspersed with steps. The alley widens within a few paces into the Bäckerstrasse, a street noted for its imposing 18th-century architecture. Architects of such minor palaces as the ones at nos. 8 and 10 adorned their facades with unusual details that could be appreciated from close up. Long ago, no. 16 contained an inn (Schmauswaberl—"The Little Feast Hive") favored at the time by university students because of its habit of serving food left over from the banquets at the Hofburg at discounted prices. Other buildings of architectural note include nos. 7, 12, and 14, whose statue of Mary in a niche above the door shows evidence of the powerful effect of the Virgin on the everyday hopes and dreams of Vienna during the baroque age.

Follow Bäckerstrasse for about a block until you reach the confines of the square that's referred to by locals as the Universitätsplatz but by virtually every map as the Dr. Ignaz Seipel-Platz (named for a theologian and priest who functioned twice as chancellor of Austria between the two world wars). The building that dominates the square is the:

⑩ Jesuitenkirche/Universitätskirche (Jesuit Church/University Church)

It was built between 1623 and 1627 and adorned with twin towers and an enhanced baroque facade in the early 1700s by those workhorses of the Austrian Counter-Reformation, the Jesuits. Ferdinand, the fervently Catholic Spanish-born emperor, invited the Jesuits to Vienna at a time when about three-quarters of the population had converted to Protestantism. It was estimated that only four Catholic priests remained at their posts in the entire city. From this building, the Jesuits spearheaded the 18th-century conversion of Austria back to Catholicism and more or less dominated the curriculum at the nearby university. The stern group of academics built an amazingly ornate church, with allegorical frescoes and all the aesthetic tricks that make visitors believe they've entered a transitional world midway between earth and heaven.

The western edge of Dr. Ignaz Seipel-Platz borders one of the showcase buildings of Vienna's university, the:

⑪ Aula (Great Hall)

Vienna's premier rococo attraction, the Aula is a precursor of the great concert halls that dot the city today. In the 1700s, musical works were presented in halls such as this one, private homes, or the palaces of wealthy patrons. Haydn's oratorio *The Creation* had its premiere here, as did Beethoven's Seventh Symphony.

Exit the Dr. Ignaz Seipel-Platz at its northwest corner, and walk along the Sonnenfelsgasse. Flanked with 15th- and 16th-century houses (which until recently drew complaints because of the number of bordellos they housed), the street is architecturally noteworthy.

The building at Sonnenfelsgasse 19, dating from 1628, was once home to the proctor (administrator) of the nearby university. Other buildings of noteworthy beauty include nos. 3, 15, and 17. The street bears the name of one of the few advisors who could ever win an argument with Maria Theresa, Josef von Sonnenfels. The son of a Viennese Christian convert, Sonnenfels was descended from a long line of German rabbis. He learned a dozen languages while employed as a foot soldier in the Austrian army and later used his influence to abolish torture in the prisons and particularly cruel methods of capital punishment. Beethoven dedicated his Piano Sonata in D Major to him.

Walk to the western terminus of the Sonnenfelsgasse, then turn left and fork sharply back to the east along the Bäckerstrasse. You will, in effect, have circumnavigated an entire medieval block.

After your exploration of Bäckerstrasse, turn south into a narrow alleyway, the Essigstrasse (Vinegar St.), and cross over the Wollzeile, centerpiece of the wool merchants and weavers' guild during the Middle Ages and now a noted shopping district. Continue your southward trek along the Stroblgasse, which leads into the Schulerstrasse. Turn right onto the Schulerstrasse, which leads within a block to a sweeping view of the side of:

⓬ St. Stephan's Cathedral

Built over a period of 400 years, and the symbol of Vienna itself, it's one of the city's most evocative and history-soaked monuments. (See "Other Top Attractions," in chapter 6.)

Shopping

Visitors can spend many happy hours shopping or just browsing in Vienna's shops, where handicrafts are part of a long-established tradition of skilled workmanship. Popular for their beauty and quality are petit-point items, hand-painted Wiener Augarten porcelain, gold and silver work, ceramics, enamel jewelry, wrought-iron articles, and leather goods, among others.

1 The Shopping Scene

The main shopping streets are in the city center (1st District). Here you'll find **Kärntnerstrasse,** between the State Opera and Stock-im-Eisen-Platz (U-Bahn: Karlsplatz); the **Graben,** between Stock-im-Eisen-Platz and Kohlmarkt (U-Bahn: Stephansplatz); **Kohlmarkt,** between the Graben and Michaelerplatz (U-Bahn: Herrengasse); and **Rotenturmstrasse,** between Stephansplatz and Kai (U-Bahn: Stephansplatz). Other destinations are **Mariahilferstrasse,** between Babenbergerstrasse and Schonbrunn, one of the longest streets in Vienna (U-Bahn: Mariahilferstrasse or Schönbrunn); **Favoritenstrasse,** between Süditrolerplatz and Reumannplatz (U-Bahn: Süditrolerplatz); and **Landstrasser Hauptstrasse** (U-Bahn: Schlachthausgasse).

The **Naschmarkt** is a vegetable-and-fruit market with a lively scene every day. To visit it, head south of the opera district. It's at Linke and Rechte Wienzeile (U-Bahn: Karlsplatz; see the box, "Open-Air Markets," later in this chapter.)

Right in the heart of the city, opening onto Stephansplatz, stands the supremely modern **Haas House,** designed by the renowned Pritzker Prize–winning Hans Hollein. You can see the mirror image of the cathedral reflected in its semicircular glass facade. Today, Haas House shelters a number of exclusive shops and boutiques, and also boasts a terrace restaurant with a panoramic view over the historic core.

SHOPPING HOURS

Shops are normally open Monday to Friday from 9am to 6pm, and Saturday from 9am to 1pm. Small shops close between noon and 2pm for lunch. Shops in the Westbahnhof and Südbahnhof railroad stations are open daily from 7am to 11pm, offering groceries, smokers' supplies, stationery, books, and flowers.

A SHOPPING CENTER

Ringstrassen-Galerien   Rental fees for shop space in central Vienna are legendarily expensive. In response, about 70 boutique-ish emporiums selling everything from key chains to evening wear have pooled their resources and moved to labyrinthine quarters near the State Opera House, midway between the Bristol Hotel and the Anna Hotel. The prominent location guarantees glamour, though the cramped dimensions of many of the stores might be a turnoff. However, the selection is broad, and no one can deny the gallery's easy-to-find location. Each shop is operated independently, but

Vienna Shopping

A.E. Köchert **21**
Agatha Paris **30**
Albin Denk **14**
Altmann & Kühne **15**
Arcadia Opera Shop **28**
Augarten Porzellan **16**
The British Bookshop **27**
Da Caruso **3**
Dorotheum **24**
D&S Antiquitäten **23**
Flohmarkt **1**
Galerie bei der Albertina **25**
Gerstner **19**
Glasgalerie Kovacek **22**
J. & L. Lobmeyr **26**
Kober **11**
Lanz **18**
Loden Plankl **4**
Mary Kindermoden **13**
Morawa **8**
Naschmarkt **2**
Niederösterreichisches
  Heimatwerk **6**
Ö.W. (Österreichische
  Werkstatten) **17**
Popp & Kretschmer **29**
Ringstrassen-Galerien **30**
Rozet & Fischmeister **5**
Shakespeare & Company **7**
Sportalm Trachtenmoden **9**
Steffl Kaufhaus **20**
Wein & Co. **10**
Zur Schwäbischen
  Jungfrau **12**

Votivkirche
Roosevelt-platz
SCHOTTENRING
Schottenring
Börse
Börse-platz
Universität Wien
Schottenstift
Freyung
RATHAUS
Rathaus
Rathaus-platz
Burgtheater
Am Hof
Minoriten-kirche
Minoriten-platz
HERREN-GASSE
Michaeler-platz
Michaeler-kirche
PARK
Parlament
VOLKSGARTEN
Ballhaus-platz
Schmerling-platz
Hofburg
Josefs-platz
Heldenplatz
Burgring
VOLKS-THEATER
Volkstheater
Naturhistorisches Museum
Neue Hofburg
BURGGARTEN
Maria-Theresien-Platz
Kunsthistorisches Museum
Museums-Quartier
Opernring
MUSEUMS-QUARTIER
Schiller-platz
Akad. der Bildenden Künste
Secession
To Westbahnhof and Schönbrunn
Mariahilfer Strasse
Theater an der Wien
Naschmarkt

0   200 yds
0   200 m

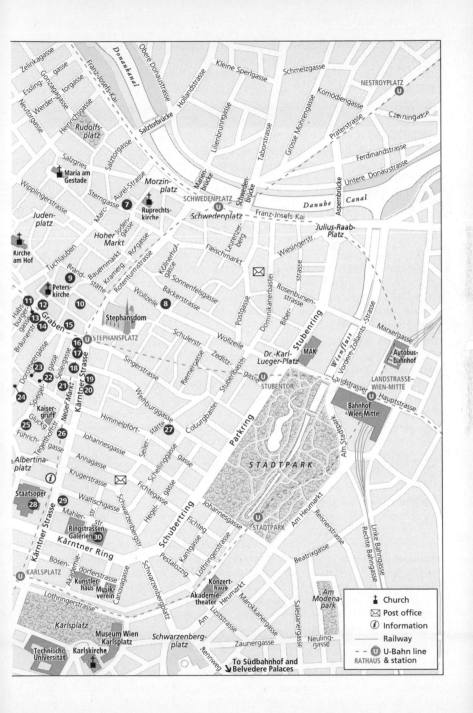

Zelinkagasse
Esslinggasse
Gonzagagasse
Werdertorgasse
Neutorgasse
Heinrichsgasse
Franz-Josefs-Kai
Donaukanal
Obere Donaustrasse
Salztorbrücke
Salztorgasse
Kleine Sperlgasse
Hollandstrasse
Lilienbrunngasse
Schmelzgasse
Schmelzgasse
Komödiengasse
Grosse Mohrengasse
Praterstrasse
NESTROYPLATZ
Czerningasse
Ferdinandstrasse
Untere Donaustrasse

Rudolfs-platz
Salzgries
Maria am Gestade
Sterngasse
Aurel-Strasse
Marc
Morzin-platz
7
Ruprechts-kirche
Marienbrücke
Schwedenbrücke
SCHWEDENPLATZ
Schwedenplatz
Franz-Josefs Kai
Danube Canal
Aspernbrücke
Julius-Raab-Platz

Wipplingerstrasse
Juden-platz
Hoher Markt
Judengasse
Rotgasse
Fleischmarkt
Leutenberg
Wiesingerstr
Strasse

Kirche am Hof
Tuchlauben
Brand-stätte
Bauernmarkt
Kramerg.
Rotenturmstrasse
Kölnerhof-gasse
Sonnenfelsgasse
Postgasse
Dominikanerbastei
Rosenbursen-strasse
Biber-

9
Peters-kirche
10
Wollzeile
Bäckerstrasse
8

11
12
Habs-burgergasse
13
14
Graben
15
Stephansdom
STEPHANSPLATZ
Schulerstr.
Wollzeile
Zedlitz-
Dr.-Karl-Lueger-Platz
Stubenring
MAK
Winzhus
Vordere-Zollamts-Strasse
Marxergasse
Autobus-bahnhof
LANDSTRASSE-WIEN-MITTE

16
17
18
19
20
21
Neuer Markt
Kärntner Strasse
Singerstrasse
Riemergasse
Zedlitz-
Stubenbastei
gasse
STUBENTOR
Landstrasser Hauptstrasse
Bahnhof Wien-Mitte
Am Stadtpark

23
22
Dorotheergasse
Sellergasse
Weihburggasse
Coburgbastei
Parkring

24
Spiegel-
Bräunerstr
Kaiser-gruft
Glückg.
Tegetthoffstr.
Führich-gasse
Johannesgasse
Annagasse
Schellinggasse
Fichtegasse
Himmelpfort-stätte
27
STADTPARK

25
26
Albertina-platz
Krugerstrasse

Staatsoper
28
29
Walfischgasse
Mahler-str.
Ringstrassen-Galerien
30
Kärntner Ring
Bösen-dorferstrasse
Akademie-
Künstler-haus
Musik-verein
KARLSPLATZ
Lothringerstrasse

Schwarzenbergstr.
Hegel-
Fichteg.
Kantgasse
Pestalozzig.
Lothringerstrasse
Schwarzenberg-platz
Schubertring
Johannesgasse
Am Heumarkt
Reisnerstrasse
Linke Bahngasse
Rechte Bahngasse
Beatrixgasse

Karlsplatz
Museum Wien Karlsplatz
Technische Universität
Karlskirche
Schwarzenberg-platz
Zaunergasse
Rennweg
Am Heumarkt
Marokkanergasse
Lisztstrasse
Konzert-haus
Akademie-theater
Salesianergasse
Neulinggasse
Am Modena-park

To Südbahnhof and Belvedere Palaces

♱	Church
✉	Post office
ⓘ	Information
——	Railway
- - Ⓤ	U-Bahn line & station
RATHAUS	

virtually all of them conduct business Monday to Friday 10am to 7pm, and Saturday 10am to 6pm. Stores here of particular interest to fashion hounds include Casselli and Agatha Paris (see listings below). In the Palais Corso and in the Kärntnerringhof, Kärntner Ring 5-13. ℂ 01/512-81-11.

2 Shopping A to Z

ANTIQUES

Vienna's antiques shops constitute a limitless treasure trove. You can find valuable old books, engravings, etchings, and paintings in secondhand shops, bookshops, and picture galleries.

D&S Antiquitäten ℛ *Finds*   Some of the greatest breakthroughs in clock-making technology occurred in Vienna between 1800 and 1840. This store, established in 1979, specializes in the acquisition, sale, and repair of antique Viennese clocks, stocking an awesome collection worthy of many world-class museums. The shop even stocks a "masterpiece" (each craftsman made only one such piece in his lifetime, to accompany his bid for entrance into the clockmakers' guild)—in this case, the work of a well-known craftsman of the early 1800s, Benedict Scheisel. Don't come here expecting a bargain—prices are astronomical—and devotees of timepieces from around the world flock to this emporium, treating it like a virtual museum of clocks. Dorotheergasse 13. ℂ 01/512-1011.

Dorotheum ℛℛ   Dating from 1707, this is the oldest auction house in Europe. Emperor Joseph I established it so that impoverished aristocrats could fairly (and anonymously) get good value for their heirlooms. Today the Dorotheum holds many art auctions. If you're interested in an item, you give a small fee to a *sensal,* or licensed bidder, and he or she bids in your name. The vast array of objects for sale includes exquisite furniture and carpets, delicate objets d'art, and valuable paintings, as well as decorative jewelry. If you're unable to attend an auction, you can browse the sale rooms, selecting items you want to purchase directly to take home with you the same day. Approximately 31 auctions take place in July alone; over the course of a year, the Dorotheum handles some 250,000 pieces of art and antiques. Dorotheergasse 17. ℂ 01/5156-0200.

Flohmarkt ℛ   You might find a little of everything at this flea market near the Naschmarkt (see the box "Open-Air Markets," below) and the Kettenbrückengasse U-Bahn station. It's held every Saturday from 6:30am to 6pm, except on public holidays. The Viennese have perfected the skill of haggling, and the Flohmarkt is one of their favorite arenas. It takes a trained eye to spot the antique treasures scattered among the junk. Everything you've ever wanted is here, especially if you're seeking chunky Swiss watches from the 1970s, glassware from the Czech Republic (sold as "Venetian glassware"), and even Russian icons. Believe it or not, some of this stuff is original; other merchandise is merely knockoff. Linke Wienzeile. No phone.

Galerie bei der Albertina   Come here for ceramics and furniture made during the early 20th century by the iconoclastic crafts group Weiner Werkstette. Its members made good use of the machinery of the emerging industrial age in the fabrication of domestic furnishings and decor. The inventory incorporates decorative objects, sculpture, paintings from the Jugendstil (Art Nouveau) age, etchings, an occasional drawing by Egon Schiele or Gustav Klimt. Lobkowitzplatz 1. ℂ 01/513-1416.

Glasgalerie Kovacek   Antique glass collected from estate sales and private collections throughout Austria takes up the ground floor. Most items date to the 19th and early 20th centuries, some to the 17th century. The most appealing pieces boast heraldic symbols, sometimes from branches of the Habsburgs. Also here is a collection of cunning glass paperweights imported from Bohemia, France, Italy, and other parts of Austria.

The upper floor holds the kind of classical paintings against which the Secessionists revolted. Look for canvases by Franz Makart, foremost of the 19th-century historic academics, as well as some Secessionist works, including two by Kokoschka. Spiegelgasse 12. ℰ **01/512-9954.**

ART

Ö.W. (Österreichische Werkstatten) ℛ   Even if you skip every other store in Vienna, check this one out. This well-run store sells hundreds of handmade art objects. Leading artists and craftspeople throughout the country organized this cooperative to showcase their wares. The location is easy to find, only half a minute's walk from St. Stephan's Cathedral. There's an especially good selection of pewter, along with modern jewelry, glassware, brass, baskets, ceramics, and serving spoons fashioned from deer horn and bone. Take some time to wander through; you never know what treasure is hidden in a nook of this cavernous three-floor outlet. Kärntnerstrasse 6. ℰ **01/512-2418.**

BOOKS

The British Bookshop   This is the largest and most comprehensive emporium of English-language books in Austria, with a sprawling ground-floor showroom loaded with American, Australian, and English books. There are no periodicals and no cute gift displays. All you'll find is enough reading material to last you for the rest of your life, and educational aids for teaching English as a second language. Weihburggasse 24-26. ℰ **01/512-1945.**

> ### VAT Refunds
>
> Fortunately for visitors to Austria, the country's Value-Added Tax (*Mehrwertsteuer Rückvergütung,* or VAT), which can be as high as 34% on some luxury goods, is refundable. See "Taxes" under the section "Fast Facts: Vienna" in chapter 3 to learn the refund procedure.

Morawa   This is a well-stocked branch of one of Austria's largest bookstore chains, with a collection of mostly German-language, and to a lesser degree English-language, books. If you're looking exclusively for English-language books, it's better to head to either the British Bookshop (see above) or Shakespeare & Company (noted below). Wollzeile 11. ℰ **01/910-76276.**

Shakespeare & Company   Established in the 1980s as a bastion of English-language reading skills, and modeled to some degree after its older and much more famous namesake in Paris, this store carries an especially good collection of English-language books and magazines. Sterngasse 2. ℰ **01/535-5053.**

CHANDELIERS

J. & L. Lobmeyr ℛℛℛ   If during your exploration of Vienna you admire a crystal chandelier, there's a good chance that it was made by this company. Designated purveyor to the Imperial Court of Austria in the early 19th century, it has maintained an elevated position ever since. The company is credited with designing and creating the

---

Fun Fact **The Austro-Hungarian Empire Lives On**

The empire of the kingdom of Austria and Hungary faded into history at the end of World War I, and Austria is only a tiny republic today. But you wouldn't know that by looking into the windows of certain shops. Many proudly display the initials "K & K," or *Kaiserlich und Königlich*. The anachronistic symbol translates as "by appointment of the Imperial and Royal Household."

---

first electric chandelier in 1883. It has also designed chandeliers for the Vienna State Opera, the Metropolitan Opera House in New York, the Assembly Hall in the Kremlin, the new concert hall in Fukuoka, Japan, and many palaces and mosques in the Near and Far East.

Behind its Art Nouveau facade on the main shopping street of the city center, you'll see at least 50 chandeliers of all shapes and sizes. The store also sells hand-painted Hungarian porcelain, along with complete breakfast and dinner services. It will engrave your family crest on a wineglass or sell you a unique modern piece of sculptured glass from the third-floor showroom. The second floor is a museum of some the outstanding pieces the company has made since it was established in 1823. Kärntnerstrasse 26. ℂ 01/512-0508.

CONFECTIONERY

Altmann & Kühne   Many Viennese adults fondly recall the marzipan, hazelnut, or nougat their parents bought for them during strolls along the Graben. Established in 1928, this cozy shop stocks virtually nothing particularly good for your waistline or your teeth, but everything is positively and undeniably scrumptious. The visual display of all things sweet is almost as appealing. The pastries and tarts filled with fresh seasonal raspberries are, quite simply, delectable. Graben 30. ℂ 01/533-0927.

Gerstner   Gerstner competes with Café Demel (see chapter 5) as one of the city's greatest pastry makers and chocolatiers. It carries some of the most delectable-looking cakes, petits fours, and chocolates anywhere. Kärntnerstrasse 11-15. ℂ 01/512-49630.

DEPARTMENT STORES

Steffl Kaufhaus   This five-story department store is one of Vienna's most visible and well advertised. You'll find rambling racks of cosmetics, perfumes, a noteworthy section devoted to books and periodicals, housewares, and thousands of garments for men, women, and children. If you forgot to pack something for your trip, chances are very good that Steffl Kaufhaus will have it. Kärntnerstrasse 19. ℂ 01/514310.

FASHION & TRADITIONAL CLOTHING

Lanz   A well-known Austrian store, Lanz specializes in dirndls and other folk clothing. This rustically elegant shop's stock is mostly for women, with a limited selection of men's jackets, neckties, and hats. Clothes for toddlers begin at sizes appropriate for a 1-year-old; women's apparel begins at size 36 (American size 6). Kärntnerstrasse 10. ℂ 01/512-2456.

Loden Plankl 🌟🌟   Established in 1830 by the Plankl family, this store is the oldest and most reputable outlet in Vienna for traditional Austrian clothing. Children's sizes usually begin with items for 2-year-olds, and women's sizes range from 6 to 20 (American). Sizes for large or tall men go up to 60. Michaelerplatz 6. ℂ 01/533-8032.

Mary Kindermoden   Here's a store specializing in children's clothing with a regional twist. In the heart of the Old Town, near St. Stephan's Cathedral, the store has two floors that stock well-made garments, including lace swaddling clothes for christenings. Most garments are for children ages 10 months to 14 years. The staff speaks English and seems to deal well with children. Graben 14. ✆ 01/533-6097.

Niederösterreichisches Heimatwerk   If you're looking for the traditional garments that Austrian men, women, and children still wear with undeniable style, this is one of the best-stocked clothing stores in Vienna. The inventory covers three full floors, and includes garments inspired by the folk traditions of Styria, the Tyrol, Carinthia, and virtually every other Austrian province. You'll also find handcrafted gift items (pewter, breadboards and breadbaskets, crystal, and tableware) laden with alpine charm. Wipplingerstrasse 23. ✆ 01/533-18990.

Popp & Kretschmer   The staff here is usually as well dressed and elegant as the clientele, and if you appear to be a bona fide customer, the sales clerks will offer coffee, tea, or champagne as you scrutinize the carefully selected merchandise. The store carries three floors of dresses, along with shoes, handbags, belts, and a small selection of men's briefcases and travel bags. You'll find it opposite the State Opera. Kärntnerstrasse 51. ✆ 01/512-78010.

Sportalm Trachtenmoden   This stylish women's store stocks a staggering collection of dirndls. Children's sizes fit girls ages 1 to 14. You'll find the store in the jarringly modern Haas Haus, across the plaza from Vienna's cathedral. Brandstätte 7-9. ✆ 01/535-5289.

JEWELRY

A. E. Köchert 🛍🛍🛍   The sixth generation of the family who served as court jewelers until the end of the Habsburg Empire continues its tradition of fine workmanship here. The store, founded in 1814, occupies a 16th-century landmark building. The firm designed many of the crown jewels of Europe, but the staff gives equal attention to customers looking only at charms for a bracelet. Neuer Markt 15. ✆ 01/512-58280.

Agatha Paris   The concept here is small scale and intensely decorative, with jewelry that manages to be both exotic and tasteful. Many pieces are inset with semiprecious (read: affordable) gemstones; others combine gold and silver into attractive ornaments, which are sometimes based on antique models. In the Ringstrassen Galerien, Kärntner Ring 5-7. ✆ 01/512-4621.

Rozet & Fischmeister 🛍   Owned by the same family since it was established in 1770, this jewelry store specializes in gold jewelry, gemstones set in artful settings, and both antique and modern versions of silver tableware. If you opt to buy an engagement ring or a bauble for a friend, you'll be following in the footsteps of Franz Joseph I. The staff will even quietly admit that he made several discreet purchases for his legendary mistress, actress Katharina Schratt. Kohlmarkt 11. ✆ 01/533-8061.

LACE & NEEDLEWORK

Zur Schwäbischen Jungfrau 🛍🛍🛍   This is one of the most illustrious shops in Austria, with a reputation that goes back almost 300 years. Here, Maria Theresa bought her first handkerchiefs, and thousands of debutantes have shopped for dresses. Come here for towels, bed linens, lace tablecloths, and some of the most elaborate needlepoint and embroidery anywhere. Service is courtly, cordial, and impeccable. Graben 26. ✆ 01/535-5356.

Moments Open-Air Markets

Since the Middle Ages, Viennese merchants have thrived by hauling produce, dairy products, and meats from the fertile farms of Lower Austria and Burgenland into the city center. The tradition of buying the day's provisions directly from street stalls is so strong, even today, that it discourages the establishment of modern supermarkets in the city center.

The largest of the city's outdoor food markets is the **Naschmarkt,** Wienzeile, in the 6th District (U-Bahn: Karlsplatz), just south of the Ring. It occupies what was originally the riverbed of a branch of the Danube, which was diverted and paved over during the massive public works projects of the 19th century. It's the most popular and colorful of the markets, as well as the most comprehensive.

Entire books have been written about the subcultures and linguistic dialects that flourish among the Naschmarkt's denizens. Observe the following unwritten rules if you want to avoid the wrath of the notoriously short-tempered women selling their goods: Never touch merchandise unless you intend to buy something. Don't try to buy less than a half-kilo (about a pound) of potatoes. And—even if your German is good—don't even try to understand the raunchy Viennese patois.

Get there early in the morning and wander through the labyrinth of outdoor food stands, and at the end of your tour, head for the nearby **Coffeehouse Drechsler** for breakfast or a cup of coffee.

Somewhat smaller and less varied are the **Rochusmarkt,** at Landstrasser Hauptstrasse at the corner of the Erdbergstrasse, in the 3rd District (U-Bahn: Rochusgasse), a short distance east of the Ring; and the **Brunnenmarkt,** on the Brunnengasse, in the 16th District (U-Bahn: Josefstädterstrasse), a subway ride west of the center and a short walk north of Vienna's Westbahnhof.

Most merchants in these markets maintain approximately the same hours: Monday to Friday from 8am to 6pm, Saturday from 8am to noon.

MUSIC

Arcadia Opera Shop   This respected record store is one of the best for classical music. The well-educated staff knows the music and performers (as well as the availability of recordings), and is usually eager to share that knowledge. The shop also carries books on art, music, architecture, and opera, as well as an assortment of musical memorabilia. The shop is on the street level of the Vienna State Opera, with a separate entrance on Kärntnerstrasse. Guided tours of the splendid opera house end here. Wiener Staatsoper, Kärntnerstrasse 40. ℰ **01/513-95680.**

Da Caruso   Almost adjacent to the Vienna State Opera, this store is known to music fans and musicologists worldwide. Its inventory includes rare and unusual recordings of historic performances by the Vienna Opera and the Vienna Philharmonic. If you're looking for a magical or particularly emotional performance by Maria Callas, Herbert von Karajan, or Bruno Walter, chances are you can get it here, digitalized on CD.

There's also a collection of taped films. The staff is hip, alert, and obviously in love with music. Operngasse 4. $\mathcal{C}$ 01/513-1326.

PORCELAIN & POTTERY

Albin Denk ꝗꝗ   Albin Denk is the oldest continuously operating porcelain store in Vienna (since 1702). Its clients have included Empress Elisabeth, and the shop you see today looks almost the same as it did when she visited. The three low-ceilinged rooms are beautifully decorated with thousands of objects from Meissen, Dresden, and other regions. Graben 13. $\mathcal{C}$ 01/512-44390.

Augarten Porzellan ꝗꝗ   Established in 1718, Augarten is the second-oldest (after Meissen) manufacturer of porcelain in Europe. This multitiered shop is the most visible and well-stocked outlet in the world. It can ship virtually anything anywhere. The tableware—fragile dinner plates with traditional or contemporary patterns—is elegant and much sought after. Also noteworthy are porcelain statues of the Lipizzaner horses. Stock im Eisenplatz 3-4. $\mathcal{C}$ 01/512-14940.

TOYS

Kober ꝗ *Kids*   Kober has been a household name, especially at Christmastime in Vienna, for more than 100 years. It carries old-fashioned wood toys, teddy bears straight out of a Styrian storybook, go-carts (assembly required), building sets, and car and airplane models. The occasional set of toy soldiers is more *Nutcracker Suite* than G.I. Joe. Graben 14-15. $\mathcal{C}$ 01/533-60180.

WINE

Wein & Co.   Since the colonization of Vindobona by the ancient Romans, the Viennese have always taken their wines seriously. Wein & Co. is Vienna's largest wine outlet, a sprawling cellar-level ode to the joys of the grape and the bounty of Bacchus. You'll also find wines from around the world, including South Africa and Chile. Jasomirgottstrasse 3-5. $\mathcal{C}$ 01/535-0916.

9

Vienna After Dark

Viennese nightlife offers something for everyone. You can dance into the morning hours, hear a concert, attend an opera or festival, go to the theater, gamble, or simply sit and talk over a drink at a local tavern.

The best source of information about the cultural scene is *Wien Monatsprogramm,* which is distributed free at tourist information offices and at many hotel reception desks. On Thursdays, *Die Presse,* the Viennese daily, publishes the major cultural events for the coming week. It's in German but might still be helpful to you.

The Viennese are not known for discounting their cultural presentations. However, *Wien Monatsprogramm* lists outlets where you can purchase tickets in advance, cutting down the surcharge imposed by travel agencies, usually by about 22%. If you're not a student and don't want to go bankrupt to see a performance at the Staatsoper or the Burgtheater, you can purchase standing-room tickets at a cost of about 5€ ($6).

Students under 27 with valid IDs are eligible for many discounts. The Burgtheater, Akademietheater, and Staatsoper sell student tickets for just 10€ ($13) the night of the performance. Theaters routinely grant students about 20% off the regular ticket price. Vienna is the home of four major symphony orchestras, including the world-acclaimed Vienna Symphony and the Vienna Philharmonic. In addition to the ÖRF Symphony Orchestra and the Niederöster-reichische Tonkünstler, there are dozens of others, ranging from smaller orchestras to chamber orchestras.

1 The Performing Arts

Music is at the heart of Vienna's cultural life. This has been true for centuries, and the city continues to lure composers, librettists, musicians, and music lovers. You can find places to enjoy everything from chamber music and pop to waltzes and jazz. You'll find small discos and large concert halls, as well as musical theaters. If you tire of aural entertainment, you'll find no shortage of theater, from classical to avant-garde. Below we describe just a few of the better-known spots for cultural recreation—if you're in Vienna long enough, you'll find many other delights on your own.

OPERA & CLASSICAL MUSIC

Musikverein   Count yourself fortunate if you get to hear a concert here. The Golden Hall is regarded as one of the four acoustically best concert halls in the world. Some 600 concerts per season (Sept–June) are presented here. Only 10 to 12 of these are played by the Vienna Philharmonic, and these are subscription concerts, so they're always sold out long in advance. Standing room is available at almost any performance, but you must line up hours before the show. The box office is open Aug 16–Sept 3 Mon-Fri 9am–noon. The rest of the year it is open Mon–Fri 9am–8pm and Sat

A Note on Evening Dress

Vienna is still not as informal as North America or the rest of Europe. Many people dress well for concerts and theaters. For especially festive occasions—such as opera premieres, receptions, and balls—tails or dinner jackets and evening dresses still appear. Younger people and visitors, however, no longer adhere to these customs. If you want to dress up, you can rent evening wear (as well as carnival costumes) from several places. Consult the telephone directory classified section (similar to the Yellow Pages in the United States) under "Kleiderleihanstalten."

9am–1pm, but closed from July–Aug 15. Dumbastrasse 3. 𝄐 01/5058190 for the box office. www.musikverein-wien.at. Tickets up to 120€ ($156) for seats, 3€ ($3.90) for standing room. U-Bahn: Karlsplatz.

Schönbrunn Palace Theater 𝄐 A gem in a regal setting, this theater opened in 1749 for the entertainment of the court of Maria Theresa. The architecture is a medley of baroque and rococo, and there's a large, plush box where the imperial family sat to enjoy the shows. Operettas and comic operas are performed in July and August. A wide variety of different art groups, each responsible for its own ticket sales, perform here. At Schönbrunn Palace, Schönbrunner Schlossstrasse. 𝄐 01/512-01-00. www.musik-theater-schoenbrunn.at. Tickets 35€–85€ ($46–$111). U-Bahn: Schönbrunn.

Staatsoper (State Opera) 𝄐𝄐𝄐 Opera is sacred in Vienna—when World War II was over, the city's top priority was the restoration of the heavily damaged Staatsoper. With the Vienna Philharmonic Orchestra in the pit, the leading opera stars of the world perform at the legendary opera house. In their day, Richard Strauss and Gustav Mahler worked as directors. Daily performances run from September 1 until the end of June. Tickets are hard to get but worth the effort. (Also see "Other Top Attractions," in chapter 6.) Opernring 2. 𝄐 01/5144-42960. www.staatsoper.at. Tickets 10€–220€ ($13–$286). Tours 6.50€ ($8.45) per person. U-Bahn: Karlsplatz.

Theater an der Wien Since opening on June 13, 1801, this theater has offered excellent opera and operetta presentations. This was the site of the premiere of Beethoven's *Fidelio* in 1805; in fact, the composer once lived in the building. The world premiere of Johann Strauss II's *Die Fledermaus* was also here. Linke Wienzeile 6. 𝄐 01/588-300. www.theateranderwien.at. Tickets 30€–90€ ($39–$117). U-Bahn: Karlsplatz.

Volksoper This opera house presents lavish productions of Viennese operettas, light opera, and other musicals daily from September 1 until the end of June. Tickets go on sale at the Volksoper only 1 hour before performances. Währingerstrasse 78. 𝄐 01/514-4430. www.volksoper.at. Tickets 7€–100€ ($9.10–$130) for seats, 2.50€–4€ ($3.25–$5.20) for standing room. U-Bahn: Volksoper.

Wiener Konzerthaus This major concert hall, built in 1912, is home to the Wiener Symphoniker. It's the venue for a wide spectrum of musical events, including orchestral concerts, chamber music recitals, choir concerts, piano recitals, and opera stage performances. Box office is open Monday to Friday 9am–7:45pm, and Saturday 9am–1pm. August hours are Monday to Friday 9am–1pm. Lothringerstrasse 20. 𝄐 01/242-002. www.konzerthaus.at. Ticket prices depend on the event. U-Bahn: Stadtpark.

The Toughest Ticket in Town

Reservations and information for the Weiner Staatsoper (Vienna State Opera), Volksoper, Burgtheater (National Theater), and Akademietheater can be obtained by contacting **Österreichische Bundestheater (Austrian Federal Theaters)**, the office that coordinates reservations and information for all four state theaters (② **01/5144-42959;** www.bundestheater.at). Call Monday to Friday 8am to 5pm. *Note:* The number is often busy; it's easier to get information and order tickets online. The major season is September to June, with more limited presentations in summer. Many tickets are issued to subscribers before the box office opens. For all four theaters, box-office sales are made only 1 month before each performance at the Bundestheaterkasse, Goethegasse 1 (② **01/51-44-40**), open Monday to Friday 8am to 6pm, Saturday 9am to 2pm, and Sunday and holidays 9am to noon. Credit card sales can be arranged by telephone within 6 days of a performance by calling ② **01/513-1513** Monday through Friday from 10am to 6pm, and Saturday and Sunday from 10am to noon. Tickets for all performances, including the opera, are also available by writing to the Österreichischer Bundestheaterverband, Goethegasse 1, A-1010 Vienna, from points outside Vienna. Orders must be received at least 3 weeks in advance of the performance to be booked, but do not send money through the mail.

Note: The single most oft-repeated complaint of music lovers in Vienna is about the lack of available tickets to many highly desirable musical performances. If the suggestions above don't produce the desired tickets, you could consult a ticket broker. Their surcharge usually won't exceed 25%, except for exceptionally rare tickets, when that surcharge might be doubled or tripled. One of the most reputable agencies is **Liener Brünn** (② **01/533-09-61**), which might make tickets available months in advance or as little as a few hours before the anticipated event.

As a final resort, remember that the concierges of virtually every upscale hotel in Vienna long ago learned sophisticated tricks for acquiring hard-to-come-by tickets. (A gratuity of at least 10€/$13 might work wonders and will be expected anyway for the phoning this task will entail. You'll pay a hefty surcharge as well.)

THEATER

Akademietheater   This theater specializes in both classic and contemporary works. The Burgtheater Company often performs here—it's the world-famous troupe's second, smaller house. Lisztstrasse 3. ② **01/5144-44740**. www.burgtheater.at. Tickets 4€–48€ ($5.20–$62) for seats, 1.50€ ($1.95) for standing room. U-Bahn: Stadtpark.

Burgtheater (National Theater)   The Burgtheater produces classical and modern plays in German. Work started on the original structure in 1776; the theater was destroyed in World War II and reopened in 1955. It's the dream of every German-speaking actor to appear here. Dr.-Karl-Lueger-Ring 2. ② **01/5144-4140**. www.burgtheater.at. Tickets 4€–48€ ($5.20–$62) for seats, 1.50€ ($1.80) for standing room. Tram: 1, 2, or D to Burgtheater.

The Sound of Music

Almost immediately after the orchestra of the Wiener Hofburgtheater (the Vienna court theater) began offering symphonic concerts on March 28, 1842, the Wiener Philharmoniker attracted lavish accolades. By 1845, the French composer Hector Berlioz had already declared that the orchestra "may have its equal, but it certainly has no superior." In 1863, Richard Wagner gushed, "I heard expressive and tonal beauty, which no other orchestra has offered me." Twelve years later, Verdi described the Wiener Philharmoniker as "a wonderful orchestra." Anton Bruckner, himself regarded as "God's musician," exclaimed that the musicians "played like gods," and Leonard Bernstein thought their excellence came from the fact that "they perform totally out of love."

Theater in der Josefstadt   One of the most influential theaters in the German-speaking world, this institution reached legendary heights of excellence under the aegis of Max Reinhardt beginning in 1924. Built in 1776, it presents a variety of comedies and dramas. Box office is open daily 10am–7:30pm. Josefstädterstrasse 26. ✆ 01/42700. www.josefstadt.org. Tickets 3€–62€ ($3.90–$81). U-Bahn: Rathaus. Tram: J. Bus: 13.

Vienna's English Theatre   This popular English-speaking theater was established in 1963. Many international actors and celebrities have appeared on the neobaroque theater's stage. The theater occasionally presents works by American playwrights. Box office is open Monday to Friday 10am–7:30pm. Josefsgasse 12. ✆ 01/402-1260-0. www. englishtheatre.at. Tickets 20€–38€ ($26–$49). U-Bahn: Rathaus. Tram: J. Bus: 13A.

Volkstheater   Built in 1889, this theater presents classical works of European theater. Modern plays and comedies are also presented. The theater's season runs September through May. Box office is open Monday to Saturday 10am–7:30pm. Neustiftgasse 1. ✆ 01/521-110. www.volkstheater.at. Tickets 7.50€–40€ ($9.75–$52). U-Bahn: Volkstheater. Tram: 1, 2, 49, D, or J. Bus: 48A.

2 The Club & Music Scene

NIGHT CLUBS

Café Leopold   No one ever expected that the city's homage to Viennese expressionism (the Leopold Museum) would ever rock 'n' roll with the sounds of dancing feet and high-energy music. But that's exactly what happens here 3 nights a week, when the museum's restaurant fills up with drinkers, wits, gossips, dancers, and people of all ilk on the make. There's a revolving cycle of DJs, each vying for local fame and approval, and a wide selection of party-colored cocktails, priced at around 9€ ($12) each. The cafe/restaurant section is open Sunday to Wednesday 10am to 2pm, Friday and Saturday 10am to 4pm. The disco operates only Thursday through Saturday 9:30pm till between 2 and 3am, depending on business. In the Leopold Museum, Museumsplatz 1. ✆ 01/523-67-32. U-Bahn: Volkstheater or Babenbergstrasse/MuseumsQuartier.

Chelsea ✦   This is the city's hottest venue for underground music. From all over the continent, the best bands and DJs are imported to entertain the gyrating throngs who gather here in a sort of techno-pop atmosphere. The pulsating club lies in one of the arches of the old railway train tracks that divide the north of the city from the historic

---

> **Fun Fact Vienna's Own Playwright**
>
> If your German is passable, try to see a play by **Arthur Schnitzler**. The mild-mannered playwright, who died in 1931, was the quintessential Viennese writer. Through his works he gave the imperial city the charm and style more often associated with Paris. Whenever possible, we attend a revival of one of his plays, such as *Einsame Weg (The Solitary Path)* or *Professor Bernhardi*. Our favorite is *Reigen*, on which the film *La Ronde* was based. The Theater in der Josefstadt often performs Schnitzler's plays.

---

core. Open nightly 7pm–4am. Lerchenfelder-Gürtel (Stadtbahnbögen 29-31). © **01/407-93-09.** Cover 6€–12€ ($7.80–$16). U-Bahn: Josefstädterstrasse/Thaliastrasse.

Club Havana ☆ The Viennese versions of Jennifer Lopez or Ricky Martin show up here for "Latinpop parties." Believe it or not, at least according to the posters, Che Guevara is still a cultural icon here. "La Vida" takes the form of everything from merengue to hip-hop. The club is located a minute's walk from the Opera House on the backside of the Ringstrassengalerien. Open nightly 8pm–4am. Depending on the night, you might be hit with a cover charge. Otherwise, Brazilian cocktails start at 8€ ($10). Mahlerstrasse 11. © **01/5132075.** Cover varies. U-Bahn: Karlsplatz.

U-4 The origins of this club go back to the 1920s, and it continues to revitalize itself with every new generation of nightclubbers. Today it's cited as one of the trendiest clubs in Vienna. Depending on the schedule, you're likely to experience such themes as Italian night, salsa/Latino night, and—every Thursday—gay night. It's open nightly 10pm to around 5am, depending on business. Schönbrunner Strasse 222. © **01/817-1192.** Cover varies from nothing to 10€ ($13). U-Bahn: Pilgrimgasse.

ROCK, SALSA, JAZZ & BLUES

Jazzland ☆ This is one of the most famous jazz pubs in Austria, noted for the quality of its U.S. and central European-based performers. It's in a deep 200-year-old cellar. Beer—which seems to be the thing to order here—costs 4€ ($5.20) for a foaming mugful. Platters of Viennese food such as *tafelspitz,* Wiener schnitzel, and roulades of beef cost 5€ to 10€ ($6.50–$13). The place is open Monday to Saturday 7pm–1am. Music begins at 9pm, and three sets are performed. Franz-Josefs-Kai 29. © **01/533-2575.** Cover 11€–20€ ($14–$26). U-Bahn: Schwedenplatz.

Loop This bar/club/lounge boasts programs self-characterized as "queer beats," "funky dope beats," "electric soul," and even "delicious tunes." Under the U-Bahn stop, this is a sleekly contemporary nighttime rendezvous, "drawing only the coolest of the cool," the bartender assured us. Regardless of how the club's owners describe their musical offerings, the night we visited was devoted to hip-hop, jazz, and funk. Open Monday to Wednesday and Sunday 7pm–2am, Thursday to Saturday 7pm–4am. Usually there's no cover, but drinks form an impressive *carte,* ranging from tequila to "wodka," costing from 4€ to 12€ ($5.20–$16). Lerchenfeldergürtel 26. © **01/4024195.** U-Bahn: Josefstädterstrasse/Thaliastrasse.

Planet Music Planet Music is a direct competitor of the also-recommended Tunnel (see below). As such, it attracts some of the same clientele, has some of the same energy, and—with perhaps a higher percentage of folk singers, reggae, soca, and new wave artists—hosts some of the same musicians. It's also about twice as large as the Tunnel, which contributes to larger crowds and louder volumes. Planet Music rocks every Monday through Friday, with the bar drawing a heavy after-work crowd after 6pm. Live concerts can take place any day of the week, so call ahead for the live music schedule. Adalbert-Stifter-Strasse 73. ℂ **01/332-46-41.** Cover charge 9€–25€ ($12–$33). Tram: 33.

Porgy & Bess ℱ   Its name may suggest an all-black classical musical in the States, but this is actually the best jazz club in the city. Its array of performers from both Europe and around the world is strictly first class. Established in 1993, the club became an instant hit and has been going strong ever since, patronized by Vienna's most avid jazz aficionados. The club opens Monday through Saturday at 7pm and Sunday at 8pm; closing times vary, often 3am or 4am. Riembergasse 11. ℂ **01/5128811.** U-Bahn: Stubentor. Tram: 1A to Riemerg.

Tunnel   Experiences like the ones created in the 1960s and 1970s by Jimi Hendrix are alive and well, if in less dramatic form, at Tunnel. In a smoke-filled cellar near Town Hall, it showcases musical groups from virtually everywhere. You'll never know quite what to expect, as the only hint of what's on or off is a recorded German-language announcement of what's about to appear and occasional advertisements in local newspapers. It's open daily 9pm–2am, with live music beginning around 10pm. Florianigasse 39. ℂ **01/405-3465.** Cover 3€–15€ ($3.90–$20). U-Bahn: Rathaus.

DANCE CLUBS

Flex ℱ   No other dance club in Vienna has a history as long, as distinguished, and as "flexible" as this one. This industrial-looking venue is set uncomfortably between the edge of the canal and the subway tracks. With exterior graffiti that includes the scrawlings of street artists going back to the '70s, it's a prime venue for post-millennium fans of electronic music. Inside, you'll find a beer-soaked, congenially battered venue where the ghosts of rock 'n' roll seem to flat restlessly above a Sputnik-era linoleum floor. It's where the young and the restless (some of them teenagers) of Vienna go for access to music that's the rage, and the rave, in places such as Berlin, London, NYC, and Los Angeles. Open daily 9am–2am. Am Donaukanal. ℂ **01/533-7525.** Cover 10€ ($13). U-Bahn: Schottenring.

Passage (Babenburger Passage)   Even the location of this pulsating dance club is an architectural oddity. It occupies what Vienna's city planners conceived as an underground pedestrian walkway (*passagen*) and a subway station for the U-2 line, deep beneath the circular network of boulevards that surrounds the southwestern perimeter of Vienna's First District. Today, sealed off from unaffiliated pedestrian traffic, its tiled surfaces reverberate every night with the amplified sounds of electronic music which, because of other bunker-like aspects of the place, can't be heard by the residents of nearby buildings. Open daily 9:30pm–midnight. Burgring 1 at the Babenbergerstrasse. ℂ **01/961-8800.** Cover 10€ ($13). U-Bahn: Babenbergerstrasse or MuseumsQuartier.

Queen Anne   Lots of fabulous people (David Bowie, 1970s metal band Deep Purple) are attracted to this nightclub and disco. The club has a big collection of the latest stateside and Italian records, as well as occasional musical acts ranging from Mick Jagger look-alikes to imitations of Watusi dancers. Open daily 10pm–6am. A cocktail goes for 8.50€ ($11); beer starts at 5.50€ ($7.15). Johannesgasse 12. ℂ **01/994-8844.** U-Bahn: Stadtpark.

Scotch Club   Except for the whisky, there's not much Scottish about this disco and coffeehouse in Vienna's most fashionable area, a 5-minute walk from many of its premier hotels and the Parkring. It welcomes a clientele of good-looking women, whose ages begin at around 20 and range upward into various states of careful preservation, and seemingly affluent men, whose ages range, in the words of a manager, from around 23 to "aggressive and elderly." There's a disco in the cellar (entrance is free, and it's open Mon to Sat 10pm–4am); a coffeehouse on the street level (open Mon to Sat 10am–4am); and a "games lounge" featuring chess boards and a bar upstairs (open Mon to Sat 8pm–4am). Parkring 10. ℭ **01/512-9417.** U-Bahn: Stadtpark or Stubentor.

Titanic   A sprawling dance club that has thrived since the early 1980s, it has two different dance areas and a likable upstairs restaurant where Mexican, Italian, and international foods provide quick energy for further dancing. You'll enter a mirrored world with strobe lights, without seating areas, which encourages patrons to dance, drink, and mingle, sometimes aggressively, throughout the evening. As for the music, you're likely to find everything from soul and house to '70s-style disco and hip-hop. The restaurant serves dinner every Friday and Saturday 7pm–3am; main courses are 10€ to 17€ ($13–$22). The dancing areas are open Friday and Saturday 10pm to around 6am, depending on business. Beer costs 3€ to 4€ ($3.90–$5.20). Theobaldgasse 11. ℭ **01/587-4758.** U-Bahn: Mariahilferstrasse.

3 The Bar Scene

Vienna's blossoming bar scene centers on the **Bermuda Triangle,** an area roughly bordered by Judengasse, Seitenstättengasse Rabensteig, and Franz-Josefs-Kai. You'll find everything from intimate watering holes to large bars with live music, a sample of which we list below. The closest U-Bahn stop is Schwedenplatz.

Barfly's Club ℛ *(Finds*   This is the most urbane and sophisticated cocktail bar in town, frequented by journalists, actors, and politicians. It's got a laissez-faire ambience that combines aspects of Vienna's *grande bourgeoisie* with its discreet avant-garde. A menu lists about 370 cocktails that include every kind of mixed drink imaginable, priced at 7€ to 11€ ($9.10–$14). The only food served is "toast" (warm sandwiches), priced at 5€ ($6.50). It's open daily 6pm to between 2 and 4am, depending on the night of the week. In the Hotel Fürst Metternich, Esterházygasse 33. ℭ **01/586-0825.** U-Bahn: Kirchengasse. Tram: 5.

Esterházykeller   The ancient bricks and scarred wooden tables of this drinking spot, famous since 1683, are permeated with the aroma of endless pints of spilled beer. An outing here isn't recommended for everyone, but if you decide to chance it, choose the left entrance (facing from the street), grip the railing firmly, and begin your descent. Wine, a specialty, starts at 1.70€ ($2.20). The place is open Monday to Friday 11am–11pm, and Saturday and Sunday 4–11pm. Haarhof 1. ℭ **01/533-3482.** U-Bahn: Stephansplatz.

Krah Krah   This place is the most animated and well-known singles bar in the area. An attractive, and sometimes available, after-work crowd fills this woodsy, somewhat battered space. Beer is the drink of choice here, with more than 60 kinds available, from 2.50€ to 4.10€ ($3.25–$5.35) each. Sandwiches, snacks, and simple platters of food, including hefty portions of Weiner schnitzel, start at 4.50€ ($5.85). It's open daily 11am–2am. Rabensteig 8. ℭ **01/533-8193.** U-Bahn: Schwedenplatz.

La Divina *𝒜𝒜*   Artful, artsy, and immediately adjacent to the side entrance of the Albertina, this is a cocktail bar that would be a lot of fun anywhere, but thanks to its links to the Vienna State Opera, it sometimes rises to "divine" levels of operatic camp. Its name derives from the moniker any opera lover associates with über-diva Maria Callas (1923–1977). The sinuous line of the bartop was inspired by the neck of a violin, and the old-fashioned red velour cubbyhole—ideal for an intimate drink—evokes one of the boxes at the Vienna State Opera. And then there's that Bösendorfer grand piano, where every Wednesday to Saturday, from 9:30 to 11:30pm, some operatic wannabe will be crashing out arias. The menu is light on food (snacks only) but rich (more than 100) in cocktails, 15 of which feature some variation of champagne. Glasses of wine and cocktails cost 3.50€ to 12€ ($4.55–$16) each, and the bar is open daily 4pm–2am. Hanuschgasse 3. ℭ 01/513-43-19. U-Bahn: Karlsplatz.

Loos American Bar *𝒜 Finds*   One of the most unusual and interesting bars in the center of Vienna, this very dark, sometimes mysterious bar was designed by the noteworthy architect Adolf Loos in 1908. At the time, it functioned as the drinking room of a private men's club, but today it's more democratic, and welcomes a mostly bilingual crowd of very hip singles from Vienna's arts-and-media scene. Walls, floors, and ceilings sport layers of dark marble and black onyx, making this one of the most expensive small-scale decors in the city. No food is served, but the mixologist's specialties include six kinds of martinis, plus five kinds of Manhattans, each 7.50€ ($9.75). Beer costs from 2.60€ ($3.40). It's open Sunday through Wednesday noon–4am and Thursday through Saturday noon–5am. Kärntnerdurchgang 10. ℭ 01/512-3283. U-Bahn: Stephansplatz.

Mocca Club   This hip, trendy coffeehouse/cafe/bar may have been born on the ruins of a failed Starbucks, but both caffeine and alcohol drinkers agree the combination here is successful. You'll select from a jumble of sofas, deep armchairs, and conventional tables and chairs, and then order the drug of your choice from a vast menu of more than 93 kinds of tea, 52 kinds of coffee, and 200 creatively defined cocktails. If you want a cocktail, try a mojito. Tea lovers should consider a delicate *Bai Mei* from China, and the Indian Monsoon Malabar coffee is soft, genteel—even heavenly. Cocktails range from 7€ to 10€ ($9.10–$13); coffees from 1.80€–2.50€ ($2.35–$3.25). Open Sunday to Thursday 10am–midnight, Friday to Saturday 10am–2am. Linke Wienzeile 4. ℭ 01/587-0087. U-Bahn: Karlsplatz.

Onyx Bar   One of the most visible and best known, though crowded, bars near the Stephansplatz is on the sixth (next-to-uppermost) floor of one of Vienna's most controversial buildings—Haas Haus. Lunch is served from noon to 3pm daily; dinner is served from 6pm to midnight. The staff serves a long and varied cocktail menu from 6pm to 2am, including strawberry margaritas and caipirinhas, each priced from 3€ to 20€ ($3.90–$26). Live and recorded music is presented, usually beginning after 8:30pm. In the Haas Haus, Stephansplatz 12. ℭ 01/53539690. U-Bahn: Stephansplatz.

Rhiz Bar Modern   Hip, multicultural, and electronically sophisticated, with no trace at all of Habsburg nostalgia, this bar is nestled into the vaulted, century-old niches created by the trusses of the U6 subway line, a few blocks west of the Ring. A TV camera constantly broadcasts images of the hipster clientele over the Internet every night from 10pm to 3am. Drinks include Austrian wine, Scottish whiskey, and beer from everywhere in Europe. A large beer costs 3€ ($3.90). It's open Monday to

Saturday 6pm–4am and Sunday 6pm–2am. Llerchenfeldergürtel 37-38, Stadtbahnbögen. ℭ 01/409-2505. www.rhiz.org. U-Bahn: Josefstädterstrasse.

Sacher Eck   Even the venerable Sacher has shown that it keeps up with the times, in the form of its street-level cafe, the Sacher-Ecke, a new "Sacher Light" that's a deliberately toned down, more youthful version of the Habsburgundian dragon represented by the hotel itself. The Sacher-Ecke (literally, "Sacher-Corner") occupies the corner of the Sacher that faces the mobs of pedestrian traffic along the Kärntnerstrasse. Rock music plays softly, and there's wine by the glass, cocktails, and Sachertorte by the slice. Accompanied with a swirl of whipped cream, it's priced at 4.80€ ($6.25). A Bellini costs 9.50€ ($12); champagne, champagne cocktails, and Sekt go from 7€ to 17€ ($9.10–$21). Breakfast costs 9.50€ ($12) and includes ham, cheese, yogurt, breads, jam, butter, and coffee. Daily 9am–1am. Kärntnerstrasse 38 (corner of Philharmoniker-strasse). ℭ 01/51-456-699. U-Bahn: Karlsplatz.

Schikaneder   If you're young and hot, and want to meet locals who share those same traits, come here. There's plenty of conversation, good drinks, and sympathetic company. The bar starts filling up by 9:30pm and by midnight it's packed, often with university students. Don't dare tell anyone in this hip crowd you're a tourist. Open daily 5:30pm–4am. There's no cover but beer starts at 2€ ($2.60). You can also order various wines by the glass. Margaretenstrasse 22-24. ℭ 01/5855888. U-Bahn: Margaretengürtel.

Sky Bar ✶   Local hipsters ridicule this place as a posh see-and-be-seen venue for Vienna's social striving *nouveaux riches*. We think the place is well designed and, under the right circumstances, can be a lot of fun, particularly when we remind ourselves that the Steffl building was erected on the site of the (long-ago demolished) house where Mozart died. Take an elevator to the top floor of the building for a sweeping view over the city. Open Monday to Wednesday 11:30am–3am, Thursday to Saturday 11:30am–4am, and Sunday 6pm–3am. Kärntnerstrasse 19. ℭ 01/513-1712. U-Bahn: Karlsplatz.

The Wine Bar at Julius Meinl   Part of its allure derives from its role as a showcase for the wine-buying savvy of Vienna's most comprehensive delicatessen (Julius Meinl) and wine shop. It's small and cozy, set in the cellar of a food shop that leaves most gastronomes salivating, and accessible through a separate entrance that's open long after the delicatessen has closed. Within a decor that evokes the interior of a farmhouse on, say, the Austro-Italian border, it features a changing array of wines from around the world, and platters of flavorful but uncomplicated food that's deliberately selected as a foil for (what else?) the wines. You'll be amply satisfied with the dozens of wines listed on the blackboard or on the menu, but if there's a particular bottle you're hankering for in the stacks of wine within the street-level deli, a staff member will sell it to you and uncork it at a surcharge of only 10% more than what you'd have paid for it retail. Glasses of wine cost 3€ to 25€ ($3.90–$33); platters of food 9€ to 15€ ($12–$20) each. Open Monday to Saturday 11am–midnight. Graben 19. ℭ 01/532-3334-6100. U-Bahn: Stephansplatz.

GAY & LESBIAN BARS

Alfi's Goldener Spiegel   The most enduring gay restaurant in Vienna (p. 103) is also its most popular gay bar, attracting mostly male clients to its position near Vienna's Naschmarkt. You don't need to come here to dine, but you can patronize the bar, where almost any gay male from abroad drops in for a look-see. The place is very cruisy, and the bar is open Wednesday to Monday 7pm–2am. Linke Wienzeile 46. ℂ 01/ 586-6608. U-Bahn: Kettenbruckengasse.

Café Savoy   Soaring frescoed ceilings and a smoke-stained beaux-arts decor that evokes the grand Imperial days of the Habsburgs make this cruisy cafe/bar an appealing setting. Open Monday to Friday 5pm–2am, Saturday 9am–2am. Linke Wienzeile 36. ℂ 01/586-7348. U-Bahn: Kettenbruckengasse.

Eagle Bar   This is one of the premier leather and denim bars for gay men in Vienna. There's no dancing, and the bar even offers a back room where free condoms are distributed. It's open daily 9pm–4am. Large beers begin at 3€ ($3.90). Blümelgasse 1. ℂ 01/587-26-61. U-Bahn: Neubaugasse.

Felixx ⭐   It's the classiest gay bar and cafe in town, thanks to a 2006 refurbishment that left the place awash in meticulously applied tones of fuchsia that emphasize turn-of-the-20th-century cove moldings, a crystal chandelier that could proudly grace any Opera Ball, and a huge late-19th-century portrait of the female cabaret entertainer who introduced *lieder* (live singing) for the first time to a generation of wine- and coffee-drinkers. Ironically, the venue is less kitschy than you'd think, managing to pull off a lasting impression of elegance and good taste. Open daily 7pm–2am. Gumpendorferstrasse 5. ℂ 01/920-4714. U-Bahn: Babenbergerstrasse or MuseumsQuartier.

Frauencafé   Frauencafé is exactly what a translation of its name would imply: a politically conscious cafe for lesbian and (to a lesser degree) heterosexual women who appreciate the company of other women. Established in 1977 in the cramped quarters of a century-old building, it's filled with magazines, newspapers, modern paintings, and a clientele of Austrian and foreign women. Next door is a feminist bookstore loosely affiliated with the cafe. Frauencafé is open Tuesday to Saturday 6:30pm–2am. Glasses of wine begin at 2€ ($2.60). Langegasse 11. ℂ 01/4063754. U-Bahn: Lerchenfelderstrasse.

4 The *Heurigen* ⭐

These *heurigen*, or wine taverns, on the outskirts of Vienna have long been celebrated in operetta, film, and song. Grinzing is the most-visited district; other *heurigen* neighborhoods include Sievering, Neustift, and Heiligenstadt.

Grinzing lies at the edge of the Vienna Woods, a short distance northwest of the center. Much of Grinzing looks the way it did when Beethoven lived nearby. It's a district of crooked old streets and houses, with thick walls surrounding inner courtyards where grape arbors shelter wine drinkers. The sound of zithers and accordions lasts long into the summer night.

If you're a motorist, don't drive to the *heurigen*. Police patrols are very strict, and you may not drive with more than 0.8% alcohol in your bloodstream. It's much better to take public transportation. Most *heurigen* are within 30 to 40 minutes of downtown.

Take tram no. 1 to Schottentor, and change there for tram no. 38 to Grinzing, no. 41 to Neustift, or no. 38 to Sievering (which is also accessible by bus no. 39A). Heiligenstadt is the last stop on U-Bahn line U4.

Alter Klosterkeller im Passauerhof   One of Vienna's well-known wine taverns, this spot maintains an old-fashioned ambience little changed since the turn of the 20th century. Specialties include such familiar fare as *tafelspitz*, an array of roasts, and plenty of strudel. Main courses range from 15€ to 25€ ($20–$33). Drinks begin at 2.50€ ($3.25). It's open daily 5pm–midnight. Live music is played from 6 to midnight. It's closed January to mid-March. Cobenzigasse 9, Grinzing. © 01/320-6345.

Altes Presshaus   The oldest *heurig* in Grinzing has been open since 1527. Ask to see its authentic cellar. The wood paneling and antique furniture give the interior character, while the garden terrace blossoms in summer. Meals cost 10€ to 15€ ($13–$20); drinks begin at 3€ ($3.90). It's open daily 4pm–midnight and is closed January and February. Cobenzlgasse 15, Grinzing. © 01/320-0203.

Der Rudolfshof 🎧   One of the most appealing wine restaurants in Grinzing dates back to 1848, when it was little more than a shack within a garden. Its real fame came around the turn of the 20th century, when Crown Prince Rudolf, son of Emperor Franz Josef, adopted it as his favorite watering hole. A verdant garden, scattered with tables, is favored by Viennese apartment dwellers on warm summer evenings. Inside, portraits of Rudolf decorate a setting that evokes an old-fashioned hunting lodge. Come here for pitchers of the fruity white wine *grüner Veltliner* and a light red, *roter Bok*. Glasses of wine cost 2.40€ to 5€ ($3.10–$6.50). The menu lists schnitzels, roasts, and soups, but the house specialty is shish kabob. The salad bar is very fresh. Main courses cost 10€ to 11€ ($13–$14). It's open from mid-March to mid-January daily 1–11:30pm, and mid-January to mid-March only Friday through Sunday 1–11:30pm. Cobenzlgasse 8, Grinzing. © 01/32021-08.

Heurige Mayer 🎧   This historic house was some 130 years old when Beethoven composed sections of his *Ninth Symphony* while living here in 1817. The same kind of fruity dry wine is still sold to guests in the shady courtyard of the rose garden. The menu includes grilled chicken, savory pork, and a buffet of well-prepared country food. Reservations are suggested. It's open Monday through Friday 4pm–midnight, and on Sunday and holidays 11am–midnight. Live music is played every Sunday and Friday 7pm–midnight. Closed Saturday. Wine sells for 3.50€ ($4.55) a glass, with meals beginning at 13€ ($17). It's closed December 21–January 15. Am Pfarrplatz 2, Heiligenstadt. © 01/3703361, or 01/370-1287 after 4pm.

Weingut Wolff   Although aficionados claim that the best *heurigen* are "deep in the countryside" of lower Austria, this one comes closest to offering an authentic experience just 20 minutes from the center of Vienna. In summer, you're welcomed into a flower-decked garden set against a backdrop of ancient vineyards. You can fill up your platter with some of the best wursts and roast meats (especially the delectable pork), along with freshly made salads. Save room for one of the luscious and velvety-smooth Austrian cakes. Find a table under a cluster of grapes and sample the fruity young wines, especially the chardonnay, sylvaner, or *grüner Veltliner*. The tavern is open daily 11am–1am, with main courses ranging from 8€ to 15€ ($10–$20). Rathstrasse 50, Neustift. © 01/440-3727.

Zum Figlmüller   One of the city's most popular wine restaurants is this suburban branch of Vienna's Figlmüller. Although there's a set of indoor dining rooms, most visitors prefer the flowering terrace with its romantic garden. The restaurant prides itself on serving wines produced only under its own supervision, beginning at 3€ ($3.60) per glass. Meals include a wide array of light salads, as well as more substantial food. Prices range from 7€ to 14€ ($9.10–$18). It's open late April to mid-November daily 11:30am–midnight. Grinzinger Strasse 55, Grinzing. © 01/320-4257.

5 More Entertainment

A CASINO

Casino Wien   You'll need to show your passport to get into this casino, opened in 1968. There are gaming tables for French and American roulette, blackjack, and chemin de fer, as well as the ever-present slot machines. The casino is open daily 11am–4am, with the tables closing at 3pm. Esterházy Palace, Kärntnerstrasse 41. ℂ 01/512-4836.

FILMS

Filmmuseum   This cinema shows films in their original languages and presents retrospectives of such directors as Fritz Lang. The museum presents avant-garde, experimental, and classic films. A monthly program is available free inside the Albertina, and a copy is posted outside. The film library inside the government-funded museum includes more than 11,000 book titles, and the still collection numbers more than 100,000. Admission costs 9.50€ ($12) for nonmembers. Membership for 24 hours costs 5.50€ ($7.15); membership for a full year costs 12€ ($16). In the Albertina, Augustinerstrasse 1. ℂ 01/533-7054. U-Bahn: Karlsplatz.

6 Only in Vienna

We've recommended a variety of nightspots, but to get a truly Viennese experience, head to one of the establishments below.

Alt Wien   Set on one of the oldest, narrowest streets of medieval Vienna, a short walk north of the cathedral, this is the kind of smoky, mysterious, and shadowy cafe that evokes subversive plots, doomed romances, and revolutionary movements being hatched and plotted. During the day, it's a busy workaday restaurant patronized by virtually everybody. But as the night progresses, you're likely to rub elbows with denizens of late-night Wien who get more sentimental and schmaltzy with each beer. Foaming mugfuls sell for 2.90€ ($3.75) each and can be accompanied by heaping platters of goulash and schnitzels. Main courses range from 5€ to 8€ ($6.50–$10). It's open daily 10am–2am. Bäckerstrasse 9 (1). ℂ 01/512-5222. U-Bahn: Stephansplatz.

Karl Kolarik's Schweizerhaus   References to this old-fashioned eating house are about as old as the Prater itself. Awash with beer and central European kitsch, it sprawls across a *biergarten* landscape that might remind you of the Habsburg Empire at its most indulgent. Indulgence is indeed the word—the vastly proportioned main dishes could feed an entire 19th-century army. The menu stresses old-fashioned

---

Moments   *The Third Man* Lives

At **Burg Kino,** Opernring 19 (ℂ 01/587-8406), the theater marquee still features English-language presentations of *The Third Man,* with the names of the stars, Joseph Cotten and Orson Welles, in lights. When it was first released, the post-war Viennese were horrified at the depiction of their city as a "rat-infested rubble heap." Over decades, they have come to love the film, which this cinema shows twice a week. Many young Viennese, as well as visitors from abroad, flock to screenings (in English) on Friday at 10:45pm, Sunday at 3:30pm, and Tuesday 4:15pm. Tickets cost 6€ to 8€ ($7.80–$10). U-Bahn: Karlsplatz.

schnitzels and its house specialty, roasted pork hocks *(Hintere Schweinsstelze)* served with dollops of mustard and horseradish. Wash it all down with mugs of Czech Budweiser. A half-liter of beer costs 3.30€ ($4.30); main courses range from 3€ to 11€ ($3.90–$14). It's open from March 15 to October 31 daily 11am–11pm. In the Prater, Strasse des Ersten Mai 116. ⓒ 01/728-01-52. U-Bahn: Praterstern.

Möbel   Locals perch along the long stainless-steel countertop for a glass of wine, a coffee, and light platters of food. But what makes this café-cum-art-gallery unusual is the hypermodern furniture that's for sale, ranging from coffee tables and reclining chairs to bookshelves and even a ceramic-sided wood-burning stove priced at 1,300€ ($1,690). Sandwiches cost 4.50€ ($5.85), and glasses of wine range from 1.50€ to 2.90€ ($1.95–$3.75). It's open daily 10am–1am. Burggasse 10. ⓒ 01/524-9497. U-Bahn: Volkstheater.

Pavillion   Even the Viennese stumble when trying to describe this civic monument from the Sputnik-era of the 1950s. During the day, it's a cozy cafe with a multigenerational clientele and a sweeping garden overlooking the Heldenplatz (forecourt to the Hofburg). Come here to peruse the newspapers, chat with locals, and drink coffee, wine, beer, or schnapps. The place grows much more animated after the music (funk, soul, blues, and jazz) begins around 8pm. Platters of Viennese food are priced from 6.50€ to 12€ ($8–$16). It's open daily 11am–2am between April and October. Burgring 2. ⓒ 01/532-0907. U-Bahn: Volkstheater.

Schnitzelwirt Schmidt   The waitresses wear dirndls, the portions are huge, and the cuisine—only pork and some chicken—celebrates the culinary folklore of central Europe. The setting is rustic, a kind of tongue-in-cheek bucolic homage to the Old Vienna Woods, and schnitzels are almost guaranteed to hang over the sides of the plates. Regardless of what you order, it will be accompanied by french fries, salad, and copious quantities of beer and wine. Go for the good value, unmistakably Viennese ambience, and great people-watching. Main courses cost 5€ to 10€ ($6.50–$13). It's open Monday to Saturday 11am–10pm. Neubaugasse 52 (7). ⓒ 01/523-3771. U-Bahn: Mariahilferstrasse. Tram: 49.

Wiener Stamperl (The Viennese Dram)   Named after a medieval unit of liquid measurement, this is about as beer-soaked and as rowdy a nighttime venue as we're willing to recommend. It occupies a battered, woodsy-looking room reeking of spilled beer, stale smoke, and the unmistakable scent of hundreds of boisterous drinkers. At the horseshoe-shape bar, order foaming steins of Ottakinger beer or glasses of new wine from nearby vineyards served from an old-fashioned barrel. The menu consists entirely of an array of coarse bread slathered with spicy, high-cholesterol ingredients, such as various wursts and cheeses and, for anyone devoted to authentic old-time cuisine, lard specked with bits of bacon. It's open Monday to Thursday 11am–2am, and Friday and Saturday 11pm–4am. Sterngasse 1. ⓒ 01/533-6230. U-Bahn: Schwedenplatz.

Side Trips from Vienna

Exciting day trips on Vienna's doorstep include the Vienna Woods; the villages along the Danube, particularly the vineyards of the Wachau; and the small province of Burgenland, between Vienna and the Hungarian border.

Lower Austria (Niederösterreich), known as the "cradle of Austria's history," is the biggest of the nine federal states that make up the country. The province is bordered on the north by the Czech Republic, on the east by Slovakia, on the south by the province of Styria, and on the west by Upper Austria.

This historic area was once heavily fortified, as some 550 fortresses and castles (often in ruins) testify. The medieval Kuenringer and Babenburger dynasties had their hereditary estates here. Vineyards cover the province, which is home to historic monasteries, churches, and abbeys. In summer it booms with music festivals and classical and contemporary theater.

Lower Austria consists of five distinct districts. The best known is the Wienerwald, or **Vienna Woods** (see "Tales of the Vienna Woods" box, in chapter 6). Although the woods have been thinned out on the eastern side, they still surround Vienna.

The district of **Alpine Lower Austria** lies about an hour's drive south of Vienna, with mountains up to 1,800m (5,905 ft.) high.

The **foothills of the Alps** begin about 48km (30 miles) west of Vienna and extend to the borders of Styria and Upper Austria. This area has some 50 open-air swimming pools and nine chairlifts to the higher peaks, such as Ötscher and Hochkar (both around 2,100m/6,890 ft.).

One of the most celebrated districts is the **Waldviertel-Weinviertel.** A *Viertel* is a traditional division of Lower Austria, and the *Wald* (woods) and *Wein* (wine) areas contain thousands of miles of marked hiking paths and many mellow old wine cellars.

Another district, **Wachau-Nibelungengau,** has both historical and cultural significance. It's a land of castles, palaces, abbeys, monasteries, and vineyards. This area on the banks of the Danube begins about 64km (40 miles) west of Vienna.

Lower Austria, from the rolling hillsides of the Wienerwald to the terraces of the Wachau, produces some 60% of Austria's grape harvest. Many visitors like to take a **"wine route"** through the province, stopping at cozy taverns to sample the vintages from Krems, Klosterneuburg, Dürnstein, Langenlois, Retz, Gumpoldskirchen, Poysdorf, and other towns.

Lower Austria is also home to more than a dozen **spa** resorts, such as Baden, the most popular. These resorts are family-friendly, and most hotels accommodate children up to 6 years old free; those between the ages of 7 and 12 stay for half price. Many towns and villages have attractions designed just for kids.

It's relatively inexpensive to travel in Lower Austria, where prices are about 30% lower than those in Vienna. Finding a hotel in these small towns isn't a problem; they're signposted at the approaches to the resorts and villages. You might not always find a room with a private bathroom in some of the area's old inns, but unless otherwise noted, all recommended accommodations have private bathrooms. Parking is also more accessible in the outlying towns, an appealing feature if you're driving. Unless otherwise noted, you park free. Note that some hotels have only a postal code for an address (if you're writing to them, this is the complete address).

Burgenland, the newest and easternmost province of Austria, is a stark contrast to Lower Austria. It's a little border region, formed in 1921 from German-speaking areas of what was once Hungary. Burgenland voted to join Austria in the aftermath of World War I, although when the vote was taken in 1919, its capital, Ödenburg, now called Sopron, chose to remain with Hungary. Sopron lies west of Lake Neusiedl (Neusiedler See), a popular haven for the Viennese.

The province marks the beginning of a flat steppe *(puszta)* that reaches from Vienna almost to Budapest. It shares a western border with Styria and Lower Austria, and the long eastern boundary separates Burgenland from Hungary. Called "the vegetable garden of Vienna," Burgenland is mostly an agricultural province, producing more than one-third of all the wine made in Austria. Its Pannonian climate translates into hot summers with little rainfall and moderate winters. You can usually enjoy sunny days from early spring until late autumn.

The capital of Burgenland is **Eisenstadt,** a small provincial city. For many years, it was the home of Joseph Haydn, and the composer is buried here. Each summer there's a festival at Mörbisch, using Lake Neusiedl as a theatrical backdrop. **Neusiedl** is the only steppe lake in central Europe. If you're visiting in summer, you'll most certainly want to explore it by motorboat. Lots of Viennese flee to Burgenland on weekends for sailing, birding, and other outdoor activities.

Accommodations in the province are extremely limited, but they're among the least expensive in the country. The area is relatively unknown to North Americans, which means fewer tourists. Like Lower Austria, Burgenland contains many fortresses and castles, often in ruins, but you'll find a few castle hotels. The touring season in Burgenland lasts from April to October.

1 The Wienerwald (Vienna Woods) ✶

The Vienna Woods—romanticized in operetta and literature, and known worldwide through the famous Strauss waltz—stretch from Vienna's city limits to the foothills of the Alps to the south. For an introduction, see chapter 6, "Exploring Vienna."

You can hike through the woods along marked paths or drive through, stopping at country towns to sample the wine and the local cuisine, which is usually hearty and reasonably priced. The Viennese and a horde of foreign visitors, principally German, usually descend on the wine taverns and cellars here on weekends—we advise you to make any summer visit on a weekday. The best time of year to go is in September and October, when the grapes are harvested from the terraced hills.

TIPS ON EXPLORING THE VIENNA WOODS

You can visit the expansive and pastoral Vienna Woods by car or by public transportation. We recommend renting a car so you can stop and explore some of the villages and vineyards along the way. Public transportation will get you around, but it will take much more time. Either way, you can easily reach all of the destinations listed below within a day's trip from Vienna. If you have more time, spend the night in one or more of the quintessential Austrian towns along the way.

Lower Austria, Burgenland & the Danube Valley

CZECH REPUBLIC

Gmünd

Retz

Laa

Horn

303

Mistelbach

WALDVIERTEL

NIEDERÖSTERREICH
(LOWER AUSTRIA)

WEINVIERTEL

303

Stockerau

7

SLOVAKIA

Ottenschlag

Krems

3

Tulln

A22

Korneuburg

OBER-
ÖSTERREICH
(UPPER
AUSTRIA)

33

Dürnstein

Danube River

Klosterneuburg

Herzogenburg

Kapelln

1

VIENNA

Marbach

Melk

St. Pölten

WIEN

3

A1

Amstetten

A1

Perchtoldsdorf
Hinterbrühl

16

10

Parndorf

NIEDERÖSTERREICH
(LOWER AUSTRIA)

Heiligenkreuz Abbey
Mayerling

A2

Baden bei Wien

Neusiedl am See

51

Waidhofen

20

Purbach am See

Eisenstadt

50

Poders-
dorf

25

Annaberg

Wiener Neustadt

Rust

Illmitz

Puchberg

17

Mattersburg

Neusiedler See

Forchtenstein

Sopron

20

Semmering

S31

BURGENLAND

115

S6

Kapfenburg

A2

A9

STEIERMARK
(STYRIA)

Oberwart

HUNGARY

335

54

Köflach

Graz

A2

KÄRNTEN
(CARINTHIA)

A9

Deutschlandsburg

Area of detail

Vienna

Maribor

AUSTRIA

SLOVENIA

Skiing

0   20 mi

0   20 km

N

VISITOR INFORMATION   Before you go, visit the tourist office for **Klosterneuburg** at Niedermarkt 4, A-3400 (℗ **02243/32038;** fax 02243/3213462; www.klosterneuburg. com). It's the best source of information for the Vienna Woods. It's open daily 10am to 7pm.

ORGANIZED TOURS   Vienna Sightseeing Tours, Starhemberggasse 25 (℗ **01/ 712-468-30,** fax 01/714 11 41; www.viennasightseeingtours.com), runs a popular 4-hour tour called "Vienna Woods–Mayerling." It goes through the Vienna Woods past the Castle of Liechtenstein and the old Roman city of Baden. There's an excursion to Mayerling. You'll also go to the Cistercian abbey of Heiligenkreuz-Höldrichsmühle-Seegrotte and take a boat ride on Seegrotte, the largest subterranean lake in Europe. The office is open for tours April to October daily 6:30am to 7:30pm, and November to March daily 6:30am to 5pm. It costs 42€ ($55) for adults and 15€ ($20) for children, including admission fees and a guide.

KLOSTERNEUBURG

On the northwestern outskirts of Vienna, Klosterneuburg is an old market town in the major wine-producing center of Austria. The Babenburgs established the town on the eastern foothills of the Vienna Woods, making it an ideal spot to stay if you want to enjoy the countryside and Vienna, 11km (7 miles) southeast.

ESSENTIALS

GETTING THERE   By **car** from Vienna, take Route 14 northwest, following the south bank of the Danube to Klosterneuburg. If you opt for public transportation, take the **U-Bahn** (U4, U6) to Heiligenstadt, and catch **bus** no. 239 or 341 to Klosterneuburg. By **train,** catch the Schnellbahn (S-Train) from Franz-Josef Bahnhof to Klosterneuburg-Kierling.

VISITOR INFORMATION   Contact the Klosterneuburg **tourist information office** at Niedermarkt 4, A-3400 (℗ **02243/32038;** fax 02243/3213462; www. klosterneuburg.com). It's open daily 10am to 7pm.

Austrians gather in Klosterneuburg annually on November 15 to celebrate St. Leopold's Day with music, banquets, and a parade.

VISITING THE ABBEY

Klosterneuburg Abbey (Stift Klosterneuburg) ⚘, Stiftsplatz 1 (℗ **02243/4110**), is the most significant abbey in Austria. It was founded in 1114 by the Babenberg margrave Leopold III, and was once the residence of the famous Habsburg emperor Charles VI.

The abbey is visited not only for its history, but also for its art treasures. The most valuable piece is the world-famous enamel altar of Nikolaus of Verdun, created in 1181. The monastery also boasts the largest private library in Austria, with more than 1,250 handwritten books and many antique paintings. Guided tours of the monastery are given daily year-round. On the tour, you visit the Cathedral of the Monastery (unless Masses are underway), the cloister, St. Leopold's Chapel (with the Verdun altar), the former well house, and the residential apartments of the emperors.

The monastery itself remains open year-round, but the museum of the monastery is closed from mid-November to April. The museum can be visited without a guide from May to mid-November Tuesday to Sunday from 10am to 5pm for 5€ ($6.50). Visits to the monastery itself, however, require participation in a guided tour. These are available at hourly intervals year-round daily from 9am to noon and 1:30 to

4:30pm. Except for a specially designated English-language tour conducted every Sunday at 2pm, most tours are conducted in German, with occasional snippets of English if the guide is able. The price is 5.50€ ($7.15) for adults and 3.20€ ($4.15) for children. Additional English-language tours can be arranged in advance. You can purchase a cost-effective combination ticket to the monastery and museum for 7€ ($9.10) for adults and 4€ ($5.20) for children under 12.

WHERE TO STAY & DINE

Hotel Josef Buschenretter   Built in 1970 1.6km (a mile) south of the town center, this hotel is white-walled with a mansard roof rising above the balcony on the fourth floor. A roof terrace and a cozy bar provide diversion for hotel guests. The well-kept medium-size bedrooms are comfortably furnished and have bathrooms equipped with shower units.

Wienerstrasse 188, A-3400 Klosterneuburg. © 02243/32385. Fax 02243/3238-5160. www.hotel-buschenretter.at. 35 units. 78€ ($101) double. Rates include buffet breakfast. AE, DC, MC, V. Free parking. Closed Dec 15–Jan 15. **Amenities:** Restaurant; bar; indoor heated pool; laundry service/dry cleaning. *In room:* TV.

Hotel Schrannenhof   Originally dating from the Middle Ages, this hotel has been completely renovated and modernized. The owners rent guest rooms with large living and sleeping rooms and small kitchens, as well as quiet and comfortable double rooms with showers. International and Austrian specialties are served in Veit, the hotel's cafe-restaurant next door. The hotel also runs the Pension Alte Mühle (see below).

Niedermarkt 17-19, A-3400 Klosterneuburg. © 02243/32072. Fax 02243/320-7213. www.schrannenhof.at. 14 units. 88€ ($114) double; 124€ ($161) suite. Rates include buffet breakfast. AE, DC, MC. Free parking. **Amenities:** Breakfast room; lounge. *In room:* A/C (in some), TV, kitchenette (in some), minibar, hair dryer, safe.

Pension Alte Mühle   Housed in a simple two-story building from the 1930s, this hotel is gracious and hospitable. The breakfast room offers a bountiful morning buffet; the comfortable restaurant-cafe, Veit, is only 800m (2,624 ft.) away. Bedrooms are furnished in a cozy, traditional style, with well-maintained, if small, private bathrooms with shower units. The Veit family owns the place, and in summer their pleasant garden lures guests.

Mühlengasse 36, A-3400 Klosterneuburg. © 02243/37788. Fax 02243/377-8822. www.hotel-altemuehle.at. 13 units. 72€ ($94) double. Rates include breakfast. AE, DC, MC. Free parking. **Amenities:** Breakfast room; laundry service. *In room:* TV, minibar, hair dryer, safe.

PERCHTOLDSDORF: A STOP ON THE WINE TOUR

This old market town with colorful buildings, referred to locally as Petersdorf, is one of the most-visited spots in Lower Austria when the Viennese go on a wine tour. You'll find many *heurigen* here, where you can sample local wines and enjoy good, hearty cuisine. Perchtoldsdorf is not as well known as Grinzing, which is actually within the city limits of Vienna, but many visitors find it less touristy. It has a Gothic church, and part of its defense tower dates from the early 16th century. A vintners' festival, held annually in early November, attracts many Viennese. Local growers make a "goat" from grapes for this festive occasion.

GETTING THERE   Perchtoldsdorf lies 18km (11 miles) from the center of Vienna (it's actually at the southwestern city limits) and 14km (8¾ miles) north of Baden. From Vienna's Westbahnhof, you can take the S-Bahn to Liesing. From here, Perchtoldsdorf is just a short taxi ride away (cabs are found at the train station).

VISITOR INFORMATION   The **tourist information office,** in the center of Perchtoldsdorf (© **01/536100;** www.noe.co.at), is open Monday to Thursday 8:30am to 5pm and Friday 8:30am to 4pm.

WHERE TO DINE

Restaurant Jahreszeiten $\bigcirc$ AUSTRIAN/FRENCH/INTERNATIONAL   Set within what was a private villa in the 1800s, this restaurant, the best in town, provides a haven for escapist Viennese looking for hints of the country life. In a pair of elegantly rustic dining rooms illuminated at night with flickering candles, you can enjoy such well-crafted dishes as rare poached salmon served with herbs and truffled noodles, Chinese-style prawns in an Asiatic sauce prepared by the kitchen's Japanese cooks, and filet of turbot with morels and asparagus-studded risotto. Try a soufflé for dessert. A tremendous effort is made to secure the freshest produce. Service is polite, hardworking, and discreet.

Hochstrasse 17. © 01/8656080. Reservations recommended. Main courses 14€–20€ ($18–$25). Set menus 25€–30€ ($33–$39). AE, DC, MC, V. Daily 11:30am–11pm. Closed 3 weeks in Aug.

HINTERBRÜHL

You'll find good accommodations and good food in this hamlet, which is really no more than a cluster of bucolic homes, favored by Viennese who like to escape the city for a long weekend. Hinterbrühl holds memories of Franz Schubert, who wrote *Der Lindenbaum* here. This tiny area is also home to Europe's largest subterranean lake (see below).

GETTING THERE   The village is 26km (16 miles) south of Vienna and 3km (2 miles) south of Mölding, the nearest large town. To reach Hinterbrühl from Vienna, take the S-Bahn from the Südbahnhof to Mölding (trip time: 15 min.) and then catch a connecting bus to Hinterbrühl, the last stop (12 min.). By car, drive southwest along the A-21, exiting at the signs to Gisshubel. From there, follow the signs to Hinterbrühl and Mölding.

VISITOR INFORMATION   The **tourist information office** in Kaiserin-Elisabeth 2, Mölding (© **02236/26727**) is open Monday to Friday 9am to 5pm.

AN UNDERGROUND LAKE

Seegrotte Hinterbrühl $\bigcirc$ *Finds*   Some of the village of Hinterbrühl was built directly above the stalactite-covered waters of Europe's largest underground lake. From the entrance a few hundred yards from the edge of town, you'll descend a steep flight of stairs before facing the extensively illuminated waters of a shallow, very still, and very cold underground lake. The famous natural marvel was the site of the construction of the world's first jet plane and other aircraft during World War II. Expect a running commentary in German and broken English during the 20-minute boat ride.

Grutschgasse 2A, Hinterbrühl. © 02235/26364. Admission and boat ride 7€ ($9.10) adult, 4.50€ ($5.85) children under 14 and students. Apr–Oct daily 9am–5pm; Nov–Mar Mon–Fri 9am–noon and 1–3pm, Sat–Sun 9am–3:30pm.

WHERE TO STAY

Hotel Beethoven   This hotel in the heart of the hamlet boasts one of the village's oldest buildings, a private house originally constructed around 1785. In 1992, the hotel renovated most of the interior and built a new wing. It was again renovated in 2002. The average-size bedrooms are cozy, traditional, and well maintained, with good beds and adequate bathrooms equipped mostly with tub/shower combinations.

There's no formal restaurant on the premises, but management maintains an all-day cafe where coffee, drinks, pastries, ice cream, salads, and platters of regional food are served daily.

Beethovengasse 8, A-2371 Hinterbrühl. ⓒ **02236/26252.** Fax 02236/277017. www.hotel-beethoven.cc. 25 units. 84€–92€ ($109–$120) double. Rates include buffet breakfast. AE, DC, MC, V. Free parking. **Amenities:** Cafe; bar. *In room:* TV, dataport, minibar, hair dryer, safe (in some).

WHERE TO DINE
Restaurant Hexensitz ⚐ AUSTRIAN/INTERNATIONAL   Featuring impeccable service, this restaurant celebrates the subtleties of Austrian country cooking. Its upscale setting is a century-old building whose trio of dining rooms are outfitted "in the Lower Austrian style" with wood paneling and country antiques. In summer, the restaurant expands outward into a well-kept garden. It offers daily changing dishes such as Styrian venison with kohlrabi, wine sauce, and homemade noodles; medallions of pork with spinach and herbs; and sea bass with forest mushrooms. The traditional desserts are luscious. The kitchen personnel are devoted and professional, and the food is savory and nearly always delightful.

Johannesstrasse 35. ⓒ **02236/22937.** Reservations recommended. Main courses 10€–22€ ($13–$29); fixed-price lunch 25€ ($33) available on Sun; fixed-price dinner 40€ ($52). MC, V. Tues 6–10pm; Wed–Sat 11:30am–2pm and 6–10pm; Sun 11:30am–2pm.

MAYERLING
This beautiful spot, 29km (18 miles) west of Vienna in the heart of the Wienerwald, is best known for the unresolved deaths of Archduke Rudolf, son of Emperor Franz Joseph, and his mistress in 1889. The event, which took place in a hunting lodge (now a Carmelite convent), altered the line of Austro-Hungarian succession. The heir apparent became Franz Joseph's nephew, Archduke Ferdinand, whose murder in Sarajevo sparked World War I.

ESSENTIALS
GETTING THERE   By **car,** head southwest on A-21 to Alland and take 210 to Mayerling. Or take **bus** no. 1123, 1124, or 1127, marked ALLAND, from Vienna's Südtirolerplatz (trip time: 90 min.). From Baden, hop on bus no. 1140 or 1141.

VISITOR INFORMATION   Contact the local authorities at the **Rathaus,** in nearby Heiligenkreuz (ⓒ **02258/8720;** www.heiligenkreuz.at). It's open Monday to Friday from 8am to noon and 2 to 5pm.

SEEING THE SIGHTS
Abbey Heiligenkreuz (Abbey of the Holy Cross)   Margrave Leopold III founded this abbey. It was built in the 12th century and subsequently gained an overlay of Gothic and baroque additions, with some 13th- and 14th-century stained glass still in place. The Romanesque and Gothic cloisters, with some 300 pillars of red marble, date from 1240. Some of the dukes of Babenberg were buried in the chapter house, including Duke Friedrich II, the last of his line. Heiligenkreuz has more relics of the Holy Cross than any other site in Europe except Rome.

Today a vital community of 50 Cistercian monks lives in Heiligenkreuz. In summer at noon and 6pm daily, visitors can attend the solemn choir prayers.

Heiligenkreuz. ⓒ **02258/8703.** Admission 6.20€ ($8.05) adults, 3€ ($3.90) children. Daily 9–11:30am and 1:30–5pm (until 4pm Nov–Feb). Tours daily 10 and 11am and 2 and 3pm, plus 4pm Easter to Sept. From Mayerling, take Heiligenkreuzstrasse 4.8km (3 miles) to Heiligenkreuz.

Twilight of the Habsburgs

On January 30, 1889, a hunting lodge in Mayerling was the setting of a grim tragedy that altered the line of succession of the Austro-Hungarian Empire and shocked the world. On a snowy night, Archduke Rudolf, the only son of Emperor Franz Joseph and Empress Elisabeth, and his 18-year-old mistress, Maria Vetsera, were found dead. It was announced that they had shot themselves, although no weapon ever surfaced for examination. All doors and windows to the room had been locked when the bodies were discovered. All evidence that might have shed light on the deaths was subsequently destroyed. Had it been a double suicide or an assassination?

Rudolf, a sensitive eccentric, was locked in an unhappy marriage, and neither his father nor Pope Leo XIII would allow an annulment. He had fallen in love with Maria at a German embassy ball when she was only 17. Maria's public snubbing of Archduchess Stephanie of Belgium, Rudolf's wife, at a reception given by the German ambassador to Vienna led to a heated argument between Rudolf and his father. Because of the young archduke's liberal leanings and sympathy for certain Hungarian partisans, he was not popular with his country's aristocracy, which gave rise to lurid speculation about a cleverly designed plot. Supporters of the assassination theory included Empress Zita von Habsburg, the last Habsburg heir, who in 1982, told the Vienna daily *Kronen Zeitung* that she believed their deaths were the culmination of a conspiracy against the family. Franz Joseph, griefstricken at the loss of his only son, ordered the hunting lodge torn down and a Carmelite nunnery built in its place.

Maria Vetsera was buried in a village cemetery in Heiligenkreuz. The inscription over her tomb reads, *Wie eine Blume sprosst der mensch auf und wird gebrochen* ("Human beings, like flowers, bloom and are crushed"). In a curious incident in 1988, her coffin was exhumed and stolen by a Linz executive, who was distraught at the death of his wife and obsessed with the Mayerling affair. It took police 4 years to recover the coffin.

Jagdschloss   A Carmelite abbey stands on the site of the infamous hunting lodge where Archduke Rudolf and his mistress supposedly committed suicide (see "Twilight of the Habsburgs," above). If it hadn't been torn down, the hunting lodge would be a much more fascinating—if macabre—attraction. Although nothing remains of the lodge, history buffs enjoy visiting the abbey.

Mayerling. ⓒ 02258/2275. Admission 2.50€ ($3.25) adults, 1.25€ ($1.65) children under 14. Daily 9am–12:30pm and 1:30–5pm (until 6pm in summer).

WHERE TO STAY & DINE

Hotel Hanner   The best hotel in town rises three stories, in a conservative but very modern format of respectability and charm. Bedrooms are streamlined, comfortable, and modern, with a color scheme that varies slightly, each from its neighbor, in its use of pastels. Guests appreciate the calm, the quiet, and the proximity to the acres of natural beauty in the surrounding region.

Mayerling #1, A-2534 Mayerling. ⓒ 02258/2378. Fax 02258/237841. 27 units. 140€–204€ ($182–$265) double. Rates include breakfast. AE, DC, MC, V. Free parking. **Amenities:** Restaurant; bar; fitness center; sauna; room service (7am–10pm); laundry; dry cleaning; nonsmoking rooms. *In room:* TV, dataport, minibar, hair dryer, safe.

Restaurant Hanner AUSTRIAN   Dignified, conservatively modern, and well managed, this is the best restaurant in a town not noted for lots of competition. Large windows take in a panoramic view over the surrounding forests, and dishes change with the seasons and according to the whim of the chef. Examples include fresh fish, goulash soup, breast of chicken with paprika-flavored noodles, and filets of venison in port-wine sauce.

In the Hotel Hanner, Mayerling #1. ⓒ 02258/2378. Reservations not necessary. Main courses 10€–25€ ($13–$33), set-price menu 98€ ($127). AE, DC, MC, V. Daily noon–2pm and 6–10pm.

2 The Spa Town of Baden bei Wien ⭐

Baden was once known as "the dowager empress of health spas in Europe." Tsar Peter the Great of Russia ushered in the town's golden age by establishing a spa here at the beginning of the 18th century. The Soviet army used the resort city as its headquarters from the end of World War II to the end of the Allied occupation of Austria in 1955.

The Romans, who didn't miss many natural attractions, began to visit what they called Aquae in A.D. 100. It had 15 thermal springs whose temperatures reached 95°F (35°C). You can still see the Römerquelle (Roman Springs) in the Kurpark, which is the center of Baden today.

This lively casino town and spa in the eastern sector of the Vienna Woods was at its most fashionable in the early 18th century, but it continued to lure royalty, sycophants, musicians, and intellectuals for much of the 19th century. For years the resort was the summer retreat of the Habsburg court. In 1803, when he was still Francis II of the Holy Roman Empire, the emperor began summer visits to Baden—a tradition he continued as Francis I of Austria after the Holy Roman Empire ended in 1806.

During the Biedermeier era (mid- to late-19th c.), Baden became known for its ochre Biedermeier buildings, which still contribute to the spa city's charm. The **Kurpark,** Baden's center, is handsomely laid out and beautifully maintained. Public concerts here keep the magic of the great Austrian composers alive.

Emperor Karl made this town the Austrian army headquarters in World War I, but a certain lightheartedness persisted. The presence of the Russians during the post–World War II years brought the resort's fortunes to their lowest ebb.

The **bathing complex** was constructed over more than a dozen sulfur springs. In the complex are some half-dozen bath establishments, plus four outdoor thermal springs. These thermal springs reach temperatures ranging from 75° to 95°F (24°–35°C). The thermal complex also has a "sandy beach" and a restaurant. It lies west of the town center in the Doblhoffpark, a natural park with a lake where you can rent boats for sailing. There's also a garden restaurant in the park. The resort is officially named Baden bei Wien, to differentiate it from other Badens not near Vienna.

ESSENTIALS

GETTING THERE   If you're driving from Vienna, head south on Autobahn A-2, cutting west at the junction of Route 210, which leads to Baden. By train, Baden is a local rather than an express stop. Trains depart daily 4:40am to midnight from Vienna's

Südbahnhof (trip time: 20 min.). For schedules, call ☎ 05/1717. By bus, the Badner Bahn leaves every 15 minutes from the Staatsoper (trip time: 1 hr.).

VISITOR INFORMATION   The **tourist information office,** at Brusattiplatz 3 (☎ 02252/22-600-600; www.baden.at), is open Monday to Saturday 9am to 6pm and Sunday 9am to noon.

SEEING THE SIGHTS

In the Hauptplatz (Main Square) is the **Trinity Column,** built in 1714, which commemorates the lifting of the plague that swept over Vienna and the Wienerwald in the Middle Ages. Also here are the **Rathaus** (☎ 02252/86800) and, at no. 17, the **Kaiserhaus,** Franz II's summer residence from 1813 to 1834.

Every summer between 1821 and 1823, Beethoven rented the upper floor of a modest house, above what used to be a shop on the Rathausgasse, in Baden, for about 2 weeks, hoping to find a cure for his increasing deafness. The site has been reconfigured by the city of Baden into a small museum commemorating the time he spent here, at **Beethovenhaus,** Rathausgasse 10 (☎ 02252/868-00230). Inside you'll find a trio of small, relatively modest rooms, furnished with one of Beethoven's pianos, his bed, several pieces of porcelain, photographs of others of his residences around the German-speaking world, some mementos, and copies of the musical folios he completed (or at least worked on) during his time in Baden. The museum is open year-round Tuesday to Friday 4 to 6pm, and Saturday and Sunday 9 to 11am and 4 to 6pm. Admission costs 2.50€ ($3.25) for adults and 1€ ($1.30) for students and children under 18. Entrance is free for children under 6.

Among the other sights in Baden, there's a celebrated death mask collection at the **Stadtisches Rolletmuseum,** Weikersdorfer-Platz 1 (☎ 02252/48255). The museum possesses many items of historic and artistic interest. Furniture and the art of the Biedermeier period are especially represented. It's open Monday to Wednesday and Friday to Sunday 3 to 6pm. Admission is 2.50€ ($3.25) for adults and 1€ ($1.30) for children. To reach the museum from Hauptplatz, go south to Josefs Platz and then continue south along Vöslauer Strasse, cutting right when you come to Elisabeth Strasse, which leads directly to the square on which the museum sits.

Northeast of Hauptplatz on the Franz-Kaiser Ring is the **Stadttheater** (☎ 02252/48338), built in 1909, and on nearby Pfarrgasse, the 15th-century parish church of **St. Stephan's** (☎ 02252/48426). Inside there's a commemorative plaque to Mozart, who allegedly composed his *Ave Verum* here for the parish choirmaster.

The real reason to come to Baden is the sprawling and beautiful **Kurpark** ✪. Here you can attend concerts, plays, and operas at an open-air theater, or try your luck at the casino (see "Baden After Dark," below). The Römerquelle (Roman Springs) can be seen gurgling from an intricate rock basin, which is surrounded by monuments to Beethoven, Mozart, and the great playwright Grillparzer. From the park's numerous paths you can view Baden and the surrounding hills.

TAKING A BATH

Kurhaus, Brussatiplatz 3 (☎ 02252/44531), is open daily 10am to 10pm for the *Römertherme* (hot mineral baths). The fee is 8.50€ ($11) for 2 hours, 10€ ($13) for 3 hours, 12€ ($16) for 4 hours, and 19€ ($25) for a full day. No reservations are necessary. Once inside, access to the sauna is an additional 3.50€ ($4.55), and any massage or health/beauty regimen costs extra. Relatively wealthy clients head for the Wellness Center, which has a wide array of facilities and operates somewhat like a medical clinic. No appointment is necessary. Monday to Friday 6am to 8:30pm, Saturday 6am to 12:30pm. Closed August 23 to September 5.

WHERE TO STAY
EXPENSIVE
Grand Hotel Sauerhof zu Rauhenstein ⍟   Although this estate dates to 1583, it became famous in 1757, when a sulfur-enriched spring bubbled up after a cataclysmic earthquake in faraway Portugal. The present building was constructed in 1810 on the site of that spring, which continues to supply water to its spa facilities today. In the past, the property served as an army rehabilitation center, a sanatorium during the two world wars, and headquarters for the Russian army. In 1978, after extravagant renovations, the Sauerhof reopened as one of the region's most upscale spa hotels.

The neoclassical building, with a steep slate roof, rambles across a wide lawn. Few of the original furnishings remain, and the management has collected a handful of vintage Biedermeier sofas and chairs to fill the elegant but somewhat underfurnished public rooms. A covered courtyard, styled on ancient Rome, has a vaulted ceiling supported by chiseled stone columns. The generous-size guest rooms, decorated in contemporary style, contain beautifully kept bathrooms with tub/shower combinations. The farmer-style restaurant serves some of the best food in town.

Weilburgstrasse 11-13, A-2500 Baden bei Wien. ⓒ **02252/412510.** Fax 02252/48047. www.sauerhof.at. 88 units. 186€–222€ ($242–$289) double; from 510€ ($663) suite. Rates include buffet breakfast; half-board 27€ ($35) per person extra. AE, DC, MC, V. Free parking. **Amenities:** 2 restaurants; bar; indoor heated pool; 2 tennis courts; fitness center; spa; sauna; salon; room service (7am–10pm); laundry service; dry cleaning; nonsmoking rooms; solarium. *In room:* TV w/pay movies, dataport, minibar, hair dryer, safe.

MODERATE
Krainerhütte (Kids)   Run by Josef Dietmann and his family, this hotel stands on tree-filled grounds 8km (5 miles) west of Baden at Helenental. It's a large A-frame chalet with rows of wooden balconies. The interior has more detailing than you might expect in such a modern hotel. There are separate children's rooms and play areas. The medium-size rooms and small bathrooms with tub/shower combinations are well maintained. In the cozy restaurant or on the terrace, you can dine on international and Austrian cuisine; the fish and deer come from the hotel grounds. Hiking in the owner's forests, hunting, and fishing are possible. *Postbus* (mail bus) service to Baden is available all day.

Helenental, A-2500 Baden bei Wien. ⓒ **02252/44511.** Fax 02252/44514. www.krainerhuette.at. 62 units. 90€– 130€ ($117–$169) double; from 160€ ($208) suite. Rates include breakfast; half-board 20€ ($26) per person extra. AE, MC, V. Parking 11€ ($14). **Amenities:** Restaurant; bar; indoor heated pool; tennis court; fitness center; sauna; room service (7am–10pm); babysitting; laundry service; dry cleaning; nonsmoking rooms. *In room:* TV, dataport, minibar, hair dryer.

Parkhotel Baden   This contemporary hotel sits in the middle of an inner-city park dotted with trees and statuary. The high-ceilinged lobby has a marble floor padded with thick oriental carpets and ringed with richly grained paneling. Most of the good-size, sunny guest rooms have their own loggia overlooking century-old trees; each contains a good bathroom with tub/shower combination and plenty of shelf space.

Kaiser-Franz-Ring 5, A-2500 Baden bei Wien. ⓒ **02252/443860.** Fax 02252/80578. www.niederoesterreich.at/park-hotel-baden. 87 units. 150€ ($195) double; 180€ ($234) suite. Rates include breakfast. AE, DC, MC, V. Free parking. **Amenities:** 2 restaurants; bar; indoor heated pool; health club; sauna; massage; room service (7am–10pm); babysitting; laundry service; dry cleaning. *In room:* TV, dataport, minibar, hair dryer.

Schloss Weikersdorf The oldest part of the hotel has massive beams, arched and vaulted ceilings, an Italianate loggia stretching toward the manicured gardens, and an inner courtyard with stone arcades. Accommodations, which include 77 bedrooms in the main house plus 27 in the annex, are handsomely furnished and most comfortable. The rooms in the newer section repeat the older section's arches and high ceilings, and sport ornate chandeliers and antique or reproduction furniture. All rooms have well-maintained bathrooms with tub/shower combinations and have been recently renovated.

Schlossgasse 9-11, A-2500 Baden bei Wien. (?) **02252/48301.** Fax 02252/4830-1150. www.hotelschlossweikersdorf.at. 104 units. 168€–185€ ($218–$241) double; 250€ ($325) suite. Rates include breakfast. AE, DC, MC, V. Free parking. **Amenities:** 2 restaurants; bar; indoor heated pool; 4 tennis courts; sauna; room service (7am-10pm); massage; laundry service; dry cleaning; nonsmoking rooms; rooms for those w/limited mobility; bowling alley. *In room:* TV, dataport (in some), minibar, hair dryer, safe.

WHERE TO DINE

Kupferdachl AUSTRIAN A local cornerstone since 1966, this family favorite serves rib-sticking fare that the locals adore, everything from cabbage soup to *apfelstrudel* for dessert. For a main dish, the chefs make the spa's best Wiener schnitzel, served with a freshly made salad and rice. Veal cutlet also appears cordon bleu. Expect good, old-fashioned Austrian cookery that was known before WWII.

Heiligenkreuzegasse 2. (?) **02252/41617.** Reservations recommended. Main courses 7€–12€ ($9.10–$16). No credit cards. Mon–Fri 8am–6:30pm; Sat–Sun 9am–4pm.

BADEN AFTER DARK

Casino Baden The town's major evening attraction is the casino, where you can play roulette, blackjack, baccarat, poker (seven-card stud), money wheel, and slot machines. Many visitors from Vienna come down to Baden for a night of gambling, eating, and drinking; there are two bars and a restaurant. Guests are often fashionably dressed, and you'll feel more comfortable if you are, too (men should wear jackets and ties). It's open daily 3pm to 3am. A less formal casino on the premises, the Casino Leger, is open daily noon to midnight.

In the Kurpark. (?) **02252/444960.** Free admission; 25€ ($33) worth of chips for 21€ ($27).

3 Wiener Neustadt

Wiener Neustadt was once the official residence of Habsburg Emperor Friedrich III, and this thriving city between the foothills of the Alps and the edge of the Pannonian lowland has a strong historic background.

The town was founded in 1192, when Duke Leopold V of the ruling house of Babenburg built its castle. He had it constructed as a citadel to ward off attacks by the Magyars from the east. From 1440 to 1493, Austrian emperors lived in this fortress, in the southeast corner of what is now the old town. Maximilian I, called "the last of the knights," was born here in 1459 and buried in the castle's Church of St. George. In 1752, on Maria Theresa's orders, the castle became a military academy.

Wiener Neustadt was a target for Allied bombs during World War II. It's where the routes from Vienna diverge, one going to the Semmering Pass and the other to Hungary via the Sopron Gate. The 200-year-old military academy that traditionally turned out officers for the Austrian army might have been an added attraction to bombers—German general Erwin Rommel ("the Desert Fox") was the academy's first commandant after the Nazi Anschluss. At any rate, the city was the target of more Allied bombing than any other in the country. It leveled an estimated 60% of its buildings.

ESSENTIALS

GETTING THERE   If you're driving from Vienna, head south along Autobahn A-2 until you reach the junction with Route 21, at which point you head east to Wiener Neustadt.

Trains leave for Wiener Neustadt daily from Vienna's Südbahnhof, from 5:30am to past midnight (trip time: 27–44 min.). For schedules, call © **05/1717** in Vienna or check www.oebb.at. Buses depart from the Wiener Mitte bus station throughout the day at 15- to 30-minute intervals (trip time: 1 hr.). The bus drops off passengers in the town center, at Ungargasse 2. Most visitors opt for the train.

VISITOR INFORMATION   The Wiener Neustadt **tourist information office,** at Hauptplatz in Rathaus (© **02622/29551**), is open Monday to Friday 8am to 5pm, Saturday 8am to noon.

SEEING THE SIGHTS

You can visit the **Church of St. George (St. Georgenkirche),** Burgplatz 1 (© **02622/ 3810**), daily from 8am to 6pm. The gable of the church is adorned with more than 100 heraldic shields of the Habsburgs. It's noted for its handsome interior, decorated in the late Gothic style.

Neukloster, Neuklostergasse 1 (© **02622/23102**), a Cistercian abbey, was founded in 1250 and reconstructed in the 18th century. The New Abbey Church (Neuklosterkirche), near the Hauptplatz, is Gothic and has a beautiful choir. It contains the tomb of Empress Eleanor of Portugal, wife of Friedrich III and mother of Maximilian I. Mozart's *Requiem* was first presented here in 1793. Admission is free, and it's open Monday to Friday 9am to noon and 2 to 5pm.

Liebfrauenkirche, Domplatz (© **02622/23202**), was once the headquarters of an Episcopal seat. It's graced by a 13th-century Romanesque nave, but the choir is Gothic. The west towers have been rebuilt. Admission is free, and the church is open daily 8am to noon and 2 to 6pm.

In the town is a **Recturm,** Babenberger Ring (© **02622/279-24**), a Gothic tower said to have been built with the ransom money paid for Richard the Lion-Hearted. It's open March to October on Tuesday to Thursday 10am to noon and 2 to 4pm, and Saturday and Sunday 10am to noon only. Admission is free.

WHERE TO STAY

Hotel Corvinus ☆   The best hotel in town, built in the 1970s, sits in a quiet neighborhood near the city park, a 2-minute walk south of the main rail station. The good-size rooms have modern comforts, such as firm beds and well-maintained bathrooms equipped with tub/shower combinations. There's also an inviting bar area, a parasol-covered sun terrace, and a lightheartedly elegant restaurant serving Austrian and international dishes.

Bahngasse 29-33, A-2700 Wiener Neustadt. © **02622/24134.** Fax 02622/24139. www.hotel-corvinus.at. 68 units. 120€ ($156) double. Rates include buffet breakfast. AE, DC, MC, V. Free parking. **Amenities:** Restaurant; bar; Jacuzzi; sauna; room service (7am–10pm); laundry service; dry cleaning; nonsmoking rooms; solarium. *In room:* TV, dataport, minibar, hair dryer.

WHERE TO DINE

Gelbes Haus ☆ *Finds* AUSTRIAN/INTERNATIONAL   Set in the historic heart of town, this long-enduring and well-respected restaurant (whose name translates as "the yellow house") takes its name from the vivid ocher color of its exterior, which is from around 1911. The Art Nouveau dining room emphasizes style and comfort. The

Austrian and international cuisine is prepared with fresh ingredients, imagination, and flair. Dishes include a succulent version of *tafelspitz;* an assortment of carpaccios arranged with herbs, truffle oil, goose liver, and exotic mushrooms; rump steak stuffed with goose liver, tomatoes, and onions; and filets of pork in red-wine sauce with cabbage and herbs. French and Italian dishes are added according to the whim of the chef.

Kaiserbrunnen 11. ℂ 02622/26400. Reservations recommended. Main courses 10€–15€ ($13–$20); fixed-price dinners 35€–55€ ($46–$72). DC, MC, V. Mon–Sat noon–2pm and 7:30–10pm. Closed Christmas, New Year's Day, and Easter.

4 The Danube Valley ★★★

The Danube is one of Europe's legendary rivers, rich in scenic splendor and surrounded by history and architecture. The Wachau, a section of the Danube Valley northwest of Vienna, is one of the most beautiful and historic areas of Austria. Traveling through the rolling hills and fertile soil of the Wachau, you'll pass ruins of castles reminiscent of the Rhine Valley, some of the most celebrated vineyards in Austria, famous medieval monasteries, and ruins from Stone Age peoples, the Celts, the Romans, and the Habsburgs. Unrelentingly prosperous, the district has won many awards for the authenticity of its historic renovations.

If you like the looks of this district, take a paddleboat steamer trip. Most of these operate only between April 1 and October 31. You can travel the countryside from an armchair on the ship's deck.

If you're really "doing the Danube," you can begin your trip at Passau, Germany, and go all the way to the Black Sea and across to the Crimean Peninsula, stopping over at Yalta. However, just the Vienna-Yalta portion of the trip takes nearly a week, and few travelers can devote that much time. Most visitors limit themselves to a more restricted look at the Danube by taking one of the many popular trips offered from Vienna. (See the "Cruising the Danube" box in chapter 6.)

TIPS ON EXPLORING THE DANUBE VALLEY

If you have only a day to see the Danube Valley, we highly recommend the tours listed below. If you have more time, rent a car and explore this district yourself, driving inland from the river now and then to visit the towns and sights listed below. You can also take public transportation to the towns we've highlighted (see individual listings).

The Wachau and the rest of the Danube Valley contain some of the most impressive monuments in Austria, but because of their far-flung locations, many prefer to participate in an organized tour. The best of these are conducted by **Vienna Sightseeing Tours,** Starhemberggasse 25 (ℂ **01/7124-6830;** fax 01/714-1141; www.vienna sightseeingtours.com), which offers guided tours by motorcoach in winter and by both motorcoach and boat in summer. Stops on this 8-hour trip include Krems, Dürnstein, and Melk Abbey. Prices are 61€ ($79) for adults and 30€ ($39) for children under 12, and do not include lunch. Prices include lunch in winter. Advance reservations are required.

Before you venture into the Danube Valley, pick up maps and other helpful information at the **tourist office for Lower Austria,** Postfach 10.000, A-1010 Vienna (ℂ **01/536-106200;** fax 01/536-106-060; www.niederoesterreich.at).

TULLN

This is one of the most ancient towns in Austria. Originally a naval base called Comagena and later a center for the Babenburg dynasty, Tulln, on the right bank of the

Danube, is "the flower town" because of the masses of blossoms you'll see in spring and summer. It's the place, according to the Nibelungen saga, where Kriemhild, the Burgundian princess of Worms, met Etzel, king of the Huns. A famous "son of Tulln" was Kurt Waldheim, former secretary-general of the United Nations and one of Austria's most controversial former presidents, due to his previous Nazi affiliations.

ESSENTIALS

GETTING THERE   Tulln lies 42km (26 miles) west of Vienna, on the south bank of the Danube, and 13km (8 miles) southwest of Stockerau, the next big town, on the north bank of the Danube. If you're driving from Vienna, head west along Route 14.

S-Bahn trains depart from the Wien Nord Station and, more frequently, from the Wien Franz-Josefs Bahnhof daily 4:30am to 8:30pm (trip time: 27–45 min.). Tulln lies on the busy main rail lines linking Vienna with Prague, and most local timetables list Gmund, an Austrian city on the border of the Czech Republic, as the final destination. For more information, call (℃ **05/1717,** or check www.oebb.at. We don't recommend taking the bus from Vienna, as it would require multiple transfers.

From mid-May to late September, river cruisers owned by the **DDSG-Blue Danube Shipping Line** (℃ **01/588800**) depart westward from Vienna on Sunday at 8:30am en route to Passau, Germany, and arrive in Tulln around 11:20am; then they continue westward to Krems, arriving there around 1:55pm. For more information, call the shipping line or the tourist office in either Tulln or Krems.

VISITOR INFORMATION   The **tourist office** in Tulln, at Minoritenplatz 2 (℃ **02272/67566;** www.tulln.at), is open November to April, Monday to Friday 8am to 3pm; and May to October, Monday to Friday 9am to 7pm, Saturday and Sunday 10am to 7pm.

SEEING THE SIGHTS

The twin-towered **Pfarrkirche (parish church)** of St. Stephan on Wiener Strasse grew out of a 12th-century Romanesque basilica dedicated to St. Stephan. Its west portal was built in the 13th century. A Gothic overlay added in its early centuries fell victim to the 18th-century baroque craze that swept the country. A 1786 altarpiece commemorates the martyrdom of St. Stephan.

Adjoining the church is the **Karner (charnel)** ☆☆. This funereal chapel is the major sight of Tulln, the finest of its kind in the entire country. Built in the mid-13th century in the shape of a polygon, it's richly decorated with capitols and arches. The Romanesque dome is adorned with frescoes.

In a restored former prison, Tulln has opened the **Egon Schiele Museum** ☆☆, Donaulände 28 (℃ **02272/645-70**), devoted to its other famous son, born here in 1890. Schiele is one of the greatest Austrian artists of the early 1900s. The prison setting might be appropriate, as the expressionist painter spent 24 days in jail in 1912 in the town of Neulengbach for possession of what back then was regarded as pornography. While awaiting trial, he produced 13 watercolors, most of which are now in the Albertina in Vienna. The Tulln museum has more than 90 of his oil paintings, watercolors, and designs, along with much memorabilia. It's open daily 10am to 6pm. Admission is 4€ ($5.20) adults and 2€ ($2.60) children. The museum is closed in December and January.

WHERE TO STAY & DINE

Gasthaus zur Sonne (Gasthaus Sodoma) ☆ AUSTRIAN   This is Tulln's finest and most famous restaurant. The 1940s building, on the main street a short walk from the railway station, looks like a cross between a chalet and a villa. Under the direction of the Sodoma family since 1968, it consists of two cozy dining rooms lined with oil paintings. Customers, including the mayor of Vienna and other Austrian celebrities, have enjoyed dishes that change with the season. The menu invariably includes well-prepared versions of dumplings stuffed with minced meat, pumpkin soup, a marvelous Weiner schnitzel, onion-studded roast beef, *tafelspitz*, and perfectly cooked zander (freshwater lake fish) served with potatoes and butter sauce.

Bahnhofstrasse 48. (℃) **02272/64616.** Reservations recommended. Main courses 8€–21€ ($10–$27). No credit cards. Tues–Sat 11:30am–2pm and 6–9:30pm.

Hotel Römerhof   Built in 1972, this hotel near the train station has a simple modern facade of white walls and unadorned windows. The interior is warmly outfitted with earth tones, a macramé wall hanging, and pendant lighting fixtures. The bedrooms are comfortable but utterly functional, with duvet-covered beds. Bathrooms have well-kept showers but limited storage space.

Langenlebarnerstrasse 66, A-3430 Tulln an der Donau. (℃) **02272/62954.** www.hotel-roemerhof.at. 51 units. 72€–90€ ($94–$117) double. Rates include buffet breakfast. MC, V. Free parking. **Amenities:** Breakfast room; bar; sauna; beer garden. *In room:* TV, minibar, hair dryer, safe.

Hotel Rossmühle   A stay at this very visible, very central hotel will almost certainly give you an insight into old-fashioned Austria at its most idiosyncratic. Rebuilt within the shells of two very old buildings in the 1970s, each within a 2-minute walk from the other, it combines many 19th-century architectural details, including wrought-iron gates, a collection of antique furniture, and crystal chandeliers. The bedrooms within the annex are smaller, less grand, and cheaper than those within the main building. Rooms in the main core have tub/shower combinations; those within the annex have only showers. The on-site restaurant offers an all-Austrian ode to wholesome food and a faded kind of country charm. It's most frequently patronized by clients of the hotel, who arrange half-board for a supplement of 15€ ($13) per person.

Hauptplatz 12, A-3430 Tulln an der Donau. (℃) **02272/624110.** Fax 02272/6241133. www.rossmuehle.at. 44 units. 76€–104€ ($99–$135) double. Rates include buffet breakfast. AE, MC, V. Free parking. From Vienna, drive 30 min. west along Rte. 14. **Amenities:** Restaurant; lounge. *In room:* TV.

HERZOGENBURG

To reach Herzogenburg from Vienna, drive 65km (40 miles) west on Autobahn A-1 to St. Pölten. The monastery is 11km (6¾ miles) north of St. Pölten. Take Wiener Strasse (Rte. 1) east from St. Pölten to Kapelln (13km/8 miles), go left at the sign onto a minor road to Herzogenburg, and follow signs.

Augustinian Herzogenburg Monastery   A German bishop from Passau founded the monastery in the early 12th century. The present complex of buildings comprising the church and the abbey was reconstructed in the baroque style (1714–40). Jakob Prandtauer and Josef Munggenast, along with Fischer von Erlach, designed the buildings. The magnificent baroque church has a sumptuous interior, with an altarpiece by Daniel Gran and a beautiful organ loft. The most outstanding art owned by the abbey is a series of 16th-century **paintings on wood** (☆); they are on display in a room devoted to Gothic art.

You can wander around on your own or join a guided tour. There's a wine tavern in the complex where you can eat Austrian specialties.

A-3130 Herzogenburg. ℂ **02782/83113.** Admission 6€ ($7.80) adults, 4€ ($5.20) seniors, 3€ ($3.90) students. Apr–Oct daily 9am–6pm. Tours daily on the hour 9–11am and 1–5pm. Closed Nov–Mar.

KREMS ✦

In the eastern part of the Wachau on the left bank of the Danube lies Krems, a city some 1,000 years old. Krems is a mellow place of courtyards, old churches, and ancient houses in the heart of vineyard country, with some partially preserved town walls. Just as the Viennese flock to Grinzing and other suburbs to sample new wine in the *heurigen,* the people of the Wachau come here to taste the vintners' products, which appear in Krems earlier in the year.

ESSENTIALS

GETTING THERE   Krems is located 80km (50 miles) west of Vienna and 29km (18 miles) north of St. Pölten. If you're driving from Vienna, drive north along the A-22 until it splits into three roads near the town of Stockerau. Here, drive due west along Route 3, following the signs to Krems.

Trains depart from both the Wien Nord Station and the Wien Franz-Josefs Bahnhof for Krems daily every hour or so from 2:30am to 11:30pm (trip time: 60–95 min.). Many are direct, although some require a transfer at Absdorf-Hippersdorf or St. Pölten. Call ℂ **05/1717** for schedules. Traveling by bus from Vienna to Krems is not recommended because of the many transfers required. Krems, however, is well connected by local bus lines to surrounding villages. From mid-May to late September, the **DDSG Blue Danube Shipping Company** (ℂ **01/588800**) runs river cruises departing Vienna on Sunday at 8:35am and arriving in Krems around 1:55pm.

VISITOR INFORMATION   The Krems **tourist office,** at Undstrasse 6 (ℂ **02732/ 82676;** www.krems.at), is open Monday to Friday 8:30am to 6pm, Saturday and Sunday 10am to noon and 1 to 4pm.

SEEING THE SIGHTS

The most interesting part of Krems today is what was once the little village of **Stein.** Narrow streets are terraced above the river, and the single main street, **Steinlanderstrasse,** is flanked with houses, many from the 16th century. The **Grosser Passauerhof,** Steinlanderstrasse 76 (ℂ **02732/82188**), is a Gothic structure decorated with an oriel. Another house, at Steinlanderstrasse 84, combines Byzantine and Venetian elements among other architectural influences; it was once the imperial tollhouse. In days of yore, the aristocrats of Krems barricaded the Danube and extracted heavy tolls from the river traffic. Sometimes the tolls were more than the hapless victims could pay, so the townspeople just confiscated the cargo. In the Altstadt, the **Steiner Tor,** a 1480 gate, is a landmark.

Pfarrkirche St. Viet (ℂ **02732/857100**), the parish church of Krems, stands in the center of town at the Rathaus, reached by going along either Untere Landstrasse or Obere Landstrasse. The overly ornate church is rich with gilt and statuary. Construction on this, one of the oldest baroque churches in the province, began in 1616. Martin Johann Schmidt, better known as Kremser Schmidt, painted many of the frescoes inside the church in the 18th century.

You'll find the **Weinstadt Museum Krems (Historical Museum of Krems),** Körnermarkt 14 (ℂ **02732/801567**), in a restored Dominican monastery. The Gothic abbey is from the 13th and 14th centuries. One of the more intriguing displays is a copy of a 32,000-year-old statuette, the country's most ancient work of art. Of further interest are the cellar tunnels from the 1500s that were excavated underneath the cloister. The complex also has an interesting **Weinbaumuseum (Wine Museum)**, exhibiting artifacts gathered from the vineyards along the Danube. Admission to both areas of the museum is 3.50€ ($4.55). It's open only from March to November Tuesday to Sunday 10am to 6pm.

Nearby Attractions

Twenty-nine kilometers (18 miles) north of Krems at St. Pölten is the Museum of Lower Austria, formerly located in Vienna. Now called **Landes Museum**, it's at Franz-Schubert-Platz (© **2742/908-090-100**). This museum exhibits the geology, flora, and fauna of the area surrounding Vienna. It also exhibits a collection of arts and crafts, including baroque and Biedermeier; temporary shows featuring 20th-century works are presented as well. Admission is 8€ ($10) for adults and 7€ ($9.10) for children. It's open Tuesday to Sunday 9am to 5pm.

WHERE TO STAY

Donauhotel Krems   This large, glass-walled hotel built in the 1970s has a wooden canopy stretched over the front entrance. The bedrooms are comfortably furnished and well maintained. They are a little small for long stays but are suitable for an overnight, as the beds are fluffy and the bathrooms (most with tub/shower combinations) are spotless. Austrian fare is available in the airy cafe, on the terrace, or in the more formal restaurant.

Edmund-Hofbauer-Strasse 19, A-3500 Krems. © **02732/87565.** Fax 02732/875-6552. donauhotel-krems@aon.at. 60 units. 84€ ($109) double. Rates include buffet breakfast; half-board 14€ ($18) per person extra. AE, DC, MC, V. No parking. **Amenities:** Restaurant; bar; fitness center; sauna; solarium (last 3 for women only). *In room:* TV, hair dryer, safe.

Gourmethotel am Förthof ⚲ *(Finds*   In the Stein sector of the city, this big-windowed hotel has white-stucco walls and flower-covered balconies. A rose garden surrounds the base of an alfresco cafe; inside are oriental rugs and a scattering of antiques amid newer furniture. Each of the high-ceilinged bedrooms has a foyer and a shared balcony. Most bedrooms are fairly spacious. Bathrooms, though small, have well-kept tub/shower combinations.

Donaulände 8, A-3500 Krems. © **02732/83345.** Fax 02732/833-4540. www.niederoesterreich.at/gourmethotel. 20 units. 90€–130€ ($117–$169) double. Rates include breakfast; half-board 25€ ($33) per person extra. AE, DC, MC, V. Free parking. **Amenities:** Restaurant; bar; outdoor pool; sauna; room service (7am–10pm); babysitting; laundry service; dry cleaning; all nonsmoking rooms. *In room:* TV, minibar, hair dryer, safe.

WHERE TO DINE

Restaurant Bacher ⚲ AUSTRIAN/INTERNATIONAL   Lisl and Klaus Wagner-Bacher operate this excellent restaurant-hotel, with an elegant dining room and a well-kept garden. Specialties include crabmeat salad dressed with nut oil, and zucchini stuffed with fish and accompanied by two kinds of sauces. Dessert might be beignets with apricot sauce and vanilla ice cream. Lisl has won awards for her cuisine, as her enthusiastic clientele will tell you. The wine list has more than 600 selections.

Eight double and three single rooms are offered. Rooms contain TVs, minibars, phones, and radios, and each is attractively furnished with good beds and well-maintained bathrooms. Rates are 120€ to 170€ ($156–$221) for a double with buffet breakfast. The establishment is 4km (2½ miles) from Krems.

Südtiroler Platz 208, A-3512 Mautern. ℂ **02732/82937.** Fax 02732/74337. Reservations required. Main courses 16€–29€ ($21–$38); fixed-price menus 58€–80€ ($75–$104). DC, MC, V. Wed–Sat 11:30am–1:30pm and 6–9:30pm; Sun 11:30am–9pm. Closed mid-Jan to mid-Feb.

DÜRNSTEIN ★★

Less than 8km (5 miles) west of Krems, Dürnstein is the loveliest town along the Danube and, accordingly, draws throngs of tour groups in summer. Terraced vineyards mark this as a Danube wine town, and the town's fortified walls are partially preserved.

ESSENTIALS

GETTING THERE   The town is 80km (50 miles) west of Vienna. If you're driving, take Route 3 west. From Krems, continue driving west along Route 3 for 8km (5 miles). Train travel to Dürnstein from Vienna requires a transfer in Krems (see above). In Krems, trains depart approximately every 2 hours on river-running routes; it's a 6km (3¾-mile) trip to Dürnstein. Call ℂ **05/1717** in Vienna for schedules. There's also bus service between Krems and Dürnstein (trip time: 20 min.).

VISITOR INFORMATION   A little **tourist office,** housed in a tiny shed in the east parking lot called Parkplatz Ost (ℂ **02711/200**), is open April to October only. Hours are daily 11am to 6pm.

SEEING THE SIGHTS

The ruins of a **castle fortress,** 159m (522 ft.) above the town, are inextricably linked to the Crusades. Here Leopold V, the Babenberg duke ruling the country at that time, held Richard the Lion-Hearted of England prisoner in 1193. For quite some time, nobody knew exactly where in Austria Richard was incarcerated, but his loyal minstrel companion, Blondel, had a clever idea. He went from castle to castle, playing his lute and singing Richard's favorite songs. The tactic paid off, the legend says, for at Dürnstein, Richard heard Blondel's singing and sang the lyrics in reply. The discovery forced Leopold to transfer Richard to a castle in the Rhineland Palatinate, but by then everybody knew where he was. So Leopold set a high ransom on the king's head, which was eventually met, and Richard was set free. The castle was virtually demolished by the Swedes in 1645, but you can visit the ruins if you don't mind a vigorous climb (allow 1 hr.). The castle isn't much, but the view of Dürnstein and the Wachau is more than worth the effort.

Back in town, take in the principal artery, **Hauptstrasse** ★, which is flanked by richly adorned old residences. Many of these date from the 1500s and have been well maintained through the centuries.

The 15th-century **Pfarrkirche (parish church)** also merits a visit. The building was originally an Augustinian monastery and was reconstructed when the baroque style swept Austria. The church tower is the finest baroque example in the whole country and a prominent landmark in the Danube Valley. Kremser Schmidt, the noted baroque painter, did some of the altar paintings.

WHERE TO STAY & DINE

Gartenhotel Weinhof Pfeffel *Value*   This black-roofed, white-walled hotel is partially concealed by well-landscaped shrubbery. One of the best bargains in town, the hotel takes its name from its garden courtyard with flowering trees, where tasty (but not fancy) meals are served. The public rooms are furnished with traditional pieces. The bedrooms are handsomely furnished in a traditional Austrian motif, with comfortable armchairs, good beds, and medium-size bathrooms equipped with tub/shower combinations. Leopold Pfeffel, your host, serves wine from his own terraced vineyard. He has also added a swimming pool.

A-3601 Dürnstein. ✆ 02711/206. Fax 02711/12068. www.pfeffel.at. 40 units. 82€–128€ ($107–$166) double; from 108€ ($140) suite. Rates include breakfast. MC, V. Free parking. Closed Dec–Feb. **Amenities:** Restaurant; bar; outdoor pool; sauna; room service (7am–10pm); laundry service; dry cleaning; nonsmoking rooms. *In room:* TV, dataport, minibar, hair dryer, safe.

Hotel-Restaurant Sänger Blondel ☆ (Finds)

Lemon-colored and charmingly old-fashioned, with green shutters and clusters of flowers at the windows, this hotel is named after the faithful minstrel who searched the countryside for Richard the Lion-Hearted. Bedrooms are furnished in a rustic style and are quite comfortable, containing small bathrooms equipped with shower units. All have good beds with fresh linens. Each Thursday, an evening of zither music is presented. If the weather is good, the music is played outside in the flowery chestnut garden near the baroque church tower. There's a good and reasonably priced restaurant serving regional cuisine.

A-3601 Dürnstein. ✆ 02711/253. Fax 02711/2537. www.saengerblondel.at. 15 units. 92€–106€ ($120–$138) double; 124€ ($161) suite. Rates include breakfast. MC, V. Parking 7€ ($9.10). Closed Dec–Feb and the first week in July. **Amenities:** Restaurant; lounge; laundry service; dry cleaning. *In room:* TV, hair dryer.

Hotel Schloss Dürnstein ☆☆

The baroque tower of this Renaissance castle rises above the scenic Danube. It's one of the best-decorated hotels in Austria, with white ceramic stoves, vaulted ceilings, parquet floors, oriental rugs, and gilt mirrors. A beautiful shady terrace is only a stone's throw from the river. Elegantly furnished bedrooms come in a wide variety of styles, ranging from those that are large and palatial to others that are rather small and modern. Modern bathrooms with tub/shower combinations are in all the bedrooms, though sometimes in cramped conditions. The restaurant serves well-prepared dishes from the kitchen of an experienced chef.

A-3601 Dürnstein. ✆ 02711/212. Fax 02711/212-30. www.schloss.at. 41 units. 205€–250€ ($267–$325) double; from 340€ ($442) suite. Rates include breakfast. AE, DC, MC, V. Free parking. Closed Nov 10–Mar 25. A pickup can be arranged at the Dürnstein rail station. **Amenities:** Restaurant; bar; 2 pools (1 heated indoor); fitness center; sauna; gymnastics center; room service (7am–10pm); massage; babysitting; laundry service; dry cleaning. *In room:* TV, dataport, minibar, hair dryer, safe.

Romantik Hotel Richard Löwenherz ☆☆

This hotel was founded in the 1950s on the site of a 700-year-old nunnery, originally dedicated to the sisters of Santa Clara in 1289. Its richly historical interior is filled with antiques, Renaissance sculpture, elegant chandeliers, stone vaulting, and paneling that's been polished over the years to a mellow patina. An arbor-covered sun terrace with restaurant tables extends toward the Danube. The spacious bedrooms, especially those in the balconied modern section, are filled with cheerful furniture. The duvet-covered beds are the finest in the area. Each unit also has a beautifully kept bathroom with a tub/shower combination. The restaurant offers a fine selection of local wines among its many regional specialties.

A-3601 Dürnstein. ✆ 02711/222. Fax 02711/22218. www.richardloewenherz.at. 38 units. 160€–180€ ($208–$234) double; 292€ ($380) suite. Rates include buffet breakfast. AE, DC, MC, V. Free parking. Closed Nov–Mar. **Amenities:** Restaurant; lounge; outdoor heated pool; room service (7am–9pm); laundry service; nonsmoking rooms. *In room:* TV, dataport, hair dryer.

MELK

The words of Empress Maria Theresa speak volumes about Melk: "If I had never come here, I would have regretted it." The main attraction is the Melk Abbey, a sprawling baroque building overlooking the Danube basin. Melk marks the western terminus of the Wachau and lies upstream from Krems.

ESSENTIALS

GETTING THERE Melk is 89km (55 miles) west of Vienna. **Motorists** can take Autobahn A-1, exiting at the signs for Melk. If you prefer a more romantic and scenic road, try Route 3, which parallels the Danube but takes 30 to 45 minutes longer. **Trains** leave frequently from Vienna's Westbahnhof to Melk, with two brief stops en route (trip time: about 1 hr.).

VISITOR INFORMATION The **Melk tourist office** at Babenbergerstrasse 1 (© 02752/52307410; www.tiscover.com/melk), in the center of town, is open April and October Monday to Friday 9am to noon and 2 to 6pm, Sunday 10am to 2pm; May, June, and September Monday to Friday 9am to noon and 2 to 6pm, Saturday and Sunday 10am to noon and 4 to 6pm; July and August Monday to Saturday 9am to 7pm, Sunday 10am to noon and 5 to 7pm.

SEEING THE SIGHTS

Melk Abbey ✦✦ One of the finest baroque buildings in the world, Melk Abbey and the **Stiftskirche (abbey church)** ✦✦✦ are the major attractions today. However, Melk has been an important place in the Danube Basin ever since the Romans built a fortress on a promontory looking out onto a tiny "arm" of the Danube. Melk also figures in the *Nibelungenlied* (the German epic poem), in which it is called *Medelike*.

The rock-strewn bluff where the abbey now stands overlooking the river was the seat of the Babenbergs, who ruled Austria from 976 until the Habsburgs took over. In the 11th century, Leopold II of the House of Babenberg presented Melk to the Benedictine monks, who turned it into a fortified abbey. Its influence and reputation as a center of learning and culture spread all over Austria, a fact that is familiar to readers of Umberto Eco's *The Name of the Rose*. The Reformation and the 1683 Turkish invasion took a toll on the abbey, although it was spared from direct attack when the Ottoman armies were repelled outside Vienna. The construction of the new building began in 1702, just in time to be given the full baroque treatment.

Most of the design of the present abbey was by the architect Jakob Prandtauer. Its marble hall, called the Marmorsaal, contains pilasters coated in red marble. A richly painted allegorical picture on the ceiling is the work of Paul Troger. The library, rising two floors, again with a Troger ceiling, contains some 80,000 volumes. The Kaisergang, or emperors' gallery, 198m (650 ft.) long, is decorated with portraits of Austrian rulers.

Despite all the adornment in the abbey, it is still surpassed in lavish glory by the Stiftskirche, the golden abbey church. Damaged by fire in 1947, the church has been fully restored, including the regilding statues and altars with gold bouillon. The church has an astonishing number of windows, and it's richly embellished with marble and frescoes. Many of the paintings are by Johann Michael Rottmayr, but Troger also contributed.

Melk is still a working abbey, and you might see black-robed Benedictine monks going about their business or students rushing out of the gates. Visitors head for the terrace for a view of the river. Napoleon probably used it for a lookout when he made Melk his headquarters during the campaign against Austria.

Throughout the year, the abbey is open every day. From May to September, tours depart at intervals of 15 to 20 minutes. The first tour begins at 9am and the last is at

5pm; guides make efforts to translate into English a running commentary that is otherwise German.

Dietmayerstrasse 1, A-3390 Melk. ℂ 02752/555-232 for tour information. Guided tours 8.80€ ($12) adults, 5.90€ ($7.65) children, unguided tours 7€ ($9.10) adults, 4.10€ ($5.35) children.

WHERE TO STAY
Hotel Stadt Melk *(★ (Value*   Just below the town's palace, this four-story hotel, with a gabled roof and stucco walls, was originally built a century ago as a private home. It was eventually converted into this cozy, family-run hotel, and now has simply furnished bedrooms that are clean and comfortable, with sturdy beds and well-maintained bathrooms that, though small, are adequate and equipped with tub/shower combinations. Rooms in the rear open onto views of the abbey. The pleasant restaurant has leaded-glass windows in round bull's-eye patterns of greenish glass. Meals, beginning at 35€ ($42), are also served on a balcony at the front of the hotel. The food is quite good.

Hauptplatz 1, A-3390 Melk. ℂ 02752/52475. Fax 02752/524-7519. www.tiscover.at/hotel-stadt-melk. 14 units. 85€ ($111) double; 150€ ($195) suite. Rates include breakfast. AE, DC, MC, V. Free parking. **Amenities:** Restaurant; bar; sauna; laundry service; dry cleaning service. *In room:* TV, minibar, hair dryer, safe.

WHERE TO DINE
Stiftsrestaurant Melk BURGENLANDER   If you're visiting Melk, this place is required dining, lying right at the entrance to the abbey. Don't let its cafeteria-like dimensions sway you from its fine cuisine. This modernly decorated restaurant is well equipped to handle large groups—some 3,000 visitors a day frequent the establishment during peak season. From the reasonable fixed-price menu you might opt for the asparagus-and-ham soup with crispy dumplings; hunter's roast with mushrooms, potato croquettes, and cranberry sauce; and the famed Sacher torte for dessert.

Abt-Berthold-Dietmayrstrasse 3. ℂ 02752/52555. Main courses 8€–13€ ($10–$17). AE, MC, V. Mid-Mar to Oct daily 8am–7pm; Nov–Jan 2 daily 9am–5pm. Closed otherwise.

5 Eisenstadt: Haydn's Home

When Burgenland joined Austria in the 1920s, it was a province without a capital. In 1924, its citizens agreed to give Eisenstadt the honor. The small town lies at the foot of the Leitha mountains, at the beginning of the Great Hungarian Plain. Surrounded by vineyards, forests, and fruit trees, it's a convenient stopover for exploring Lake Neusiedl, 9.6km (6 miles) east.

Even before assuming its new administrative role, Eisenstadt was renowned as the place where the great composer Joseph Haydn lived and worked while under the patronage of the aristocratic Esterházy family.

ESSENTIALS
GETTING THERE   Board one of the many trains heading toward Budapest from the Südbahnhof (South Railway Station) in Vienna, and change trains in the railway junction of Neusiedl am See. Connections are timed to link up with the 16 or so trains that continue on to Eisenstadt (trip time: 90 min.). Call ℂ 05/1717 in Vienna for schedules.

From the Vienna International Airport, you can take a bus to the City Air Terminal at the Vienna Hilton. From this station, buses depart for Eisenstadt every 20 minutes during the day. The sign on the bus reads EISENSTADT-DOMPLATZ (there's no number).

If you're driving from Vienna, take Route 10 east to Parndorf Ort, and then head southwest along Route 50 to Eisenstadt.

VISITOR INFORMATION   The **Eisenstadt tourist office,** Schloss Esterházy (*©* **02682/67390**), distributes information (in English), and will make hotel reservations for you at no charge.

SEEING THE SIGHTS

Bergkirche (Church of the Calvary)   This church contains Haydn's white marble tomb. Until 1954, only the composer's headless body was here. His skull was in Vienna's Sammlung alter Musikinstrumente (see "Neue Hofburg," p. 113), where curious spectators were actually allowed to feel it. Haydn's head had been stolen a few days after his death and wasn't reunited with his body for 145 years. In a long and complicated journey, the head traveled from one owner to another before finally, we hope, coming to rest with the other part of Haydn's remains at Eisenstadt.

Joseph-Haydn-Platz 1. *©* **02682/62638.** Church free admission; Haydn's tomb 2.50€ ($3.25) adults, 2€ ($2.60) seniors, 1€ ($1.20) students. Daily 9am–noon and 1–5pm. Closed Nov–Mar. From Esterházy Platz at the castle, head directly west along Esterházystrasse, a slightly uphill walk.

Haydn Museum   The little home of the composer from 1766 to 1778 is now a museum honoring its former tenant. Although he appeared in court nearly every night, Haydn actually lived very modestly when he was at home. A little flower-filled courtyard is one of the few luxuries. The museum has collected mementos of Haydn's life and work.

Haydn-Gasse 21. *©* **02682/7193900.** Admission 3.50€ ($4.55) adults; 3€ ($3.90) children, seniors, and students. Daily 9am–5pm. Closed Nov–Mar. Pass Schloss Esterházy and turn left onto Haydn-Gasse.

Schloss Esterházy *(★)*   Haydn worked in this château built on the site of a medieval castle and owned by the Esterházy princes. The Esterházy clan was a great Hungarian family who ruled over Eisenstadt and its surrounding area. They claimed descent from Attila the Hun. The Esterházys helped the Habsburgs gain control in Hungary. So great was their loyalty to Austria, when Napoleon offered the crown of Hungary to Nic Esterházy in 1809, he refused it.

The castle was designed by the Italian architect Carlo Antonio Carlone, who began work on it in 1663. Subsequently, many other architects have remodeled it, resulting in sweeping alterations to its appearance. In the late 17th and early 18th centuries, it was given a baroque pastel facade. On the first floor, the great baronial hall was made into the Haydnsaal, where the composer conducted the orchestra Prince Esterházy had provided for him. The walls and ceilings of this concert hall are elaborately decorated, but the floor is of bare wood, which, it is claimed, is the reason for the room's acoustic perfection.

Esterházy Platz. *©* **2682/7193000.** Admission 6€ ($7.80) adults; 5€ ($6.50) children, seniors, and students; 14€ ($18) family ticket. Sat–Tues and Thurs 9am–7pm; Wed and Fri 9am–8pm. From the bus station at Domplatz, follow the sign to the castle (a 10-min. walk).

WHERE TO STAY & DINE

Gasthof Öhr   Although the rooms of this pleasant inn are clean and comfortable, with exposed paneling, comfortable beds, and a sense of old-fashioned charm, the place is more famous and more consistently popular as a restaurant, where main courses cost 8€ to 20€ ($10–$26) each, and where the kitchen consistently turns out flavorful portions of *tafelspitz,* Wiener schnitzel, and such freshwater fish dishes as zander in white wine with capers, and pan-fried trout, sometimes with almonds, sometimes with white wine and butter. These are served within any of four old-fashioned dining rooms accented with wood trim, or during clement weather, within a garden in back. The restaurant is open Tuesday to Sunday 11am to 10pm. This inn was built just after the end of World War II, and is located just across from Eisenstadt's bus station, behind a white facade.

Ruster Strasse 51, 7000 Eisenstadt. © 02682/62460. www.hotelohr.at. 30 units. 95€–105€ ($124–$137) double. DC, MC, V. **Amenities:** Restaurant; limited room service; babysitting. *In room:* TV.

Hotel Burgenland Hotel Burgenland opened in 1982 and quickly established itself as the best in Eisenstadt. A mansard roof, white stucco walls, and big windows form the exterior of this hotel located directly northeast of the bus station at Domplatz. The comfortable rooms have lots of light, comfortable beds, functional furniture, and neatly kept bathrooms with tub/shower combinations.

One of the best restaurants in Burgenland is the hotel's Bienenkorb. The bright and airy restaurant serves traditional dishes such as cabbage soup and veal steak with fresh vegetables, along with some Hungarian specialties.

Schubertplatz 1, A-7000 Eisenstadt. © 02682/6960. Fax 02682/65531. www.hotelburgenland.at. 88 units. 135€ ($176) double; from 195€ ($254) suite. Rates include buffet breakfast. AE, DC, MC, V. Parking 10€ ($13). **Amenities:** 2 restaurants; bar; indoor heated pool; fitness center; sauna; room service (7am–10pm); babysitting; laundry service; dry cleaning; nonsmoking rooms. *In room:* TV w/pay movies, dataport, minibar, hair dryer, trouser press, safe.

6 Lake Neusiedl ✫

The Lake Neusiedl region is a famous getaway for the Viennese, but those from around the globe will find it just as desirable. The lake offers countless diversions, making it an ideal destination for families and active travelers. The steppe landscape is great for strolls and hikes, and the geological anomaly of Neusiedler See (see box below) will intrigue you.

NEUSIEDL AM SEE

This crowded summer weekend spot lies on the northern bank of Lake Neusiedl. Watersports prevail; you can rent a sailboat and spend the day drifting across the lake. The Gothic parish church is noted for its "ship pulpit." A watchtower from the Middle Ages still stands guard over the town, although it's no longer occupied. If you plan to be here on a summer weekend, make advance reservations.

ESSENTIALS

GETTING THERE Neusiedl am See lies 45km (28 miles) southeast of Vienna, 359km (223 miles) east of Salzburg, and 34km (21 miles) northeast of Eisenstadt. This town is your gateway to the lake, as it's less than an hour by express train from Vienna. If you're driving from Vienna, take the A-4 or Route 10 east. If you're in Eisenstadt, head northeast along Route 50, cutting east along Route 51 for a short distance. It's better to have a car if you're exploring Lake Neusiedl, although there are bus connections that depart several times daily from the Domplatz bus station at Eisenstadt.

VISITOR INFORMATION The **Neusiedl am See tourist office,** in the Rathaus (town hall), Hauptplatz 1 (© 02167/2229), distributes information about accommodations and boat rentals. Open July and August Monday to Friday 8am to 6pm, Saturday 10am to noon and 2 to 6pm; September to June Monday to Thursday 8am to noon and 1 to 4:30pm, Friday 8am to 1pm.

Fun Fact **The Capricious Lake**

Neusiedler See (Lake Neusiedl) is a popular steppe lake in the northern part of Burgenland. This strange lake should never be taken for granted—in fact, from 1868 to 1872, it completely dried up, as it has done periodically throughout its history. This creates intriguing real estate disputes among landowners. The lake was once part of a body of water that blanketed all of the Pannonian Plain. It's 6.8 to 15km (4¼–9¼ miles) wide and about 35km (22 miles) long. Today it's only about 1.8m (6 ft.) deep at its lowest point, and the wind can shift the water dramatically, even causing parts of the lake to dry up.

A broad belt of reeds encircles its huge expanse, about 185 sq. km (115 sq. miles). This thicket is an ideal habitat for many species of waterfowl. In all, some 250 species of birds inhabit the lake, including the usual collection of storks, geese, ducks, and herons. The Neusiedler See possesses no natural outlets; it is fed by underground lakes. The water is slightly salty, so the plants and animals here are unique in Europe. Alpine, Baltic, and Pannonian flora and fauna meet in its waters.

The Viennese come to the lake throughout the year, in summer to fish and windsurf and in winter to skate. Nearly every village has a beach (although on any given day it might be swallowed up by the sea or end up miles from the shore, depending on which way the wind blows). Washed in sun, the vineyards in Rust produce award-winning vintages.

WHERE TO STAY & DINE

Gasthof zur Traube   This small hotel stands on the town's bustling main street. The pleasant ground-floor restaurant is filled with country trim and wrought-iron table dividers. You can stop in for a meal from 11am to 10pm, or book one of the cozy upstairs rooms. Both the rooms and shower-only bathrooms are a bit on the small size. In summer, guests can relax in the garden. Franz Rittsteuer and his family are the owners.

Hauptplatz 9, A-7100 Neusiedl am See. © **02167/2423**. Fax 02167/24236. www.zur-traube.at. 7 units. 58€ ($75) double; 75€ ($98) triple. Rates include breakfast. MC, V. Free parking. **Amenities:** Restaurant; bar. *In room:* TV.

Hotel Wende   This place is actually a complex of three sprawling buildings interconnected by rambling corridors. Set at the edge of town on the road leading to the water, the hotel is almost a village unto itself. The bedrooms are well furnished, with well-maintained bathrooms containing tub/shower combinations.

The best food and best service, as well as the most formal setting, are found in the hotel's restaurant. Under a wood-beamed ceiling, the rich and bountiful table of Burgenland is set to perfection. In summer, tables are placed outside overlooking the grounds. Because Burgenland is a border state, the menu reflects the cuisines of Hungary and Austria. The menu includes a savory soup made with fresh carp from nearby lakes; pork cutlets with homemade noodles, bacon-flavored *rösti* (fried potatoes), baby carrots, and fresh herbs; Hungarian crepes stuffed with minced veal and covered with paprika-cream sauce; and, for dessert, a strudel studded with fresh dates and topped with marzipan-flavored whipped cream.

Seestrasse 40-50, A-7100 Neusiedl am See. © **02167/8111.** Fax 02167/811-1649. www.hotel-wende.at. 106 units. 134€–154€ ($174–$200) double; 290€–308€ ($377–$400) suite. Rates include half-board. AE, DC, MC, V. Parking garage 10€ ($12). Closed last week in Jan and first 2 weeks in Feb. Free pickup at the train station. **Amenities:** Restaurant; bar; indoor heated pool; 3 tennis courts; fitness center; Jacuzzi; sauna; salon; room service (7am–10pm); massage; babysitting; laundry service; dry cleaning; nonsmoking rooms. *In room:* TV, dataport, minibar, hair dryer.

PURBACH AM SEE

If you take Route 50 south from the northern tip of Lake Neusiedl, your first stop might be this little resort village, which has some nice accommodations. Purbach boasts a well-preserved circuit of town walls, which were built to stop Turkish invasions during the 16th and 17th centuries. It's also a market town, where you can buy some of Burgenland's renowned wines from local vendors.

ESSENTIALS

GETTING THERE   Purbach is 50km (31 miles) southeast of Vienna and 18km (11 miles) northeast of Eisenstadt. From Eisenstadt, you can take a daily bus that leaves from the station at Domplatz. If you're driving from Eisenstadt, head northeast along Route 50; if you're coming from Vienna, cut southeast along Route 10.

VISITOR INFORMATION   Contact the **Neusiedler See tourist office** in Neusiedl am See, Hauptplatz 1 (© **02167/2229**). It's open July and August, Monday to Friday 8am to 7pm, Saturday 10am to noon and 2 to 6pm, Sunday 4 to 7pm; September to June, Monday to Thursday 8am to noon and 1 to 4:30pm, Friday 8am to 1pm.

WHERE TO STAY

Am Spitz   The main building of this hotel has a gable trimmed with baroque embellishments, lying 2km (1¼ miles) from the center. The Holzl-Schwarz family is your host here, where a hotel has stood for more than 600 years. The current incarnation includes accommodations with wonderful views of the lake. The hotel staff takes care and pride in the maintenance of its average-size rooms and small but quite serviceable shower-only bathrooms. The hotel is well directed, conservative, and deserving of its three-star government rating. The adjoining restaurant is one of the best places in the region for Burgenland cuisine.

Waldsiedlung 2, A-7083 Purbach am See. © **02683/5519.** Fax 02683/551920. www.klosteramspitz.at. 15 units. 100€–120€ ($130–$156) double. Rates include buffet breakfast. MC, V. Free parking. Closed Christmas–Easter. The hotel will pick up guests at the bus station. **Amenities:** Restaurant; lounge; room service (7am–10pm); coin-operated laundry. *In room:* TV, dataport, minibar, hair dryer.

WHERE TO DINE

Am Spitz Restaurant   BURGENLAND/PANNONIAN   The regional artifacts that adorn the space and the excellent waitstaff make this restaurant a warm and inviting place. Chefs borrow heavily from the recipes of Burgenland and the neighboring province of Pannonia. The setting, in a former 17th-century abbey with a flower garden extending in summer to the lake itself, is beautiful.

The menu changes daily but always features the catch of the day (from the nearby lake) that can be prepared to your desires. Meat and poultry are other main dishes, and we're especially fond of their pan-fried chicken schnitzel or their perfectly grilled tender beef. Roast veal steak is another menu highlight. Most diners prefer to begin with a bowl of the spicy Hungarian-inspired fish soup. All the luscious desserts are made fresh daily. The wine cellar stocks hundreds of bottles—in fact, the hotel owns around 14 hectares (35 acres) of vineyards and produces its own wines.

Waldsiedlung 2. © 02683/5519. Reservations recommended. Main courses 10€–22€ ($13–$29); fixed-price menus 50€–60€ ($65–$78). Mid-Mar to mid-Dec Thurs–Sun noon–2pm and 6–9pm.

RUST

South of Purbach, Rust is a small resort village with limited accommodations. It's famous for its stork nests, which perch on chimneys throughout the town. The antiquated, charming town center is well preserved and clean. Its walls were built in 1614 for protection against the Turks.

Lush vineyards that produce the Burgenlander grape surround Rust, capital of the Burgenland lake district. If it's available, try Blaufränkisch, a red wine that seems to be entirely consumed by locals and visiting Viennese. Sometimes you can go right up to the door of a vintner's farmhouse, especially if it displays a green bough, and sample the wine before buying it on the spot.

Rust has a warm and friendly atmosphere, especially on weekends. Summers are often hot, and the lake water can get warm. You can rent sailboats and windsurfers on the banks of the shallow Neusiedler See.

ESSENTIALS

GETTING THERE   The village is 18km (11 miles) northeast of Eisenstadt, 71km (44 miles) southeast of Vienna, and 349km (216 miles) east of Salzburg. There's no train station, but buses connect Eisenstadt with Rust. For bus information, call © 01/ 526-6048. If you're headed out of Eisenstadt by car, go east on Route 52. From Purbach, take Route 50 south toward Eisenstadt. At Seehof, take a left fork to Oggau and Rust.

VISITOR INFORMATION   The **Rust tourist office,** in the Rathaus (town hall) in the center of the village (© 02685/502), can arrange inexpensive stays with English-speaking families. It's open Monday to Friday 9am to noon and 1 to 6pm, Saturday 1 to 4pm, and Sunday 9am to noon.

WHERE TO STAY & DINE

Hotel-Restaurant Sifkovitz ✦   Attracting summer visitors from Vienna and Hungary, this hotel consists of an older building with a new wing. Rooms get a lot of sun and are comfortably furnished, if rather functional. There's no great style here, but the beds are firm and the bathrooms, although not large, are well maintained and equipped with tub/shower combinations. There is access to tennis courts, but they're on the grounds of another hotel nearby (the staff will make arrangements). Food, both Austrian and Hungarian, is served daily.

Am Seekanal 8, A-7071 Rust. © 02685/276. Fax 02685/36012. www.sifkovits.at. 35 units. 82€–122€ ($106–$159) per person double. Rates include buffet breakfast. AE, DC, MC, V. Closed Dec–Mar. **Amenities:** Restaurant; bar; fitness center; sauna; room service (7am–10pm); laundry service; dry cleaning; nonsmoking rooms. In room: TV, dataport, minibar, hair dryer, safe.

Mooslechner's Burgerhaus ✦ AUSTRIAN/CONTINENTAL   Rust has several other restaurants fixated on innovative and more expensive cuisine, but we prefer this *gemütlich,* middle-bracket tavern in the heart of town. Within a venue that dates from the 1530s, it provides plenty of old-fashioned charm. The food, focused on traditional preparations of zander, goose and, in season, game dishes, evokes traditional Austria at its best. The cook here is particularly proud of the terrines of gooseliver that emerge

from the kitchen. With room for only about 60 to 80 diners at a time, the venue is cozy and rather charming.

Hauptstrasse 1. © **02685/6416**. Reservations recommended only in midsummer. Set-price menus 31€–76€ ($40–$99). DC, MC, V. Tues–Sun noon–2pm and 6–10pm. Closed Feb.

Seehotel Rust ⊕   Seehotel Rust is one of the most attractive hotels in the lake district, set on a grassy lawn at the edge of the lake. This well-designed hotel remains open year-round, and offers pleasantly furnished bedrooms and clean bathrooms equipped with a shower unit. The rooms are a little too "peas-in-the-pod" for most tastes; however, an overnight stopover can be just fine.

Offerings in the restaurant include *tafelspitz* with chive sauce, calves' brains with a honey vinegar, watercress soup, and sole meunière. A Gypsy band provides entertainment.

Am Seekanal 2-4, A-7071 Rust. © **02685/3810**. Fax 02685/381419. www.seehotel-rust.at. 110 units. 150€–182€ ($195–$237) double; 185€–195€ ($241–$254) suite. Rates include half-board. AE, DC, MC, V. Free parking. **Amenities:** Restaurant; bar; indoor heated pool; 4 tennis courts (2 indoor); squash court; sauna; boat rental; room service (7am–10pm); babysitting; laundry service; dry cleaning; nonsmoking rooms. *In room:* TV, dataport, minibar, hair dryer.

ILLMITZ

This old *puszta* (steppe) village on the east side of the lake has grown into a town with a moderate tourist business in summer. By **car** from Eisenstadt, take Route 50 northeast, through Purbach, cutting southeast on Route 51 via Podersdorf to Illmitz.

NEARBY ATTRACTIONS

Leaving Illmitz, head east on the main route and then cut north at the junction with Route 51. From Route 51, both the little villages of St. Andrä bei Frauenkirchen and Andau are signposted. Near the Hungarian border, the hamlet of **St. Andrä bei Frauenkirchen** is filled with thatch houses. Known for its basket weaving, the town makes for a nice shopping expedition.

A short drive farther on is **Andau,** which became the focus of world attention in 1956 during the Hungarian uprising. Through this town, hundreds of Hungarians dashed to freedom in the West, fleeing the Soviet invasion of Budapest.

Starting in the late 1940s, the border with Hungary was closely guarded, and people who tried to escape into Austria were often shot. But now all that has changed. In 1989, the fortifications were rendered obsolete as hundreds of East Germans fled across the border to the West and freedom. Before the year was out, the Iron Curtain had fallen.

The surrounding marshy area of this remote sector of Austria, called **Seewinkel,** is a haven for birds and rare flora, plus many small *puszta* animals. This large natural wildlife sanctuary is dotted with windmills and huge reed thickets, used for roofs.

WHERE TO STAY & DINE

Weingut-Weingasthof Rosenhof ⊕   This charming baroque hotel stands in a gardenlike setting. Through the arched gateway, framed by a gold-and-white facade, is a rose-laden courtyard filled with arbors. The tile-roofed building, capped with platforms for storks' nests, contains cozy, perfectly maintained bedrooms and bathrooms with shower units.

In an older section, you'll find a wine restaurant whose star attraction is the recent vintage produced by the Haider family's wine presses. The restaurant serves Hungarian and Burgenland specialties to its guests and much of the neighborhood. Dishes might be as exotic as wild boar cooked in a marinade and thickened with regional walnuts. Local fish, such as carp and the meaty zander from the Danube, are available. In autumn, the inn serves *traubensaft*—delectable juice made from freshly harvested grapes that is consumed before it becomes alcoholic. In the evening, musicians fill the air with Gypsy music.

Florianigasse 1, A-7142 Illmitz. © 02175/2232. Fax 02175/22324. www.rosenhof.cc. 15 units. 78€–86€ ($101–$112) double. Rates include buffet breakfast. MC, V. Closed Nov to Easter. **Amenities:** Restaurant; bar; laundry service; dry cleaning. *In room:* TV, hair dryer.

PODERSDORF

Podersdorf am See is one of the best places for swimming in the mysterious lake—its shoreline is relatively free of reeds. As a result, the little town has become a modest summer resort. The parish church in the village dates from the late 18th century. You'll see many storks nesting atop chimneys and some cottages with thatched roofs. The Viennese like to drive out here on a summer Sunday to go for a swim and to purchase wine from the local vintners.

ESSENTIALS

GETTING THERE   Podersdorf lies 14km (8¾ miles) south of the major center along the lake, Neusiedl am See (see above). It's easiest to drive here, although buses run throughout the day from Eisenstadt, going via Neusiedl am See. If you're driving from Eisenstadt, head northeast along Route 50, via Purbach, cutting southeast at the junction with Route 51; you'll go via Neusiedl am See before cutting south along the lake to Podersdorf.

VISITOR INFORMATION   In summer, a small **tourist office** at Hauptstrasse 2 (© **02177/2227**) dispenses information daily 8am to 5pm.

WHERE TO STAY

Gasthof Seewirt   This hotel sits at the edge of the lake, within a short walk of a great swath of marshland. Rooms are clean, comfortable, and utilitarian, but only medium in size. Duvets cover the comfortable beds, and the shower-only bathrooms are a bit cramped but spotlessly kept. Public areas bear the owners' personal touch and include one of the best restaurants in town (see below).

Strandplatz 1, A-7141 Podersdorf. © 02177/2415. Fax 02177/246530. 35 units. 95€–170€ ($124–$221) double. Rates include half-board. AE, DC, V. Closed Nov–Mar. **Amenities:** Restaurant; lounge; indoor heated pool; Jacuzzi; sauna; room service (7am–10pm); nonsmoking rooms; rooms for those w/limited mobility. *In room:* TV, hair dryer, safe.

Haus Attila   Newer and more recently renovated than its sibling, the Seewirt, this hotel was renovated and enlarged in 2004, with new rooms overlooking the lake. The light-grained balconies are partially shielded by a row of trees, and many overlook the lake. Rooms are clean and comfortable, and the tiny shower-only bathrooms are well maintained. Many visitors who check in for a couple of days of lakeside relaxation never move too far, consuming their meals in the dining room of the Seewirt, less than 91m (298 ft.) away. In the basement of a nearby annex is a well-stocked wine cellar, where a member of the Karner family can take you for a wine tasting. Some of the vintages are produced from their own vineyards.

Strandplatz 8, A-7141 Podersdorf. © 02177/2415. Fax 02177/246530. www.seewirtkarner.at. 38 units. 97€–159€ ($126–$207) double. Rates include breakfast. AE, MC, V. Closed Nov 1–Mar 30. **Amenities:** Lounge; indoor heated pool; sauna; room service (7am–10pm); nonsmoking rooms; rooms for those w/limited mobility. *In room:* TV, hair dryer, safe.

Seehotel Herlinde   An excellent government-rated two-star choice, this vacation spot is on the beach of Lake Neusiedl away from the main highway. All the functionally furnished rooms have their own balconies; the best have views of the lake. Room size is only adequate; the beds are nothing special, though the mattresses are firm. The shower-only bathrooms are small but are polished brightly every day. The food and wine are plentiful, the latter often enjoyed on a 200 seat terrace.

Strandplatz 17, A-7141 Podersdorf. (2) **02177/2273.** Fax 02177/2430. 40 units. 106€ ($138) double. Rates include breakfast and lunch. MC, V. **Amenities:** Restaurant; bar; sauna; laundry service; all nonsmoking rooms. *In room:* TV, minibar, hair dryer.

WHERE TO DINE

Gasthof Seewirt Café Restaurant ⨪ BURGENLANDER/INTERNATIONAL
The preferred place for dining at the resort is this likable and unpretentious hotel restaurant that prepares bountiful dishes served by formally dressed waiters who are eager to describe the local cuisine. The Karner family—well-known vintners whose excellent Rieslings, red and white pinots, and Weisburgunders are available for consumption—are proud of their long-established traditions and a local cuisine that in some ways resembles that of neighboring Hungary. A house specialty is *Palatschinken Marmaladen,* consisting of tender roast beef glazed with apricot jam, and a dessert called *Somloer Nockerl,* made of vanilla pudding, whipped cream, raisins, and nuts in a biscuit shell.

Strandplatz 1. (2) **02177/2415.** Main courses 8€–22€ ($10–$29). MC, V. Daily 11:30am–2:30pm and 6-9:30pm. Closed Nov–Mar.

7 Forchtenstein

This town resembles so many others along the way that you could easily pass through it without taking much notice. However, Forchtenstein is home to one of the most famous of the Esterházy castles, which is reason enough make it a stop on your trip.

ESSENTIALS

GETTING THERE   From Eisenstadt, take Route S-31 southwest to Mattersburg, and from there follow the signs along a very minor road southwest to Forchtenstein. Three buses per day (only one on Sun) run from Vienna to Forchtenstein. There are no direct trains; the nearest railway station is 10km (6¼ miles) away, in Mattersburg. From here, take a taxi or one of the three daily buses that go to Forchtenstein.

VISITOR INFORMATION   In lieu of a tourist office, the **town council** in the mayor's office at Hauptstrasse 52 (© **02685/7744**) provides information Monday to Friday 9am to 2pm.

SEEING THE SIGHTS

The castle **Burg Forchtenstein,** Burgplatz 1 (© **02626/81212**), 14km (8¾ miles) southeast of Wiener Neustadt in Lower Austria, was constructed on a rocky base by order of the counts of Mattersdorf in the 13th century. The Esterházy family had it greatly expanded around 1636. From its belvedere, you can see as far as the Great Hungarian Plain.

The castle saw action in the Turkish sieges of Austria in 1529 and in 1683. A museum since 1815, it now holds the Prince Esterházy collections, which consist of family memorabilia, a portrait gallery, large battle paintings, historical banners, and Turkish war booty and hunting arms. It's the largest private collection of historical arms in Austria. Legend has it that Turkish prisoners carved the castle cistern out of the rock, more than 137m (449 ft.) deep.

Admission is 7€ ($9.10) for adults, 6€ ($7.80) for students and children 6 to 15, free for children under 6. The castle is open April to October daily 9am to 5pm; November to March, tours are offered only when requested in advance. A guide shows you through.

WHERE TO STAY

Gasthof Sauerzapf   This hotel has two stories of weathered stucco, renovated windows, and a roofline that's red on one side and black on the other. The updated interior is cozy and attractive, albeit simple, and is kept immaculate. Anna Daskalakis-Sauerzapf, the owner, rents modestly furnished rooms that are reasonably comfortable for the price. Their style is reminiscent of your great-aunt's house—comfortable beds and just-adequate shower-only bathrooms, inviting nonetheless. The restaurant serves good food and an array of local wines.

Rosalienstrasse 39, A-7212 Forchtenstein. ⓒ/fax **02626/81217.** 12 units. 44€ ($57) double. Rates include breakfast. No credit cards. Free parking. **Amenities:** Restaurant (closed Wed); lounge. *In room:* No phone.

WHERE TO DINE

Reisner *(Value* AUSTRIAN   The area's best restaurant has expanded over the years from its original century-old core. Here you'll find good food, particularly the regional specialties and Burgenland wines. Our favorite area is the cozy, rustic, smaller room, which the locals prefer as well. Besides the especially good steaks, you might enjoy trout filet served with a savory ragout of tomatoes, zucchini, potatoes, and basil. The five-course fixed-price meal is gargantuan.

Hauptstrasse 141. ⓒ **02626/63139.** Reservations recommended. Main courses 8€–19€ ($10–$25); fixed-price dinner menus 20€–42€ ($26–$55). No credit cards. Wed–Sun 9am–2:30pm and 6–10pm.

Appendix A:
Vienna in Depth

As Vienna moves deeper into a new millennium, it's good to look back at its rich classical, culinary, and historical legacy to appreciate its present more deeply. The royal seat of the Habsburgs for 600 years, Vienna has always stood out as a center of art and music, as well as architecture.

1 Vienna Today

As the capital of Austria, Vienna lives with its legacy. The little country was the birthplace of Mozart, Freud, Hitler, and the Wiener schnitzel.

In 2004, recognition came on two fronts: Elfriede Jelinek, the controversial writer, won the Nobel Prize for literature. On another front, Charles I, the last Habsburg to rule as emperor, was beatified by the pope.

Like the United States, Austria remains deeply polarized, and along similar lines. The establishment of the far-right Freedom Party in 2000 has brought Austria worldwide condemnation. In contrast, many citizens of Vienna, and Austria in general, are among the most liberal, advanced, well informed, and tolerant on earth.

As one example of the newer, more left-wing Austria, environmental awareness is on the rise. Recycling is more evident in Vienna than in any other European capital—in fact, recycling bins are commonplace on the city's streets. The Viennese

are often sorting their paper, plastic, and aluminum and steel cans.

Visitors today will find a newer and brighter Vienna, a city with more *joie de vivre* than it's had since before World War II. It's still the city where the music never stops. In spite of two world wars, much of the empire's glory and grandeur remain. Its treasures now stock the museums, and its palaces are open to visitors. Vienna has been called an "architectural waltz"— baroque buildings, marble statues, lovely old squares, grand palaces, and famous concert halls are all still here, as if the empire were still flourishing.

Wolfgang Seipel, who waits tables in a local cafe, told us, "We have our guilt, the famous Viennese schizophrenia. We've condoned atrocities, and there have been some embarrassing Nazi revelations. If Freud were still with us, I'm sure he'd wear out a couch every month. But in spite of it all, Vienna still knows how to show you a hell of a good time."

2 History 101

Vienna's history has been heavily influenced by its position astride the Danube, midway between the trade routes linking the prosperous ports of northern Germany with Italy. Its location at the crossroads of three great European cultures (Slavic, Teutonic, and Roman/Italian) transformed the settlement into a melting

pot and, more often than not, a battlefield, even in prehistoric times.

EARLY TIMES The 1906 discovery of the Venus of Willendorf, a Stone Age fertility figurine, in the Danube Valley showed that the region around Vienna was inhabited long before recorded history. It's known that around 1000 B.C., the mysterious Indo–European Illyrians established a high-level barbarian civilization around Vienna. After them came the Celts, who migrated east from Gaul around 400 B.C. They arrived in time to greet and resist the Romans, who began carving inroads into what is now known as Austria.

Around A.D. 10, the Romans chose the site of modern-day Vienna for a fortified military camp, Vindobona. This strategic outpost is well documented—its location is bordered today by Vienna's Rotenturmstrasse, St. Rupert's Church, the Graben, and Tiefer Graben. Vindobona marked the northeast border of the Roman Empire, and it functioned as a buffer zone between warring Roman, Germanic, and Slavic camps.

BABENBERGS & BOHEMIANS   In 803, the Frankish emperor Charlemagne swept through the Danube Valley, establishing a new territory called Ostmark (the Eastern March). When Charlemagne died in 814 and his once-mighty empire disintegrated, Vindobona struggled to survive. The earliest known reference to the site by the name we know today (Wenia) appeared in a proclamation of the archbishop of Salzburg in 881.

In 976, Leopold von Babenberg established control over Austria, the beginning of a 3-century rule. Commerce thrived under the Babenbergs, and Vienna grew into one of the largest towns north of the Alps. By the end of the 10th century, Ostmark had become Ostarrichi, which later changed to Österreich (Austria).

Toward the end of the 12th century, Vienna underwent an expansion that would shape its development for centuries to come. In 1200, Vienna's ring of city walls was completed, financed by the ransom paid by the English to retrieve their king, Richard Coeur de Lion (the Lion-Hearted), who had been seized on Austrian soil in 1192. A city charter was granted to Vienna in 1221, complete with trading privileges that encouraged the town's further economic development.

In 1246, when the last of the Babenbergs, Friedrich II, died without an heir, the door was left open for a struggle between the Bohemian, Hungarian, and German princes over control of Austria. The Bohemian king Ottokar II stepped into the vacuum. However, Ottokar, who controlled an empire that extended from the Adriatic Sea to Slovakia, refused to swear an oath of fealty to the newly elected emperor, Rudolf I of Habsburg, and the opposing armies joined in one of Vienna's pivotal conflicts, the Battle of Marchfeld, in 1278. Though Ottokar's administration was short, he is credited with the construction of the earliest version of Vienna's Hofburg.

Dateline

- 23,000 B.C. Venus of Willendorf, a representative of a Danubian fertility goddess, is crafted near Vienna.
- 1000 B.C. Illyrian tribes establish a society near Vienna.
- 400 B.C. Vendi tribes migrate from Gaul eastward to regions around Vienna.
- 100 B.C. Romans make military inroads into southern Austria.
- A.D. 10 Vindobona (Vienna) is established as a frontier outpost of the Roman Empire. Within 300 years, it's a thriving trading post.
- 400 Vindobona is burnt and rebuilt, but the event marks the gradual withdrawal of the Romans from Austria.
- 500 Vienna is overrun by Lombards.
- 630 The Avars take Vienna.
- 803 Charlemagne conquers the Danube Valley and site of Vienna, labeling what's now Austria Ostmark.
- 814 Death of Charlemagne signals dissolution of his empire.
- 881 First documented reference to Vienna (Wenia) appears.
- 955 Charlemagne's heir, Otto I, reconquers Ostmark.
- 962 Otto I is anointed the first official Holy Roman Emperor by the pope.

continued

THE HABSBURG DYNASTY Under Rudolph of Habsburg, a powerful European dynasty was launched, one of the longest lived in history. The Habsburg grip on much of central Europe would last until the end of World War I in 1918. During the next 2 centuries a series of annexations and consolidations of power brought both Carinthia (1335) and the Tyrol (1363) under Habsburg control.

Many of these Habsburg rulers are long forgotten, but an exception is Rudolf IV (1339–65). Known as "The Founder," he laid the cornerstone of what was later consecrated as St. Stephan's Cathedral. He also founded the University of Vienna as a response to the university in neighboring Prague.

A turning point in the dynasty came in 1453, when Friedrich II was elected Holy Roman Emperor. He ruled from a power base in Vienna. By 1469, Vienna had been elevated to a bishopric, giving the city wide-ranging secular and religious authority.

Friedrich's power was not always steady—he lost control of both Bohemia and Hungary, each of which elected a king. In 1485, he was driven from Vienna by the Hungarian king Matthias Corvinus, who ruled for a 5-year period from Vienna's Hofburg.

In 1490, Corvinus died and civil war broke out in Hungary. Maximilian I (1459–1519), Friedrich's son, took advantage of the situation in Hungary to regain control of much of the territory his father had lost.

The Habsburgs did not always conquer territory. Sometimes they succeeded through politically expedient marriages, a series of which brought Spain, Burgundy, and the Netherlands into their empire. In 1496, 4 years after Spanish colonization of the New World, a Habsburg, Phillip the Fair, married the Spanish *infanta* (heiress), a union that produced Charles I (Carlos I), who became ruler of Spain and its New World holdings in 1516. Three years later, he was crowned Holy Roman Emperor as Charles V. Charles ceded control of Austria to his Vienna-based younger brother, Ferdinand, in 1521. Ferdinand later married Anna Jagiello, heiress to Hungary and Bohemia, adding those countries to the empire.

In 1526, discontent in Vienna broke into civil war. Ferdinand responded with brutal repression and a new city charter that placed the city directly under Habsburg control.

PLAGUES & TURKISH INVASIONS
In 1529, half of the city was destroyed by fire. Also during that year, Turkish armies laid siege to the city for 18 anxious days. They left Vienna's outer suburbs in smoldering ruins when they withdrew, but they never breached the inner walls.

- **976** Leopold von Babenberg rises to power in the Danube Valley.
- **996** Austria is referred to for the first time with a derivation of its modern name (Ostarrichi).
- **1030** After Cologne, Vienna is the largest town north of the Alps.
- **1147** A Romanesque predecessor of St. Stephan's Cathedral is consecrated as the religious centerpiece of Vienna.
- **1192** English king Richard the Lion-Hearted is arrested and held hostage by the Viennese. His ransom pays for construction of the city's walls, completed in 1200.
- **1221** City charter is granted to Vienna, with trading privileges.
- **1246** Last of the Babenbergs, Friedrich the Warlike, dies in battle. Bohemian king Ottokar II succeeds him.
- **1278** Ottokar II is killed at Battle of Marchfeld. Rudolf II of Habsburg begins one of the longest dynastic rules in European history.
- **1335 and 1363** Habsburgs add Carinthia and the Tyrol to Austrian territory.
- **1433** Central spire of St. Stephan's is completed.

Partly as a gesture of solidarity, Ferdinand I declared Vienna the site of his official capital in 1533.

In the 16th century, the Protestant Reformation shook Europe. In the second half of the century, under the tolerant Maximilian II, Vienna was almost 80% Protestant and even had a Lutheran mayor. However, Ferdinand II was rigorous in his suppression of Protestantism, and returned Vienna to Catholicism. By the first half of the 17th century, Vienna was a bastion of the Counter-Reformation.

Incursions into the Balkans by Ottoman Turks continued to upset the balance of power in Central Europe. During the same period, there were outbreaks of the Black Death; in 1679, between 75,000 and 150,000 Viennese died. Leopold I commemorated the city's deliverance from the plague with the famous Pestaule column. It stands today on one of Vienna's main avenues, the Graben.

The final defeat of the Turks and the end of the Turkish menace came in September 1683. Along with a decline in plague-related deaths, the victory revitalized the city.

MARIA THERESA & POLITICAL REFORM Freed from military threat, the city developed under Charles VI (1711–40) and his daughter, Maria Theresa, into a "mecca of the arts." Architects like Johann Bernhard Fischer von Erlach and Johann Lukas von Hildebrandt designed lavish buildings, and composers and musicians flooded into the city.

In 1700, Charles II, last of the Spanish Habsburgs, died without an heir, signaling the final gasp of Habsburg control in Spain. Fearful of a similar fate, Austrian emperor Charles VI penned the Pragmatic Sanction, which ensured that his daughter, Maria Theresa, would follow him. Accordingly, Maria Theresa ascended to power in 1740 at the age of 23, and retained her post for 40 years. The only glitch was the War of the Austrian Succession (1740–48), which contested her coronation.

Austria entered a golden age of the baroque. During Maria Theresa's reign, the population of Vienna almost doubled, from 88,000 to 175,000. Her most visible architectural legacies include sections of Vienna's Hofburg and her preferred residence, Schönbrunn Palace, completed in 1769. Modern reforms were implemented in the National Army, the economy, the civil service, and education.

Maria Theresa was succeeded by her son, Joseph II. An enlightened monarch who eschewed ritual, he introduced many reforms—especially in the church—made himself available to the people, and issued an "Edict of Tolerance."

NAPOLEON & THE CONGRESS OF VIENNA The 19th century had a

- **1453** Friedrich II is elected Holy Roman Emperor and rules from Vienna.
- **1469** Vienna is elevated to a bishopric.
- **1485–90** Hungarian king Matthias Corvinus occupies Vienna's Hofburg.
- **1490** Maximilian I recaptures Hungary and lost dominions.
- **1496** A Habsburg son marries the *infanta* of Spain, an act that eventually places a Habsburg in control of vast territories in the New World.
- **1519** Charles I, Habsburg ruler of Spain, is elected Holy Roman Emperor as Charles V.
- **1521** Charles V cedes Vienna to his brother for more effective rule.
- **1526** Rebellion in Vienna leads to brutal repression by the Habsburgs.
- **1529** In the first Turkish siege, fire destroys half of Vienna.
- **1533** Vienna is declared the official Habsburg capital.
- **1556** Charles V cedes his position as Holy Roman Emperor to his brother Ferdinand, the Austrian king.
- **1560** Vienna's city walls are strengthened.
- **1571** Ferdinand grants religious freedom to all Austrians. Before long, 80% of Austrians have converted to Protestantism.

continued

turbulent start. Napoleon's empire building wreaked havoc on Vienna's political landscape. His incursions onto Habsburg territories began in 1803 and culminated in the French occupation of Vienna in 1805 and 1809. Napoleon dissolved the Holy Roman Empire and ordered the new Austrian emperor, Franz I, to abdicate his position as Holy Roman Emperor. The Viennese treasury went bankrupt in 1811, causing a collapse of Austria's monetary system.

In one of the 19th century's more bizarre marriages, Napoleon married the Habsburg archduchess Marie-Louise by proxy in 1810. His days of success were numbered, however, and he was finally defeated in 1814.

METTERNICH Organized to pick up the pieces and to redefine national borders after Napoleon's defeat, the pivotal Congress of Vienna (1814–15) included representatives of all Europe's major powers. The Congress was a showcase for the brilliant diplomacy and intrigue of Austria's foreign minister, Klemens von Metternich, who restored Austria's pride and influence within a redefined confederation of German-speaking states.

Metternich's dominance of Austria between 1815 and 1848 ushered in another golden age. The Biedermeier period was distinguished by the increased prosperity of the middle class. Virtually kept out of politics, the bourgeoisie concentrated on culture. They built villas and the first big apartment houses and encouraged painting, music, and literature.

Advancing technology changed the skyline of Vienna as the 19th century progressed. The first steamship company to navigate the Danube was established in 1832, and Austria's first railway line opened in 1837.

In the meantime, despite his brilliance as an international diplomat, Metternich enacted domestic policies that almost guaranteed civil unrest. They led to the eradication of civil rights, the postwar imposition of a police state, and the creation of an economic climate that favored industrialization at the expense of wages and workers' rights.

In March 1848, events exploded not only in Vienna and Hungary, but also across most of Europe. Metternich was ousted and fled the city (some of his not-so-lucky colleagues were lynched). In response to the threat of revolutionary chaos, the Austrian army imposed a new version of absolute autocracy.

Emperor Franz Joseph I, the last scion of the Habsburg dynasty, was the beneficiary of the restored order. At the age of 18, he began his autocratic 68-year reign in 1848.

THE METROPOLIS OF EUROPE Franz Joseph I's austere comportment

- **1572** The Spanish Riding School is established.
- **1576** A reconversion to Catholicism of all Austrians begins. The Counter-Reformation begins.
- **1600–50** Hundreds of Catholic monks, priests, and nuns establish bases in Vienna as a means of encouraging the reconversion and strengthening the Habsburg role in the Counter-Reformation.
- **1618–48** The Thirty Years' War almost paralyzes Vienna.
- **1679** In the worst year of the plague, 75,000 to 150,000 Viennese die.
- **1683** Turks besiege Vienna but are routed by the armies of Lorraine and Poland.
- **1699** Turks evacuate strongholds in Hungary, ending the threat to Europe.
- **1700** The last of the Spanish Habsburgs dies, followed a
- year later by the War of the Spanish Succession.
- **1740** Maria Theresa ascends the Austrian throne despite initial tremors from the War of the Austrian Succession (1740–48).
- **1769** Schönbrunn Palace is completed.
- **1770** The marriage of a Habsburg princess (Marie Antoinette) to Louis XVI of France cements relations between Austria and France.

created the perfect foil for an explosion of artistic development in the newly revitalized city. A major accomplishment was the vast Ringstrasse, the boulevard that encircles Vienna's 1st District. Franz Joseph ordered it built over the old city walls, and the construction of the "Ringstrassenzone" became a work of homogeneous civic architecture unparalleled throughout Europe.

Meanwhile, advanced technology helped launch Vienna into the Industrial Age, transforming the city into a glittering showcase. The empire's vast resources were used to keep theaters, coffeehouses, concert halls, palaces, and homes well lit, cleaned, and maintained. The water supply was improved, and the Danube regulated. A new town hall was built, and a new park, the Stadtpark, opened.

The foundations of the Habsburg monarchy were shaken again in 1889 by the mysterious deaths of 30-year-old Crown Prince Rudolf, an outspoken and not particularly stable liberal, and his 18-year-old mistress at the royal hunting lodge of Mayerling. The possibility that they were murdered, and the insistence of his family that every shred of evidence associated with the case be destroyed, led to lurid speculation.

In 1890, many of the city's outer suburbs were incorporated into the City of Vienna, and in 1900 a final 20th district, Brigittenau, was also added. In 1906, women received the right to vote. By 1910, Vienna, with a population of 2 million, was the fourth-largest city in Europe, after London, Paris, and Berlin.

WORLD WAR I & THE VERSAILLES TREATY During the Belle Epoque, Europe sat on a powder keg of frustrated socialist platforms, national alliances, and conflicting colonial ambitions. The Austro-Hungarian Empire was linked by the Triple Alliance to both Germany and Italy. Europe leapt headfirst into armed conflict when Franz Joseph's nephew and designated heir, the Archduke Ferdinand, was shot to death by a Serbian terrorist as he and his wife, Sophie, rode through Sarajevo on June 28, 1914. Within 30 days, the Austro-Hungarian Empire declared war on Serbia, signaling the outbreak of World War I. An embittered Franz Joseph died in 1916, midway through the conflict. His successor, Charles I, the last of the Habsburg monarchs, was forced to abdicate in 1918 as part of the peace treaty.

The punitive peace treaty concluded at Versailles broke up the vast Austro-Hungarian territories into the nations of Hungary, Poland, Yugoslavia, and Czechoslovakia. The new Austria would adhere to the boundaries of Charlemagne's Ostmark. This overnight collapse of the empire caused profound dislocations of

- **1780** Maria Theresa dies, and her liberal son, Joseph II, ascends to power.
- **1789** Revolution in France leads to the beheading of Marie Antoinette.
- **1805 and 1809** Armies of Napoleon twice occupy Vienna.
- **1810** Napoleon marries Habsburg archduchess Marie-Louise.

- **1811** Viennese treasury is bankrupted by military spending.
- **1814–15** Congress of Vienna rearranges the map of Europe following the defeat of Napoleon.
- **1815–48** Vienna's Biedermeier period, supervised by Klemens von Metternich, marks the triumph of the bourgeoisie.

- **1832** First steamship company is organized to ply the Danube.
- **1837** Austria's first railway line is created.
- **1848** Violent revolution in Vienna ousts Metternich, threatens the collapse of Austrian society, and ushers 18-year-old Franz Joseph I into power.

continued

populations and trade patterns. Some of the new nations refused to deliver raw materials to Vienna's factories or, in some cases, food to Vienna's markets. Coupled with the effects of the Versailles treaty and the massive loss of manpower and resources during the war, Vienna soon found itself on the brink of starvation. Despite staggering odds, the new government—assisted by a massive loan in 1922 from the League of Nations—managed to stabilize the currency while Austrian industrialists hammered out new sources of raw materials.

THE ANSCHLUSS   In 1934, social tensions broke out into civil war, Europe's first confrontation between fascism and democracy. Austrian nationalism under the authoritarian chancellor, Engelbert Dollfuss, put an end to progressive policies. Later that year, Austrian Nazis assassinated Dollfuss, and Nazis were included in the resultant coalition government. In 1938, Austria united with Nazi Germany (the Anschluss). Hitler returned triumphantly to Vienna, several decades after he had lived there as an impoverished and embittered artist. In a national referendum, 99.75% of Austrians voted their support.

WORLD WAR II & ITS AFTERMATH   The rise of Austria's Nazis devastated Vienna's academic and artistic communities. Many of their members, including Sigmund Freud, fled to safety

elsewhere. About 60,000 Austrian Jews were sent to concentration camps, and only an estimated 2,000 survived; Austria's homosexual and Gypsy populations were similarly decimated.

Beginning in 1943, Allied bombing raids demolished vast neighborhoods of the city, damaging virtually every public building of any stature. The city's most prominent landmark, St. Stephan's Cathedral, suffered a roof collapse and fires in both towers. The city's death rate was one of the highest in Europe. For the Viennese, at least, the war ended abruptly on April 11, 1945, when Russian troops moved into the city from bases in Hungary.

During a confused interim that lasted a decade, Austria was divided into four zones of occupation, each controlled by one of the four Allies (the United States, the Soviet Union, Britain, and France). Vienna, deep within the Soviet zone, was also subdivided into four zones, each occupied by one of the victors. Control of the inner city alternated every month between each of the four powers. It was a dark and depressing time in Vienna; rubble was slowly cleared away from bomb sites, but the most glorious public monuments in Europe lay in ashes. Espionage, black-market profiteering, and personal betrayals proliferated, poisoning the memories of many older Viennese even today.

- **1859** Austria loses control of its Italian provinces, including Venice and Milan.
- **1862** Flooding on the Danube leads to a reconfiguration of its banks to a channel in Vienna's suburbs.
- **1867** Hungary and Austria merge, becoming the Austro–Hungarian Empire, headed by the emperor Franz Joseph I.
- **1869** Vienna's State Opera House is completed.

- **1873** Vienna hosts the World's Fair.
- **1889** Crown Prince Rudolf dies at Mayerling, sparking controversy.
- **1890–1900** Vienna's outer suburbs are incorporated into the city as Districts 11 to 20.
- **1914** Assassination of the heir to the Habsburg Empire, Archduke Ferdinand, sparks World War I.

- **1916** Franz Joseph dies and is succeeded by Charles I, last of the Habsburg monarchs.
- **1918** World War I ends, Austria is defeated, Charles I abdicates, and the Austro-Hungarian Empire is radically dismantled.
- **1919** Liberalization of Austrian voting laws enacts monumental changes in the social structure of Vienna. "Red Vienna" period begins; the city swings radically to the left.

POSTWAR TIMES On May 15, 1955, Austria regained its sovereignty as an independent, perpetually neutral nation. As a neutral capital, Vienna became the obvious choice for meetings between John Kennedy and Nikita Khrushchev (in 1961) and Leonid Brezhnev and Jimmy Carter (in 1979). Many international organizations (including OPEC and the Atomic Energy Authority) established branches or headquarters there.

Once again part of a republic, the Viennese aggressively sought to restore their self-image as cultural barons. Restoring the State Opera House and other grand monuments became a top priority.

However, Vienna's self-image suffered a blow when scandal surrounded Austria's president, Kurt Waldheim, elected in 1986. Waldheim had been an officer in the Nazi army and had countenanced the deportation of Jews to extermination camps. The United States declared him persona non grata. Many Austrians stood by Waldheim; others were deeply embarrassed. Waldheim did not seek reelection, and in May 1992, Thomas Klestil, a career diplomat, was elected president, supported by the centrist Austrian People's Party.

In 1989, the last heiress to the Habsburg dynasty, Empress Zita of Bourbon-Parma, in exile since 1919, was buried in one of the most lavish and emotional funerals ever held in Vienna. At age 96,

the last empress of Austria and queen of Hungary had always been held in some degree of reverence, a symbol of the glorious days of the Austrian empire.

In the spring of 1998, the Austrian government stunned the art world by agreeing to return artworks confiscated from Jews by the Nazis. Many Jewish families, including the Austrian branch of the Rothschilds, had fled into exile in 1938. Although they tried to regain their possessions after the war, they were not successful. Austrian journalist Hubertus Czernin wrote, "The art was stolen by the Nazis and stolen a second time by the Austrian government." One museum director claimed Austria had "a specific moral debt," which it was now repaying.

In 1999 elections, the Freedom Party won notoriety—and 27% of the vote—by denouncing the presence of foreigners in Austria. Echoing Nazi rhetoric, the party blames foreigners for drugs, crime, welfare abuse, and the spread of tuberculosis. The party remains racist and Nazi-admiring in spite of the resignation of its leader, Jörg Haider, its most controversial member.

After first announcing punishing sanctions against Austria for its tilt to the far right, the European Union in September of 2000 lifted those sanctions while vowing to keep a special eye on Austria's song and dance into right-wing politics. E.U. officials concluded that in spite of earlier

- **1927** Violent discord rocks Vienna.
- **1929** Worldwide economic depression occurs.
- **1933** Austria's authoritarian chancellor, Engelbert Dollfuss, outlaws the Austrian Nazi party.
- **1934** Dollfuss is assassinated by Nazis.
- **1938** German Nazi troops complete an amicable invasion of Austria that leads to the union of the two nations

(Anschluss) through World War II.
- **1943–45** Massive bombings by Allied forces leave most public monuments in ruins.
- **1945** Allied forces defeat Germany and Austria. Vienna is "liberated" by Soviet troops on April 11. On April 27, Austria is redefined as a country separate from Germany and divided, like Germany, into four zones of

occupation. Vienna also is subdivided into four zones.
- **1955** Allied forces evacuate Vienna; Vienna is the capital of a neutral Austria.
- **1961** Summit meeting in Vienna occurs between John F. Kennedy and Nikita Khrushchev.
- **1979** Summit meeting in Vienna occurs between Leonid Brezhnev and Jimmy Carter.

continued

defiance, the Austrian government in Vienna had taken "concrete steps to fight racism, xenophobia, and anti-Semitism."

News of an expat Austrian, a citizen of Graz, made the biggest headlines in both Vienna and the country itself in 2004. Their homegrown son, muscleman/movie star Arnold Schwarzenegger, swept into the governor's office in California in a recall vote. Even though he's married to a Kennedy, Maria Shriver, Schwarzenegger is a Republican, and lent the prestige of his name in the campaign of George W. Bush for reelection. For his efforts, he told a stunned nation, he was denied sex for 2 weeks.

In October of 2006, Austria's opposition Social Democrats won nationwide elections, swinging the country to the center-left after more than six years of influence by the extreme right. Immigration was a central theme in the campaign (sound familiar?), and the far right wants to reduce the number of foreigners in Austria by 30 percent. The Social Democrats on the other hand promised to lower the number of unemployed and reduce salary differences between men and women.

3 Exploring Vienna's Architecture

Vienna is best known for the splendor of its baroque and rococo palaces and churches. It also contains a wealth of internationally renowned Gothic and modern architecture.

GOTHIC ARCHITECTURE

Although Vienna holds no remains of early medieval buildings, a number of Gothic buildings rest on older foundations. During the 1300s, ecclesiastical architecture was based on the Hallenkirche (hall church), a model that originated in Germany. These buildings featured interiors that resembled enormous hallways, with nave and aisles of the same height. The earliest example of this style was the choir added in 1295 to an older Romanesque building, the abbey church of Heiligenkreuz, 15 miles west of Vienna.

The most famous building in the Hallenkirche style was the first incarnation of St. Stephan's Cathedral. Later modifications greatly altered the details of its original construction, and today only the foundations, the main portal, and the modestly proportioned western towers remain. Much more dramatic is the cathedral's needle-shaped central spire, completed in 1433, which still soars high above Vienna's skyline. St. Stephan's triple naves, each the same height, are a distinctive feature of Austrian Gothic. Other

- **1986** Investigations into the wartime activities of Austrian chancellor Kurt Waldheim profoundly embarrass Austria.
- **1989** The last heiress to the Habsburg dynasty, Empress Zita of Bourbon-Parma, in exile since 1919, dies and is buried in one of the most elaborate funerals in Viennese history.
- **1995** Austria, Sweden, and Finland are admitted to the European Union.
- **1997** After 10 years, long-time chancellor Franz Vranitzky steps down, turning over leadership of Social Democratic Party.
- **1998** Austria decides to return art that Nazis plundered (much of it in museums).
- **1999** Right-wing Freedom Party stirs worldwide protests against Austria.
- **2000** The E.U. issues sanctions against Austria, and then rescinds them.
- **2004** Celebrations throughout Austria as its homegrown son, Arnold Schwarzenegger, is elected governor of California.
- **2006** Center-Left opposition wins in Austria.

examples of this construction can be seen in the Minorite Church and the Church of St. Augustine.

During the late 1400s, Gothic architecture retreated from the soaring proportions of the Hallenkirche style, and focus turned to more modest buildings with richly decorated interiors. Stone masons added tracery (geometric patterns) and full-rounded or low-relief sculpture to ceilings and walls. Gothic churches continued to be built in Austria until the mid-1500s.

FROM GOTHIC TO BAROQUE

One of the unusual aspects of Vienna is its lack of Renaissance buildings. The Turks besieged Vienna periodically from 1529 until the 1680s, forcing planners to use most of their resources to strengthen the city's fortifications.

Although Vienna itself has no Renaissance examples, Italian influences were evident for more than a century before baroque gained a true foothold. Late in the 16th century, many Italian builders settled in the regions of Tyrol, Carinthia, and Styria. In these less-threatened regions of Austria, Italian influence produced a number of country churches and civic buildings in the Renaissance style, with open porticoes, balconies, and loggias.

THE FLOWERING OF THE BAROQUE

The 47-year rule of Leopold I (1658–1705) witnessed the beginning of the golden age of Austrian baroque architecture. Italian-born Dominico Martinelli (1650–1718) designed the **Liechtenstein Palace,** built between 1694 and 1706 and inspired by the Renaissance-era Palazzo Farnese in Rome.

Austria soon began to produce its own architects. **Johann Bernhard Fischer von Erlach** (1656–1723) trained with both Bernini and Borromini in Rome. His style was restrained but monumental, drawing richly from the great buildings of antiquity. Fischer von Erlach knew how to transform the Italianate baroque of the south into a style that suited the Viennese. His most notable work is the **Karlskirche,** built in 1713. He also created the original design for Maria Theresa's **Schönbrunn Palace.** He had planned a sort of super-Versailles, but the project turned out to be too costly. Only the entrance facade remains of Fischer von Erlach's design. The **Hofbibliothek (National Library)** on Josephsplatz and the **Hofstalungen** are other notable buildings he designed.

Fischer von Erlach was succeeded by another great name in the history of architecture: **Johann Lukas von Hildebrandt** (1668–1745). Von Hildebrandt's design for Prince Eugene's **Belvedere Palace**—a series of interlocking cubes with sloping mansard-style roofs—is the culmination of the architectural theories initiated by Fischer von Erlach. Other von Hildebrandt designs in Vienna include the **Schwarzenberg Palace** (now a hotel) and **St. Peter's Church.**

The **rococo style** developed as a more ornate, somewhat fussier progression of the baroque. Gilt stucco, brightly colored frescoes, and interiors that drip with embellishments are its hallmarks. Excellent examples include the **Abbey of Dürnstein** (1731–35) and **Melk Abbey,** both in Lower Austria. One of the most powerful proponents of rococo was Maria Theresa, who used its motifs so extensively within Schönbrunn Palace during its 1744 renovation that the school of Austrian rococo is sometimes referred to as "late-baroque Theresian style."

In response to the excesses of rococo, architects eventually turned to classical Greece and Rome for inspiration. The result was a restrained neoclassicism that transformed the skyline of Vienna and lasted well into the 19th century. The dignified austerity of Vienna's **Technical University** is a good example.

ECLECTICISM & VIENNA'S RING

As Austria's wealthy bourgeoisie began to impose their tastes on public architecture, 19th-century building grew more solid and monumental. The neoclassical style remained the preferred choice for government buildings, as evidenced by Vienna's **Mint** and the **Palace of the Provincial Government.**

The 19th century's most impressive Viennese architectural achievement was the construction of the **Ringstrasse** (1857–91). The medieval walls were demolished, and the Ring was lined with showcase buildings. This was Emperor Franz Joseph's personal project and his greatest achievement. Architects from all over Europe answered the emperor's call, eager to seize the unprecedented opportunity to design a whole city district. Between 1850 and the official opening ceremony in 1879, the Ring's architecture became increasingly eclectic: French neo-Gothic (the Votivkirche), Flemish neo-Gothic (the Rathaus), Greek Revival (Parliament), French Renaissance (Staatsoper), and Tuscan Renaissance (Museum of Applied Arts). While the volume of traffic circling Old Vienna diminishes some of the Ring's charm, a circumnavigation of the Ring provides a panorama of eclectic yet harmonious building styles.

SECESSIONIST & POLITICAL ARCHITECTURE

By the late 19th century, younger architects were in rebellion against the pomp and formality of older architectural styles. In 1896, young **Otto Wagner** (1841–1918) published a tract called *Moderne Architektur,* which argued for a return to more natural and functional architectural forms. The result was the establishment of **Art Nouveau (Jugendstil,** or, as it applies specifically to Vienna, **Sezessionstil**). The Vienna Secession architects reaped the benefits of the technological advances and the new building materials that became available after the Industrial Revolution.

Wagner, designer of Vienna's **Kirche am Steinhof** and the city's **Postsparkasse** (Post Office Savings Bank), became a founding member of the movement.

Joseph Hoffman (1870–1955) and **Adolf Loos** (1870–1933) promoted the use of glass, newly developed steel alloys, and aluminum. In the process, they discarded nearly all ornamentation, a rejection that contemporary Vienna found profoundly distasteful and almost shocking. Loos was particularly critical of the buildings adorning the Ringstrasse. His most controversial design is the **Michaelerplatz Building.** Sometimes referred to as "the Loos House," it was erected on Michaelerplatz in 1908. The streamlined structure was bitterly criticized for its total lack of ornamentation and its similarities to the "gridwork of a sewer." According to gossip, the emperor found it so offensive that he ordered his drivers to avoid the Hofburg entrance on Michaelerplatz altogether.

Architectural philosophies were also affected during the "Red Vienna" period by the socialist reformers' desire to alleviate public housing shortages, a grinding social problem of the years between world wars. The Social Democratic Party began erecting "palaces for the people." The most obvious example is the **Karl-Marx-Hof** (Heiligenstadterstrasse 82-92, A-1190), which includes 1,600 apartments and stretches for more than half a mile.

TO THE PRESENT DAY

After World War II, much of Vienna's resources went toward restoring older historic buildings to their prewar grandeur. New buildings were streamlined and functional; much of Vienna today features the same kind of neutral modernism you're likely to find in postwar Berlin or Frankfurt.

Postmodern masters, however, have broken the mold of the 1950s and 1960s. They include the iconoclastic mogul Hans Hollein, designer of the silvery, curved-sided **Haas Haus** (1990) adjacent to St. Stephan's Cathedral. The self-consciously avant-garde **Friedensreich Hundertwasser** is a multicolored, ecologically inspired apartment building at the corner of Löwengasse and Kegelgasse that appears to be randomly stacked.

Lately, **Hermann Czech** has been stirring architectural excitement, not so much by building new structures as developing daring interiors for boutiques and bistros; examples are the **Kleines Café** (Franziskanerplatz 3) and **Restaurant Salzamt** (Ruprechtsplatz 1).

4 Art through the Ages

Vienna's location at the crossroads of the Germanic, Mediterranean, and eastern European worlds contributed to a rich and varied artistic heritage.

EARLY ECCLESIASTICAL ART

Most art in the early medieval period was church art. From the Carolingian period, the only survivors are a handful of **illuminated manuscripts,** now in Vienna's National Library. The most famous is the *Cutbercht Evangeliar* from around 800, a richly illuminated copy of the four gospels.

The Romanesque period reached its peak between 1000 and 1190. Notable from this time is the Admont Great Bible, crafted around 1140, one of the prized treasures of Vienna's National Library. In 1181, the famous goldsmith Nicolas de Verdun produced one of the finest **enamel works** in Europe for the pulpit at Klosterneuburg Abbey. Verdun's 51 small panels, crafted from enamel and gold, depict scenes from the religious tracts of the Augustinians. After a fire in the 1300s, the panels were repositioned onto an altarpiece known as the Verdun Altar at Klosterneuburg, where they can be seen today.

THE GOTHIC AGE

The Gothic age in Austria is better remembered for its architecture than its painting and sculpture. Early Gothic sculpture was influenced by the **Zachbruchiger Stil** (zigzag style), identified by vivid angular outlines of forms against contrasting backgrounds. The era's greatest surviving sculptures date from around 1320 and include *The Enthroned Madonna* of *Klosterneuburg* and *The Servant's Madonna,* showcased in Vienna's St. Stephan's Cathedral.

By the late 1300s, Austrian sculpture was strongly influenced by Bohemia. The human form became elongated, exaggerated, and idealized, often set in graceful but unnatural S curves. Wood became increasingly popular as an artistic medium and was often painted in vivid colors. A superb example of **Gothic sculpture** is *The Servant's Madonna* in St. Stephan's Cathedral. Carved around 1320, it depicts Mary enthroned and holding a standing Christ child.

FROM THE RENAISSANCE TO THE 18TH CENTURY

During most of the Renaissance, Vienna was too preoccupied with fending off invasions, sieges, and plagues to produce the kind of painting and sculpture that flowered in other parts of Europe. As a result, in the 17th and 18th centuries, Vienna struggled to keep up with cities like Salzburg, Munich, and Innsbruck.

Most painting and sculpture during the baroque period was for the enhancement of the grandiose churches and spectacular palaces that sprang up across Vienna. Artists were imported from Italy; one, **Andrea Pozzo** (1642–1709), produced the masterpiece *The Apotheosis of Hercules* that appears on the ceilings of Vienna's Liechtenstein Palace. Baroque painting emphasized symmetry and unity, and *trompe l'oeil* was used to give extra dimension to a building's sculptural and architectural motifs.

The first noteworthy Austrian-born baroque painter was **Johann Rottmayr** (1654–1730), the preferred decorator of the two most influential architects of the age, von Hildebrandt and Fischer von Erlach. Rottmayr's works adorn some of the ceilings of Vienna's Schönbrunn Palace and Peterskirche. Countless other artists contributed to the Viennese baroque style. Notable are the frescoes of **Daniel Gran** (1694–1754), who decorated the Hofbibliothek. He also has an altarpiece in the Karlskirche.

Vienna, as it emerged from a base of muddy fields into a majestic fantasy of baroque architecture, was captured on the canvas in the landscapes of **Bernardo Bellotto** (1720–80), nephew and pupil of the famous Venetian painter Canaletto. Brought to Vienna at the request of Maria Theresa, Bellotto managed to bathe the city in a flat but clear light of arresting detail and pinpoint accuracy. His paintings today are valued as social and historical as well as artistic documents.

Dutch-born, Swedish-trained **Martin van Meytens** (1695–1770), court painter to Maria Theresa, captured the lavish balls and assemblies of Vienna's aristocracy. His canvases, though awkwardly composed and overburdened with detail, are the best visual record of the Austrian court's balls and receptions. In 1730, van Meytens was appointed director of Vienna's Fine Arts Academy.

Sculptors also made their contribution to the baroque style. **Georg Raphael Donner** (1693–1741) is best known for the remarkable life-size bronzes of the Fountain of Providence in the Neuer Markt. **Balthasar Permoser** (1651–1732) is responsible for the equestrian statues of Prince Eugene of Savoy in the courtyard of the Belvedere Palace. The famous double sarcophagus in the Kapuzinerkirche designed for Maria Theresa and her husband, Francis Stephen, is the masterpiece of **Balthasar Moll** (1717–85).

Equally influential was **Franz Xaver Messerschmidt** (1737–83), the German-trained resident of Vienna who became famous for his portrait busts. His legacy is accurate and evocative representations of Maria Theresa, her son Joseph II, and other luminaries.

THE REVOLT FROM "OFFICIAL ART"

In rebellion against "official art," a school of **Romantic Realist** painters emerged, drawing on biblical themes and Austrian folklore. Scenes from popular operas were painted lovingly on the walls of the Vienna State Opera. The 17th-century Dutch masters influenced landscape painting.

Georg Waldmüller (1793–1865), a self-proclaimed enemy of "academic art" and an advocate of realism, created one of the best pictorial descriptions of Viennese Biedermeier society in his *Wiener Zimmer* (1837). More than 120 of his paintings are on display at the Upper Belvedere museum.

Another realist was **Carl Moll** (1861–1945), whose graceful and evocative portrayals of everyday scenes are prized today. **Joseph Engelhart** (1864–1941) was known for his voluptuous renderings of Belle Epoque coquettes flirting with Viennese gentlemen.

THE SECESSIONIST MOVEMENT

Young painters, decorators, and architects from Vienna's Academy of Fine Arts founded the Secessionist Movement (Sezessionstil) in 1897. The name captures their retreat (secession) from the Künstlerhaus (Vienna Artists' Association), which they considered pompous, sanctimonious, artificial, mediocre, and mired in the historicism favored by Emperor Franz Joseph. Their artistic statement was similar to that of the Art Nouveau movement in Paris and the Jugendstil movement in Munich.

The Secessionist headquarters, on the Friedrichstrasse at the corner of the

Opernring, was inaugurated in 1898 as an exhibition space for avant-garde artists. Foremost among the group was **Gustav Klimt** (1862–1918), whose work developed rapidly into a highly personal and radically innovative form of decorative painting based on the sinuous curved line of Art Nouveau. His masterpieces include a mammoth frieze, 33m (110 ft.) long, encrusted with gemstones, and dedicated to Beethoven. Executed in 1902, it's one of the artistic focal points of the Secessionist Pavilion. Other pivotal works include *Portrait of Adèle Bloch-Bauer* (1907), an abstract depiction of a prominent Jewish Viennese socialite. Its gilded geometric form is reminiscent of ancient Byzantine art.

THE MODERN AGE

Klimt's talented disciple was **Egon Schiele** (1890–1918). Tormented, overly sensitive, and virtually unknown during his brief lifetime, he is now considered a modernist master whose work can stand alongside that of van Gogh and Modigliani. His works seem to dissolve the boundaries between humankind and the natural world, granting a kind of anthropomorphic humanity to landscape painting. One of his most disturbing paintings is the tormented *The Family* (1917), originally conceived as decoration for a mausoleum.

Modern sculpture in Vienna is inseparable from the international art trends that dominated the 20th century. **Fritz Wotruba** (1907–75) introduced a neo-cubist style of sculpture. Many of his sculptural theories were manifested in his Wotruba Church (Church of the Most Holy Trinity), erected toward the end of his life in Vienna's outlying 23rd District. Adorned with his sculptures and representative of his architectural theories in general, the building is an important sightseeing and spiritual attraction.

Oskar Kokoschka (1886–1980) was one of Vienna's most important contemporary painters. Kokoschka expressed the frenzied psychological confusion of the years before and after World War II. His portraits of such personalities as the artist Carl Moll are bathed in psychological realism and violent emotion.

5 Musical Vienna

Music is central to Viennese life. From the concertos of Mozart and Johann Strauss's waltzes to opera and folk tunes, the Viennese are surrounded by music—and not only in the concert hall and opera house, but at the *heurige* as well.

THE CLASSICAL PERIOD

The classical period was a golden age in Viennese musical life. Two of the greatest composers of all time, Mozart and Haydn, worked in Vienna. Maria Theresa herself trilled arias on the stage of the Schlosstheater at Schönbrunn, and she and her children and friends often performed operas and dances.

Classicism's first great manifestation was the development of *Singspiele*, a reform of opera by **Christoph Willibald Ritter von Gluck** (1714–87). Baroque opera had become overburdened with ornamentation, and Gluck introduced a more natural musical form. In 1762, Maria Theresa presented Vienna with the first performance of Gluck's innovative opera *Orpheus and Eurydice*. It and *Alceste* (1767) are his best-known operas, regularly performed today.

Franz Joseph Haydn (1732–1809) is the creator of the classical sonata, which is the basis of classical chamber music. Haydn's patrons were the rich and powerful Esterházy family, whom he served as musical director. His output was prodigious. He wrote chamber music, sonatas, operas, and symphonies. His strong faith is in evidence in his oratorios; among the greatest are *The Creation* (1798) and *The Seasons* (1801). He also is the composer of the Austrian national anthem (1797), which he later elaborated in his quartet, Opus 76, no. 3.

The most famous composer of the period was **Wolfgang Amadeus Mozart** (1756 91). The prodigy from Salzburg charmed Maria Theresa and her court with his playing when he was only 6 years old. His father, Leopold, exploited his son's talent—"Wolferl" spent his childhood touring all over Europe. Later, he went with his father to Italy, where he absorbed that country's fertile musical traditions. Leaving Salzburg, he settled in Vienna, at first with great success. His influence effected fundamental and widespread changes in the musical life of the capital. Eccentric and extravagant, he was unable to keep patronage or land any lucrative post; he finally received an appointment as chamber composer to the emperor Joseph II at a minimal salary. Despite hard times, Mozart refused the posts offered him in other cities, possibly because in Vienna he found the best of all musical worlds—the best instrumentalists, the finest opera, the most talented singers. He composed more than 600 works in practically every musical form known to the time; his greatest compositions are unmatched in beauty and profundity. He died in poverty, buried in a pauper's grave in Vienna, the whereabouts of which are uncertain.

THE ROMANTIC AGE

Franz Schubert (1797–1828), the only one of the great composers born in Vienna, was of the Biedermeier era and the most Viennese of musicians. He turned *lieder,* popular folk songs often used with dances, into an art form. He was a master of melodic line, and he created hundreds of songs, chamber music works, and symphonies. At the age of 18, he showed his genius by setting the words of German poet Goethe to music in *Margaret at the Spinning Wheel* and *The Elf King*. His *Unfinished Symphony* remains his best-known work, but his

great achievement lies in his chamber music and song cycles.

THE 19TH CENTURY

After 1850, Vienna became the world's capital of light music, exporting it to every corner of the globe. The **waltz,** originally developed as a rustic Austrian country dance, was enthusiastically adopted by Viennese society.

Johann Strauss (1804–49), composer of more than 150 waltzes, and his talented and entrepreneurial son, **Johann Strauss the Younger** (1825–99), who developed the art form further, helped spread the stately and graceful rhythms of the waltz across Europe. The younger Strauss also popularized the operetta, the genesis of the Broadway musical.

The tradition of Viennese light opera continued to thrive, thanks to the efforts of **Franz von Suppé** (1819–95) and Hungarian-born **Franz Lehár** (1870–1948). Lehár's witty and mildly scandalous *The Merry Widow* (1905) is the most popular and amusing light opera ever written.

Vienna did not lack for important serious music in the late 19th century. **Anton Bruckner** (1824–96) composed nine symphonies and a handful of powerful masses. **Hugo Wolf** (1860–1903), following in Schubert's footsteps, reinvented key elements of the German lieder with his five great song cycles. Most innovative of all was **Gustav Mahler** (1860–1911). A pupil of Bruckner, he expanded the size of the orchestra, often added a chorus or vocal soloists, and composed evocative music, much of it set to poetry.

THE NEW VIENNA SCHOOL

Mahler's musical heirs forever altered the world's concepts of harmony and tonality, and introduced what were then shocking concepts of rhythm. **Arnold Schoenberg** (1874–1951) expanded Mahler's style in such atonal works as *Das Buch der Hangenden Garten* (1908) and developed a 12-tone musical technique referred to as "dodecaphony" (*Suite for Piano*, 1924). By the end of his career, he pioneered "serial music," series of notes with no key center, shifting from one tonal group to another. **Anton von Webern** (1883–1945) and **Alban Berg** (1885–1935), composer of the brilliant but esoteric opera *Wozzeck,* were pupils of Schoenberg's. They adapted his system to their own musical personalities.

Finally, this discussion of Viennese music would not be complete without mention of the vast repertoire of folk songs, Christmas carols, and country dances that have inspired both professional musicians and ordinary folk for generations. The most famous Christmas carol in the world, *"Stille Nacht, Heilige Nacht"* ("Silent Night, Holy Night"), was composed and performed for the first time in Salzburg in 1818 and heard in Vienna for the first time that year.

6 A Taste of Vienna

It's pointless to argue whether a Viennese dish is of Hungarian, Czech, Austrian, Slovenian, or even Serbian origin. Personally, we've always been more interested in taste. Our palates respond well to *Wienerküche* (Viennese cooking), a centuries-old blend of foreign recipes and homespun concoctions. Viennese cooking tends to be rich and heavy, with little regard for cholesterol levels.

FROM WIENER SCHNITZEL TO SACHERTORTE

Of course everyone knows Wiener schnitzel, the breaded veal cutlet that has achieved popularity worldwide. The most authentic local recipes call for the schnitzel to be fried in lard, but everyone agrees on one point: The schnitzel should have the golden-brown color of a Stradivarius violin.

Another renowned meat specialty is boiled beef, or *tafelspitz,* said to reflect "the soul of the empire." This was Emperor Franz Joseph's favorite dish. For the best, try it at Hotel Sacher; if you're on a budget, then order *tafelspitz* at a *beisl,* cousin of the French bistro.

Roast goose is served on festive occasions, such as Christmas, but at any time of the year you can order *eine gute fettgans* (a good fat goose). After such a rich dinner, you might want to relax over some strong coffee, followed by schnapps.

For a taste of Hungary, order a goulash. Goulashes (stews of beef or pork with paprika) can be prepared in many different ways. The local version, *Wiener gulasch,* is lighter on the paprika than most Hungarian versions. And don't forget *gulyassuppe* (a Hungarian goulash soup), which can be a meal in itself.

Viennese pastry is probably the best in the world, both rich and varied. The familiar strudel comes in many forms; *apfelstrudel* (apple) is the most popular, but you can also order cherry and other flavors. Viennese cakes defy description—look for *gugelhupf, wuchteln,* and *mohnbeugerl.* Many of the *torten* are made with ground hazelnuts or almonds in the place of flour. You can put whipped cream on everything. Don't miss *rehruken,* a chocolate "saddle of venison" cake that's studded with almonds.

Even if you're not addicted to sweets, there's a gustatory experience you mustn't miss: the Viennese Sachertorte. Many gourmets claim to have the authentic, original recipe for this "king of tortes," a rich chocolate cake with a layer of apricot jam. Master pastry baker Franz Sacher created the Sachertorte for Prince von Metternich in 1832, and it is still available in the Hotel Sacher. Outstanding imitations can be found throughout Vienna.

COFFEE

Although it might sound heretical, Turkey is credited with establishing the famous Viennese coffeehouse. Legend holds that Turks retreating from the siege of Vienna abandoned several sacks of coffee, which, when brewed by the victorious Viennese, established the Austrian passion for coffee for all time. The first *kaffeehaus* was established in Vienna in 1683.

In Vienna, *Jause* is a 4pm coffee-and-pastry ritual that is practiced daily in the city's coffeehouses. You can order your coffee a number of different ways—everything from *verkehrt* (almost milk pale) to *mocca* (ebony black). Note that in Vienna, only strangers ask for *einen kaffee* (a coffee). If you do, you'll be asked what kind you want. Your safest choice is a large or small *brauner*—coffee with milk. *Kaffee mit schlagobers* (with whipped cream) is perfect for those with a sweet tooth. You can even order *doppelschlag* (double whipped cream).

BEER, WINE & LIQUEURS

Vienna imposes few restrictions on the sale of alcohol, so except in alcohol-free places, you should be able to order beer or wine with your meal—even if it's 9am. Many Viennese have their first strong drink in the morning, preferring beer over coffee to get them going.

In general, **Austrian wines** are served when new, and most are consumed where they're produced. We prefer the white wine to the red. More than 99% of all Austrian wine is produced in vineyards in eastern Austria, principally Vienna, Lower Austria, Styria, and Burgenland. The most famous Austrian wine, Gumpoldskirchen, which is sold all over Vienna, comes from Lower Austria, the country's largest wine producer. At the heart of the Baden wine district of Sudbahnstrecke is the village of Gumpoldskirchen, which gives the wine its name. This white wine is heady, rich, and slightly sweet.

Located in an outer district of Vienna, Klosterneuburg, an ancient abbey on the right bank of the Danube, produces the finest white wine in Austria. Monks have made Klosterneuburger at this monastery for centuries. The Wachau district, west of Vienna, also produces some fine delicate wines, including Loibner Kaiserwein and Duernsteiner Katzensprung, which are fragrant and fruity.

By far the best red wine—on this there is little disagreement—is Vöslauer from Vöslau. It's strong but not quite as powerful as Gumpoldskirchen and Klosterneuburger. From Styria comes Austria's best-known rosé, Schilcher, which is slightly dry, fruity, and sparkling.

Because many Viennese visiting the *heurigen* outside the city didn't want to get too drunk, they started diluting the new wine with club soda or mineral water. Thus the spritzer was born. The mix is best with a very dry wine.

In all except the most deluxe restaurants, it's possible to order a carafe of wine, *offener Wein*, which will be much less expensive than a bottle.

Austrian beers are relatively inexpensive and quite good, and they're sold throughout Vienna. Vienna is home to what we believe is the finest beer in the region, Schwechater. Gösser, produced in Styria, is one of the most favored brews and comes in both light and dark. Adambräu, another native beer, is also sold in Vienna's bars and taverns, along with some lighter, Bavarian-type beers such as Weizengold and Kaiser. For those who prefer the taste without the alcohol, Null Komma Josef is a local alcohol-free beer.

Two of the most famous and favored **liqueurs** among Austrians are *slivovitz* (a plum brandy that originated in Croatia) and *barack* (made from apricots). Imported whisky and bourbon are likely to be lethal in price. When you're in Vienna, it's a good rule of thumb to drink the "spirit of the land."

The most festive drink is **Bowle** (pronounced *bole*), which is often served at parties. It was first made for us by the great Austrian chanteuse Greta Keller, and we've been devotees ever since. She preferred the lethal method of soaking berries and sliced peaches overnight in brandy, adding three bottles of dry white wine, and letting it stand for another 2 to 3 hours. Before serving, she'd pour a bottle of champagne over it. In her words, "You can drink it as a cocktail, during and after dinner, and on . . . and on . . . and on!"

THE *HEURIGEN*

In 1784, Joseph II decreed that each vintner in the suburbs of Vienna could sell his own wine right on his doorstep. A tradition was born that continues today.

Heurig means "new wine" or, more literally, "of this year."

The *heurigen,* or wine taverns, lie on the outskirts of Vienna, mainly in Grinzing. In summer, in fair weather, much of the drinking takes place in vine-covered gardens. In some old-fashioned places, on a nippy night, you'll find a crackling fire in a flower-bordered ceramic stove. There's likely to be a Gypsy violinist, an accordionist, or perhaps a zither player entertaining with Viennese songs. Most *heurigen* are rustic, with wooden benches and tables, and it's perfectly acceptable to bring your own snacks. But today, many are restaurants, serving buffets of meats, cheeses, breads, and vegetables. For more information, see chapter 9. **Beware:** The wine is surprisingly potent, in spite of its innocent taste.

Appendix B:
Useful Terms & Phrases

Though German is the national language, English is widely spoken throughout Austria (children learn English in school), especially in cities such as Vienna. However, when you encounter someone who doesn't speak it, or if you're trying to read a menu or sign, the following might be useful.

1 Glossary

Altstadt old part of a city or town
Anlage park area
Apotheke pharmacy
Bad spa
Bahn railroad, train
Bahnhof railroad station
Beisl Viennese bistro, usually inexpensive
Berg mountain
Brücke bridge
Brunnen spring or well
Burg fortified castle
Dom cathedral
Domplatz cathedral square
Drogerie shop selling cosmetics, sundries
Evergreen (Schrammel) alpine traditional music
Gasse lane
Gasthof inn
Gemütlichkeit (adj. gemütlich) comfort, coziness, friendliness
Graben moat
Gutbürgerliche Küche home cooking
Hauptbahnhof main railroad station
Heurige traditional wine tavern
Hof court (of a prince), mansion
Insel island
Jugendstil Art Nouveau
Kai quay
Kammer room in public building
Kanal canal
Kapelle chapel
Kaufhaus department store
Kino cinema
Kirche church
Kloster monastery
Konditorei pastry shop

Kunst art
Marktplatz market square
Neustadt new part of city or town
Oper opera
Platz square
Rathaus town or city hall
Ratskeller restaurant in Rathaus cellar serving traditional German food
Reisebüro travel agency
Saal hall
Schauspielhaus theater for plays
Schloss palace, castle
See lake (*der* See) or sea (*die* See)
Sezessionstil Viennese art movement
Spielbank casino
Stadt town, city
Stadtbahn (S-Bahn) commuter railroad
Steg footbridge
Strand beach
Strasse street
Strassenbahn streetcar, tram
Tankstelle service station
Tor gateway
Turm tower
Ufer shore, riverbank
Untergrundbahn (U-Bahn) subway, underground transportation system in a city
Verkehrsamt tourist office
Weg road
Zimmer room

2 Menu Terms

SOUPS (SUPPEN)

Erbsensuppe pea soup
Gemüsesuppe vegetable soup
Gulaschsuppe goulash soup

Kartoffelsuppe potato soup
Linsensuppe lentil soup
Nudelsuppe noodle soup

MEATS (WURST, FLEISCH & GEFLÜGEL)

Aufschnitt cold cuts
Brathuhn roast chicken
Bratwurst grilled sausage
Ente duck
Gans goose
Gulasch Hungarian stew
Hammel mutton
Kalb veal
Kaltes geflügel cold poultry
Kassler rippchen pork chops

Lamm lamb
Leber liver
Nieren kidneys
Rinderbraten roast beef
Rindfleisch beef
Schinken ham
Schweinebraten roast pork
Truthahn turkey
Wiener schnitzel veal cutlet
Wurst sausage

FISH (FISCH)

Forelle trout
Hecht pike
Karpfen carp
Krebs crawfish

Lachs salmon
Makrele mackerel
Schellfisch haddock
Seezunge sole

EGGS (EIER)

Eier in der schale boiled eggs
Mit speck with bacon
Rühreier scrambled eggs

Spiegeleier fried eggs
Verlorene eier poached eggs

SANDWICHES (BELEGTE BROTE)

Käsebrot cheese sandwich
Schinkenbrot ham sandwich

Schwarzbrot mit butter pumpernickel
  with butter
Wurstbrot sausage sandwich

VEGETABLES (GEMÜSE)

Artischocken artichokes
Blumenkohl cauliflower
Bohnen beans
Bratkartoffeln fried potatoes
Erbsen peas
Grüne bohnen string beans
Gurken cucumbers
Karotten carrots
Kartoffelbrei mashed potatoes
Kartoffelsalat potato salad
Knödel dumpling

Kohl cabbage
Reis rice
Rotkraut red cabbage
Salat lettuce
Salzkartoffeln boiled potatoes
Sauerkraut sauerkraut
Spargel asparagus
Spinat spinach
Tomaten tomatoes
Vorspeisen hors d'oeuvres
Weisse rüben turnips

DESSERTS (NACHTISCH)

Blatterteiggebäck puff pastry
Bratapfel baked apple
Käse cheese
Kompott stewed fruit

Obstkuchen fruit tart
Obstsalat fruit salad
Pfannkuchen sugared pancakes
Torten pastries

FRUITS (OBST)

Ananas pineapple
Apfel apple
Apfelsine orange
Banane banana
Birne pear

Erdbeeren strawberries
Kirschen cherries
Pfirsich peach
Weintrauben grapes
Zitrone lemon

BEVERAGES (GETRÄNKE)

Bier beer
Kaffee coffee
Milch milk
Rotwein red wine

Schokolade hot chocolate
Tee tea
Wasser water

CONDIMENTS & TABLE ITEMS

Brot bread
Brötchen rolls
Butter butter
Eis ice
Essig vinegar
Gabel fork
Glas glass
Loffel spoon

Messer knife
Pfeffer pepper
Platte plate
Sahne cream
Salz salt
Senf mustard
Tasse cup
Zucker sugar

COOKING TERMS

Gebacken baked
Gebraten fried
Gefüllt stuffed
Gekocht boiled

Geröstet roasted
Gut durchgebraten well done
Nicht durchgebraten rare
Paniert breaded

Index

See also Accommodations and Restaurant indexes, below.

GENERAL INDEX

A
AARP, 23
Abbey Heiligenkreuz (Abbey of the Holy Cross), 187
Abbey of Dürnstein, 221
Abercrombie and Kent, 32
Above and Beyond Tours, 22
Access-Able Travel Source, 21
Access America, 19
Accessible Journeys, 21
Accommodations, 49–80. See also Accommodations Index
  agencies, 49
  airport, 80
  Alsergrund (9th District), 77–78
  Baden bei Wien, 191–192
  best, 7–8
  Eisenstadt, 203
  family-friendly, 72
  Forchtenstein, 211
  Hinterbrühl, 186–187
  Illmitz, 208–209
  Innere Stadt (Inner City), 50–67
  Josefstadt (8th District), 76–77
  Klosterneuburg, 185
  Krems, 198
  Landstrasse (3rd District), 70–71
  Leopoldstadt (2nd District), 67, 70
  Mariahilf (6th District), 72–74
  Mayerling, 188–189
  Melk, 202
  Neubau (7th District), 74–76
  Podersdorf, 209–210
  private homes and furnished apartments, 50
  Purbach am See, 206
  near Schönbrunn, 79–80
  seasonal hotels, 49–50
  surfing for, 25

Tulln, 195–196
Westbahnhof (15th District), 79
what's new in, 1–3
Wieden and Margareten (4th & 5th Districts), 71–72
Wiener Neustadt, 193
Active pursuits, 137–140
Addresses, finding, 38
A. E. Köchert, 165
Agatha Paris, 165
Airfares
  surfing for, 24–25
  tips for getting the best, 28–29
Airlines, 27–28, 34
  bankrupt, 19
Airport, 34
  getting into town from, 28
  hotel, 80
  security procedures, 27, 28
Air Tickets Direct, 29
Akademie der Bildenden Künste (Fine Arts Academy), 120, 149
Akademietheater, 170
Albertina, 110–111, 142
Albin Denk, 167
Alfi's Goldener Spiegel, 176–177
Alpine Lower Austria, 181
Alsergrund (9th District), 40
  accommodations, 77–78
  restaurant, 107–108
Alter Klosterkeller im Passauerhof, 177–178
Alter Steffl (Old Steve), 117
Altes Presshaus, 178
Altes Rathaus, 153
Altmann & Kühne, 164
Alt Wien, 179
American Airlines, 28
American Express, 14
  office, 44
  traveler's checks, 16
American Express Travel, 32

American Foundation for the Blind (AFB), 21
Andau, 208
The Anschluss, 218
Antiques, 162–163
Arcadia Opera Shop, 166
Architecture, 220–223
Art, 223–225
Art museums
  Albertina, 110–111
  Barockmuseum (Museum of Baroque Art), 124
  Ephesos-Museum (Museum of Ephesian Sculpture), 115
  Gemäldegalerie der Akademie der Bildenden Künste (Gallery of Painting and Fine Arts), 120, 149
  Kunsthalle Wien, 116
  Kunsthistorisches Museum (Museum of Fine Arts), 120–121
  Leopold Museum, 116–117
  Liechtenstein Museum, 121–122
  MUMOK (Museum of Modern Art Ludwig Foundation), 117
  Museum Mittelalterlicher Kunst (Museum of Medieval Art), 124
  Österreichische Galerie Belvedere, 122, 124
  Österreichisches Museum für Angewandte Kunst (Museum of Applied Art), 129
  Secession Building, 122
Art Nouveau, 222
Askoe-Tennis-Centrum-Schmelz, 140
Askoe Wien, 140
ATMs (automated teller machines), 15
Augarten Porzellan, 167

Augustinerkirche (Church of the Augustinians), 111–112
Augustinian Herzogenburg Monastery, 196–197
Aula (Great Hall), 157–158
Australia
  customs regulations, 13
  embassy of, 45
  health-related travel advice, 21
Austrian Airlines, 27, 28
Austrian Derby, 140
Austrian Federal Theaters (Österreichische Bundestheater), 170
Austrian National Library (Österreichische Nationalbibliothek), 115
Austrian National Tourist Office, 11, 35
  hotel reservations, 49
Austrobus, 49
Austropa, 49
Avis, 44

Babenbergs, The, 213
Babysitters, 44
Baden bei Wien, 189–192
Barfly's Club, 174
Barockmuseum (Museum of Baroque Art), 124
Baroque architecture, 221
Bars, gay and lesbian, 176–177
Basilikenhaus, 156
Beer, 228
Beethoven, Ludwig van, 136, 152, 169
  Beethovenhaus (Baden bei Wien), 190
  Pasqualati House, 136
Beethovenhaus (Baden bei Wien), 190
Bellotto, Bernardo, 224
Bergkirche (Church of the Calvary; Eisenstadt), 203
Bermuda Triangle, 174
Bicycle Rental Hochschaubahn, 137
Bicycling, 43, 137
Biking, 5
Blaguss Reisen, 49
Blogs and travelogues, 25
Boating, 138
Boat trips and cruises, 4, 32, 138
Bohemians, 213
Boingo, 26
Books, recommended, 33

Botanischer Garten (Botanical Garden of the University of Vienna), 132
British Airways, 27, 28
British Airways Holidays, 32
The British Bookshop, 163
Bruckner, Anton, 112
Bruegel, Pieter, the Elder, 121
Brunnenmarkt, 166
Bucket shops, 29
Budget Rent-a-Car, 44
Burgenland, 2, 182
Burg Forchtenstein, 210–211
Burggarten, 132
Burgkapelle (Home of the Vienna Boys' Choir), 112–113
Burg Kino, 179
Burgtheater (National Theater), 145, 170
Business hours, 44
Bus travel, 32, 35, 42–43
  from the airport, 28

Café Leopold, 171
Café Savoy, 177
Café Stein, 45
Calendar of events, 17–18
Canada
  airlines from, 28
  customs regulations, 12–13
  embassy of, 45
  health-related travel advice, 21
  tourist information, 11
Capuchin Friars, Church of the, 142
Car rentals, 43–44
  surfing for, 25
Carriage Museum (Wagenburg), 125
Car travel, 31–32, 43
Casino Baden, 192
Casino Wien, 179
Cellphones, 26–27
Centers for Disease Control and Prevention, 20
Chancellery, 144–145
Charlemagne, 115, 127, 145, 213
Charles VI, 128, 150, 184, 215
Chelsea, 171–172
Children, families with
  information and resources, 23–24
  restaurant, 101
  sights and attractions, 134–135
Christkindlmärkt, 18

Chunnel, 29–31
Churches, 125–128
Church of the Jesuits (Jesuitenkirche/Universitätskirche, 128, 157
Church of the Teutonic Order (Deutschordenskirche), 125–126
Cinema, 179
Circus and Clown Museum (Zirkus und Clownmuseum), 135
City Air Terminal, 28, 34
City Bus Terminal, 35
City code, 47
Climate, 16
Clock Museum, Municipal (Uhrenmuseum der Stadt Wien), 129–130
Club and music scene, 171–174
Club Havana, 172
Coffee, 228
Coffeehouses and cafes, 5–6, 98–99
Connection kit, 26
Consolidators, 29
Consulates, 45
Country code, 47
Cranach, Lucas, the Elder, 120
Credit cards, 16
Cuisine, 227
Currency and currency exchange, 13–15
Customs regulations, 11–13
Cybercafes, 26

Da Caruso, 166–167
Damron guides, 22
Dance clubs, 173–174
D&S Antiquitäten, 162
Danube (Donau), 4. *See also* Boat trips and cruises
Danube Canal (Donaukanal), 38
Danube Tower (Donauturm), 133
The Danube Valley, 194–202
DDSG Blue Danube Shipping Company, 4, 32, 138
Delta Vacations, 32
Dentists, 45
Department store, 164
Der Rudolfshof, 178
Deutschordenskirche (Church of the Teutonic Order), 125–126
Die Burgkapelle (Home of the Vienna Boys' Choir), 112–113
Die Presse, 168

Dining, 81–109. *See also*
   Restaurant Index
   Alsergrund (9th District),
      107–108
   Baden bei Wien, 192
   best, 8–10
   by cuisine, 81–83
   family-friendly, 101
   Forchtenstein, 211
   Hinterbrühl, 187
   Illmitz, 208–209
   Innere Stadt (Inner City),
      86–100
   Josefstadt (8th District),
      106–107
   Klosterneuburg, 185
   Krems, 198–199
   Landstrasse (3rd District),
      101–102
   Leopoldstadt (2nd District),
      100–101
   Mariahilf (6th District),
      103–104
   Mayerling, 189
   meals and dining customs, 81
   Melk, 202
   Neubau (7th District),
      104–105
   in the outer districts and out-
      skirts, 109
   Podersdorf, 210
   Purbach am See, 206–207
   near Schönbrunn, 108–109
   vegetarian, 103
   Westbahnhof (15th District),
      108
   Wieden and Margareten (4th
      & 5th Districts), 102–103
   Wiener Neustadt, 193–194
Disabilities, travelers with,
   21–22
Doctors, 45
Dominikanerkirche, 156–157
Domkirche St. Stephan (St.
   Stephan's Cathedral), 6–7,
   117, 146, 158
Donaukanal (Danube Canal), 38
Donaupark, 132–133
Donauturm (Danube Tower), 133
Donner, Georg Raphael, 224
Donner Fountain, 142
Dorotheum, 5, 144, 162
Driving and traffic
   regulations, 44
Drug laws, 45
Drugstores, 45
Dürer, Albrecht, 110, 121
Dürnstein, 199–200

Eagle Bar, 177
Egon Schiele Museum
   (Tulln), 195
Eisenstadt, 182, 202–204
Eistraum (Dream on Ice), 17
Elderhostel, 23
ElderTreks, 23
Electricity, 45
Elisabeth, Empress (Sissi), 114
Elite Tours, 137
ELTExpress, 29
Embassies and consulates, 45
Emergencies, 45
Emerging Horizons, 22
Engelhart, Joseph, 224
Entry requirements, 11
Ephesos-Museum (Museum of
   Ephesian Sculpture), 115
Ernst-Happel-Stadion, 140
Esterházykeller, 174
Eurailpass, 30–31
Euro, 13–14
Eurolines, 32
Expedia, 24

Families with children
   information and resources,
      23–24
   restaurant, 101
   sights and attractions,
      134–135
Familyhostel, 23
Family Travel Files, 24
Family Travel Forum, 23
Family Travel Network, 23–24
Fasching, 17
Fashions (clothing), 164–165
Felixx, 177
Festivals and special events,
   17–18
Film Festival, Music, 18
Filmmuseum, 179
Films, 179
Fischer von Erlach, Johann
   Bernhard, 128, 142, 150, 196,
   221, 224
Fleischmarkt, 154
Flex, 173
Flights.com, 29
Flohmarkt, 152, 162
FlyCheap, 29
Flying Wheels Travel, 21
Football, 140
Forchtenstein, 210–211
Franz Ferdinand, Archduke,
   113, 124, 131

Franz-Josef Bahnhof, 35
Franz Joseph I, Emperor, 126,
   148, 216–217, 222, 224, 227
   statue of, 132
Frauencafé, 177
Frederick III, Emperor, tomb
   of, 117
Freihaus, 151
Frequent-flier clubs, 29
Freud, Sigmund, 33, 99, 129
   Haus, 131
Friends of Music Building
   (Musikvereinsgebäude), 150
Frommers.com, 25
*Frommer's Gay & Lesbian
   Europe,* 22

Galerie bei der Albertina, 162
Galerie des 19. und 20.
   Jahrhunderts (Gallery of
   19th-and 20th-Century
   Art), 124
Gallery of Painting and Fine
   Arts (Gemäldegalerie der
   Akademie der Bildenden
   Künste), 120, 149
Gay and lesbian travelers, 22
Gay.com Travel, 22
Gemäldegalerie der Akademie
   der Bildenden Künste
   (Gallery of Painting and Fine
   Arts), 120, 149
Gerstner, 106, 164
Glasgalerie Kovacek, 163
Gloriette, 125
Gluck, Christoph Willibald
   Ritter von, 225
Golf, 138
Golfplatz Föhrenwald, 138
Golfplatz Wien-Freudenau, 138
Gothic architecture, 220–221
Gothic sculpture, 223
Gran, Daniel, 196, 224
Griechengasse, 154
Grinzing, 133
   Heurigen (wine taverns),
      177–178
Grosser Passauerhof
   (Krems), 197
Gumpendorferstrasse, 152

Haas House, 159
The Habsburgs, 5, 33, 188, 214
Hauptstrasse (Dürnstein), 199
Haus der Musik, 120

Haydn, Franz Joseph, 33, 112, 225–226
  Museum (Eisenstadt), 203
  tomb of (Eisenstadt), 203
  Wohnhaus (Haydn's House), 135
Health & Fitness (Living Well Express), 138–139
Health clubs, 138–139
Health concerns, 20–21
Health insurance, 19
Heeresgeschichtliches Museum (Museum of Military History), 131
Heiligenkreuzerhof, 156
Heldenplatz, 144
Hertz, 44
Herzogenburg, 196–197
Heurige Mayer, 178
Heurigen (wine taverns), 5, 177–178, 229
Hiking, 139
Hildebrandt, Johann Lukas von, 122, 127, 128, 221, 224
Hinterbrühl, 186–187
Historisches Museum der Stadt Wien (Historical Museum of Vienna), 131
History of Austria, books about, 33
History of Vienna, 212–220
  the Anschluss, 218
  Babenbergs and Bohemians, 213
  early times, 212–213
  Franz Joseph I, 216–217
  the Habsburgs, 214
  Maria Theresa and political reform, 215
  Metternich, 216
  Napoleon and the Congress of Vienna, 215–216
  plagues and Turkish invasions, 214–215
  World War I and the Versailles Treaty, 217–218
  World War II and its aftermath, 218–219
Hitler, Adolph, 124
Hofburg, 110–116, 144
Hoffman, Joseph, 222
Hofmusikkapelle, 113
Hoher Markt, 153–154
Holiday Care Service, 22
Holidays, 16
Horr Stadion, 140
Horse-drawn carriages (fiaker), 43

Horse racing, 140
Hospitals, 45
Hotel Bristol, 148
Hotels, 49–80. See also Accommodations Index
  agencies, 49
  airport, 80
  Alsergrund (9th District), 77–78
  Baden bei Wien, 191–192
  best, 7–8
  Eisenstadt, 203
  family-friendly, 72
  Forchtenstein, 211
  Hinterbrühl, 186–187
  Illmitz, 208–209
  Innere Stadt (Inner City), 50–67
  Josefstadt (8th District), 76–77
  Klosterneuburg, 185
  Krems, 198
  Landstrasse (3rd District), 70–71
  Leopoldstadt (2nd District), 67, 70
  Mariahilf (6th District), 72–74
  Mayerling, 188–189
  Melk, 202
  Neubau (7th District), 74–76
  Podersdorf, 209–210
  private homes and furnished apartments, 50
  Purbach am See, 206
  near Schönbrunn, 79–80
  seasonal hotels, 49–50
  surfing for, 25
  Tulln, 195–196
  Westbahnhof (15th District), 79
  what's new in, 1–2
  Wieden and Margareten (4th & 5th Districts), 71–72
  Wiener Neustadt, 193
Hotel Sacher, 141
Hot lines, 45
Hundertwasser, Friedensreich, 131
Hundertwasserhaus, 122
Hungarian Embassy, 145

IAMAT (International Association to Medical Assistance to Travelers), 20
iCan, 22
Ice skating, 139
Illmitz, 208–209

Imperial Apartments (Kaiserappartements), 113
Imperial Ball, 17
Imperial Furniture Collection (Kaiserliches Hofmobiliendepot), 120
Imperial Gardens, 125
Imperial Silver and Porcelain Collection, 113
Imperial Treasury (Schatzkammer), 115
Informationdienst der Wiener Verkehrsbetriebe (Vienna Public Transport Information Center), 41
Information sources, 11, 35
Information-Zimmernachweis, 32
Inner City (Innere Stadt; 1st District), 35, 38, 39
  accommodations, 50–67
  restaurants, 86–100
  sights and attractions, 117, 120–122
    churches, 125–128
    museums and galleries, 129–130
    parks and gardens, 132
Insurance, 18–19
InsureMyTrip.com, 18
International Association for Medical Assistance to Travelers (IAMAT), 20
International Gay and Lesbian Travel Association (IGLTA), 22
International Music Festival, 17
International Society of Travel Medicine, 21
International Student Identity Card (ISIC), 24
International Youth Travel Card (IYTC), 24
Internet access, 25–26, 45
InterRail Pass, 31
InTouch USA, 27
INTRAV, 23
IPass network, 26
Ireland, embassy of, 45
i2roam, 26

Jagdschloss (Mayerling), 188
J. & L. Lobmeyr, 163
Jazz clubs, 172–173
Jazz Festival, Vienna, 18
Jazzland, 172
Jesuitenkirche/Universitätskirche (Jesuit Church/University Church), 128, 157

Jewelry, 165
Jews in Vienna, 130, 218
  Judenplatz, 130
  Jüdisches Museum Wien, 129
  Museum Judenplatz, 130
Johann-Strauss Memorial
  Rooms, 136
Josefsplatz, 144
Josefstadt (8th District), 40
  accommodations, 76–77
  restaurants, 106–107
Joseph II, Emperor, 6, 154, 155,
  215, 229
  equestrian statue of
    (Josefsplatz), 144
Judenplatz, 130
Jüdisches Museum Wien, 129

Kahlenberg, 133
Kaiserappartements (Imperial
  Apartments), 113
Kaiserhaus (Baden bei
  Wien), 190
Kaiserliches Hofmobiliendepot
  (Imperial Furniture
  Collection), 120
Kapuzinerkirche, 126
Karl Kolarik's Schweizerhaus,
  179–180
Karl-Marx-Hof, 222
Karlskirche (Church of St.
  Charles), 128, 150–151
Karlsplatz, 150
Karner (Tulln), 195
Kärntnerstrasse, 6, 146
Kids
  information and resources,
    23–24
  restaurant, 101
  sights and attractions,
    134–135
Klimt, Gustav, 122, 124, 131,
  149, 162, 225
Klosterneuburg, 184–185
Klosterneuburg Abbey (Stift
  Klosterneuburg), 184–185
Kober, 167
Kokoschka, Oskar, 111, 116,
  122, 163, 225
Köllnerhofgasse, 156
Konditorei Oberlaa, 106
Krah Krah, 174
Krems, 197–199
Kunsthalle Wien, 2, 116
KunstHausWien, 131

Kunsthistorisches Museum
  (Museum of Fine Arts),
  120–121
Künstlerhaus, 150
Kurhaus (Baden bei Wien),
  190–191
Kurpark, Baden bei Wien,
  189, 190
Kurzpark scheine (short-term
  parking voucher), 44

Lace and needlework, 165
La Divina, 2, 175
Lainzer Tiergarten, 139
Landes Museum (Krems), 198
Landstrasse (3rd District), 39
  accommodations, 70–71
  restaurants, 101–102
Language, 46
Lanz, 164
Legal aid, 46
Leopold Museum, 2, 116–117
Leopoldstadt (2nd District), 39
  accommodations, 67, 70
  restaurants, 100–101
Liebfrauenkirche (Wiener
  Neustadt), 193
Liechtenstein Museum,
  121–122
Liechtenstein Palace (Palais
  Liechtenstein), 145, 221, 223
Liener Brünn, 170
Lipizzaner Museum, 113
Lipizzaner stallions, 115–116
Liquor laws, 46
Lobkowitz Palace, 142
Loden Plankl, 164
Loop, 172
Loos, Adolf, 222
Loos American Bar, 175
Loos House (Michaelerplatz
  Building), 144, 222
Lost-luggage insurance, 19
Lower Austria (Niederöster-
  reich), 181
Lower Belvedere (Unteres
  Belvedere), 124
Lufthansa, 27
Luggage Express, 30
Luggage storage and
  lockers, 46

Magna Racino, 140
Mail, 46
Majolikahaus, 152

Maps, street, 39
Margareten (5th District), 39
  accommodations, 71–72
  restaurants, 102–103
Maria am Gestade (Maria-
  Stiegen-Kirche; St. Mary's on
  the Bank), 126, 153
Maria Christina, Tomb of, 111
Mariahilf (6th District), 40
  accommodations, 72–74
  restaurants, 103–104
Maria Theresa, Empress, 111,
  120, 125, 126, 129, 132, 135,
  142, 144, 165, 192, 200, 215,
  221, 224–226
Markets, 166
Mary Kindermoden, 165
MasterCard, traveler's
  checks, 16
Mayerling, 187–189
Medallion House, 152
MEDEX Assistance, 19
Medic Alert Identification
  Tag, 20
Medical insurance, 19
Medieval Synagogue (Mittelal-
  terliche Synagogue), 130
Melk, 200–202
Melk Abbey, 201, 221
Messerschmidt, Franz Xaver,
  146, 224
Metternich, Klemens von, 216
Michaelerkirche (Church of
  St. Michael), 126–127, 145
Michaelerplatz Building (Loos
  House), 144, 222
Military History, Museum of
  (Heeresgeschichtliches
  Museum), 131
Minoritenkirche (Church of the
  Minorites), 127, 145
Mittelalterliche Synagogue
  (Medieval Synagogue), 130
Möbel, 180
Mocca Club, 2, 175
Moll, Balthasar, 224
Moll, Carl, 224
Money matters, 13–16
Morawa, 163
Moss-Rehab, 21
Mozart, Wolfgang Amadeus, 4,
  33, 152, 190, 193, 226
  Mozart-Wohnung/Figarohaus
    (Mozart Memorial),
    135, 136
Mozart Concerts (website), 11

MUMOK (Museum of Modern Art Ludwig Foundation), 2, 117
Museum für Völkerkunde (Museum of Ethnology), 115
Museum Judenplatz, 130
Museum Mittelalterlicher Kunst (Museum of Medieval Art), 124
Museum of Baroque Art (Barockmuseum), 124
Museum of Ephesian Sculpture (Ephesos-Museum), 115
Museum of Ethnology (Museum für Völkerkunde), 115
Museum of Fine Arts (Kunsthistorisches Museum), 120–121
Museum of Military History (Heeresgeschichtliches Museum), 131
MuseumsQuartier Complex, 2, 116–117
Music
    classical, 168–170
    Haus der Musik, 120
    history of, 225–227
    sights and attractions, 135–136
    special events and festivals, 17–18
Music Film Festival, 18
Music stores, 166–167
Musikverein, 168–169
Musikvereinsgebäude (Friends of Music Building), 150

Napoleon, 117, 201, 215–216
Naschmarkt, 10, 106, 151, 159, 166
National Library, Austrian (Österreichische Nationalbibliothek), 115
National Rail Inquiries, 31
National Theater (Burgtheater), 145, 170
Naturhistorisches Museum (Natural History Museum), 129
Neighborhoods, 39–40
Neubau (7th District), 40
    accommodations, 74–76
    restaurants, 104–105
Neue Hofburg, 113
Neukloster (Wiener Neustadt), 193
Neusiedl, 182
Neusiedl, Lake, 204–210
Neusiedl am See, 204–206

Neusiedler See (Lake Neusiedl), 205
Newspapers and magazines, 46
New Year's Eve/New Year's Day, 17
New Zealand
    customs regulations, 13
    embassy of, 45
Niederösterreich Information, 35
Niederösterreichisches Heimatwerk, 165
Night clubs, 171–172
Nightlife, 168–180
    bars, 174–177
    club and music scene, 171–174
    gay and lesbian bars, 176–177
    Heurigen (wine taverns), 177–178
    performing arts, 168–171
    what's new in, 2
Now, Voyager, 22

ÖAMTC (Österreichischer Automobil-, Motorrad- und Touringclub), 43
Oberes Belvedere (Upper Belvedere), 124
Odysseus: The International Gay Travel Planner, 22
Old Steve (Alter Steffl), 117
Olivia Cruises & Resorts, 22
Onyx Bar, 175
Open-air markets, 166
Open World Magazine, 22
Opera Ball, 17
Orbitz, 24
Organized tours, 137
    Vienna Woods, 184
Österreichische Bundestheater (Austrian Federal Theaters), 170
Österreichische Galerie Belvedere, 122, 124
Österreichische Nationalbibliothek (Austrian National Library), 115
Österreichischer Automobil-, Motorrad- und Touringclub (ÖAMTC), 43
Österreichisches Museum für Angewandte Kunst (Museum of Applied Art), 129
Österreichische Werkstatten (Ö.W.), 163

Otto Wagner Pavilions, 150
Ö.W. (Österreichische Werkstatten), 163

Package tours, 32
Palace Theater (Schlosstheater), 125
Palais Liechtenstein (Liechtenstein Palace), 145, 221, 223
Parkgarage Am Hof, 44
Parkgarage Freyung, 44
Parking, 44
Parks and gardens, 132–134
Pasqualati House, 136
Passage, 2
Pavillion, 180
Pedal Power, 43, 137
Perchtoldsdorf, 185–186
Performing arts, 168–171
Permoser, Balthasar, 224
Peterskirche (St. Peter's Church), 127, 145
Pfarrkirche (parish church)
    Dürnstein, 199
    St. Viet (Krems), 197
    Tulln, 195
Piaristenkirche (Church of the Piarist Order), 128
Picnics, 106
Plague Column, 145
Planet Music, 172–173
Podersdorf, 209–210
Police, 46
Popp & Kretschmer, 165
Porcelain and pottery, 167
Porgy & Bess, 173
Pozzo, Andrea, 121, 128, 223
Praterverband (The Prater), 6, 133–134
Prescription medications, 20
Purbach am See, 206–207

RADAR (Royal Association for Disability and Rehabilitation), 22
Radio, 46
RailEurope, 30
Rail passes, 30–31
Rainbow Online, 22
Rainfall, average monthly, 17
Rapide-Wien, 140
Rathaus (Baden bei Wien), 190
Recturm (Wiener Neustadt), 193
Rennbahn Freudenau, 140
Rennbahn Krieau, 140

Restaurants, 81–109. *See also* Restaurant Index
Alsergrund (9th District), 107–108
Baden bei Wien, 192
best, 8–10
by cuisine, 81–83
family-friendly, 101
Forchtenstein, 211
Hinterbrühl, 187
Illmitz, 208–209
Innere Stadt (Inner City), 86–100
Josefstadt (8th District), 106–107
Klosterneuburg, 185
Krems, 198–199
Landstrasse (3rd District), 101–102
Leopoldstadt (2nd District), 100–101
Mariahilf (6th District), 103–104
Mayerling, 189
meals and dining customs, 81
Melk, 202
Neubau (7th District), 104–105
in the outer districts and outskirts, 109
Podersdorf, 210
Purbach am See, 206–207
near Schönbrunn, 108–109
vegetarian, 103
Westbahnhof (15th District), 108
Wieden and Margareten (4th & 5th Districts), 102–103
Wiener Neustadt, 193–194
Restrooms, 46
Rhiz Bar Modern, 175–176
Richard the Lion-Hearted, 199
Riesenrad, 134
Ringstrasse, 38, 222
Ringstrassen-Galerien, 159, 162
RoadPost, 27
Rochusmarkt, 166
Rococo style, 221
Romans, 189, 213
Römerquelle (Roman Springs), 189, 190
Rottmayr, Johann, 127, 128, 145, 201, 224
Royal Association for Disability and Rehabilitation (RADAR), 22
Rozet & Fischmeister, 165
Rudolf, Archduke, 188

Ruesch International, 15
Ruprechtskirche (St. Rupert's Church), 127–128
Rust, 207–208

Sacher Eck, 176
Safety, 21, 46
St. Andrä bei Frauenkirchen, 208
St. Charles, Church of (Karlskirche), 128, 150–151
St. George, Church of (St. Georgenkirche; Wiener Neustadt), 193
St. Joseph, Church of (Kahlenberg), 133
St. Mary's on the Bank (Maria am Gestade), 126, 153
St. Michael, Church of (Michaelerkirche), 126–127, 145
St. Peter's Church (Peterskirche), 127, 145
St. Rupert's Church (Ruprechtskirche), 127–128
St. Stephan, parish church of (Tulln), 195
St. Stephan's (Baden bei Wien), 190
St. Stephan's Cathedral (Domkirche St. Stephan), 6–7, 117, 146, 158
St. Viet, Pfarrkirche (Krems), 197
Sammlung alter Musikinstrumente, 114
SATH (Society for Accessible Travel and Hospitality), 21
Savoy Foundation for Noble Ladies (Savoysches Damenstift), 146
Schatzkammer (Imperial Treasury), 115
Schiele, Egon, 93, 116, 124, 149, 162, 225
Museum (Tulln), 195
Schikaneder, 176
Schloss Esterházy, 203
Schloss Schönbrunn Experience, 125
Schlosstheater (Palace Theater), 125
Schneeberg, Mount, 139
Schnellbahn (S-Bahn), 28, 34
Schnitzelwirt Schmidt, 180
Schnitzler, Arthur, 172
Schoenberg, Arnold, 226–227
Schönbrunner Tiergarten, 135

Schönbrunn Palace, 124–125, 221
accommodations near, 79–80
restaurants near, 108–109
Schönbrunn Palace Theater, 169
Schönlaterngasse, 156
Schubert, Franz, 112, 132, 156, 186, 226
Museum, 136
Schumann, Robert, 156
Scotch Club, 174
Seasons, 16
Secession Building, 122
Secessionist movement (Sezessionstil), 124, 149, 163, 222, 224–225
Seegrotte Hinterbrühl, 186
Seewinkel, 208
Semmering, Mount, 139
Senior travel, 23
Shakespeare & Company, 163
Shipping your luggage, 30
Shopping, 159–167
hours, 159
Short-term parking voucher (*kurzpark scheine*), 44
Sights and attractions, 110–137
churches, 125–128
for kids, 134–135
MuseumsQuartier, 116–117
musical landmarks, 135–136
new, 2
organized tours, 137
parks and gardens, 132–134
Sigmund Freud Haus, 131–132
Sissi (Empress Elisabeth), 114
Skiing, 139
Sky Bar, 2, 176
SkyCap International, 30
Soccer, 140
Society for Accessible Travel and Hospitality (SATH), 21
Spanish Riding School (Spanische Reitschule), 4–5, 113, 115–116, 144
Spa resorts, 181
Baden bei Wien, 189–192
Spartacus International Gay Guide, 22
Special events and festivals, 17–18
Spectator sports, 140
Sportalm Trachtenmoden, 165
Sports and active pursuits, 137–140
Sports Express, 30
Spring Festival, 17

Staatsoper, 6
Stadtisches Rolletmuseum (Baden bei Wien), 190
Stadtpark, 132
Stadttheater (Baden bei Wien), 190
Stadt-Wander-Wege, 139
State Apartments, 125
State Opera House (Wiener Staatsoper), 122, 141, 148, 169
STA Travel, 24, 29
Steffl Kaufhaus, 164
Stein, 197
Steiner Tor (Krems), 197
Steinlanderstrasse (Krems), 197
Stift Klosterneuburg (Klosterneuburg Abbey), 184–185
Stiftskirche (abbey church), Melk, 201–202
Stock-im-Eisen, 146
Strauss, Johann, Jr., Johann-Strauss Memorial Rooms, 136
Streetcar Museum (Wiener Straasenbahnmuseum), 135
Street food, 106
Street maps, 39
Student travel, 24
Südbahnhof, 28, 34
Swimming, 139–140
Swiss Court, 110
Synagogue, Medieval (Mittelalterliche Synagogue), 130

*T*afelspitz, 5
Taxes, 47
Taxis, 43
    from the airport, 28
Technische Universität (Technical University), 151
Telegrams, telex and fax, 47
Telephone, 47–48
Television, 46
Temperature, average daytime, 17
Tennis, 140
Teutonic Order, Church of the (Deutschordenskirche), 125–126
Theater, 170–171
Theater an der Wien, 151–152, 169
Theater in der Josefstadt, 171
The Third Man (film), 6, 33, 154, 179
Thomas Cook, 14

Thomas Cook European Timetable of Railroads, 29
Tief-garage Kärntnerstrasse, 44
Time zone, 48
Tipping, 48
Titanic, 174
Tourist information, 11, 35
    Baden bei Wien, 190
    Danube Valley, 194
    Dürnstein, 199
    Eisenstadt, 203
    Forchtenstein, 210
    Hinterbrühl, 186
    Klosterneuburg, 184
    Krems, 197
    Mayerling, 187
    Melk, 201
    Neusiedl am See, 204
    Perchtoldsdorf, 186
    Podersdorf, 209
    Purbach am See, 206
    Rust, 207
    Tulln, 195
    Vienna Woods, 184
Tours, 137
    organized, Vienna Woods, klosterneuburg, 184
    package, 32
    walking, 141–158
        back streets, 153–158
        Imperial Vienna, 141–146
        south of the Ring, 146–152
Toys, 167
Train travel, 29–31, 34–35
    from the airport, 28
Trams (streetcars), 42
Transit information, 48
Transportation, 40–44
Travel Assistance International, 19
Travel blogs and travelogues, 25
Travel CUTS, 24
Traveler's checks, 16
Travelex Insurance Services, 19
Travel Guard International, 19
Traveling Internationally with Your Kids, 24
Traveling to Austria, 11
    by boat, 32
    by bus, 32
    by car, 31–32
    customs regulations, 11–13
    entry requirements, 11
    with minors, 24
    by plane, 27–29
    pre-departure checklist, 12
    by train, 29, 34

Travel insurance, 18–19
Travel Insured International, 19
Travelocity, 24
Treasury, Imperial (Schatzkammer), 115
Trinity Column (Baden bei Wien), 190
Trip-cancellation insurance, 18–19
Tulln, 194–196
Tunnel, 173
Turkish invasions, 214–215

U-Bahn (subway), 42
U-4, 172
Uhrenmuseum der Stadt Wien (Municipal Clock Museum), 129–130
United Kingdom
    airlines from, 28
    customs regulations, 12
    disabled travelers, 22
    embassy of, 45
    health-related travel advice, 21
    rail passes, 31
United States
    airlines from, 27–28
    customs regulations, 11–12
    embassy of, 45
    health-related travel advice, 21
    tourist information, 11
Universitätskirche (Jesuitenkirche/Church of the Jesuits), 128, 157
Unteres Belvedere (Lower Belvedere), 124
Upper Belvedere (Oberes Belvedere), 124
USIT, 24
U.S. State Department, 21

*V*acationVillas.net, 50
Van Dyck, 120, 121
Van Meytens, Martin, 224
VAT refunds, 163
Venus of Willendorf, 129
Vetsera, Maria, 188
Vienna A to Z, 35
Vienna Boys' Choir (Wiener Sängerknaben), 6, 112, 113
Vienna Card, 42
Vienna Festival, 17–18
Vienna International Airport, 34
Vienna Jazz Festival, 18

Vienna Public Transport Information Center (Informationdienst der Wiener Verkehrsbetriebe), 41
Vienna's English Theatre, 171
Vienna Sightseeing Tours (Wiener Rundfahrten), 137, 104, 194
Vienna Spring Festival, 17
Vienna State Opera (Wiener Staatsoper), 122, 141, 148, 169
Vienna Tourist Board, 11, 35
Vienna Tourist Information Office, 34
Vienna Woods (Wienerwald), 132, 133, 182–189
Vienna Workshop (Wiener Werkstatte), 129
Virtual Bellhop, 30
Visa, traveler's checks, 16
Visitor information, 11, 35
    Baden bei Wien, 190
    Danube Valley, 194
    Dürnstein, 199
    Eisenstadt, 203
    Forchtenstein, 210
    Hinterbrühl, 186
    Klosterneuburg, 184
    Krems, 197
    Mayerling, 187
    Melk, 201
    Neusiedl am See, 204
    Perchtoldsdorf, 186
    Podersdorf, 209
    Purbach am See, 206
    Rust, 207
    Tulln, 195
    Vienna Woods, 184
Volksgarten (People's Park), 132
Volksoper, 169
Volkstheater, 171
Votivkirche (Votive Church), 128

Wachau-Nibelungengau, 181
Wagenburg (Carriage Museum), 125
Wagner, Otto, 120, 152, 222
    Pavilions, 150
Waldmüller, Georg, 224
Waldviertel-Weinviertel, 181
Walking tours, 141–158
    back streets, 153–158
    Imperial Vienna, 141–146
    south of the Ring, 146–152
Wayport, 26
Websites, 11

Wedding and honeymoon packages, 55
Wein & Co., 167
Weinbaumuseum (Wine Museum; Krems), 198
Weiner Stadion, 140
Weingut Wolff, 178
Weinstadt Museum Krems (Historical Museum of Krems), 197–198
Westbahnhof (15th District), 28, 34
    accommodations, 79
    restaurant, 108
Western Union, 13
Wheelchair accessibility, 21
Wieden (4th District), 39
    accommodations, 71–72
    restaurants, 102–103
Wiener Eislaufverein, 139
Wiener Konzerthaus, 169
Wiener Neustadt, 192–194
Wiener Neustadt altarpiece, 117
Wiener Philharmoniker, 171
Wiener Rundfahrten (Vienna Sightseeing Tours), 137, 184, 194
Wiener Sängerknaben (Vienna Boys' Choir), 6, 112, 113
Wiener Staatsoper (Vienna State Opera), 122, 141, 148, 169
Wiener Stamperl (The Viennese Dram), 180
Wiener Straasenbahnmuseum (Streetcar Museum), 135
Wienerwald (Vienna Woods), 132, 182–189
Wiener Werkstatte (Vienna Workshop), 129
Wien Mitte, 28, 35
Wien Mitte/Landstrasse rail station, 28, 34
Wien Modern, 18
Wien Monatsprogramm, 35, 168
Wien Nord, 28
Wien Tourist-Information, 35
Wi-Fi access, 26
The Wine Bar at Julius Meinl, 176
Wines, 167, 228
Wine taverns *(Heurigen),* 5, 177–178, 229
World War II, 121, 192
Worldwide Assistance Services, 19
Wotruba, Fritz, 225
Würstelstand, 106

Zirkus und Clownmuseum (Circus and Clown Museum), 135
Zoo, Schönbrunner Tiergarten, 135
Zum Figlmüller, 178
Zur Schwäbischen Jungfrau, 165

ACCOMMODATIONS

Academia Hotel, 49–50
Altwienerhof, 79–80
Am Spitz (Purbach am See), 206
Atlas Hotel, 49–50
Austria Trend Hotel Albatros, 77
Avis Hotel, 49–50
Best Western Hotel Tigra, 61
Cordial Theaterhotel Wien, 76
Do & Co. Hotel, 1, 50
Donauhotel Krems, 198
Dorint Hotel Biedermeier, 55, 70–71
Drei Kronen, 64
Fürst Metternich Hotel, 73
Gartenhotel Weinhof Pfeffel (Dürnstein), 199–200
Gasthaus zur Sonne (Gasthaus Sodoma; Tulln), 195–196
Gasthof Öhr (Eisenstadt), 203–204
Gasthof Sauerzapf (Forchtenstein), 211
Gasthof Seewirt (Podersdorf), 209
Gasthof zur Traube (Neusiedl am See), 205
Golden Tulip Wien City, 73–74
Gourmethotel am Förthof (Krems), 198
Graben Hotel, 61
Grand Hotel Sauerhof zu Rauhenstein (Baden bei Wien), 191
Grand Hotel Wien, 50–51, 55
Haus Attila (Podersdorf), 209
Hilton International Vienna Plaza, 51
Hilton Vienna, 8, 70
Hilton Vienna Danube, 67
Hotel Amadeus, 58–59
Hotel Ambassador, 8, 51
Hotel Am Parkring, 61–62
Hotel Am Schubertring, 62, 72
Hotel Astoria, 59
Hotel Austria, 64
Hotel Beethoven (Hinterbrühl), 186–187

Hotel Bellevue, 77–78
Hotel Bristol, 7, 51, 54
Hotel Burgenland (Eisenstadt), 204
Hotel Capricorno, 62
Hotel Corvinus (Wiener Neustadt), 193
Hotel Das Triest, 7, 59
Hotel Das Tyrol, 1, 72–73
Hotel de France, 8, 54
Hotel Erzherzog Rainer, 71
Hotel Graf Stadion, 72, 77
Hotel Hanner (Mayerling), 188–189
Hotel Ibis Wien, 74
Hotel Imperial, 7, 54–55
Hotel Inter-Continental Wien, 55–56
Hotel Josef Buschenretter (Klosterneuburg), 185
Hotel Kaiserin Elisabeth, 59–60
Hotel Kärntnerhof, 7, 64–65, 72
Hotel König Von Ungarn, 60
Hotel Kummer, 73
Hotel Mercure Josefshof, 72, 78
Hotel Mercure Secession, 74
Hotel Opernring, 62–63, 72
Hotel Parliament Levante, 1, 76
Hotel-Pension Arenberg, 63
Hotel-Pension Barich, 71
Hotel-Pension Museum, 75
Hotel-Pension Shermin, 65
Hotel-Pension Suzanne, 7–8, 65, 72
Hotel Post, 65
Hotel Prinz Eugen, 71–72
Hotel Regina, 78
Hotel-Restaurant Sänger Blondel (Dürnstein), 200
Hotel-Restaurant Sifkovitz (Rust), 207
Hotel Römerhof (Tulln), 196
Hotel Römischer Kaiser, 60, 72
Hotel Rossmühle (Tulln), 196
Hotel Royal, 7, 63
Hotel Sacher Wien, 56
Hotel Savoy, 75–76
Hotel Schloss Dürnstein, 200
Hotel Schrannenhof (Klosterneuburg), 185
Hotel Stadt Melk, 202
Hotel Stefanie, 67, 70
Hotel Viennart, 63
Hotel Wandl, 65–66
Hotel Wende (Neusiedl am See), 205–206
Hotel Zipser, 77
K + K Hotel Maria Theresia, 74–75

K + K Palais Hotel, 61
Krainerhütte (Baden bei Wien), 191
Le Meridien Vienna, 56–57
Mailberger Hof, 63–64
Mercure Wien Westbahnhof, 79
NH Vienna Airport Hotel, 80
Palais Coburg Hotel Residenz, 1, 7, 57
Parkhotel Baden (Baden bei Wien), 191
Parkhotel Schönbrunn, 79
Pension Alte Mühle (Klosterneuburg), 185
Pension Altstadt Vienna, 8, 75
Pension Dr. Geissler, 66
Pension Neuer Markt, 66
Pension Nossek, 66
Pension Pertschy, 66–67
Radisson/SAS Palais Hotel Vienna, 57–58
Radisson/SAS Style Hotel, 1, 58
Rathauspark Hotel, 76–77
Rathaus Wein & Design Hotel, 78
Renaissance Penta Vienna Hotel, 71
Romantik Hotel Richard Löwenherz (Dürnstein), 200
Schloss Weikersdorf (Baden bei Wien), 192
Seehotel Herlinde (Podersdorf), 210
Seehotel Rust, 208
Vienna Marriott, 8, 58
Weingut-Weingasthof Rosenhof (Illmitz), 208–209
Zur Wiener Staatsoper, 67

RESTAURANTS

Abend-Restaurant Feuervogel, 107–108
Akakiko, 92
Alfi's Goldener Spiegel, 103
Alte Backstube, 106
Altes Jägerhaus, 100–101
Altwienerhof, 9, 108
Amerlingbeisl, 105
Am Spitz Restaurant (Purbach am See), 206–207
Augustinerkeller, 92–93, 142
Bauer, 87–88
Blaustern, 109
Bohème, 104
Buffet Trzésniewski, 93, 146
Café Central, 10, 98
Café Cuadro, 102

Café Demel, 5, 10, 98
Café Diglas, 98
Café Dommayer, 98
Café Frauenhuber, 98–99
Café Imperial, 10, 99
Café Landtmann, 99
Café Leopold, 93
Café Restaurant Halle, 93–94
Café-Restaurant Kunsthaus, 101–102
Café Sperl, 99, 152
Café Tirolerhof, 99
Cantinetta Antinori, 89–90
Demmers Teehaus, 99
Die Fromme Helene, 106–107
Do & Co., 1, 88
Dubrovnik, 94
Fabios, 1, 88
Figlmüller, 94
Firenze Enoteca, 9, 90, 103
Gasthaus Lux, 104–105
Gasthaus Ubl, 103
Gasthof Öhr (Eisenstadt), 2
Gasthof Seewirt Café Restaurant (Podersdorf), 210
Gelbes Haus (Wiener Neustadt), 193–194
Gergely's, 103
Gösser Bierklinik, 94–95
Gräfin vom Naschmarkt, 103–104
Griechenbeisl, 90, 154
Gulaschmuseum, 9, 95, 101
Hansen, 95
Hietzinger Brau, 108–109
Hotel-Restaurant Sänger Blondel (Dürnstein), 200
Hotel-Restaurant Sifkovitz (Rust), 207
Julius Meinl, 2, 90–91
Kardos, 9, 95
Karl Kolarik's Schweizerhaus, 179–180
Kern's Beisel, 96
Kervansaray und Hummer Bar, 9–10, 86
König von Ungarn (King of Hungary), 86
Korso bei der Oper, 9, 86–87
Kupferdachl (Baden bei Wien), 192
Leupold's Kupferdachl, 91
Mooslechner's Burgerhaus (Rust), 3, 207–208
Mörwald im Ambassador, 9, 87
Motto, 102
Niky's Kuchlmasterei, 101
Ofenloch, 91

Österreicher im MAK Gasthof &
Bar, 2, 96–97
Palmenhaus, 9, 96
Piaristenkeller, 107
Plachutta, 89
Plutzer Bräu, 105
Reisner (Forchtenstein), 211
Restaurant Dacher (Krems),
198–199
Restaurant Hanner
(Mayerling), 189
Restaurant Hexensitz
(Hinterbrühl), 187
Restaurant Jahreszeiten
(Perchtoldsdorf), 186

Restaurant Salzamt, 97
Restaurant Taubenkobel, 109
Sacher Hotel Restaurant, 8, 87
Schnattl, 107
Seehotel Rust, 208
Siebenstern-Bräu, 10, 105
Silberwirt, 102
Steirereck, 9, 101
Stiftsrestaurant Melk, 202
Vestibül, 91
Vikerl's Lokal, 108
Vincent, 100
Weibels Wirtshaus, 9, 89

Weingut-Weingasthof Rosenhof
(Illmitz), 208–209
Wiener Rathauskeller, 9, 10, 89
Zu den 3 Hacken (at the Three
Axes), 97
Zum Finsteren Stern, 91–92
Zum Kuchldragoner, 97, 100
Zum Schwarzen Kameel
(Stiebitz), 92
Zum Weissen Rauchfangkehrer,
92
Zwölf-Apostelkeller, 100

FROMMER'S® COMPLETE TRAVEL GUIDES

Alaska
Amalfi Coast
American Southwest
Amsterdam
Argentina & Chile
Arizona
Atlanta
Australia
Austria
Bahamas
Barcelona
Beijing
Belgium, Holland & Luxembourg
Belize
Bermuda
Boston
Brazil
British Columbia & the Canadian
 Rockies
Brussels & Bruges
Budapest & the Best of Hungary
Buenos Aires
Calgary
California
Canada
Cancún, Cozumel & the Yucatán
Cape Cod, Nantucket & Martha's
 Vineyard
Caribbean
Caribbean Ports of Call
Carolinas & Georgia
Chicago
China
Colorado
Costa Rica
Croatia
Cuba
Denmark
Denver, Boulder & Colorado Springs
Edinburgh & Glasgow
England
Europe
Europe by Rail
Florence, Tuscany & Umbria

Florida
France
Germany
Greece
Greek Islands
Hawaii
Hong Kong
Honolulu, Waikiki & Oahu
India
Ireland
Israel
Italy
Jamaica
Japan
Kauai
Las Vegas
London
Los Angeles
Los Cabos & Baja
Madrid
Maine Coast
Maryland & Delaware
Maui
Mexico
Montana & Wyoming
Montréal & Québec City
Moscow & St. Petersburg
Munich & the Bavarian Alps
Nashville & Memphis
New England
Newfoundland & Labrador
New Mexico
New Orleans
New York City
New York State
New Zealand
Northern Italy
Norway
Nova Scotia, New Brunswick &
 Prince Edward Island
Oregon
Paris
Peru
Philadelphia & the Amish Country

Portugal
Prague & the Best of the Czech
 Republic
Provence & the Riviera
Puerto Rico
Rome
San Antonio & Austin
San Diego
San Francisco
Santa Fe, Taos & Albuquerque
Scandinavia
Scotland
Seattle
Seville, Granada & the Best of
 Andalusia
Shanghai
Sicily
Singapore & Malaysia
South Africa
South America
South Florida
South Pacific
Southeast Asia
Spain
Sweden
Switzerland
Tahiti & French Polynesia
Texas
Thailand
Tokyo
Toronto
Turkey
USA
Utah
Vancouver & Victoria
Vermont, New Hampshire & Maine
Vienna & the Danube Valley
Vietnam
Virgin Islands
Virginia
Walt Disney World® & Orlando
Washington, D.C.
Washington State

FROMMER'S® DAY BY DAY GUIDES

Amsterdam
Chicago
Florence & Tuscany

London
New York City
Paris

Rome
San Francisco
Venice

PAULINE FROMMER'S GUIDES! SEE MORE. SPEND LESS.

Hawaii
Italy
New York City

FROMMER'S® PORTABLE GUIDES

Acapulco, Ixtapa & Zihuatanejo
Amsterdam
Aruba
Australia's Great Barrier Reef
Bahamas
Big Island of Hawaii
Boston
California Wine Country
Cancún
Cayman Islands
Charleston
Chicago
Dominican Republic

Dublin
Florence
Las Vegas
Las Vegas for Non-Gamblers
London
Maui
Nantucket & Martha's Vineyard
New Orleans
New York City
Paris
Portland
Puerto Rico
Puerto Vallarta, Manzanillo &
 Guadalajara

Rio de Janeiro
San Diego
San Francisco
Savannah
St. Martin, Sint Maarten, Anguila &
 St. Bart's
Turks & Caicos
Vancouver
Venice
Virgin Islands
Washington, D.C.
Whistler

FROMMER'S® CRUISE GUIDES

Alaska Cruises & Ports of Call   Cruises & Ports of Call   European Cruises & Ports of Call

FROMMER'S® NATIONAL PARK GUIDES

Algonquin Provincial Park
Banff & Jasper
Grand Canyon

National Parks of the American West
Rocky Mountain
Yellowstone & Grand Teton

Yosemite and Sequoia & Kings
  Canyon
Zion & Bryce Canyon

FROMMER'S® MEMORABLE WALKS

London
New York

Paris
Rome

San Francisco

FROMMER'S® WITH KIDS GUIDES

Chicago
Hawaii
Las Vegas
London

National Parks
New York City
San Francisco

Toronto
Walt Disney World® & Orlando
Washington, D.C.

SUZY GERSHMAN'S BORN TO SHOP GUIDES

France
Hong Kong, Shanghai & Beijing
Italy

London
New York

Paris
San Francisco

FROMMER'S® IRREVERENT GUIDES

Amsterdam
Boston
Chicago
Las Vegas

London
Los Angeles
Manhattan
Paris

Rome
San Francisco
Walt Disney World®
Washington, D.C.

FROMMER'S® BEST-LOVED DRIVING TOURS

Austria
Britain
California
France

Germany
Ireland
Italy
New England

Northern Italy
Scotland
Spain
Tuscany & Umbria

THE UNOFFICIAL GUIDES®

Adventure Travel in Alaska
Beyond Disney
California with Kids
Central Italy
Chicago
Cruises
Disneyland®
England
Florida
Florida with Kids

Hawaii
Ireland
Las Vegas
London
Maui
Mexico's Best Beach Resorts
Mini Mickey
New Orleans
New York City

Paris
San Francisco
South Florida including Miami &
  the Keys
Walt Disney World®
Walt Disney World® for
  Grown-ups
Walt Disney World® with Kids
Washington, D.C.

SPECIAL-INTEREST TITLES

Athens Past & Present
Best Places to Raise Your Family
Cities Ranked & Rated
500 Places to Take Your Kids Before They Grow Up
Frommer's Best Day Trips from London
Frommer's Best RV & Tent Campgrounds
  in the U.S.A.

Frommer's Exploring America by RV
Frommer's NYC Free & Dirt Cheap
Frommer's Road Atlas Europe
Frommer's Road Atlas Ireland
Great Escapes From NYC Without Wheels
Retirement Places Rated

FROMMER'S® PHRASEFINDER DICTIONARY GUIDES

French   Italian   Spanish

THE NEW TRAVELOCITY GUARANTEE

EVERYTHING YOU BOOK WILL BE RIGHT, OR WE'LL WORK WITH OUR TRAVEL PARTNERS TO MAKE IT RIGHT, RIGHT AWAY.

*To drive home the point,
we're going to use the word "right" in every single sentence.*

Let's get right to it. Right to the meat! Only Travelocity guarantees everything about your booking will be right, or we'll work with our travel partners to make it right, right away. Right on!

Here's a picture taken smack dab right in the middle of Antigua, where the guarantee also covers you.

The guarantee covers all but one of the items pictured to the right.

For example, what if the ocean view you booked actually looks out at a downright ugly parking lot? You'd be right to call – we're there for you. And no one in their right mind would be pleased to learn the rental car place has closed and left them stranded. Call Travelocity and we'll help get you back on the right track.

Now, you may be thinking, "Yeah, right, I'm so sure." That's OK; you have the right to remain skeptical. That is until we mention help is always right around the corner. Call us right off the bat, knowing that our customer service reps are there for you 24/7. Righting wrongs. Left and right.

Now if you're guessing there are some things we can't control, like the weather, well you're right. But we can help you with most things – to get all the details in righting,* visit **travelocity.com/guarantee**.

*Sorry, spelling things right is one of the few things not covered under the guarantee.

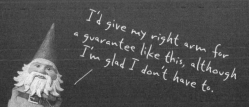

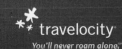

You'll never roam alone.

IF YOU BOOK IT, IT SHOULD BE THERE.

Only Travelocity guarantees it will be, or we'll work
with our travel partners to make it right, right away.
So if you're missing a balcony or anything else you
booked, just call us 24/7. **1**-888-TRAVELOCITY.

travelocity
You'll never roam alone.